T0325645

Managing Enterprise Information Technology Acquisitions:

Assessing Organizational Preparedness

Harekrishna Misra
Institute of Rural Management – Anand, India

Hakikur Rahman
University of Minho, Portugal

A volume in the Advances in Business
Information Systems and Analytics
(ABISA) Book Series

An Imprint of IGI Global

Managing Director:	Lindsay Johnston
Editorial Director:	Joel Gamon
Production Manager:	Jennifer Yoder
Publishing Systems Analyst:	Adrienne Freeland
Development Editor:	Austin DeMarco
Assistant Acquisitions Editor:	Kayla Wolfe
Typesetter:	Lisandro Gonzalez
Cover Design:	Jason Mull

Published in the United States of America by
Business Science Reference (an imprint of IGI Global)
701 E. Chocolate Avenue
Hershey PA 17033
Tel: 717-533-8845
Fax: 717-533-8661
E-mail: cust@igi-global.com
Web site: http://www.igi-global.com

Library of Congress Cataloging-in-Publication Data

Misra, H. K. (Harekrishna)
  Managing Enterprise information technology acquisitions : assessing organizational preparedness / by Harekrishna Misra and Hakikur Rahman.
      pages cm
  Includes bibliographical references and index.
  Summary: "This book provides leaders and innovators with research and strategies to make the most of their options involving IT and organizational management approaches"--Provided by publisher.
    ISBN 978-1-4666-4201-0 (hardcover) -- ISBN 978-1-4666-4202-7 (ebook) -- ISBN 978-1-4666-4203-4 (print & perpetual access) 1. Information technology--Management. 2. Information technology--Planning. I. Rahman, Hakikur, 1957- II. Title.

HD30.2.M57 2013
004.068--dc23

2013009758

This book is published in the IGI Global book series Advances in Business Information Systems and Analytics (ABISA) Book Series (ISSN: 2327-3275; eISSN: 2327-3283)

British Cataloguing in Publication Data
A Cataloguing in Publication record for this book is available from the British Library.

All work contributed to this book is new, previously-unpublished material. The views expressed in this book are those of the authors, but not necessarily of the publisher.

Advances in Business Information Systems and Analytics (ABISA) Book Series

Madjid Tavana
La Salle University, USA

ISSN: 2327-3275
EISSN: 2327-3283

MISSION

The successful development and management of information systems and business analytics is crucial to the success of an organization. New technological developments and methods for data analysis have allowed organizations to not only improve their processes and allow for greater productivity, but have also provided businesses with a venue through which to cut costs, plan for the future, and maintain competitive advantage in the information age.

The **Advances in Business Information Systems and Analytics (ABISA) Book Series** aims to present diverse and timely research in the development, deployment, and management of business information systems and business analytics for continued organizational development and improved business value.

COVERAGE

- Big Data
- Business Decision Making
- Business Information Security
- Business Process Management
- Business Systems Engineering
- Data Analytics
- Data Management
- Decision Support Systems
- Management Information Systems
- Performance Metrics

IGI Global is currently accepting manuscripts for publication within this series. To submit a proposal for a volume in this series, please contact our Acquisition Editors at Acquisitions@igi-global.com or visit: http://www.igi-global.com/publish/.

Titles in this Series

For a list of additional titles in this series, please visit: www.igi-global.com

Managing Enterprise Information Technology Acquisitions Assessing Organizational Preparedness
Harekrishna Misra (Institute of Rural Management Anand, India) and Hakikur Rahman (Institute of Computer Management & Science, Bangladesh)
Business Science Reference • copyright 2013 • 345pp • H/C (ISBN: 9781466642010) • US $185.00 (our price)

Information Systems and Technology for Organizations in a Networked Society
Tomayess Issa (Curtin University, Australia) Pedro Isaías (Universidade Aberta, Portugal) and Piet Kommers (University of Twente, The Netherlands)
Business Science Reference • copyright 2013 • 432pp • H/C (ISBN: 9781466640627) • US $185.00 (our price)

Cases on Enterprise Information Systems and Implementation Stages Learning from the Gulf Region
Fayez Albadri (ADMO-OPCO, UAE)
Information Science Reference • copyright 2013 • 370pp • H/C (ISBN: 9781466622203) • US $185.00 (our price)

Business Intelligence and Agile Methodologies for Knowledge-Based Organizations Cross-Disciplinary Applications
Asim Abdel Rahman El Sheikh (The Arab Academy for Banking and Financial Sciences, Jordan) and Mouhib Alnoukari (Arab International University, Syria)
Business Science Reference • copyright 2012 • 370pp • H/C (ISBN: 9781613500507) • US $185.00 (our price)

Business Intelligence Applications and the Web Models, Systems and Technologies
Marta E. Zorrilla (University of Cantabria, Spain) Jose-Norberto Mazón (University of Alicante, Spain) Óscar Ferrández (University of Alicante, Spain) Irene Garrigós (University of Alicante, Spain) Florian Daniel (University of Trento, Italy) and Juan Trujillo (University of Alicante, Spain)
Business Science Reference • copyright 2012 • 374pp • H/C (ISBN: 9781613500385) • US $185.00 (our price)

Electronic Supply Network Coordination in Intelligent and Dynamic Environments Modeling and Implementation
Iraj Mahdavi (Mazandaran University of Science and Technology, Iran) Shima Mohebbi (University of Tehran, Iran) and Namjae Cho (Hanyang University, Korea)
Business Science Reference • copyright 2011 • 434pp • H/C (ISBN: 9781605668086) • US $180.00 (our price)

Enterprise Information Systems Design, Implementation and Management Organizational Applications
Maria Manuela Cruz-Cunha (Polytechnic Institute of Cavado and Ave, Portugal) and Joao Varajao (University of Tras-os-Montes e Alto Duoro, Portugal)
Information Science Reference • copyright 2011 • 622pp • H/C (ISBN: 9781616920203) • US $180.00 (our price)

www.igi-global.com

701 E. Chocolate Ave., Hershey, PA 17033
Order online at www.igi-global.com or call 717-533-8845 x100
To place a standing order for titles released in this series, contact: cust@igi-global.com
Mon-Fri 8:00 am - 5:00 pm (est) or fax 24 hours a day 717-533-8661

Table of Contents

Section 2
Technology Issues in IT Acquisition Preparedness

Section 3
Modeling Process

Chapter 9

Chapter 10

Section 4
Application of Model

Preface

With the emergence of new technologies and due to the prevailing economic crisis, utilization of Information Technology (IT) has become indispensable for almost every organization. In this aspect, giving proper attention to the process of IT acquisition has become an important task of strategic decision makers in the organization. Further, due to the immense and inherent benefits, investments in IT acquisitions have grown significantly around the world. IT is also being considered as an important factor for all strategic decisions in most of the organizations today to meet the challenges of modern business and market. Emergence of IT components in the areas of resource planning, forecasting, and decision modeling has ensured the acceptability of IT as an infrastructure across various sectors including business, government, academia, and development. One of the major contributions of the IT-oriented services is towards formalization of processes, services, and establishing control and measurements of organizational performance. Along this discourse, IT-enabled Balanced Score Cards (BSC) and dash boards have led to wide acceptance of Enterprise Resource Planning (ERP).

However, due to strategic reasons and high investments in IT, organizations are now encouraged to measure and audit infrastructure created, services rendered, and the benefits accrued. This measurement includes all IT components like hardware, systems software, middleware, application software, user interfaces, networks, and communication systems. Quality models, standards, and various measurement systems have evolved to support this measurement.

IT acquisitions have brought in many improvements in organizations. However, there are many instances of post acquisition shocks in acquiring organizations do exist. IT acquisition failures are attributed to inadequate articulation of strategic needs, changes in the organizational priorities, and other influencing issues related to market. In many cases, failures are quite phenomenal in terms of return on investments, unrealistic service levels, poor usability, and inadequate User-Centered Designs (UCD). These failures have led to shorter lifecycles of IT infrastructures created. Another dimension that complicates the IT acquisition scenario is the release of continuous upgrades and updates in products and services. All these dimensions of performance measurements for IT acquisitions relate to organizational imperatives. IT acquisition generally includes strategizing, planning, acquiring and developing, deployment, and use of IT infrastructure. All these activities need a roadmap with clearly defined strategies and goals on a long-term basis.

Organizations today are mostly change oriented, and they face dynamic environment. Many organizations follow responsive strategies while some include preventive and proactive strategies of varying degree. In order to have continuity in business and stay competitive in the market (with market leadership as a long-term goal!) organizations strive for performance management and control over resources. However, establishing organization-wide standards for measurements and infusing controls in a transparent and efficient manner is quite challenging. This is because organizations not only need to consider people, process, and technologies involved, but also manage culture, climate, and other related behavioral issues. BSC-based organizational performance measurement principles, software metrics and measurements, and various quality models have evolved for implementation of measurements and controls organization-wide. These approaches argue for understanding the interface between the organizational behaviour, systems approaches, and IT infrastructures created. This interface provides the scope for studying the importance of Information Systems (IS).

IS has emerged as a discipline that involves a deeper understanding on the organizational issues and maps them through a systems approach so that an IT plan could emerge for acquisition. Systems approach deals with strategies for alignment among the organization, its business processes, and the technology. This approach also provides insights to distinguish the routine and predictable performance and control management scenarios (systematic) in an organization from the unpredictable situations (systemic) which are often negotiated by the strategic decision makers. Thus, IS-centric study facilitates the process to understand the organization in a better manner, to allow the organization to strategically prepare itself for installing performance and measurement controls, and then direct the IT acquisition process.

Systems approach that has been used for studying organizational behaviour reveals that each organization displays unique strategies to have its business continuity. Due to this uniqueness, it is quite reasonable to study the systems well before embarking on the IT acquisition process for the particular organization. Besides, each organization has its own life cycles, including processes and products. These life cycles provide ample indications about the systemic and systematic behaviour of the organization. Study on these life cycles with IS perspectives provides the base and establishes a pattern for management of information, knowledge, and decision support mechanisms for effective deployment of IT-enabled services. An insight to this pattern helps identify common attributes across the spectrum and provides scope to apply best practices to conceptualize, develop, and implement common strategies for replication.

Various models have been developed to understand, analyze, and interpret organizational performance measurement patterns and acquisition of IT process with specific contributions to setting patterns and deploying desired infrastructures to enhance organizational performance. There are many models to recommend proper procedures and methods for evaluation of IT acquisition processes with IS perspectives. In models like Capability Maturity Model – Integrated (CMMI), International Standards Organization (ISO), and Strategic Alignment Model (SAM), some of these issues are addressed. CMMI outlines procedures to acquire products, systems, and services, and to manage the acquisition process. In the ISO models, process as well as product-specific acquisition principles are prescribed. In the SAM, though role of the acquiring organization is discussed, the importance of the various stakeholders in the acquisition process is weakly elaborated. However, most of these models recognize the necessity of a feasibility study, and proper approach to assess organizational needs leading to the determination of IT requirements. There is also a need for coordinated effort to align the organizational objectives with the systemic and systematic requirements of the organization and map them for implementation on a continuous basis. This alignment is dependent on the capabilities in the organization and is influenced by people, processes, and technologies.

ABOUT THE BOOK

This book is a reflection of our experiences in managing IT acquisition life cycles for over thirty years in the industry, government establishments, and academic institutions. In most of these organizations we worked with, it has been observed that IT acquisition has started by some champions that are leading the processes. In some cases, dire needs for managing volumes of transactions in functional areas like finance, accounting, costing, production, human resources, etc., led to introduction of IT infrastructure. In a few cases, IT vendors (manufacturers and service providers) showcase the products and services they offer with expected benefits and impress upon the procurement. However, in almost all these cases there was a lack of clear understanding about the organization holistically by the IT service providers and the people involved in IT acquisition processes. Each acquisition process was taken up as a project and it passed through an acquisition cycle having distinct stages, such as conceptualization, requirement determination, acquisition, and post acquisition. Each proposed project was evaluated through standard physical and financial parameters and was declared feasible. Most of these projects passed through the stages as defined above as per the policy of the acquiring organization. During feasibility assessment, the focus was on project proposed, assessment of hardware, software, funds, etc. However, in this process a few essential variables, which are very much related to the organization's preparedness, were not considered. These factors attributed post acquisition shocks in many IT projects among these organizations. Furthermore, lack of this preparedness resulted in deploying IT-enabled services without providing better insights to performance and measurements in the organization. This also led to shorter life cycles of IT infrastructures deployed. In these cases, application software, databases, and other business intelligence tools underwent drastic changes frequently because of the dynamic requirements in the functional and strategic levels in the organization, thus resulting in elevated operational costs.

This experience provided us the motivation to examine the feasibility of assessing preparedness in the organization for IT acquisitions. It was apparent that there was a need to apply management principles for providing a systems approach to the organization before embarking on IT acquisitions. This systems approach aims to provide better insights to the organizational life cycles. Each organization displays its life cycle distinctly for its own life, organization structures, products, services, processes, and systems it handles. Overall, organizational life cycles are influenced by these individual life cycles. In order to have effective systems life cycles, it is essential that all these life cycles are studied in detail before IT acquisition is initiated and during subsequent stages of the IT acquisitions. Because of these complexities, it is pertinent to ensure that the life cycles of the organization, including the systems and IT, are well managed in an organization. This management needs preparedness to establish procedures for alignments among all the stated life cycles. Preparedness in these areas is expected to provide the impetus to establish systems in the organization and clarity in role management. Such clarity would support the organization in establishing organization-wide systems without least interference from the people who manage the roles. Well-articulated systems will also lead to areas of process improvements and value additions through IT interventions. Foremost, treating people and processes independently of the specified roles makes the systems more resilient. These features are part of enterprise IT acquisition process.

The book discusses various aspects of preparedness for the organization intending to acquire IT or wishes to assess preparedness at any stage of its life cycle. This book equips the readers with relevant inputs on the following issues to appreciate the preparedness of the organization in managing IT acquisitions:

- **Organizational Issues in IT Acquisitions:** It includes understanding the evolution, existence, life cycles, and continuity in organizations. This will provide the rationale behind establishing systems in organizations.
- **Understanding Systems in Organization:** This examines establishment of performance, control, and measurement systems in organizations. Organization's preparedness in establishing systems is also discussed.
- **Understanding IT Issues in Organizations:** This relates to preparedness among the IT service providers (including IT department employees) to understand the organizational needs in each of the stages of IT acquisition life cycle. Evaluation of all IT components is considered important during each stage of acquisition. Preparedness in this area is expected to enhance the possibility of successful alignment between organizational priorities, systems, and the technology being used for value added services.
- Gather understanding on modeling process using Structural Equation Modelling (SEM) techniques and quantitative methods.

This book discusses various metrics used in each of the acquisition process. These metrics are related to organization, systems, and technologies as desirable for understanding the overall preparedness of the acquiring organization. A model is conceptualized, designed, and tested for its fitness to predict the organizational preparedness for IT acquisitions. Some cases are discussed to understand the applicability of the model. This book is expected to contribute to the overall preparedness exercise that an organization wishes to adopt during the IT acquisition life cycle. It aims to support the practitioners, researchers, users, and planners of IS engaged in the IT acquisition process. The book is expected to benefit the readers in evaluating overall organizational preparedness in acquiring and managing IT life cycles. The model developed can be used for predicting preparedness of the organization to meet the complexities in managing IT acquisition life cycles across all its stages. The reader will also benefit in evaluating strength and weakness in each of the acquisition stages of IT acquisition life cycle with a suggestion to improve upon.

ORGANIZATION OF THE BOOK

This book discusses two frontiers of IT acquisition management: one relates to "management in organizations" and the other covers "software engineering in computer science." The motivation behind this discussion is to generate holistic "information generators" and "information users" in an enterprise environment and through their active collaboration. The main focus is on assessment of the preparedness of an organization to manage these "information generators" and "information users" and their role in IT acquisition processes. The book emphasizes the organizational preparedness that needs to be technology independent, even though substantial investments are to be made in terms of collaborating efforts of IT and non-IT human resources. This capability is expected to develop through a better climate, culture, and strategic choice made in the organization. It is believed that lack of such preparedness may affect the IT acquisition process. Thus, the book also discusses the stages of the IT acquisition process and the preparedness of the organization in each of the stages. Three stages of the IT acquisition life cycle in an organization are considered important, pre-acquisition, acquisition, and post-acquisition. In each of these stages, the organization needs to display specific preparedness traits to manage the IT infrastructures effectively. In each of these stages, understanding organization through sound management principles, understanding systems through appropriate IS, and software engineering approaches are essential features of the preparedness exercise. Organizing IT preparedness in all stages of the acquisition life cycle is also an important aspect for consideration.

The book is organized in four sections. They include "Organizational Issues in IT Acquisition Preparedness," "Technology Issues in IT Acquisition Preparedness," "Modeling Process," and "Application of the Model." Section one includes two chapters to understand the organizational issues and rationale behind understanding the preparedness of IT acquiring organization. Chapter one discusses management of organizations, which includes the motivation for creation of organizations, the desire to exist in the market with a better life cycle, and the role of management to ensure organizational continuity. The objective of this chapter is to provide insights to understand the role of performance management, control systems, and their measurement to support organizational continuity. Organizational continuity is necessary because of its socio-economic and cultural contributions to foster prosperity.

In chapter two, performance management and control systems are discussed in order to establish system thinking in the organization. System thinking is considered contemporary because of the market dynamics and the need for change management in the organization. System thinking includes organizational issues defined through systematic and systemic behaviour, which are measured by standard metrics. It is thus necessary for the IT acquiring organization to translate its preparedness for articulating appropriate performance and control systems. The role of scorecards and dashboards are discussed in this chapter to support the role of system thinking in managing organizations.

Section two deals technology issues in IT acquisition processes. It has three chapters. Chapter three discusses organizational, technological, and quality perspectives of IT acquisition preparedness. This chapter puts forward that preparedness of IT acquiring organization is quite important in terms of creating abilities to understand the process for integration of IT components with information systems, to manage acquiring process, and assess users' requirements and their preparedness to accept the computer-based information system.

Chapter four includes discussion on associated models for understanding various IT acquisition approaches, understanding organizational issues, capturing and analyzing user behaviour, analyzing usability of the IT resources in order to appreciate the acquisition holistically. These models include pre-acquisition-oriented quality and post-acquisition acceptance. This chapter focuses on three stages of the IT acquisition life cycle and discusses pay-off strategies of IT investments.

Chapter five focuses on IT acquisition life cycle and a possible approach in modeling the preparedness across all the stages. This chapter discusses strategic alignment exercises for the IT acquisition organization and conceptualizes the need for establishing a framework for assessment of organizational preparedness. The chapter is built on the strengths of various life cycle approaches discussed in previous chapters and reflects their behaviour in the assessment framework. The framework also included strengths of various model for assessment of quality and user capabilities.

Section three includes discussion on the modeling exercise and techniques adopted. This section has four chapters. Chapter six discusses modeling of IT acquisition process, measurement of the model fitness and its validation including the use of appropriate statistical methods with the perspective of measurement and architectures. Furthermore, the developed model is supported with suitably formulated hypotheses and enumerated variables to support the measurements of the output of the model with a formal proven method.

Chapter seven is devoted for discussing the validation process and its rationale. The readers will get the insights to the way the model is subjected to various parameters of validation notwithstanding their exposure to various techniques used in software engineering process assessments. Various metrics used in the model are presented and discussed. Formulation of hypotheses to justify and establish relationships among metrics and related variables are part of this chapter. This chapter discusses the role of influencers for the model and the way they are organized with the architectural imperatives (interchangeably the term variables are used for influencers). These influencers are placed in three tiers in order to showcase the hierarchical and architectural layering of the management control systems in the organization through systems thinking.

In chapters eight and nine, validation processes for Tiers-I and II are presented for preparing the base for fitness assessment of the model. Chapter eight illustrates the validation of Tier-I variables. Methods used for understanding questions, variables, and especially reliability of questions are discussed. Reliability of questions and multidimensionality of questions are tested for validation of Tier-I variables for further use.

Chapter nine discusses the validation processes for Tier-II. In this chapter, all the null hypotheses are tested with the help of dummy variables, since unequal sample sizes are dealt with in addition to the fact that the sample respondents are in distinct groups with specific deliverables.

In chapter ten, fitness of the model is discussed with various hypotheses formulated. This chapter discusses all the thirteen organizations that participated in this process and shared their data to test the model.

Advancing towards the final stage, section four is devoted to applying the model through an analytical framework. It has two chapters. Chapter eleven discusses the framework for analyses and application of the model, and two cases are presented with detailed organizational behaviour with specific references to their IT acquisition process and the consequences. The model is applied to showcase the observed weaknesses and strengths that the IT acquisition process has developed in the organization.

Chapter twelve includes methods to apply the model in the software engineering process modeling exercises. In particular, the Systems Development Life Cycle (SDLC) model is chosen as an example to map to the model developed and represent them in UML and SPEM languages. The UML-driven model presented in this chapter explains an approach to understanding the capabilities of IT users and non-IT users to collaborate. However, future work may include planning of capability thresholds, examining the capability parameters, and preparing a decision tree to track incapability and address it at the organizational level.

Harekrishna Misra
Institute of Rural Management – Anand, India

Hakikur Rahman
University of Minho, Portugal

Section 1
Organizational Issues in IT Acquisition Preparedness

Chapter 1
Managing Organizations

ABSTRACT

Managing organizations has always remained a challenge for its stakeholders. Challenges are not restricted only to managing factors of production like human resources, capital, and materials in the supply chain, but they also include important determinants for having a better culture, strategies for market and customer orientation, product innovations, and others. Life cycles in organizations are generally influenced by its products and services they deliver because they are to be accepted by the market, processes they adopt to meet the market-oriented product and services, and structures because of corrective measures adopted during every evolutionary phase organizations go through. Because of these effects in an organizational life cycle, organizations need to look after the systemic behaviors in order to ensure that continuity in the systems is retained. In order to achieve these objectives, there is need for the organization to remain prepared to seamlessly integrate organizational behavior with that of process, technology, and people. This chapter discusses these dimensions related to management of organizations, including motivation for creation of organizations, the desire to exist in the market with a better life cycle, and the role of management to ensure organizational continuity.

EVOLUTION OF ORGANIZATIONS

Understanding organizations and at the same time managing organizations are always complex in nature. These dimensions have attracted attention of practitioners, academia and others having interest in strategizing organizational life cycle management. Organizations are termed as human creations (Chandler, 1977). Over the last two decades, a major focus of organization theory has been on understanding the dynamic relation-

ships among individuals, organizations and their environments (Smith, 2008; DHS, 2008). It is argued that individuals are generally asocial and so are organizations. In other words humans tend to create, develop and manage organizations. Organizations influence the way individuals contribute to its goal and vice versa. Thus there is a need to estimate the boundaries in which organizations are created and managed keeping in view the goals and aspirations of individuals. This approach has an implicit ramification in understanding behavior of organization which may unfold the rationale behind adopting management techniques

DOI: 10.4018/978-1-4666-4201-0.ch001

and to look for value additions through systemic approaches. Since organizations are asocial, it is imperative that few human beings collectively create organizations irrespective of their forms. These individuals intend to perform in a certain way to meet common objectives and/or goals (Hicks and Gullet, 1976; Marble, 1992; Budhwar, Varma, Katou and Narayan, 2009). These individuals and created organizations continue to function in an environment. They also tend to establish systems, subsystems, and processes. In many cases organizations are built to meet objectives of individuals who form them. Because of these cohesive relationships, organizations and individuals engage in the process of "organizing," which involves creation of structure and infusing standard operating systems for internal performance management. Besides, organizations interact with the environment for its existence. Managing organizations is a continuous process in which systems, processes, strategies and structure undergo formal and informal changes to meet the overall objective of the organization. One of the critical elements other than the systems, process, and structure is "resources." Organizations strategically identify, acquire and use these resources for its existence either with a motive of "Return on Investment (RoI)" or otherwise (Clegs, 1990). Besides, these acquisitions of resources are influenced by "structures" and "strategies." It is often argued that strategies and structures should follow some sequences depending on the organizational climate. There is another school of thought in favor of a complementing mix between both structure and strategies for attaining synergy. Such divergence contributes adversely to the "systems theory" which largely draws inspirations from the synergic effects while designing systems for organizations. Besides, this confusion makes an organization complex since RoI urges the organization to go to the market and continue to exist. However, such a goal may be difficult to achieve without strategy and structures.

In this aspect, organization theory is not merely a collection of facts, but it is a way of thinking about organizations. Organization theory is rather a way to observe and analyze organizations more accurately and deeply than otherwise possible. The way to observe and think about organizations is largely based on patterns and regularities in organizational design and behavior. Normally organization scholars look for these regularities, define the, measure them, and make them available to the rest of the community. The facts from the finding are not as important as the general patterns and insights into organizational functioning. The insights from organization design research can assist managers improve organizational efficiency and effectiveness, including strengthening the quality of organizational life (Dunbar & Starbuck, 2006).

Evolution of organizations is critically influenced by "internal" and external factors. Market orientation, optimal utilization of resources, maintaining the organizational culture and processes largely influence internal processes. External influences include change in environment and market. Besides, organization also needs to carefully manage its resources, which are mostly market oriented for its existence. Thus organizations need to embrace continuous development process to remain engaged in dynamically changing external and internal environment. This process refers to "change management" in organizations (Sahgal, 1998). Systemic views continue to draw inspirations from the change management principles and capture dynamic behavior of the organization. Well-planned systems with adequate inclusion of change management indicators lead to development of resilient systems and process for garnering the strengths of organization for attaining the goals set.

Change management includes all areas of social, behavioural, economic, political, and scientific sciences that modern organizations practice today. This basket of inter-disciplinary linkages to manage modern organizations has increased complexities (Weber, 1978). Such complexities have provided the basis of systemic views, information management, and induction of technology mediated process improvement methods. In post-modernism, organizations have evolved out of traditional thinking or managing "factors of production", centralization of systems and process, generic command and control management style to move decentralized, facilitating and empowering, formal and informal communication and knowledge influencing environment as presented in Table 1.

In a classic environment, economical consideration provided the organizations to adopt mass production strategies in order to maximize returns. This approach led to large-scale adoption of bureaucratic processes involving specialization, standardization, formalization, centralization and configuration (Webber, 1978). Enterprise Resource Planning (ERP) principles augmented these practices through IT mediation and process automation like Computer Aided Design and Manufacturing (CAD&M). This evolution in organizations is dominated by machine bureaucracy, which influenced organization structure, line of control and work flow and concentration of authority. This evolution also led to a pattern having varying degree of dependencies on technology. It revealed that dependence on technology was low in small batch production units whereas large batch, mass and continuous production organizations had highest level of dependencies on technology. Technologies in this evolution path were seen as tools for improving efficiency, productivity, quality while ensuring mass production. In post-modern era, however, this concept is changed to mass customization, click-n-mortar, business with flexible manufacturing systems etc. This calls for highest degree of dependencies in technologies in general and IT in particular (Clegs, 1990; Awazu et. al., 2009; Standing and Kiniti, 2011).

The classical perception, which sought to make organizations run like efficient, smoothly functioning machines, is associated with the development of hierarchy and bureaucratic organizations and remains the basis of much of modern management theory and practice (Daft, 2008).

In this post-modern era, organizations deal with more uncertain market, high entry barriers for production and services offered by organizations, short transaction life cycles, and above all imperfect markets. Thus in post-modernism era, organizations have evolved to "there is no alternative (TINA)" tendency which professes contingency adjustments to organization structure, to regain effective fit between organizational form and performance function. This flexibility is now contingent upon IT adoption in varying degrees in the organizations (Clegg, 1990; Awazu et. al., 2009). This TINA strategy involves multipronged approach like functional, divisional (either product based or spatial), and matrix structure. Such dynamic restructuring strategy looks for more IT mediated environment to dynamically adjust its processes, information systems.

Table 1. Evolution of organizations (adapted from Petligrew, et al., 2003)

Sl.No.	Classic Organization	Post Modern Era
1.	Centralized	Decentralized
2.	Hierarchical	Inter-functional
3.	Command and control	Facilitating and empowered
4.	Traditional system and process	a) Technology mediation b) Knowledge influenced systems and processes
5.	Factor of production centric	Economy of complementarities and post modernism
6.	Localizing focus	Globalization
7.	Individualized economic focus	Networks and socially embedded
8.	Product orientation	Market orientation
9.	Mass production	Mass customization
10.	Process specific	Innovation orientation

Another set of challenges faced by organization in this post-modernization era is networking among stake holders through a dynamic performance based measurement system. These stakeholders are (internal as well as external) owners, suppliers, clients, partners, competitors, professional bodies, government and regulatory, and media. This network is now well supported by IT mediated supplying chain and value chain models with advent of contemporary IT components and methods. This environmental shift in organizations has necessitated strategic approach to continuously interact with internal and external environment to change processes, change boundaries, remain performance oriented, practice complementarities linked process value additions with minimum redundancies (Petligrew et al., 2005; Dodgson, Gann and Salter, 2006).

EXISTENCE OF ORGANIZATIONS

Society and organizations have been co-existing and complementing each other since evolution of society itself. While organizations have taken various forms in order to meet the ever dynamic requirements of society, existence of society has always been consistently demanding value additions to the quality of life of people in particular and the eco-systems in general.

Emergence of society has been credited to individual humans who form various groups for co-existence. Society ensures ties between individuals and also experiences severance of those ties as well. The social space dynamically experiences conflicts and exchanges while providing scope for individuals and groups to sustain existence. Thus society at large has remained as a ground for organizations to thrive and maintain its life cycle. In other words, organizations emerge with the support of individuals and society. Individuals with common objectives form organizations in order to accomplish certain tasks which may not be otherwise difficult to negotiate individually. Such "anticipatory" motives bring individuals together to form organizations which may include objectives related to economic considerations, institutional purposes (fairness, rationalities) or moral and political (values, rules, norms) (Masav, 1984; Drucker, 1990; Lichtenthaler, 2007; Standing and Kiniti, 2011).

Emergence of organizations has strong relationships with management principles since these forms of group behavior not only include individuals but also use various resources to meet the needs of the groups who collectively nurture their objectives. The intrinsic motivation in individuals to form organizations lies in harnessing collective power to use the resources at disposal to meet set objectives which are generally futuristic. Future is uncertain and historical perspectives, experiential learning and anticipatory approaches of individuals, society as well organizations provide the impetus to tackle these uncertainties. However, inadequacies do exist in such approaches. In order to establish an optimized environment to overcome inadequacies and remain prepared to meet the challenges, organizations continue to exist with the support of individuals who have common goals. This continuity of cohesiveness between organizations and individuals is managed through continuous deliberations and sustained strategies formulated by the organizations. Strategies are translated into action through use of resources available at the disposal of organizations. Thus systems approach (Champian, 1975) becomes essential to interface between strategy and the process through which actionable steps are taken. One of the major strengths that individuals draw through organizational arrangement is to establish systems approach which otherwise would not have been possible for them to handle complexities of society at large. Existence of organizational arrangement provides the basis for having cooperation, developing skills to learn and acquire knowledge to manage future challenges. Establishment of systems is possible through organizations and this is one of the most critical reasons for existence of organizations.

Another dimension that contributes to the existence of organizations is to provide the opportunity to develop historical perspective for the individuals who manage the organization. This perspective leads to development of experiential learning through event databases created in the organizations. Access to these events provides the right tool to establish intelligent scenarios for the individuals and groups in organizations to build scenarios and predict possible solution to future challenges. In modern organizations deployment of systems approaches in these areas have equipped the individuals and groups with decision making tools such as data warehousing, data-mining, business intelligence and modeling approaches. These tools primarily use IT extensively.

Organizations also exist to manage economies of scale and economies of integration to meet the growing demand of individuals and groups who form and continue to grow. Economies of scale bring in a cohesive relationship between organizations, individuals and market. This complex relationship which needs to be market oriented desires that all organizational elements work in tandem to manage factors of production, establish dynamic linkages when the market to innovate, design and produce desired products and services. These elements require systems, processes and measurement standards to encourage individuals and groups to work in a transparent environment for delivery of set results productively. This phenomenon is termed as management of integration. Systems perspectives support these areas adequately. IT also has been playing vital role in managing complex scenarios during growth.

MANAGING LIFE CYCLES IN ORGANIZATIONS

Managing organizations has always remained a challenge for its stakeholders. Challenges are not restricted to only managing factors of production like human resource, capital and materials in the supply chain. They also include important determinants for having a better culture, strategies for market and customer orientation, product innovations, etc. Thus, there is need for establishing a mechanism to understand how all these factors are managed and whether these factors surface cyclically for the organization to consider proactive decisions during evolution followed by revolution (Greiner, 1997; Pereira, 2009; Li, Liu and Liu, 2011; Mukherji, 2012). Understanding this trend provides a better insight to the systems planners to assess and leverage the decision styles in organization. This analysis also provides the systems planner to understand the possible life cycle of the systems being acquired for the organization.

It is argued that organizations undergo changes because of various economical, technological, informational and political factors (Petligrew et al., 2003). Even pressures to stay in business with competition, managing cost of production, facing the regulatory and policy related changes in the sector forces the organization to innovate and manage the life cycles of processes, structures and systems in place. Systems life cycles which follow the organizational life cycles due to the obvious reasons as stated above tend to influence the life cycle of IT deployed. Researchers often recognize that appreciation of organizational life cycles can be through various stages. While there are arguments in identifying various stages, researchers acknowledge that stages of life cycles are mostly irreversible since they follow a progression path and are sequential (Quinn and Cameron, 1993; Lavole and Culbert, 1978). Generically there are four stages involved in an organizational life cycle (Chin, 1994; Jones, 2004). They are "Inception," "Growth," "Maturity," and "Decline." At each stage of this cycle, organization strives to sustain in the entire life cycle to ensure that decline does not creep in easily. This needs a continuous evaluation of the set measurement parameters across the organization at each stage. Information management in each stage becomes very vital for the organization to align itself to the emerging environment and remain in the business for a longer life cycle. In Table 2 each stage is discussed with the information imperatives.

As presented in Table 2, there is scope for information management in each stage of the organizational lifecycle. Thus, the systems planner needs to continuously evaluate the need for organizational changes required and provide newer dimensions to the information management so that organizational continuity is maintained. As explained in Table 1, the inception stage of the organization needs an adequate support of the information systems planners to provide the right knowledge on market, products, and above all the possible directions for the management. At this stage, "liability of newness" is strongly associated with the organization. Thus business modeling approaches are essential to aid the decision making process. Role of information systems at this stage are mostly related to identifying best scenarios to identify products, processes, enumerate the cost and value propositions that each product and process would contribute for overall existence of the organization. These measurement criteria evolve at this stage and thus involvement of information systems planners provide the desired insights to systems development.

The growth stage of the organization seeks intensive engagement with information systems planners since the growth includes the products,

processes, and resource management. At this stage, management of volume is the key to success. IT has proved beneficial in managing volumes of transactions, information created through process interfaces and the roles the organization structure provides. Enterprise wide information management becomes the most desired deliverables of the information systems planners in the organization. Consolidation of information systems infrastructure becomes necessary to direct the return on investments in the areas of information consolidation, management of supply chain and customer relationships.

Maturity stage in the organization relates to learn from the experiences of the growth stage. At this stage, organization needs to stress on the cost optimization, optimizes resource utilization, and inculcate the habit of lean production and processes. Thus, strategic imperatives for the organization are focused on formalized performance measurements. Routine information systems management is the deliverable for the information systems planner at this stage.

Decline stage in the organization is the most unwanted situation. It needs a careful consideration in terms of analyzing the fall in market shares, increased competition, employee turnover, increased costs of production and above all the strategic failures. This stage is the end results of the failures that might have resulted in each of the earlier

Table 2. Organizational life cycle and information imperatives

Stage of life Cycle	Organizational Issues	Information Imperatives
Inception	Understanding the market	Market Information, Knowledge acquisition on product, processes, competition and uncertainty
	Providing Structure	Establishment of Standard Operating Procedures, Performance Measurements
Growth	Resource Management, Control over Cost, Margin and Market Share	Enterprise Resource Planning, Decision Modeling
Maturity	Formalization of Standard Operating Procedures, Deliverables and Benchmarking Performance	Information management through coordination, Collaboration; formalized information flow, Lean Structures and Processes
Decline	Market Behaviour, Adaptation to internal and external pressure, Liability of complacency	Information on innovation, new markets, products and processes, Business Process Re-engineering

three stages. Information systems planners have the toughest challenges at this stage. These challenges include revisiting the systems, processes, market oriented information and the infrastructure that are created over the organizational life cycle. This infrastructure needs to be re-oriented again to ensure that market intelligence is captured for speedy recovery. It calls for process reengineering, restructuring, and providing a new direction to the information infrastructure.

Nolan's stage theory on IT infrastructure acquisition life cycle follows the organizational life cycle closely (Nolan, 1979; Davis and Olson, 2000). Nolan's stage theory included four stages i.e. "Initiation," "Expansion," "Control," and "Maturity." Introduction of computing environment in an organization, as per the model, is based on the basic needs with little planning and control. This step is adopted in the organization to help the employees appreciate the role of computing environment and the way it helps improve processes. Mostly, the aim is to manage the initial resistance to change in the organizational processes due to introduction of automation. Such an approach often leads to isolated efforts in IT acquisition. However, in the inception stage of organizational life cycle as presented in Table 2, the requirements of IT infrastructure is critical. This is because of the benefits of IT to capture market information and introduce products and services as per demand. In this stage, organization provides a structure to formalize the deliverables and thus IT infrastructure needs to take formalized path through responsive information systems.

The second stage of IT infrastructure acquisition and computing environment is related to expansion. In this stage, the organization capitalizes the experiences of first stage and extends it further across the whole organization. At this stage, organization needs control over the resources in view of the fact that it is in growth stage of the organizational life cycle. This stage requires comprehensive resource planning at the enterprise level. Thus, the first stage needs to extend

adequate support through adoption of enterprise IT infrastructure. This consolidation is needed in the second stage so that growth in the organization is managed professionally.

The third stage of Nolan's stage theory suggests that active control is imposed by the organization to protect investments made in this area. Because of this control, benefits accrued in the previous two stages are not realized adequately. Financial controls and performance measurements on IT infrastructure investments are imposed. But at this stage of the organizational life cycle, maturity is attained and this requires further consolidation of IT infrastructure. Maturity in organization deals with adoption of best practices and benchmarking efforts with internal and external interfaces. Thus IT infrastructure set up so far needs to provide this support through adoption of decision models. Thus tight controls may not be in tune with the organizational objectives.

The fourth stage of the Nolan's stage theory is maturity of the IT infrastructure acquired. This calls for adjustments of controls established in the control stage. Most of the applications, services and IT infrastructure enter into an era of complacency as observed in the decline stage of organizational life cycle. At this stage however, organizational life cycle tend to enter into decline stage. This stage is quite critical for the organization since innovative practices need to be adopted for better market orientation and introduction of customer centric products and services. Role of IT infrastructure is also important at this stage to bring the desired steady state in the organizational life cycle. Thus IT infrastructure maturity should be construed as strength to foster the change that organization requires at the decline stage for sustainability.

It is noted that organizational uncertainty increases tremendously in the inception and decline phases and thus role of IT acquisition is very critical in these phases. In these stages volume of information processing is very high. Besides, during growth and maturity stages organizations strive to sustain their activities through continuous improvements. Therefore, in all the stages of the organizational life cycle, IT acquisition needs to be consistently assessed. This will aid the process of organizational continuity.

MANAGEMENT OF ORGANIZATIONAL CONTINUITY

As discussed earlier organizational life cycle needs to influence the IT acquisition life cycle. However, at times there are dissociative relationships between life cycles of organization and IT acquisition. Fundamentally organizations need to be "built to change" in this modern era. This change is related to the continuous improvements in products, processes, structures and systems in the organization to sustain the market pressure (Lawler III and Worley, 2006). This "built to change" approach is highly dependent on the organizational designs through which the life cycles in the products, processes, structures and systems are managed. The rationale behind such management is to understand the organizational response to continuity in its overall designed objectives. In order to maintain the organizational continuity, an organization may have various life cycles of products, processes, structures and

systems. However, organization needs to ensure the overall continuity among these life cycles through an organized effort so that organizational knowledge base is created for better reuse of the efforts and resources. It is therefore, important that each of these life cycles (products, processes, structures and systems) is discussed to understand their effects on organizational continuity and its resilience in managing change. It is also important to reflect on the role of IT infrastructure life cycle in maintaining continuity for each of these life cycles in organization.

- **Product Life Cycle Management:** Typically, a product undergoes five stages in its entire life cycle. In each phase there is scope to garner information for better analyses and decision making. These stages are "Development," "Introduction," "Growth," "Maturity," and "Decline" (Kotler and Keller, 2011; Chin, 1994; Levie and Lichtenstein, 2008). It is argued that at each stage of the Product Life Cycle (PLC) management, there is a scope to gather information and process them.

In Table 3, information imperatives are discussed. It is also noted that during the decline stage, organizations need to renew the profiling of

Table 3. Information imperatives in PLC management

Stage of PLC	Organizational Issues	Information Imperatives
Development	Make your product known and establish a test period	Information sharing through Web technologies; Computer aided modeling, design and engineering
Introduction	Acquire a strong market position	E-Commerce, E-Cataloguing
Growth	Maintain your market position and build on it	Click-n-Mortar Services, e-Supply Chain (Lean)
Maturity	Defend market position from competitors and improve your product	Decision Support Systems for competitor analyses on pricing and Market Behavior through data warehousing and mining
Decline	Product innovation and improvement	Customer interfaces through e-commerce activities as explained in stage-I. Processing of information gathered through all the previous stages for effective modeling and decision making

the product, market and customer so as to provide a new life cycle to the product. Innovation management is an essential input to provide cyclical continuity for the PLC in the organization. IT provides the right ambience for the organization to manage all the related challenges.

Process Life Cycle Management

Process precedes information and organizations need to process information continuously for managing continuity (Ould, 1995). Processes are defined as the formalized approach adopted in an organization to inculcate the habit of transparency, standardization, and formalization. This helps in measurement and quality improvement efforts in the entire organizational life cycle. Three major pillars of the organizational performance are "people," "process," and "technology." Processes are identified through an agreed structure in the entire organization. Each process has unique objectives, ownership, and deliverables. The processes are also repetitive in nature and each cycle brings in expected value additions to the inputs provided to it. Thus, people who own the process need to understand how the process is organized and activated to keep control over the deliverables. Processes in organizations are however, people independent and thus it enables implementation standards across the organizational set up. This standardization also helps formalize the processes to attain maturity over a period of time. An evolved and matured process does not remain as a "black box" for the people who own or operate it. Thus, scope for automation of the process through technology interventions emerges in order to improve upon the management of quality, productivity and volume. But it is argued that technology interventions should follow a suitable process audit and verification of rules and logics through which the process operates (Jeston and Nelis, 2008).

Understanding process life cycles from the organizational viewpoints are quite critical. Organizations, as they grow, create formalized

environments with distinct layers. These layers are "operational," tactical," and "strategic" (Loudon, Loudon and Dass, 2010; Davis and Olson, 2000). These layers also mature over a period of time with clarified roles, responsibilities and delivery mechanism to continuously monitor the stated objectives of the organization. This continuous evaluating approach provides scope for establishment of processes. In each layer therefore, a set of processes emerge for carrying out process specific objectives. Three types of processes are "core," "support," and "management" (Ould, 1995).

Core processes relate to the centrality of the organizational objectives. It means organizational existence is dependent on the very success of the core process management. For example, basic philosophy of a commercial manufacturing organization is to ensure that its customers are satisfied with the product and services and they continue to stay associated with the organization. The life cycle of core processes is quite high and is independent of the other organizational life cycles being discussed in this chapter. It is therefore, essential that these core processes are identified early in the life cycle of the organization and systems are developed to manage them.

Support processes relate to the structural foundations of the organization. Domain expertise emerge out of this life cycle and these process aim to support the management of core processes and provide necessary dynamic inputs to the management in the strategic layer. For example, in a commercial manufacturing organization, the strategic managers may work on introduction of product in the market and may like to assess its feasibility. This process, though not frequent, would demand the inputs from various domains like costing, accounting, marketing, production, and human resource. These domains carry out their respective processes and support the management. Therefore, there is a likely hood that the domain specific process in the tactical layer would also have larger life cycles. In order to provide adequate technology mediated support to these domains various products and services are now available in the market including Enterprise Resource Planning (ERP), process automation products like Supervisory Control And Data Acquisition (SCADA), Computer Aided Manufacturing (CAM), and Computer Aided Designs (CAD) (Loudon and Loudon, (2006)). It is often argued that better life cycles of domain specific processes with necessary integration and interface tools would provide desired results strategically (Lorange and Vancil, 1977; Ward and Peppard, 2000; Flynn, 1998). However, process life cycles are often influenced by strategic decisions related to improvements, re-engineering and replacements of processes.

Management processes organized for supporting strategic decisions in the organization. These processes are used on adhoc basis and they may have very shorter life cycles with reduced scope for reuse. For example, addition of a product in the portfolio requires a process that calls for market research and ends with a decision on this matter. This process is normally infrequent. However, it needs domain specific support and needs to be well organized (Ould, 1995).

Life Cycle Management of Organization Structure

Structure of the organization evolves as a necessity for managing tasks, responsibilities and delivers the desired result as set objectives. Organization structure reflects the arrangements made for the purpose and especially information management principles originate from this structural view (Minzberg, 1979). One of the major applications of Mintzberg model is that it considers managers as "information processors" and they need information as per their need, their role, as well as the organization's delivery systems. Mintzberg also argued that organizational life cycles and structural foundations influence each other for better management of information. His model suggests that information flow should be maintained as per the hierarchy; standardisation of outputs is done

in the organization so that information flow is well coordinated and expectations are well shared among the peers, subordinates as well as superiors. Mintzberg argued in favour of establishing distinct structure for the organizations to provide transparency in information management. He established that there are five types of organization structure and each of them displays certain traits.

Information management in organizations is dependent on the types of structures as presented in Table 4. These structural types influence the style of information flow. Organizations embrace a structure initially and migrating from one to the other type is normally infrequent since it needs investments in all resources. Thus there is strength in learning from these structures and appropriately design the information flow for better decision support. In Table 4 these types and information flow are presented.

There is challenge in maintaining the structure for an organization in the entire life cycle. This is because of the various forces influencing on the existence of the organization. Forces include internal structural pressures due to growth. For example a centralized organization (simple) structure set up in the initiation stage may demand decentralized set up in the future during growth stage. Each stage of organizational life cycle would induce effect on the possible structural assessment in the organization (Greiner, 1997). External forces including competition may also influence the organization structure to implement strategy related to cost optimization, competitiveness, and performance of market oriented deliveries (Lester et al., 2003). Re-organization of resources involved in factors of production during any stage of the organizational life cycle may demand structural re-adjustment. Thus there is continuous pressure on the strategic managers to oversee and proactively align structural changes with that of demand across all stages of the life cycle. Such alignment exercise has bearing the information infrastructure as shown in Table 4. Information imperatives need to ensure that structural adjustments in organizational life cycle do not severely affect the informa-

Table 4. Organization structure and information imperatives (adapted from Mintzberg, 1979)

Organization Structure Types	Representation	Information Imperatives
Simple Structures		Information is centralized. Roles are reactive in nature since few people control information.
Machine Bureaucracy		Information Management is domain specific. Information remains in islands leaving scope to integrate. But the strength in this structure is that standards emerge with clarity. Roles are well clarified.
Professional Bureaucracy		Each individual remains in isolation since they are experts by themselves. Information flow is very seldom in nature. Support staffs are marginalized since their work is minimal in managing information.
Divisionalized		Each division is a replica of the organization. Information flow across divisions is minimal. But upward movement to apex in the organization is very frequent. Each division may have independent task to perform.
Adhocracy		This is complex since knowledge is the main issue. Information remains secondary and supportive in nature. Knowledge workers are the main employees and are mobile.

tion system and IT infrastructure. Re-use of the information systems and IT infrastructure is quite essential since information processing tend to get affected during restructuring. It is thus imperative that organization needs to consider these effects during re-organization, alignment and improvement exercises for sustenance of organizational life cycle. Besides strategic planners need to take note of the implications on choosing organizational types and their effect on information imperatives so as to manage the changes effectively.

LIFE CYCLE MANAGEMENT OF SYSTEMS IN ORGANIZATION

Systems approach to organizations is not a new phenomenon. General Systems Theory (GST) and cybernetics have provided insights to the systems approach to understand the organizational

behavior and the rationale behind development of systems (Jackson, 2000). It is often accepted that organizations and even individuals tend to adopt "reductionist" approach to solve complex issues. Complex issues, as per reductionist approach, can be looked upon as a combination of richly defined smaller parts which can be "interrelated". This approach provides scope for establishing better control, feedback and decision making scenarios in the organization. GST argues in favour of "organic systems" in organization rather than establishing "mechanistic systems". Process life cycles profess in the direction of mechanistic systems in order to provide maturity to the way organizational tasks are carried out. However, in contemporary organizations are not free from market orientation and thus need to be organic. This imposes severe restrictions on process approaches because of the challenges to create "negative entropy" and "steady state" conditions in almost all situations

(Stoyanov et al., 2005). In order to inculcate the habit of attaining "steady state" organizations continuously work for change management involving people, process and technology. This holistic approach is possible through "systems thinking" and therefore, a systems approach to the organization is absolutely necessary.

Systems life cycle is based on the systems thinking. Systems thinking, as a prime mover for holistic approach, generate scenarios wherein all the individualistic approaches merge to meet the overall organizational objectives. This is possible only through the cooperation of people who collaborate to manage the organization. Because of the presence of humans in organizations, all the predicted results are mostly non-linear and thus process approach as explained in earlier section will not remain valid. This non-linearity also enhances the complexity because of "intellectual inertia" and "organizational inertia" (Pfeffer, 1997; Barnett et al., 2000; Jenkins, 1969; Kast and Rosenzweig, 1972). Intellectual inertia in an organization stems from the processes handled over a period of time and people who handle these processes with their explicit and tacit knowledge. These people tend to resist changes during imposition of systems thinking which demands integrated approach cutting across other domains. This resistance to change leads to overall organizational inertia and thus negative entropy creeps into the organization. At this stage systems life cycle is threatened since holistically organization may not be able to sustain the emerging organic behavior.

Another dimension that affects the systems life cycle is the process component in the organization. Processes, since formalized, are designed to manage the repetitive tasks with precision. Processes also are organized to display mechanistic behavior diligently. Because of these situations, organizations tend to create closed systems. The closed systems create entropy in the organization leading to management crisis though these systems work towards adherence to quality, productivity and transactional leaderships (Robbins and Judge,

2008). In order to extend these strengths of the closed systems organizational leadership aims to include control, feedback, and performance measurement parameters. These parameters transform the closed system to an open system. The open system influences the systems life cycle critically since the leadership changes from transactional phase to a transformational scenario. Decision making process at the strategic level imposes constraints of time, integrative approach and non-repetitiveness to make the organization more organic. Various decision models are frequently used with active and integrated support of domain specific services available in the organization.

The third dimension that influences the systems life cycle is the technology. Technology has remained an integral part of development of organization. The very purpose of technology induction in organizations is for enhancing efficiency, reducing repetitive manual processes and human errors, and bringing in overall organizational competitiveness in the market. Contemporary organizational performance measurements have argued in favour of enterprise architectures and business models for integrated systems management. This approach calls for technology mediated processes and enterprise driven information systems (Peters, 1995). This environment influences the organization structure, culture and decision making process involving people. Therefore, systems life cycles are constrained by such influences (Mintzberg, 1979; Flynn, 1998). Systems follow the organization closely to ensure that information is delivered in its true form to the decision makers. Technology enabled systems provide a newer environment in which people engaged in dissemination information feel loss of authority leading to discontinuity in the process management, social structure and the trust prevailing in the organization (Davis and Olson, 2000). Structural changes at times are inevitable due to technology induction. These changes influence the way organization attempts to collaborate with various components and therefore systems behaviour also changes. For example, a centralized organization having an enterprise system may find it difficult to accommodate the changes due to decentralized decision making processes imposed by technology induction (Orlikowski, 1992; Stephen et al., 2009).

SUMMARY

Organizations expect to perform well in its entire life cycle. The continuity in desired performance levels is influenced by various connected life cycles that organization strives to manage and these life cycles are related to products, processes, organization structures and systems. Organizational performance continuum is also influenced by people who grow with the organization. In order to stay competitive and market oriented organization also strives continuously to manage external influences. Thus, internal adjustments with reference to external forces create complex situations for the organization. Technology mediated processes, structures and systems in organization help manage these challenges with great extent. However, technology life cycles impose restrictions in organizational behavior and continuity to meet the set objectives. Thus, there is a need for the organization to remain prepared to seamlessly integrate organizational behavior with that of process, technology and people so that organizational life cycles are maintained for a longer period without decay.

REFERENCES

Awazu, Y., Baloh, P., Desouza, K. C., Wecht, C. H., Kim, J., & Jha, S. (2009). Information-communication technologies open up innovation. *Research Technology Management*, *52*(1), 51–58.

Barnett, W. P., Mischke, G. A., & Ocasio, W. (2000). The evolution of collective strategies among organizations. *Organization Studies*, *21*(2). doi:10.1177/0170840600212002.

Brown, D. R., & Harvey, D. (2006). *Experiential approach to organizational development*. Upper Saddle River, NJ: Prentice Hall.

Budhwar, P. S., Varma, A., Katou, A. A., & Narayan, D. (2009). The role of HR in cross-border mergers and acquisitions: The case of Indian pharmaceutical firms. *Multinational Business Review*, *17*(2), 89–110. doi:10.1108/1525383X200900011.

Champian, D. J. (1975). *The sociology of organizations*. New York: McGraw-Hill Book Company.

Chandler, A. D. (1977). *The visible hand: The managerial revolutions in American business*. Cambridge, MA: Harvard Business.

Chin, D. C.W. (1994, December). Organizational life cycle: A review and proposed directions for research. *Mid-Atlantic Journal of Business*.

Clegs, S. R. (1990). *Modern organizations*. New Delhi: Sage Publications.

Daft, R. L. (2008). *Organization theory and design* (10th ed.). Cengage Learning.

Davis, G. B., & Olson, M. H. (2000). *Management information systems*. New Delhi: Tata McGraw-Hill Publishing Company.

DHS. (2008). *Department of homeland security acquisition instruction/guidebook #102-01-001: Appendix B interim version 1.9 November 7 2008*. Washington, DC: DHS.

Dodgson, M., Gann, D., & Salter, A. (2006). The role of technology in the shift towards open innovation: the case of Proctor & Gamble. *R & D Management*, *36*(3), 334–346. doi:10.1111/j.1467-9310.2006.00429.x.

Drucker, P. F. (1990). *Managing the non-profit organizations practices and principles*. New Delhi: Macmillan India Limited.

Dunbar, R. J. M., & Starbuck, W. H. (2006). Learning to design organizations and learning from designing them. *Organization Science*, *17*(2), 171–178. doi:10.1287/orsc.1060.0181.

Flynn, D. J. (1998). *Information systems require-ments: Determination and analysis*. Berkshire, UK: McGraw-Hill Publishing Company.

Greiner, L. E. (1997). Evolution and revolution as organizations grow: A company's past has clues for management that are critical to future success. *Family Business Review*, *10*(4). doi:10.1111/j.1741-6248.1997.00397.x.

Haag, S., Baltzan, P., & Phillips, A. (2009). Business driven technology. New Delhi: Tata McGraw-Hill Education Private Limited. ISBN: 13: 978-0-07-067109-6

Hicks, H. G., & Gullet, C. R. (1976). *Organiza-tions: Theory and behavior*. Singapore: McGraw-Hill International Book Co..

Jackson, M. C. (2000). *Systems approach to man-agement*. New York: Plenum Publishers.

Jenkins, G. M. (1969). The systems approach. *Journal of Systems Engineering*, *1*, 3–49.

Jeston, J., & Nelis, J. (2008). *Business process management*. New York: Elsevier.

Jones, G. R. (2004). *Organizational theory, design and change*. New Delhi: Pearson Education.

Kast, F. E., & Rosenzweig, J. E. (1972). *General systems theory: Applications for organization and management*.

Kotler, P., & Keler, K. (2011). *Marketing man-agement* (14th ed.). Hoboken, NJ: Prentice Hall.

Lavole, D., & Culbert, S. A. (1978). Stages in organization and development. *Human Relations*, *31*, 417–438. doi:10.1177/001872677803100503.

Lawler, E. E. III, & Worley, C. G. (2006). *Built to change*. San Francisco, CA: Jossey-Bass.

Lester, D. L., Parnell, J. A., & Carraher, S. (2003). Organizational life cycle: A five-stage empirical scale. *The International Journal of Organizational Analysis*, *11*(4). doi:10.1108/eb028979.

Levie, J., & Lichtenstein, B. B. (2008). *From stages of business growth to a dynamic states model of entrepreneurial growth and change (WP08-02)*. Glasgow, UK: Hunter Centre for Entrepreneur-ship, University of Strathclyde.

Lichtenthaler, U. (2007). Managing external technology commercialisation: A process per-spective. *International Journal of Technology Marketing*, *2*(3), 225–242. doi:10.1504/IJTM-KT.2007.015202.

Lorange, P., & Vanicl, R. F. (1977). *Strategic planning systems*. Englewood Cliffs, NJ: Prentice-Hall Inc..

Loudon, K. C., & Loudon, J. P. (2006). *Essentials of business information systems*. Upper Saddle River, NJ: Prentice Hall.

Loudon, K. C., Loudon, J. P., & Dass, R. (2010). *Management information systems*. New Delhi: Dorling Kindersley.

Masav, D. E. (1984). *Voluntary non-profit en-terprise management*. New York: Plenum Press.

Mintzberg, H. (1979). *The structuring of organi-zations: A synthesis of the research*. Englewood Cliffs, NJ: Prentice Hall.

Mukherji, S. (2012). A framework for manag-ing customer knowledge in retail industry. *IIMB Management Review*, *24*, 95–103. doi:10.1016/j.iimb.2012.02.003.

Nolan, R. L. (1979). Managing the crises in data processing. *Harvard Business Review*.

Orlikowski, W. J. (1992). The duality of tech-nology: Rethinking the concept of technology in organizations. *Organization Science*, *3*(3). doi:10.1287/orsc.3.3.398.

Ould, M. A. (1995). *Business process: Modelling and analysis for re-engineering and improvement*. London: John Wiley and Sons.

Pereira, J. V. (2009). The new supply chain's frontier: Information management. *International Journal of Information Management, 29,* 372–379. doi:10.1016/j.ijinfomgt.2009.02.001.

Peters, L. S. (1995). *The dimensions of strategic leadership in technical hybrid organizational relationships.* Advances in Global High-Technology Management.

Petligrew, A. M., Whittington, R., Melin, L., Sanchez-Runde, C., Ruigrok, W., & Numagami, T. (2003). *Innovative forms of organizing.* New Delhi: Sage Publications.

Pfeffer, J. (1997). *New directions for organizational theory: Problems and prospects.* New York: Oxford University Press.

Quinn, R. E., & Cameron, K. S. (1983). Organizational life cycles, and shifting criteria of effectiveness: Some preliminary evidence. *Management Science, 29,* 33–51. doi:10.1287/mnsc.29.1.33.

Robbins, S. P., & Judge, T. A. (2008). *Essentials of organizational behavior.* New Delhi: PHI Learning Private Limited.

Sahgal, J. L. (1988). *Organization development.* Jaipur, India: Rupa Books International.

Smith, W. E. (2008). *The creative power: Transforming ourselves, our organizations, and our world.* London: Routledge. doi:10.4324/9780203888780.

Standing, C., & Kiniti, S. (2011). How can organizations use wikis for innovation? *Technovation, 31,* 287–295. doi:10.1016/j.technovation.2011.02.005.

Stoyanov, E. A., Wischy, M. A., & Roller, D. (2005). Cybernetics and general systems theory (GST) principles for autonomic computing design. In *Proceedings of the Second International Conference on Autonomic Computing (ICAC'05).* IEEE.

Ward, J., & Peppard, J. (2000). *Strategic planning for information systems.* New York: John Wiley and Sons.

Weber, M. (1978). *Economy and society: An outline of interpretive sociology* (Roth, G., & Wiffich, C., Eds.). Berkeley, CA: University of California Press.

Chapter 2
Management and Control:
Organizational Preparedness

ABSTRACT

Systems follow an organization through its phases, products, processes, and structures. Life cycles for systems, therefore, are manageable if other supporting lifecycles of the organization are predictable. In absence of predicting capabilities among the decision makers in the organization, ageing of the systems is obvious. This ageing process leads to decay in information generation and affects organizational intelligence gathering process. Lack of intelligence in the organization impedes the process of growth and sustenance. Intelligence gathering is a continuous process that is based on information generation through establishment of management controls systems in reactive, predictive, and proactive modes of evaluation. It is imperative that a dynamic and strategic fit is achieved, arranged between management and control systems and the strategy formulation and the task control. This dynamic and strategic fit is an indicator of organizational preparedness to manage its system and likely involves articulation of performance measurements by encompassing appropriate financial and non-financial dimensions. This chapter discusses performance management and control system, systemic and systematic behavior in order to establish improved systems thinking and preparedness in the organization.

INTRODUCTION

Managing organizations is a challenging task for the managers working at all levels in the organization. Complexity of this task grows with growth in organization related to volume of productions, and services it handles and structure of the organization that gets changed in its life cycle. Providing a static approach to management of organization is likely to provide undesirable results. Thus, it

DOI: 10.4018/978-1-4666-4201-0.ch002

is quite important to discuss the underpinnings of the management systems in the organization leading to better control over the resources and organizational excellence. This chapter initiates discussion on the management and control mechanisms that organizations adopt for sustained excellence. Exercising controls over resources in the organization is a continuous process for the strategic managers who conceptualize, design and implement control mechanism in the organization for ensuring overall success. It is also equally important for other employees in the organization to understand the features of control mechanisms and monitor the performances across the organization in a transparent manner. Thus, an overall mechanism needs to evolve in the organization for strategizing control systems. This strategy includes preparedness of all stakeholders for better execution of the strategy.

Preparedness implicitly indicates a proactive scenario in which predictive decisions are taken for excellence. It applies to individuals, groups, and organizations. Complexities involved in remaining proactive and prepared to face unpredictable situations with possible solutions are quite enormous. The degree of complexities however, varies with strategies adopted by organizations, individuals, and groups and thus there are no generic "fit-for-all" solutions to all challenges. Thus, preparedness needs to be understood with the context and viewpoints of the entities involved in the problem solving process. Since we are discussing organizational preparedness, it is relevant to contextually focus on the available approaches. This chapter includes discussions on preparedness with three perspectives i.e. organization, systems and technology. It is noted that sequenced approach to understand preparedness in organization, its systems and technology would lead to a better result. This chapter also discusses various barriers in organizing preparedness at the levels of organization leading to better systems with prescribed action plan for technology induction.

Organizations strive for inculcating the habit of standardized measurement and control systems. Contemporary approaches for developing standards for measurements and controls include development of scorecards and dashboards. Role of IT in managing organization wide scorecards and dashboards are quite evident in the context of effective decision making. IT is emerging as an effective contributor to organizational effectiveness. It is frequently argued that success of the IT induction in organization is attributed to strategy, consistent delivery, and systems usability. In this context, IT acquisitions are quite productive in

supporting transactions and in aiding coordination mechanism provided the organizational resources and business processes are properly aligned with the IT. However, many IT acquisition projects fail due to improper alignment of the business process with IT (Misra, 2006). Similarly, moderate preparedness does exist in project management and user motivation (Misra et al., 2005). This chapter discusses measurement issues with specific reference to preparedness in the organization for understanding role of IT.

MANAGEMENT AND CONTROL IN ORGANIZATIONS

Organizations are manmade and a single person is incapable of carrying out all the tasks in the organization. Therefore, many people come together with common goals and perform their duties as per agreed terms of reference. This gives rise to organization structure which could be formal or informal. The organization as it strives to exist, encounters various challenges which are driven by internal and external environment. In order to manage the dynamic situations, management control systems emerge in the organization. This management control system provides directions for the organization. Structures and processes are designed to support the management to ensure that organization traverses the directed path. This desired behaviour is managed and controlled through a mechanism which is acceptable to all stakeholders in the organization. All the elements in the structure of the organization aim to achieve the desired performance individually or collectively so as to ensure that organization continues to exist (Eilon, 1979). Furthermore, a growing number of Emerging Market (EM) firms is showing extraordinary competitiveness in the global market scenario (Stucci, 2012).

Existence and continuity in organization are dependent on purposeful resource planning and management, informed decisions and a transparent span of control. Parkinson's Law and Contingency theory argue that organizations tend to become hierarchical with its growth and thus there is need to focus on task oriented performance management and controls so that organizations can measure and keep control over the resources (Fiedler, 1964; Jones, 2004). This approach is absolutely essential for the contemporary organizations that face uncertain market behavior including customers and competition. Dynamic behavior of these attributes creates challenging situations for the managers in the organization to keep control over resources and their utilization effectively. Thus information management is quite critical to support the managerial decision making process (Merchant and Steede, 2007; Ali and Kumar, 2011). Managers across the hierarchy need to stay prepared for making informed decisions as applicable.

Each stage in organizational life cycle provides a scope to organize span of control and structural approach for effective decision making. Strategically, the management of the organization needs to plan proactively and design communication system across the span of control so that resources are utilized properly for meeting the organizational objective. Growth in the organization creates complex situation to organize control systems for monitoring performance measures which also influences the communication systems. Besides, organizational growth has effects on its structure which may take the forms like functional, divisional, geographical and matrix. Another dimension that influences the management and control is the process in the organization. Processes undergo changes keeping in view the changes that occur in the organizational environment including the technology induction and process improvement imperatives (Dressler, 2004).

Management and control systems fits between strategy formulation and task control (Anthony and Govindarajan, 2004). These systems look for systematic behaviour in the organization for better articulation performance measures encompassing financial and non-financial dimensions. Infor-

mation imperatives emerge out of this strategic approach leading to rule-based and task-oriented performance measures which are mostly controlled and monitored by human resources deployed. In order to ease the pressure on the human resources, reduce human errors for adhering to quality control measures, many tasks are technology induced. This is a part of strategic approach and thus organization needs to prepare itself to foresee the areas of technology intervention through proper analysis of management and control systems.

Systems design for establishing management and control in organizations needs to follow the organizational goals. In no case this sequence should be altered. Thus before strategizing systems design for performance management, and establishing control mechanisms through thresholds it is desirable that organization chooses the best practices and adopts benchmarking procedures. This approach would facilitate better predictability of desired organizational effectiveness. Cybernetic paradigm argues in favour of organizational preparedness for effective decision making through inculcation of habits for establishment of benchmarks and control systems. This cybernetic paradigm indicates that organizational goals should be transformed to measurable performance indicators which should be transparently made available across the organization. These indicators are to be compared with actual performances at a set frequency and reports need to be generated for organizational decision making. Systems design should therefore, formally incorporate the causal behaviour of the variances and record feedbacks for attaining steady states in each segment of the process (Maciarielo and Kirby, 2000). Cybernetics argues in favour of seamless and systemic integration between management and control. It recognizes the fact that systems need to react to the situations arising out of external and/or internal factors, provides a feedback mechanism to the control system and adopts corrective measures to attain a steady state in the organization. The structures and processes in the organization are elements in the systems which contribute to the reaction time and thus there is systems latency for such situations. Management control systems in the organization therefore, need to stay prepared to adapt itself to the situation by accounting the latency period adequately for ensuring steady state (Eilon, 1979; Yong et al., 2011).

DEFINING PREPAREDNESS

Management control systems in organization are part of the preparedness exercise that strategic leadership would like to practice continuously. Preparedness emerges out of proactive planning, creating ability to prevent crisis situations and create infrastructure and processes to manage the crisis occurred despite all steps taken. The crisis or organizational challenges surface due to external pressure or internal environment, leadership, structures and processes leading to a threat to destabilize the set directions in the organization (Shimizu and Hitt, 2004). Thus, strategic flexibility should be there in the organization to predict such crises and prepare itself to maintain steady continuously (King, 2009).

PREPAREDNESS: ORGANIZATIONAL PERSPECTIVES

An organization can be examined with the viewpoints of architectures. Architecture looks for interrelated components which are arranged in a desired fashion (Shaw and Garlan, 1996). In the context of defining preparedness in an organization, it is essential to understand various components that the organizations are made of. Organization structure indicates that generically it can be divided into three distinct layers i.e., "strategic", "tactical" and "operational" (Davis, and Olson, 2000; Loudon et al., 2010; Mintzberg, 1979). As

a first step towards appreciating organizational preparedness, it is essential that preparedness in each layer is assessed.

Strategic preparedness refers to the capability of the strategic managers in the organization to clearly plan and provide a roadmap for the organization. Systematically organizations use methods of establishing standard operating procedures, management feedback and control systems as a part of their preparedness exercise. Role of employees in displaying the eagerness to provide solutions to critical problems, continuously working for mitigating external pressures arising out of competition and technology mediated changes are also part of the preparedness exercise for the organizations. Strategic preparedness needs to address cultural barriers that may emerge due to inflexibility in the organizational structure which may lead to fear of committing mistakes and getting punished. Such apprehensive environment will lead to suppression of mistakes which may have adverse effects in process quality, productivity and efficiency. Thus strategically, there should be transparent mechanism for effective implementation of information and decision management across the hierarchy in the organization. Innovation, incubation and piloting ideas for new processes, products and services through collaborative efforts of all stakeholders are also part of the strategic preparedness in the organization. This would help prepare the organization to have effective measures to address likely problems (Shimizu and Hitt, 2004).

Strategic level preparedness also includes tasks related to taking up corrective measures in the entire organizational life cycle in which change management across employees, domain experts and other stakeholders are inculcated as a habit. This change management covers the entire gamut of exercises including recruitment, training, development and other human resource activities so as to manage the innovation cycles for value added products, services and processes (Deming,

2000; Drucker, 1999; Stamm, 2008). In order to accomplish this, strategic layer in the organization needs to stay prepared to manage changes at short notice without compromising on the culture, best practices and value systems in the organization.

Tactical layer refers to the support structure for the organization. This layer engages in carrying out the strategies and transforms them in to measurable value additions to the products, services and processes. Continuous upgradation in the processes through expert supervision, managing quality across all the factors of production and bridging the inter-functional coordination are the deliverables of this layer for effective delivery of the enterprise wide objectives. Maturity at this level brings in necessary synergy in the value chain. Functional preparedness is absolutely essential for organizational sustenance throughout its life cycle (Davis and Olson, 2000; Loudon et al., 2010).

Tactical layer preparedness contributes immensely towards enterprise level performance through provisioning flexible process environment leading to better and improved customer satisfaction; and managing changes in the entire business which is driven by enterprise wide strategy. This layer also needs to display its preparedness to take care of the strategic alignment priorities arising out of compulsions due to market dynamics and adopt necessary changes in the structures and processes internally. (Tamm et al., 2011; Radeke, 2011). Technological advancement in managing Business Process Re-engineering (BPR) challenges to introduce vale management in products, process and services are to be consciously guided in the organization through tactical preparedness. Non-availability of continuous evaluation and self regulation in this layer would tantamount to degeneration in organizational life cycle at faster pace than expected. Some of the systems oriented tools like Enterprise resource planning (ERP), Decision Support Systems (DSS) and Business Intelligence (BI) are chosen by this layer for continuous engagement with the environment and providing the

right support to the strategic layer (Dressler, 2004; Turban et al., 2008). One of the most important deliveries of the well prepared tactical layer is related to organizational knowledge management. This layer needs to create knowledge repositories and manage best case scenarios as per demand of the strategic layer so as to take informed decisions at a short notice. This organizational knowledge management is possible through coordinated efforts of all functional layers and establishment of well designed process parameters (Fernandez and Sabherwal, 2010, Loudon et al., 2010). Organizational knowledge management is a continuous process and it needs to be an enterprise wide strategy making it person independent. However, care should be taken to ensure that individuals contribute to this repository continuously through parametric driven attributes.

Operational layer is the most formalized layer in the organization. It refers to actual implementation of strategies through predetermined processes. Failure in this layer may lead to catastrophic effects at the organizational level. Preparedness of this layer is quite critical in terms of organizational continuity in its entire life cycle. This layer takes care of repetitive transactions with utmost precision at all times. This layer also continuously support the knowledge repository and information warehouse through the established interface mechanisms across process, systems, and structures in the organization. Successful transactions can effectively take place with the support from tactical layer which needs to specify the processes, identify process owners, design process rules and establish logics for information generation. This preparedness influences the activities in the operational layer. Besides, technology induction is quite critical to manage the repetitive transactions and operations to ensure quality, productivity, and efficiency of factors of production. Operational layer includes a critical mass of human resource that needs motivation to adapt to the changes due to technology induction, process improvement and product portfolio management arising out of the strategic needs in the organization (Gallo, 1988; Davis and Olson, 2000; Dressler, 2004; Fernandez and Sabherwal, 2010). Because of strict formalization in this layer, its preparedness to manage changes is also quite challenging for the organization. Thus it is quite important that BPR strategy takes into consideration the effects of limitations related to human resource engaged in this layer, process rules and logics including interface mechanism for suppliers, customers and other external stakeholders in the supply chain (Gunasekaran, 2009; Cassidy, 2002; Simchi-Levi et al., 2004).

PREPAREDNESS: SYSTEMS PERSPECTIVES

General Systems Theory (GST) describes organizations as systems. A system is identified to be an association of some components which work together to meet the systems objectives. System also organizes feedback and control mechanisms for maintaining steady state and creates negative entropy in the system so that managers could take corrective measures proactively (Gallo, 1988). System has many subsystems to relate to each other for a coherent and macro level information management to provide systematic deliveries and to meet the overall objectives of the system (Turban et al., 2008). Organizations resemble systems characteristics in many ways. Generically, organizations are created with a structure and formalized relationship among various elements as per the structural guidelines. These components perform as per agreed terms of references and deliver the results so as to meet the organizational objectives. Though there are resemblances between organization and systems, there is a need to sequence the availability of systems after the organizational existence. It means systems need to follow the organization so that effective communication management takes place across the organization (Millett, 1998). In Figure 1, the relationship between organization and system is presented.

There are various approaches to organize a system. In this chapter input-process-output framework is adopted for simple approach to the

Figure 1. Organization and systems linkage (adapted from Millett, 1998)

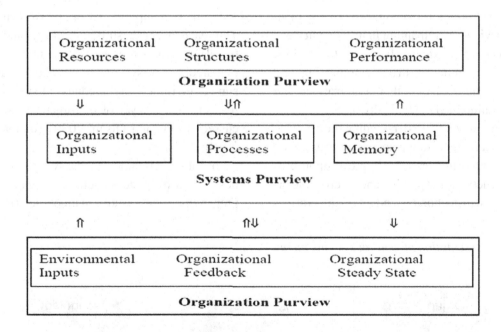

complex phenomenon. In Figure 1 it is presented that organizations use various resources and orient this use across the organization through a structural arrangement for better clarity and transparency in managing flow of information. This information flow is used to measure the organizational performance as per set objectives. Organizational inputs are received as resources from internal and external arrangements. Therefore, it resembles the systems characteristics because systems always take environmental inputs for correcting itself to attain its goals. Organizations, like systems, have various processes which are well organized and provide indications on the variances of desired outputs. All the processes are also interlinked which provides a scope to create a repository on variances and identified causes leading to organizational memory. Structure and feedback at the organizational level influence the rationale on process life cycles and thus leads to adopt process re-engineering activities for better performance. Organizational memory also contributes to attainment of steady state in the organization in order to maintain the desired performance level by taking note of the environment variations and internal resources availability. System designed for the organization needs to have a continuous dialogue with organizational purviews by remaining in its own purview. This purview specific interface aims to establish performance indicator driven monitoring and evaluation mechanism so that organizational life cycle is maintained dynamically.

GST approach for understanding the relationship between organization and systems designed aims for exploring scope to improve upon processes, structures and performances across the organization with technology induction imperatives

(Jackson, 2000; Stoyanov et al., 2005). Technology imperatives may include IT in addition to other technologies available for organizational process improvement. GST argues in favour of technology induction because of the benefits that technology brings in terms of causal analyses vis-à-vis the organizational goals, managing entropy, establishing communication and supporting decision making process (Bertalanffy, 1956). Thus system acts and interface between the organization and technology imperatives as shown in Figure 2.

Generically, systems need to interact with organization and follow the strategic directives and recommends the specific areas of technology interventions as shown in Figure 2. However, research reveals that there are many barriers the systems planners face during the phases related to understand the organizational issues including road maps, strategic directions that decision makers share keeping in view the organizational life cycle and specifying organization-wide performance indicators with clarity (Mockler, 1975; Dressler, 2004; Robbins and Judge, 2008; Jeston and Nelis, 2008; Davis and Olson, 2000; Katsuhiko and Michael, 2004; Loudon et al., 2010). This clarity emerges with the preparedness among the stakeholders managing and collaborating with each other to support the organizational goals. Thus each layer (i.e. strategic, tactical and operational) in organization needs to contribute to the preparedness of systems being planned and designed. In Table 1 preparedness of systems with respect to each layer of the organization is discussed (Davis and Olson, 2000; Loudon et al., 2010).

In Table 1 it is indicated that systems preparedness is entirely dependent on organizational preparedness and systems planners need to ensure

Figure 2. Presentation of general systems theory

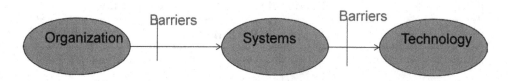

Table 1. Preparedness mapping (organization and systems)

Organizational Layer	Organizational Preparedness Attributes	Systems Preparedness Attributes
Strategic	Organization Structure, Decision Style, Maintenance of organization culture, Formalization of organizational Performance Indicators	Environmental Feedback mechanism, Procedures for internal resource management and external interfaces, Systems Modeling
Tactical	Process preparedness, Establishment process rules and logics, process parameters related to organizational performance, Process interface mechanisms as per the organization structure, establishing role clarity in organization as per organization structure	Organizing process rules and logics with integrated views, establishment of process interface mechanisms, identification areas where entropy could be managed on priority and sequencing the factors responsible for steady state, Process modeling
Operational	Transaction preparedness, Identification of transaction owners and their roles in the organization	Identification of modes of transaction, mapping the frequencies and volume of transaction, formalizing transaction cycles, generation of information with the support of process rules, logics and transactions

that barriers are proactively bridged. This activity should also include an architectural fitness between organization and systems (Shaw and Garlan, 1996; Maier and Rechtin, 2009).

PREPAREDNESS: TECHNOLOGY PERSPECTIVES

As shown in Figure 2, Systems and technology are related in a sequence. It means there are various barriers between systems established and technology being inducted in the organization. These barriers include procedures adopted by the systems planners, decision makers and technology planners in the organization. Fitness among organization, systems and technology is also essential for enhancing organizational performance (Strong and Volkoff, 2010). Due to prolific advancements in technology, there are occasions in which organization tends to outsource the technology acquisition (dependence on technology suppliers and ignoring systems planning) and acquire of technology embedded processes, and equipments (dependence of equipment suppliers). In such types of scenarios barriers creep

into the organization in the form of technology oriented process knowledge, development of human resource, effect in performance indicators in the organization and short technology life cycles (Davis and Olson, 2000; Kalusopa, 2005; Loudon et al., 2010; Jeston and Nelis, 2008; Gollakota,, 2008; Gómez and Vargas, 2012). Technology obsolescence is an important dimension which draws attention of technology planners continuously. Thus preparedness exercise is essential in the organization to ensure that barriers between systems and technology are proactively addressed. Organization needs to continuously evaluate the appropriateness of latest technologies and their likely effects on the process improvement parameters influencing overall business imperatives. In Table 2 some of the preparedness attributes are discussed to appreciate the relevance of the exercise.

Technology perspectives have direct relationships with the perspectives of organization and systems in a sequence as explained in Figure 2. Technology in general and IT in particular (for this book) intends to optimize costs of transaction, coordination and agency involved in the system designed for the organizational performance as-

Table 2. Preparedness mapping (systems and technology)

Organizational Layer	Systems Preparedness Attributes	Technology Preparedness Attributes
Strategic	Environmental Feedback mechanism, Procedures for internal resource management and external interfaces, Systems Modeling	Technology for Decision Support Systems and Executive Support Systems as applicable to systems modeled
Tactical	Organizing process rules and logics with integrated views, establishment of process interface mechanisms, identification areas where entropy could be managed on priority and sequencing the factors responsible for steady state, Process modeling	Enterprise Resource Planning (ERP), Tools for managing organizational memory (Explicit and Tacit), Managing internal and external information through organization wide databases, networks and applications as relevant to the architectures of organization and systems, preparation of process and data models to optimize costs on transactions, agency and coordination; Technology for Data Mining and Warehousing
Operational	Identification of modes of transaction, mapping the frequencies and volume of transaction, formalizing transaction cycles, generation of information with the support of process rules, logics and transactions	Adoption of suitable transaction modes with technology induction imperatives, managing transaction volumes with concurrency, latency, accuracy and timeliness of transaction cycles.

sessment. Various theories have evolved to showcase the benefits if IT induction over the years (Loudon et al, 2010). Most prominent among these theories are "micro-economic theory," "agency cost theory," and "transaction cost theory." Micro-economic theory suggests that information is acknowledged as factor of production and is extensively used in support of establishing perfect market where all the stakeholders in the supply chain can benefit through transparency and lean supply chain systems. Agency cost theory suggests that because of information management through the use of IT, market orientation can be implemented in the organization leading lean production systems and establishment of lean supply chains (Pereira, 2009). E-Commerce, M-Commerce, and E-Business suites are now available to support the organization immensely with the support from ERP solutions in the backend (Turban et al., 2008; Loudon et al., 2010; Ward and Peppard, 2000; Cassidy, 2002). It is argued that IT preparedness in the organization can reap the benefits of improving customer "management capability," "process management capability," and "performance management capability," leading to overall organization "capabilities" (Mithas et al., 2011).

MANAGING ORGANIZATIONAL DECISIONS AND CONTROLS

Management control has remained a challenging area for all the organizations despite advancements in technology, management theories and approaches to the organizational performance measurement. Keeping control over factors of production; establishing proactive, preventive, active and reactive decision making processes are parts of the organizational performance measurement designs (Hatry, 2006; Mockler, 1975). Effective management is solely dependent on organization's set goals, established control and decision support structures at all levels in the organization. These elements are inseparable and absence of one may imbalance the expected organizational performance. But the challenge is to bind the people at all levels who contribute to the effective management of the set goals in the organization. This binding force is dependent on the way the organization is preparing itself continuously to establish transparent and agreed standards for management controls and performance measurement procedures. This preparedness is strategic exercise in the organization (Davis and Olson, 2000; Maciarielo, and Kirby, 2000).

Role of information management in the areas of management control and performance measurement is quite critical. Strategic approach to Information management to deal with proactive, preventive and reactive decisions across the organization is unique and each of these scenarios requires specific resource. There are various generic approaches leading to these decision scenarios. These approaches consider quantitative methods, qualitative parameters and operational thresholds for supporting performance measurement in the organization. It is argued that performance measurement in the organization is possible for those areas where the outcomes can be tracked, analyzed, projected and predicted (Mockler, 1979; Hatry, 2006; Lokshin, Hagedoorn and Letterie, 2011). All these activities relate to information management, management control and decision theory (Hansson, 2005).

Information generated from the organizational structure, roles and processes help track outcome and analyze the behaviour of the tasks at hand. In many occasions people specific information is needed because of their roles in the organization. But organization wide information relates to standard operating behaviour and control systems which are generally accepted at all levels. Such organization wide operational behaviour and control measures are normative in nature which leads to an "evaluation-choice" routine (Hansson, 2005). These normative measurements provide an insight to the desired performance oriented decisions across the organization and also establish information management principles to control the rational decision making. This measurement has a limitation of undermining alternative choices. Such choices arising out of "evaluation-choice" routine approaches can restrict the intelligence gathering in the organization. However, such a practice provides the inherent preparedness in the organization to make the routine decisions more formal, preventive and predictive. Modern organizations today have IT supported decision making tools that support routine decisions. ERP and BI tools are part of this category which has matured to a level of product orientation with standard delivery modules fitting into generic business scenarios. Modern sequential decision models have supported these products as well (Hansson, 2005; Turban et al., 2008). Organizational preparedness therefore, is quite essential in this area to identify decision criteria, establish routine methods for formalizing "evaluation-choice" decision scenarios, and adopt IT enabled processes in order to enhance organizational performance.

According to Simon, organizations expect that its executives in the hierarchy need to spend more time on intelligence gathering (Simon, 1960; Hansson, 2005). This proactive decision making preparedness in the organization is a continuous process and needs dynamic inputs from the information management principles designed for the purpose. In order to sustain this preparedness, executives need to interface with market for intelligence gathering and related the inputs to the internal information resources to bridge the "design-reality" gaps. Normally, this proactive decision making process is based on probabilistic decision models, domain specific explicit knowledge and tacit knowledge based experiential analyses of the executives. Organizational preparedness in these areas influences the quality of decisions taken by executives leading to organizational performance. Qualitative decisions mostly are pursued in this scenario. On many occasions, searches for ideal solutions to the pre-defined problems available in the organizational repository are made for references. At times, non-sequential decision models with intuitive inputs of the decision analyzer with alternatives are also adopted for taking proactive decisions. Expert systems, decision support systems, and executive support systems are few of the models with active support from data mining and warehousing principles have emerged as standard tools for decision making. Organizations need to align their capabilities and preparedness to choose the right IT enabled services and products for enhancing effectiveness of organizational performance (Mockler, 1975; Beer, 1974; Ward and Peppard, 2000; Turban et al., 2008; Abramovsky, et al., 2009).

It is important to note that organization's situation specific decision making scenarios are modeled in its entire life cycle. In the process, various decision models are innovated, applied and modified to settle for benchmarks and attain maturity in the decision making process. Levels of maturity in making decisions and adopting decision tools are influenced by the organizational priorities. These priorities include decision styles (reactive, preventive, and proactive) among the executives, ability to understand internal and external environment seamlessly. The organization therefore, needs to stay prepared to use models that can support the decision styles meeting the dynamic requirements. In the Table 3, various approaches are listed to explain the rationale behind adopting decision styles in the organization.

It is noted that organizations face dynamic situations and complex decision making scenarios to sustain the set goals. Styles of decision making as presented in Table 3 depend on the structuredness of the problems identified. Degree of structuredness varies with respect to the internal and external environment and the preparedness of the organization to make rational choices based on normative-affective factors. Structuredness also depends on the degree of formalization in the organization. During this process of formalization, the limitations of aggregation arising out of individual decision making processes vis-à-vis organizational priorities. Extrapolation errors are quite normal in this process of aggregation at organization level. In certain cases benchmarking representative and ideal decision styles are adopted to assess the success factors for an organization. As such this approach also is not free from errors. Computing environment however, needs well designed performance measurement indicators in order to provide better control systems for the organization. Various tools have been developed for capturing the measured performances at the levels of individuals and the organization systematically. This systematic approach provides scope for managing overall efficiency and effectiveness in the organization. Systemic approach to the organization on the other hand, explores the probabilistic situations for the organization while taking into account the inputs from the systematic processes established for performance

Table 3. Decision styles and the rationale (adapted from Hansson, 2005)

Decision Style	Rationale for Decision Styles	References
Reactive	Collaborative Resolutions	Hansson, 2005
	Explicit and Tacit Knowledge based Problem Solving tools – Structured Approaches	Davis and Olson, 2000; Turban et al, 2008; Klein and Methile, 1992
Preventive	Intelligence Gathering through information retrieval techniques and searches for best practices	Mintzberg et al, 1976
	Designed parametric evaluation mechanisms through benchmarking, Structured Approaches to Problems	Davis and Olson, 2000; Ward and Peppard, 2000; Luftman, 2003
	preparing choices and alternatives with explicit and tacit knowledge	Simon, 1960; Fernandez and Sabhrewal, 2010
Proactive	Intelligence Gathering through information retrieval techniques and searches for best practices	Mintzberg et al, 1976
	Infusing Systems Thinking	Midgley, 2003
	Probabilistic Decision Modeling for managing uncertainty, Unstructured Environment	Hansson, 2005; Zeleny, 2005; Zey, 1992

measurements. Systemic assessment is holistic and proactive and preventive decision styles are included in this assessment. Systematic assessment includes the reactive decision styles and explicit behaviour of the organizational processes is taken care of continuously. In this context, organizational preparedness is an essential issue for establishing a mechanism to assess the organizational priorities. These priorities need to be included in the systems established for their internalization organization-wide. This inclusion will enable the strategic planners to have a roadmap for technology acquisitions in general with specific emphasis on IT infrastructure acquisitions.

TRANSLATING ORGANIZATIONAL PREPAREDNESS INTO ACTION

Transforming strategies into actionable parameters is a challenge for the organization. Overall strategies formulated at the organizational level need careful translations into actionable objectives which are verifiable against set parameters. The process of translation however, is quite complex. Various approaches have evolved so far to address

this challenge including BPR, balanced scorecard and workflow management. Initially, organizations look for performance measures based on factors of production. This approach provides domain specific results through effective and parameter centric matured processes.

Though this scenario brings in expertise and maturity in understanding and improving businesses, a careful balancing between external and internal environment has become essential for contemporary organizations. Organizations today need more Business Intelligence (BI) than typical data management and process improvement tools. IT has transformed the organizational decision making process through BI approaches (Turban et al., 2008).

In Figure 3 the role of BI architecture in organizational decision making process is presented including a sequential flow of the architecture for an active BI scenario. Organizational preparedness to put BI scenario in place for effective decision making requires a series of internal exercises. In the first step of the exercise, data management comes in. But there are divergent views on data management. One school of thought refers to information systems needs of the organization to

Figure 3. Business intelligence architecture (adapted from Turban, et al., 2008)

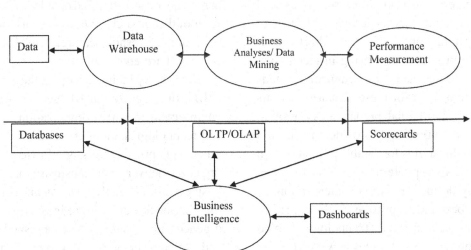

steer the data management scenario (top-down approach) whereas in other it is argued in favour of having bottom-up planning. In a top-down approach the challenge lies in forecasting the data requirements keeping in view the dynamic requirements and building a responsive database. In bottom-up planning process data are populated independent of organizational requirements which may be managed with tools for retrieval, extraction, and mining of data. In contemporary computing scenario both the options are feasible. However, organization needs to prepare for data management scenario professionally. It is desirable that all the three layers in the organizational hierarchy as discussed in Table 2 are prepared for organizing data management principles and creating ownerships for the organizational databases.

The second step in the architectural exercise refers to data warehousing. This requires architectural preparedness at the organizational level . The geographical and structural arrangements need to be reflected with a roadmap so as to establish data warehousing principles with appropriate technology adoption. This requires a fitness exercise between organization, systems and technology layers as explained in Figure 1.

The third step involves business analyses and relationship among processes in the organization. This includes a preparedness exercise to ensure that transparent business processes, rules and performance indicators are articulated prior to technology induction. In absence of this technology service providers may bring in technology enabled processes and the organization needs to adopt them. Each of these scenarios has its own advantage. Internal preparedness prior to technology adoption may provide the desired control and thresholds for establishing clarity in delivery and appropriate decision can be taken to explicitly define the areas of intervention. In other case, best and innovative practices may be a part of the vendor driven technology enabled products and services. This may however, require Business Process Re-engineering (BPR). ERP

with On-Line-Transaction-Processing (OLTP) and On-Line-Analytical-Processing (OLAP) tools can be part of this delivery process. In either case however, organization needs to stay prepared (Loudon et al, 2010; David 2004).

The fourth step includes holistic performance measurement in the organization. This is a critical job to accomplish in contemporary organizations who strive for standard performance measures. But market dynamics, competition, lower life cycles in business and technologies influence the performance measurements scenarios in the organization. Despite these challenges, it is essential that organizations strive for establishing standards for processes, workflows, transactions and related activities to support performance measurements designed for routine and structured decisions. This is likely to provide scope for the strategic managers to invest more time for unstructured decisions. During this process, efficiency of operational managers is likely to improve with respect to the workflows managed by them and extending desired support to the tactical managers. These tactical managers are engaged in reactive and preventive decisions environment and support of operational managers is quite essential (Davis and Olson, 2000). One way of dealing with this challenge is to conceptualize, design and develop scorecards with active inputs from all domains across the organization and people working in each layer of the hierarchy. Management Controls and operational thresholds are reflected in the design process (Parmenter, 2007).

The last step includes scoping the development of BI in the organization. BI looks for an integrated environment in which organization, its systems and technologies adopted are in sync with each other. This preparedness is reflected through an organized delivery mechanism in which databases, business process, analytical tools and performance measurement standards are implemented in congruence with organization's established structures and decision styles. In order to have an effective BI tools implementation, it is necessary to install organization-wide scorecards and dashboards for better decision making. This process supports the systems preparedness as explained in Figure 2 and the barriers between "organization-systems" and "systems-technology" can be narrowed down considerably leading to better performance management.

ORGANIZING SCORECARDS

Modern organizations are continuously working towards performance measurement to foster sustainable growth. In this process each organization faces a distinct set of challenges to infuse matured decision making processes for establishing organization-wide performance management systems. Developing scorecard and utilizing them organization-wide are considered as important tools for performance management. Business metrics are used as part of this process for effective deployment of scorecards (Phelps, 2004). Scorecards are used for display of progress, summaries and snapshots, thresholds with benchmarked targets and are linked to objectives. This linkage and assessment instrument in scorecard enables the decision maker to take preventive,

reactive and proactive decisions. Scorecards are mostly data intensive and they provide insights to the business performance analyses with the applications of tacit and explicit knowledge of the scorecard user.

As explained in Table 1 each layer in the organization is likely to have a set of scorecards i.e., operational, tactical and strategic layers. All the layer specific scorecards have their own data management principles with set benchmarks.

The scorecards in the organization are expected to bring clarity in roles, accountability and preparedness to take informed decisions by individual scorecard owners. Scorecards also are intended for improvement in communications across all the layers in the organization.

In Figure 4 scorecard management principles are presented. Scorecards emerge from the strategies formulated for the organization. In the process, key performance indicators / measures are listed for effective utilization of scorecards. Scorecards are also influenced by objectives set for each task evolving from the strategic initiatives. For example, profit could be a business metrics developed for the effective utilization of resources and the scorecards supporting profit measurement may lead a series of indicators re-

Figure 4. Scorecard management (Kaplan & Norton, 1996)

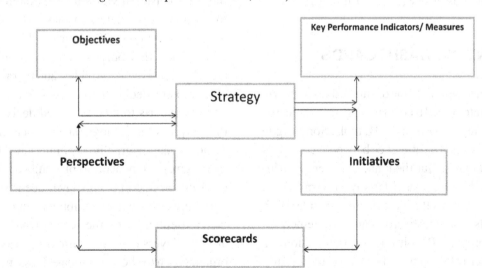

lated to financial, human resources, inventory of raw materials, finished goods and work-in-process materials. Each of these indicators may undergo benchmarked thresholds for evaluation continuously. Pure databases and related applications may support this performance management with greater degree of perfection.

Evolution of metrics driven scorecards has now been towards "balanced scorecards" (Kaplan and Norton, 1996). Balanced scorecard approach provides a holistic view on integrated business metrics deployed organization-wide. This also brings in preparedness at the levels of organization and systems leading identification of scopes for technology mediation with specific reference to IT. The purview of balanced scorecard includes identification of key drivers to the overall success of business. The balanced scorecard is structured around the measures related to financial, customer, learning and operational dimensions of the organization. It assumes to be a top-driven strategic initiative. The intention of balanced scorecard driven performance measurement is to create value added information management in the organization through investment in customers, suppliers, employees, processes, technology and innovation (Kaplan and Norton, 1996). It is observed that balanced scorecard driven performance management systems in organizations have led to sustainable business with larger life cycles.

ORGANIZING DASHBOARDS

BI tools have embraced the dashboards as a generic tool for strategic and tactical managers. Scorecards are also integral parts of the BI tools. Some argue that there is a subtle difference between scorecards and dashboards. But the small difference influences the decision maker largely in terms of the support structures that dashboards provide. Both scorecards and dashboards can complement to form a complete BI toll for the organization. IT has a larger role to play in both areas of decision

making process. Unlike scorecards, dashboards are used with graphics supported by real-time data. These dashboards can be well interpreted by the domain experts with their tacit and explicit knowledge to interpret the information retrieved holistically. One example of a dashboard is the cockpit of an airplane and the user is the pilot having adequate knowledge to interpret and take informed decisions instantly. Thus role of IT is quite critical in design, development, and implementation of dashboards.

Applications of dashboards in organizations have long-term influences in the decision making process. Dashboard designs encourage organization-wide business process and information systems alignment, establishment of coordination and collaborative methods and auditing strategies for better performance management. Dashboards also supports establishment of procedures for multi-dimensional analyses with convergence like balanced scorecards and alerts etc., for proactive decision making (Eckerson, 2006).

Dashboards have three generic layers. The first layer is operational layer. It has all the properties of scorecards that would indicate all results based on benchmarked thresholds. It encourages data warehouse concepts for better coordination and control over databases. The second layer is the tactical layer which enhances the scope for multi-dimensional views for the domain experts to summarize, collate and take a holistic view on a specified task. OLAP principles are largely adopted for this purpose and the applications are IT intensive. It provides an interactive and probabilistic decision making scenario for the domain experts to take informed decisions. The third layer is the strategic layer which involves a BI portal having graphic user interfaced business metrics management principles embedded for better decision making. This layer needs snapshots with little or no text and numbers, but with lots of tacit presentations for the decision maker. Across all these layers there is an important task for the organization to show its preparedness in structure

Figure 5. Barriers in managing organizational preparedness (adapted from Kaplan & Norton, 1996)

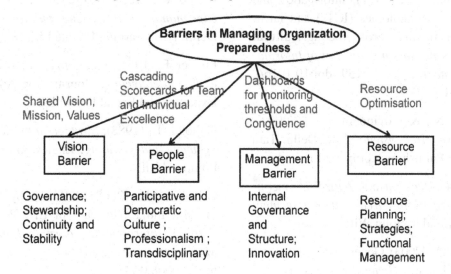

and systems to adopt IT strategy appropriately (Eckerson, 2006; Kaplan and Norton, 1996, Turban et al., 2008).

As shown in Figure 5, organizational preparedness is a continuous process which has to ensure that all the barriers related to vision, people, management and resources are neutralized professionally. Role of scorecards, dashboards, and IT enabled services is noteworthy in addressing these barriers.

SUMMARY

In this chapter, it is clarified that assessing organizational preparedness in managing IT acquisitions is a complex phenomenon. Assessment of organizational preparedness includes establishment of systems and delve into prioritized areas for technology induction with a proper roadmap. While doing so, organization is expected to address various barriers which may include human resources and other stakeholders like suppliers, customers and technology providers. Challenges to address these barriers are multi-dimensional and organization needs to stay prepared for man-

aging them for better IT acquisition life cycles. This requires a logical and sequential approach and this preparedness needs be organization-wide with transparent management control systems. Organizing scorecards and dashboards is one of the approaches for instilling better measurement and controls. Conceptualization, design, and development of scorecards and dashboards are integral constituents of organization and systems preparedness. Thus preparedness for management of IT acquisition life cycles can draw useful insights through scorecards and dashboards.

REFERENCES

Abramovsky, L., Kremp, E., Lopez, A., Schmidt, T., & Simpson, H. (2009). Understanding cooperative R&D activity: Evidence from four European countries. *Economics of Innovation and New Technology, 18*(3), 243–265. doi:10.1080/10438590801940934.

Ali, J., & Kumar, S. (2011). Information and communication technologies (ICTs) and farmers' decision-making across the agricultural supply chain. *International Journal of Information Management, 31*, 149–159. doi:10.1016/j.ijinfomgt.2010.07.008.

Anthony, R. N., & Govindarajan, V. (2004). *Management control systems*. New Delhi: Tata McGraw-Hill Publishing Company Limited.

Beer, S. (1974). *Decision and control: The meaning of operational research and management cybernetics*. London: John Wiley & Sons.

Bertalanffy, L. V. (2003). General systems theory. In Midgley, G. (Ed.), *General Systems (Vol. 1)*. London: Sage Publications.

Bruce, M. (1998). Understanding organizations: The dominance of systems theory. *International Journal of Organisational Behaviour, 1*(1), 1–12.

Cassidy, A. (2002). *A practical guide to planning for e-business success: How to e-enable your enterprise*. Boca Raton, FL: CRC Press.

Davis, G. B., & Olson, M. H. (2000). *Management information systems*. New Delhi: Tata McGraw-Hill Publishing Company.

Deming, E. E. (2000). *Out of crisis*. Cambridge, MA: The MIT Press.

Dressler, S. (2004). *Strategy, organization and performance management: From basics to best practices*. Boca Raton, FL: Universal Publishers.

Drucker, P. F. (1999). *Management challenges for the 21ˢᵗ century*. New York: Harper Business.

Eckerson, W. W. (2006). *Performance dashboards: Measuring, monitoring and managing your business*. New York: John Wiley & Sons.

Eilon, S. (1979). *Management control*. Oxford, UK: Pergamon Press.

Fernandez, I. B., & Sabhrewal, R. (2010). *Knowledge management: Systems and processes*. New Delhi: PHI Learning Private Limited.

Fiedler, E. (1964). *A contingency model of leadership effectiveness*. Journal for Advances in Experimental Social Psychology.

Gallo, T. E. (1988). *Strategic information management and planning*. Englewood Cliffs, NJ: Prentice Hall.

Gollakota, K. (2008). ICT use by businesses in rural India: The case of EID Parry's Indiagriline. *International Journal of Information Management, 28*, 336–341. doi:10.1016/j.ijinfomgt.2008.04.003.

Gómez, J., & Vargas, P. (2012). Intangible resources and technology adoption in manufacturing firms. *Research Policy, 41*, 1607–1619. doi:10.1016/j.respol.2012.04.016.

Gunasekaran, A. (Ed.). (2009). *Advances in enterprise information systems*. Hershey, PA: IGI Global.

Hansson, S. O. (2005). Decision theory – A brief introduction. Stockholm, Sweden: Royal Institute of Technology (KTH).

Hatry, H. P. (2006). *Performance measurement: Getting results*. Washington, DC: The Urban Institute Press.

Jackson, M. C. (2000). *Systems approach to management*. New York: Plenum Publishers.

Jeston, J., & Nelis, J. (2008). *Business process management*. New York: Elsevier.

Jones, G. R. (2004). *Organizational theory, design and change*. New Delhi: Pearson Education.

Kalusopa, T. (2005). The challenges of utilizing information communication technologies (ICTs) for the small-scale farmers in Zambia. *Library Hi Tech, 23*, 414–424. doi:10.1108/07378830510621810.

Kaplan, R. S., & Norton, D. P. (1996). *Balanced scorecard: Translating strategy into action*. Boston: Harvard.

King, W. R. (Ed.). (2009). *Planning for information systems*. New Delhi: PHI Learning Pvt. Ltd..

Klein, M., & Methile, L. B. (1992). *Expert systems: A decision support approach*. Cornwall, UK: Addison-Wesley Publishing Company.

Linthicum, D. S. (2004). *Enterprise application integration*. New Delhi: Pearson Education Inc..

Lokshin, B., Hagedoorn, J., & Letterie, W. (2011). The bumpy road of technology partnerships: Understanding causes and consequences of partnership mal-functioning. *Research Policy*, *40*, 297–308. doi:10.1016/j.respol.2010.10.008.

Loudon, K. C., Loudon, J. P., & Dass, R. (2010). *Management information systems*. New Delhi: Dorling Kindersley.

Luftman, J. (2003). Assessing IT/business alignment. *Information Systems Management*, *20*(4), 9–21. doi:10.1201/1078/43647.20.4.20030901/77287.2.

Maciarielo, J. A., & Kirby, C. J. (2000). *Management control systems: Using adaptive systems to attain control*. New Delhi: Prentice-Hall of India Private Limited.

Maier, M. W., & Rechtin, E. (2009). *The art of systems architecting*. Boca Raton, FL: CRC Press.

Merchant, K. A., & Van der Steede, W. A. (2007). *Management control systems – Performance, measurement, evaluation and incentives* (2nd ed.). Essex, UK: Prentice Hall.

Midgley, G. (2003). *Systems thinking: An introduction and overview*. London: Sage Publications.

Millett, B. (1998). Understanding organisations: The dominance of systems theory. *International Journal of Organisational Behaviour*, *1*(1), 1–12.

Mintzberg, H. (1979). *The structuring of organizations: A synthesis of the research*. Englewood Cliffs, NJ: Prentice Hall.

Mintzberg, H., Dury, R., & Andre, T. (1976). The structure of 'unstructured' decision processes. *Administrative Science Quarterly*, 21.

Misra, H. K. (2006). Role of human reource in information technology alignment in organizations: A metric based strategic assessment framework. *Journal of Information Technology Management*, *17*(3).

Misra, H. K., Satpathy, M., & Mohanty, B. (2005). Assessment of IT acquisition process: A metrics based measurement approach. *Vilakshan: XIMB Journal of Management*, *2*(2), 23–54.

Mithas, S., Ramasubbu, N., & Sambamurthy, V. (2011). How information management capability influences firm performance. *Management Information Systems Quarterly*, *35*(1), 237–256.

Mockler, R. T. J. (1975). *The management control process*. New Delhi: Prentice-Hall Inc..

Parmenter, D. (2007). *Key performance indicators: Developing, implementing, and using wining KPIs*. New York: John Wiley & Sons.

Pereira, J. V. (2009). The new supply chain's frontier: Information management. *International Journal of Information Management*, *29*, 372–379. doi:10.1016/j.ijinfomgt.2009.02.001.

Phelps, B. (2004). *Smart business metrics*. London: Pearson Education Limited.

Radeke, F. (2011). Toward understanding enterprise architecture management's role in strategic change: Antecedents, processes, outcomes. In *Proceedings of Wirtschaftinformatik*. Wirtschaftinformatik.

Robbins, S. P., & Judge, T. A. (2008). *Essentials of organizational behavior*. New Delhi: PHI Learning Private Limited.

Seddon, P. B., Shanks, G., & Reynolds, P. (2011). How does enterprise architecture add value to organisations? *Communications of the Association for Information Systems*, 28.

Shaw, M., & Garlan, D. (1996). *Software architecture: Perspectives on an emerging discipline*. New York: Prentice Hall.

Shi, Y., Tian, Y., Kou, G., Peng, Y., & Li, J. (2011). *Optimization based data mining: Theory and applications*. New York: Springer. doi:10.1007/978-0-85729-504-0.

Shimizu, K., & Hitt, M. A. (2004). Strategic flexibility: Organizational preparedness to reverse ineffective strategic decisions. *The Academy of Management Executive*, *18*(4), 44–59. doi:10.5465/AME.2004.15268683.

Simchi-Levi, D., Wu, D. S., & Shen, Z.-J. (Eds.). (2004). Handbook of quantitative supply chain analysis: Modeling in the e-business era. New York: Springer Science + Business Media Inc.

Simon, H. A. (1960). *The new science of management decision*. New York, NY: Harper and Row. doi:10.1037/13978-000.

Stamm, B. V. (2008). *Managing innovation, design and creativity*. Hoboken, NJ: John Wiley and Sons.

Stoyanov, E. A., Wischy, M. A., & Roller, D. (2005). Cybernetics and general systems theory (GST) principles for autonomic computing design. In *Proceedings of the Second International Conference on Autonomic Computing (ICAC'05)*. IEEE.

Strong, D., & Volkoff, O. (2010). Understanding organization-enterprise system fit: A path to theorizing the information technology artifact. *Management Information Systems Quarterly*, *34*(4), 731–756.

Stucci, T. (2012). Emerging market firms: Acquisitions in advanced markets: Matching strategy with resource, institution and industry-based antecedents. *European Management Journal*, *30*, 278–289. doi:10.1016/j.emj.2012.03.011.

Turban, E., Sharda, R., Aronson, J. E., & King, D. (2008). *Business intelligence: A managerial approach*. Upper Saddle River, NJ: Prentice Hall.

Ward, J., & Peppard, J. (2000). *Strategic planning for information systems*. New York: John Wiley and Sons.

Zeleny, M. (2005). *Human systems management: Integrating knowledge, management and systems*. Singapore: World Scientific Publishing. doi:10.1142/9789812703538.

Zey, M. (1992). *Decision making: Alternatives to rational choice models*. Thousand Oaks, CA: Sage Publications.

Section 2
Technology Issues in IT Acquisition Preparedness

Chapter 3
Understanding IT Acquisitions Preparedness:
Organizational Perspectives

ABSTRACT

It is generally experienced that every organization develops its own approach for IT acquisitions with varying degrees of emphasis on organizational priorities, systems, and technologies. Organizations involved in the IT acquisitions process pursue various perspectives depending on their strategy and implementation plans leading to varying degrees in IT preparedness. IT preparedness measurements may involve various stakeholders including employees and vendors. It is important to note that stakeholder preparedness is likely to vary in its intensity, but will eventually contribute to the overall organizational IT acquisition preparedness. In this chapter, these perspectives are discussed with a focus on IT as a form of technology acquisition, organizational processes, and quality improvement.

INTRODUCTION

IT acquisition is a complex phenomenon and organizations need to nurture their preparedness to manage this process. Ever since IT started to become essential and strategic assets in organizational practices, systems acquisitions have been a challenging and complex endeavor (Thomsen, 2010; John2010). It is also observed that IT acquisition needs to follow a sequence starting with preparedness exercises at the organizational level followed by systems and technology. Generally speaking, in the present scenario, organizations do

not need to justify IT acquisition processes seriously as was being done in early stages of business computing. Total Cost of Ownership (TCO) was quite high in the initial stages of IT evolutions. During this period, cost of IT components vis-à-vis performance of business computing was a predominant factor for justifications in IT infrastructure investments. Contemporary business computing environment has been experiencing phenomenal growth in IT adoption because of low cost of computing and TCOs. Today, IT components have been intrinsically embedded in all the functional areas including production, accounting, costing, finance etc. Many IT products are developed in providing seamless interfaces among

DOI: 10.4018/978-1-4666-4201-0.ch003

them to realize overall set goals in the organizations. Similarly, various frameworks are available that provide a structure to help property owners, managers, overseers and others determine and manage the TCO to best support their particular organization's overall business or mission (IFMA, 2011). Variants of these products include ERP, EIA, business modeling, simulations, scorecards and dashboards as discussed in chapter-1. Apart from this development, end user computing has also gained momentum to enable common user to use IT enabled services and develop own applications for better usability of IT without having formal exposures to computing, use IT

It is important to note that individual capabilities in using IT resources have grown manifold with great success. Common usability and usefulness of such capabilities are visible in mobile and Web services. However, similar success is yet to be achieved organizationally because of various issues interlinked with the IT infrastructure created for meeting strategic needs. It is quite mandatory for the organizations to ensure individual capabilities in contributing to the organizational goal. But overall organizational strategy needs to consider macro level issues which are beyond the purviews of individuals. Organizational resources in general and ICT infrastructure in particular, brings in challenging environment in which individuals, groups, departments, spatially dispersed and location specific entities under the organization structure perform to meet the common set goals. Technology acceptance is largely controlled by the possession of certain complementary resources that are difficult to acquire or copy, such as technological, human and marketing resources (Gómez and Vargas, 2012).Therefore, it is imperative for an organization to understand the implications of IT infrastructure acquisitions and stay prepared adequately to manage the acquired IT infrastructure effectively.

This chapter emphasizes on the preparedness of the organizations in managing IT infrastructure acquisitions and their life cycles. Organizations

involved in IT acquisitions process have various perspectives depending on their strategy and implementation plans. In this chapter these perspectives are discussed with focus on IT as a form of technology, organizational processes and quality. Discussions on IT perspectives include scenarios in which generic approaches made by organizations in IT acquisitions, in terms of asymmetries, opportunities and internationalizations (Lewis, 2007; Madhok and Keyhani, 2012). Discussions present eight different scenarios of IT acquisition process is managed in the organization and discusses strengths, weaknesses and challenges in the acquisition process. These scenarios provide insights to various stages involved in IT acquisitions that an organization may adopt. It is also important to note that stages of IT acquisitions are different across organizations and strategic inputs direct the adoption stages. Each of the scenarios discussed provide insights to the rationale for having organizational preparedness.

In order to address the challenges that organizations face to stay prepared for successfully managing IT acquisitions, a framework is presented in the next section. The framework recognizes role of various stakeholders who engage in the IT acquisition process. Their preparedness in collaborating in various stages of the acquisition process is an important factor and the framework intends to capture, assess, and monitor in the IT acquisition life cycle of the organization. The preparedness assessment framework includes three important stakeholders in the process. These stakeholders are IT acquiring organization, IT service providers who decide the way in which IT acquisition needs to be managed and Users who form integral parts of organization and service providers. Preparedness of IT acquiring organization discusses various issues related to organization's ability to understand product, process and quality attributes to achieve desired performance. This needs articulation of clearly defined areas for which information systems can be developed and option for IT adoption can be examined. Besides, preparedness exercise includes assessment of users' requirement and their preparedness to accept the IT-enabled systems. Preparedness of IT service providers is also another dimension of the exercise. To understand their preparedness, two scenarios emerge which are product and process based. These two scenarios are discussed in this section in detail to explain the ramifications of exercising these options. The third stakeholder is the user. Purviews of users are quite expansive in nature in this framework. Users may be internal or external to the organization in the form of employees, stock holders, customers and suppliers who need to collaborate for effectiveness of the organization whereas these users in IT acquisition process would include systems specific domain service providers. This wide range of users having varying degrees of IT orientation makes the IT acquisition scenario very complex. The following section delves into dimensions related to preparedness attributes of these users. Another perspective of IT acquisition in the organization is the quality. Quality management is an important agenda in any acquisition and IT acquisition is no different in this context. In computing environment, quality has assumed a very important role and the perspectives are fast evolving especially in the areas of product development, design and service orientation. Though there are various approaches in quality management specific to IT components under study, organizational issues in this context have played a crucial role in managing quality.

INFORMATION TECHNOLOGY ACQUISITION PROCESS

Role of ICT in the history of corporate evolution has been phenomenal. It has changed the face of corporate world, functioning of government and other organizations in a very significant manner. IT has provided enormous power to the decision makers such as corporate executives, administrators and even people in other spheres of work. It

has made virtual systems possible in every sector. With worldwide network and databases, it has made possible for decision makers to make quick and informed decisions. Response time in every decision has also reduced considerably due to phenomenal increase in the computing ability of IT components. Use of IT has also resulted in improving efficiency and exercising better control over the business processes. Future of IT holds out potential which is beyond imagination of a decision maker.

IT is commonly understood to be consisting of two major components i.e., "hard components" and "soft components". These components have undergone revolutionary changes in their computing, storage and communication capabilities. New dimensions to these components have emerged due to continuous research and the boundary between these two components has reduced progressively. The Application Specific Integrated Circuits (ASIC) technology has paved the way for this revolution leading to mobile services, remote management of appliances and services. Virtual networks and World Wide Web services have made the life of common citizen easier to conduct essential transactions with the service providing agencies, organizations such as banks, railways etc. Business through the net has become a reality today due to the IT orientation of the business processes.

IT provides capabilities that can assist organizations in appreciating the dynamic realities of emergencies more clearly and help formulate better decisions timely. Making good decisions and taking appropriate action during routine management and emergency events require access to communications, data, and computational resources in the organization. In this context IT can be used to effectively coordinate geographically dispersed assets, and manage other resources in diverse situations. (Rao et al., 2007).

Despite experiencing the huge benefits from the use of IT many organizations have failed to leverage the full potential of the technology. Studies reveal that 80 to 90 percent of application software do not meet performance goals, 80 percent of them are delivered late and over budget, 40 percent of developments fail or are abandoned, less than 25 percent of systems properly integrate business and technology objectives and only 10 to 20 percent meet their success criteria (Lycett et al.,2003). Thus there has been a growing concern over evaluating, managing and measuring effectiveness of IT infrastructure (Pervan, 1998; Luftman, 2003). While this failure is less attributed to hard components, the soft issues involving identification of need specific infrastructure and overall skill to own and manage the acquired IT are significant contributors (Drucker, 1969; Handy, 1989; Scarbrough, 1996; Herron, 2002; Arvanitis and Louikis, 2009). Another important soft issue that influences use of IT infrastructure is to build information systems (Davis and Olson, 2000). Success of ICT largely depends on how successfully Information System (IS) planning is done in an organization and this IS planning process is a complex phenomenon (Miller and Toulouse, 1986). Since IT is deployed for supporting the information systems, it inherently brings in complexity in the organization. It not only reorients the input and output environment, but also changes the way processes are handled. This change affects the people who manage these processes and provides a cascading effect on functioning of the organization (Sohal and Ng, 1998; Kohli and Devaraj, 2004; Hoving, 2003; Weill and Vitale, 2002). Acquisition of IT to manage the processes is therefore, a risky proposition despite advancement in this field of technology. It is necessary that adequate care should be taken before initiating the acquisition process.

Acquisition of IT refers to a process by which its various components are selected, obtained and used for achieving the business objectives. Normally key decision makers (individually or collectively) and in some situations business environment influence the IT acquisition process.

In some cases there is a policy that determines the IT acquisition process in the organization as well. Some of these scenarios are explained hereunder:

1. **CEO-Led Scenario:** Scenario-1 suggests that the Chief Executive Officer (CEO) is inclined towards acquisition of IT in the organization and there is a close coordination between him/her and the Chief Information Officer (CIO). The CEO may be driven by the feeling that IT acquisition may help in certain activities or processes. At times decisions on IT acquisition are taken for new systems development, procuring a product (application software) directly for the process, upgrading existing network, hardware and communication setup, and even with a motive to reduce and/or effectively utilize manpower (Bacon, 1992). The CEO led scenario is depicted in Figure 1.

2. **CIO-Led Scenario:** Scenario-2 provides a condition that is CIO-led. In this scenario, the CEO accepts the technology proposal without any active involvement in the process. The technology as recommended by the CIO is acquired. Involvement of the business process owners is solicited at a later stage of the project execution schedule. The scenario is shown in Figure 2.

3. **Process Technology Led Scenario:** Scenario-3 suggests that business process owners at times initiate a proposal in order to automate their processes either due to induction of a technology for the process (process improvement) and/or ideas mooted for providing better services through IT-alignment (Strong and Volkoff, 2004). This proposal is either routed through the CIO or the CIO initiates the project keeping in view the desired benefits of IT adoption. This is shown in Figure 3.

4. **Competitor/External Force Led Scenario:** Competitor's proven competence in providing better service encourages the orga-

nization to upgrade their process with IT interventions in the similar way. At times these organizations also benchmark before embarking on such project. This scenario is explained in Figure 4.

5. **Consultant Led Scenario:** In some cases organization takes some interest in information systems planning and prepare a policy document providing a possible road map. A consultant plays a dominant role in these cases. The CIO of course, plays a vital role in leading this activity. The process is shown in Figure 5.

6. **User-Driven Scenario:** In certain situations, existing users demand upgradation of the infrastructure because of the expected success in leveraging the IT infrastructure. This is normally CIO-driven, but mostly it is initiated by the users. This type of situation is scarce. This is shown in Figure 6.

7. **Policy-Driven Acquisition Scenario:** MIS plan is prepared by a steering committee in the organization. The CIO thereafter prepares a plan for acquisition and then the acquisition takes place as per the plan. Figure 7 explains the sequence of this acquisition process.

8. **Process Outsourcing Driven Scenario:** Business process outsourcing is the main objective in this case. Standard and matured operations are taken over by the IT service provider including setting-up the IT infrastructure, and maintaining it. The sequence of the process is shown in Figure 8.

In most cases, organizations acquire IT without having any plan or control programmes initially. At a later stage they find it difficult to derive actual benefits of integration (Kanter, 1983). Scenarios explained in Figure 1 through Figure 8 suggest the same which is either CIO-led or

Figure 1. CEO-led acquisition scenario

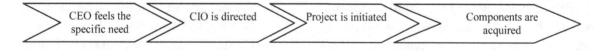

Figure 2. CIO-led acquisition scenario

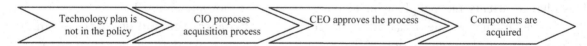

Figure 3. Process technology-led acquisition scenario

Figure 4. Competitor/external force-led acquisition scenario

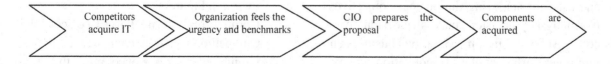

Figure 5. Consultant-led acquisition scenario

Figure 6. User-driven acquisition scenario

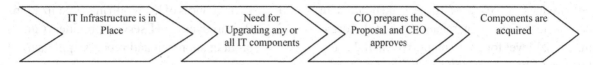

Figure 7. Policy-driven acquisition scenario

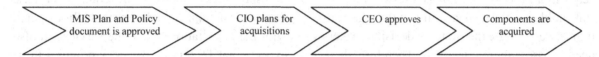

Figure 8. Process out-sourcing-driven acquisition scenario

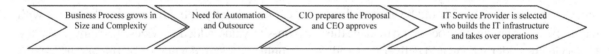

CEO-led without much planning in place. While it is always not possible to have involvement of the CEO in the process which is rather CIO-centric most of the time, it is the prime responsibility of the organization to provide a roadmap declaring clarity in intentions and providing guideline for such acquisitions. Mostly IT acquisition in an organization is seen with the following perspectives:

- Enabling certain processes and bringing in process improvement.
- Upgrading transactions at the operational level.
- Creating an integrated environment for having an effective Management Information System (MIS).

IT ACQUISITION PREPAREDNESS: ORGANIZATIONAL PERSPECTIVES

IT acquisition process in an organization is a collaborative effort like any other process (Ould, 1995). In order to have a successful collaboration, role of stakeholders is quite important. Irrespective of the scenarios for IT acquisition discussed above, it is essential to identify the stakeholders who are likely to collaborate and support the acquisition process. Especially capabilities of these stakeholders need to be assessed to facilitate organization of the acquisition process in a better way.

These stakeholders need to understand their role in the process and perhaps it is a tricky situation for the organization to formulate a strategy so that these stakeholders share the responsibility collectively. Broadly, the stakeholders are "IT-Service providers/ Product providers/ Product suppliers", "Users" and the "organization" itself. Figure 9 suggests that in an acquisition process, the roles of an organization and the suppliers are quite specific. In order to provide better preparedness for the organization one needs to assess preparedness of each of these stakeholders in detail and probably aggregate these at the organizational level for assessment. We shall discuss the research done in this regard progressively. The framework discusses relationship between two major groups of stakeholders involved in an acquisition process. Managing these two groups of stakeholders is the responsibility of the organization and especially the strategic decision makers need to assess them effectively. Therefore, there should be an evaluation process for the purpose. This evaluation process can have two elements i.e., acquisition and delivery. In the acquisition process, the stakeholders should be able to elicit requirement, organize the process and manage the IT service provider who would deliver the product and services meant for the business process. Similarly, in the delivery process, the IT service provider needs to display its credibility, capability and satisfy the IT acquirer through this evaluation process. Appreciating roles of these stakeholders and understanding their capability to effectively discharge their responsibilities in the acquisition process are quite essential. This appreciation is based on the following attributes:

1. Preparedness of IT Acquiring Organization.
2. Preparedness of IT service providers (under product approach and process approach).

Broadly IT acquiring organization involves in the acquiring process whereas the service provider is responsible for delivery of required services. Acquiring organization desires that IT is acquired with the expectation to use the services. It also expects that IT service provider provides these services including components like hardware, operating systems, databases, networks, middleware, application software including ERP applications directly delivered and implemented with on-site value-added services. In many cases the applications are developed at site under systems development life cycles and services are rendered as per specific requirements of the acquiring organization. In all these situations however, capacity

Figure 9. An acquisition process preparedness framework (Misra et al., 2004)

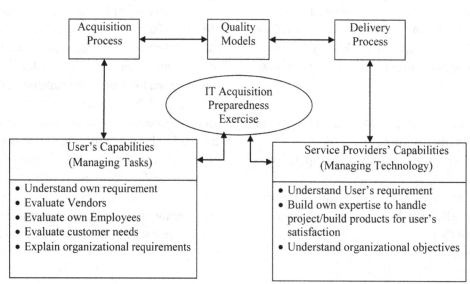

of these two major stakeholders needs scrutiny (Broadbent et al., 1999). The evaluation process is discussed below.

PREPAREDNESS OF IT ACQUIRING ORGANIZATION

Organizations with high IT capability tend to outperform the organizations without IT capability. Despite the widely held belief that IT is fundamental to the organization's survival and growth, scholars are still struggling to link this to financial performance. Studies indicate that effective and efficient use of IT is key factor differentiating successful organizations from their less successful counterparts (Bharadwaj, 2000). At the same time there is also evidence that organizations with high investments in IT fall out without deriving any benefit from IT. It is essential that IT acquisition in an organization takes place with full preparedness, because it remains as a key resource and it should be acquired with conscious decisions and involvement. Competent IT skills (human IT asset), a reusable technology base (technical asset) and a strong partnering relationship between an organization's IT and business unit management (relationship asset) influence organization's ability to deploy IT for strategic objectives (Ross et al., 1996). Besides, several organizational intangible factors such as know how, corporate culture and environmental orientation have been recognized as key-drivers for enhancing capability of IT use. It is viewed that strong IT capability enhances organization's ability to effectively leverage its IT investments (Datnthanam, and Hartono, 2003; Misra et al., 2003; Koellinger, 2008).

Preparedness of the IT acquiring organization is, therefore, one of the critical issues for a successful IT acquisition (Misra et al., 2004). Various quality models are available for the IT service provider to market and establish its credibility for wooing a prospective acquirer. However, it should be the responsibility of the acquiring organization to understand the need and rightly identifying a suitable service provider. It is increasingly becoming easier for an organization to acquire IT and no longer is limited to involvement of IT professionals. This has become possible due to availability of component based technologies with product orientation. In many cases due to non-availability of internal specialists and pressure of immediate solutions as too complex, but at the same time productive process automation, IT vendors and consultants also play an important role in IT acquisition (Yap et al., 1992; Chau, 1994; Sinha & Noble, 2008; Johnson, 2011). The possible ways for understanding capability of IT acquiring organization are:

1. Ability to understand product, process and quality attributes.
2. Ability to understand the process for integration of IT components with the information systems.
3. Ability to manage acquiring process.
4. Ability to assess users' requirement and preparedness to accept the IT-enabled systems.

Preparedness to Understand Infrastructure

IT acquiring organization needs to organize its various stakeholders while initiating any IT acquisition process. There are quality models in an IT acquisition scenario which is understood from the perspectives of IT acquirers (Geraldi, Kutsch and Turner, 2011). There are various products in the market that are to be acquired in this process. These stakeholders need to have adequate knowledge on these products and processes in order to have better results in the acquisition process. An overall increase in efficiency will bring synergy in the process of acquisition. Failure of any or all these stakeholders to perform may lead to following problems:

- **Mismatch in Requirement of Acquirer and Delivery of Supplier:** Suppliers could be the internal IT cell or a vendor. Irrespective of the status of a supplier (external/internal) a quality model applied for the user and supplier for assessing its process requirements as well as ensuring quality in delivery process. This will also ensure a quality product leading to quality in acquisition.
- **Different Methods:** For a certain delivery process different suppliers might bring in their own process and users might use certain and different standards and models to test the particular process. An acceptable and proven quality model can overcome all these hurdles.
- **Inadequacy in Capacity Building of User and Vendors:** In absence of a quality system in place, vendors and users may play their role without any focus and relevance to the requirement of an IT project. Because of this inadequacy assessment of product being delivered and product in the process, awareness among users may fall short of expectations of the deliverables designed through information systems.

Preparedness to Understand Information Systems

IT components encompass a broad range of technologies that support developing and manufacturing hardware, system and application level software, communication equipments and other various complementary product and processes to counterpart many challenges (Huff, and Munro, 1985; Gómez and Vargas, 2009). "Integration" and "fit" among all the IT components at all levels of acquisition are two critical areas in any organization. Despite advancements in technologies, methodologies and process improvement tools, success of IT and IS projects is not as expected at the organizational level. It is seen that 56 percent

of problems are generated during requirement determination and 82 percent of effort is given to correct those errors (Flynn, 1998). This will perhaps lead to a catastrophic situation if the systems are not examined at the organizational level and proper care is not taken. Though there are methods that are applied to execute a project, these have serious limitations in ensuring quality that an IT acquiring organization must be aware of. Some of these are:

1. Poor analysis of organizational issues.
2. IT components are at times complicated for a common user to understand.
3. Lack of a good developer might lead to poor adherence to quality execution of stages in a particular method.
4. Object oriented methods including Unified Modelling Languages (UML) do have limitations and disadvantages over structured systems.

These methods primarily remain process specific and do not address organizational issues. The responsibility of the IT acquiring organization therefore, is to understand organizational issues prior to embarking on such processes.

Preparedness to Manage Acquiring Process

Information has long been felt as a factor of production in many organizations and its importance is understood by many. It is also a reality that IT is not an end in itself but a means to achieve organizational goals (Bakopoulos, 1985; Casper & Ghassan, 2000). However, in this context of IT acquisition in an organization, there is much awareness. In most of the organizations today, IT has emerged as a function. Product based approaches of vendors along with various component based technologies have brought in a major support for IT acquisition in organizations. Computer Based Information Systems (CBIS) are flooding the market and acquiring organizations are not averse to adopting such systems since the benefits are handy and they are easy to install. This allows a user to procure, install, and operate its automated process thereby forcing "information islands." Due to this, IT as a technology has not only played an important role to enable business alignment depending on process of acquisition (Luftman et al., 2002), but at times it has inhibited.

Successful utilization of IT infrastructure largely depends on the effective deployment of IS based application software reflecting business processes and rules. Software plays the lead role in whole IT acquisition process. Utilizing the scope for application software to become agile, easy to deploy and adaptable to dynamic requirement enhances prospects of re-use. This benefit provides a less lead time in delivery and ease in management becomes prominent in this environment (Monarch et al., 2004). Despite these, it is clear that though decades have passed and there is quite good amount of investment on information technology, process of acquisition has not been quite successful in many of the cases.

IT infrastructure is the foundation for the IT portfolio, which is shared throughout the organization in the form of reliable services and is usually, coordinated by IS group (Broadbent et al., 1999). IT infrastructure capability includes both the technical and managerial expertise required to provide reliable physical services and extensive electronic connectivity within and outside the firm. There is a well accepted iterative relationship between the strategic context of the firm, the nature of business processes, and the significance of IT investments. These can be barriers and enablers for changing business processes. Improving processes usually involves implementing systems and process management across business function boundaries rather than within functions. IT, in the form of communication networks and shared databases, often underpins the "architecture" of business process redesign. The capability of the IT infrastructure is one of the most important is-sues for information system executives (Martin et al., 2003; Becerra et al., 2010; Marti, 2009; Jim and Michael, 2010). IT infrastructure investments can be a constraint where systems are not compatible, or where inconsistent data models have been used in different parts of business. Process oriented architectures necessary for business process redesign emphasize lateral data models, integration and interfaces systems and would take time to build. Extensive IT infrastructure capabilities facilitate both simplification and innovation in processes. This has a direct bearing on the organizational readiness and therefore process readiness is mandatory before any investment in IT infrastructure is made.

User Preparedness

User is a broad representation of the stakeholders in the IT acquisition process. A "buyer," a "supplier," or a "technology provider" provide user profiles with different objectives (Weill, and Vitale, 2002). In an acquisition process, user's role is quite wide spread. An end-user in the process could be broadly defined as the users in the organization (the acquirer) or the strategic, functional, and operational end-users, who ultimately use the technology acquired. Suppliers of the IT might involve in-house IT developers/ outside IT vendors, but their roles are limited to using the tools and technologies and therefore, are the intermediate users. All of them use IT for a common cause related to the success of the acquiring organization. Contemporary organizations support dynamic roles of users which lead to shorter life cycles of IT deliverables because of changes in process parameters. Therefore, achieving a "fit" among the business practices, IT solutions are important. In this scenario, it becomes necessary for the acquiring organization to assess user roles at various levels while entering into any stage of acquisition (Torkzadeh and Lee, 2003; Umanath, 2003; Weill and Vitale, 2002). Another way (but very important) of building user capabilities in an organization in IT acquisition process is to understand the "business process" and formalizing it before considering process the automation and innovation (Anderson and Felici, 2001; Halle, 2002; Lichtenthaler, 2010). It would be better that these processes are formalized before initiation of IT acquisition process. Business process owners and system developers (software engineering in particular) benefit from the "business rules approach." Some of the immediate benefits are: closer control over systems specifications, infrequent changes in system requirement, shortened development time, easy implementation of CBIS and fewer codes.

User-Preparedness to Adopt and Use IT-Enabled Systems

IT acquisition in an organization is to be successful if its users are able to leverage the presence of IT through effective use and to understand the way IT is to be used (Weill and Vitale, 2002). Definition of user is broad based in an IT acquisition process. The users assume the role of end-users, technology managers, and technology suppliers as well. The purview of the user we discuss in this section is that of an acquiring organization. These set of users span across all levels in the organization i.e. "strategic", "tactical" and "operational" levels.

Figure 10 suggests that users perform their role differently at different levels in the organization and their requirement varies. This is also true when we discuss about the IT requirements. One of the issues in the acquisition process is to increase capability of the user to understand the purpose of providing a systemic environment for their work. Operational users in the organization take care of routine operations and transactions. These transactions might grow in volume and frequency. However, users need to perform the task with ease provided there is structuredness in managing transactions. Structuredness calls for predicted behavior of the transactions and provide a path for traceability in case there is a need to do so. Ownership of these users provides an indication on the preparedness. This preparedness helps IT service provider to capture the transactions well. Maturity at this level provides the organization a tool to organize data processing effectively. This in turn would help the next upper layer of users called "Tactical users."

Figure 10. End users of IT and decision making process (Davis & Olson, 2000)

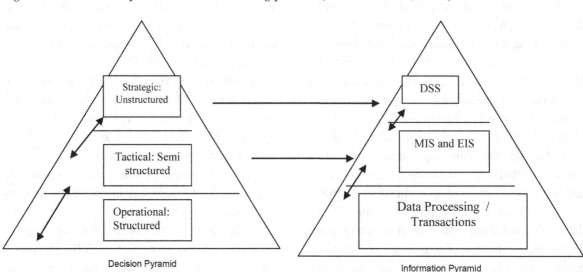

Tactical users are the functional users in the organization that provide domain knowledge to the system of decision making process. Capability of these users leads to understand the behavior of the information systems and organization of transactions and analyzing the behavior as well. This capacity provides a leadership to the operational users and monitors the requirements of strategic users. IT acquisition largely depends on the systemic approach provided by these users. Strategic users often involved in the decision making process tend to use the IT infrastructure sparingly, but depends heavily on the tactical users to feed on. This segment of users provides a dynamic ambient condition to the information management issue and therefore, must be well aware of exactly what IT being acquired is going to deliver. The unstructured-ness leads to a dynamic reporting structure with no standard pattern to follow and it compels the tactical users to meet the requirement at short notice. With the functional expertise, they tend to focus on the structured reports generated at the operational level, their evaluations and analyses. Tactical users form an interface with the strategic and operational users. Therefore, these users play a critical role in the decision-making process. Requirement analysis in this layer provides the basis for holistic views on MIS and CBIS. It also provides a direction for the IT acquisition process with experiential learning (Lee, 2001; Corbett, 2005).

Another set of users in this layer who should not be ignored in the organization are the IT managers and related workforce (Powell and Dent-Micallef, 1997; Quinn and Baily, 1994). These users are not only the immediate beneficiary of the IT acquired but their role in the pre-acquisition process also is of paramount importance as they influence directly on the technology components. Capacity building of these users would enhance the pre-acquisition of IT planning process; manage IS-IT alignment process effectively at the strategic level and attempt at bridging the gap between IS and IT planned (Peppard, 2001). Tactical level IT experts form

the backbone of the IT architecture providing an interface between the tool specific users for developing the IT component based infrastructure. Exposure of these set of users to business planning and strategies would enhance the interaction. If managed properly during pre-acquisition process, organization would draw "business maxim" as well as the "IT maxim" through these set of users in association with the business domain functional users (Broadbent et al., 1996; Curtis et al., 1995). Discussion above clarifies that there are various users in an organization who are involved in the acquisition process. The best possible way of understanding a successful IT acquisition is to capture these users (end users) early in the process. Identifying them and understanding their requirement would provide a better scope to reflect these in the system developed and IT enable them effectively. These users are categorized in Table 1.

Importance of users in an acquisition process for the organization has been discussed by many researchers (Marple et al., 2001; Luftman, 2003; Davis, 1989; Ditsa and MacGregor, 1995). Role of user depends on the stage of the acquisition scenario that exists in the organization and can vary depending on the level of association in the decision making process. Successful IT acquisition in an organization can be thought at enterprise level on the basis of "operational", "managerial", "strategic", "IT infrastructure" and "organizational" dimensions (Ross et al., 1996; Shang and Seddon, 2002). Any technology acquisition needs innovation at the user-level (Sharma and Rai, 2003; Rastogi, 1995). Innovation is a key concept in technology development and needs to be demand driven. This will determine the type of technology, and its use. The effectiveness of technology depends on its capacity to meet perceived needs and also other non-technical factors. Thus management of technology focuses on the principles of strategy.

Figure 11 explains the relationship of various technical and non-technical elements involved in its management. Having established strategies

Table 1. End-user profiling for IT use in the organization (Davis & Olson, 2000)

Type of User	Description	Domain
Operational end-users	Accesses the system through a pre-determined and structured interface, do not have adequate knowledge in programming	Moderate exposure to Business, Least on IT
Command level end-user	Some exposure to high level commands; Appreciate Use of IT, but limited in identifying the IT components	High exposure to Business Process, Low on IT
Programmer/ Component users	Operational level, with high exposure to tools, equipments; Least on Business Process	High exposure to IT Component specific use
Functional Support	IT: system developers/ analysts/ architects	High exposure to IT Component specific use, Understand the requirements of IS
	Business: Functional users	High exposure to Business, Understand s the use of IT
Strategic	IT: CIO	High exposure to IT Strategy
	Business: CEO	High exposure to Business Strategy

Figure 11. Management of technology (Eskelin, 2001; Misra et al., 2004)

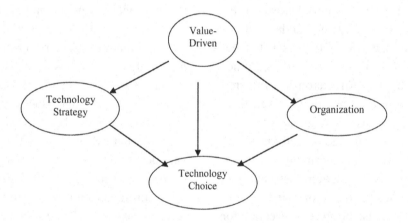

related to CBIS, organization needs to consider IT acquisitions. Alike any technology as explained above, IT requires a path to successfully meet the purpose for which it is being acquired. Mostly this stage in the acquisition process assumes a project status (Eskelin, 2001). A project initiated with a requirement should fit in to the roadmap prepared with IS-IT alignment for the organization in order to raise the expectancy level for success. Software engineering projects (Pressman, 1997) though regarded as "layered-technology" projects; it considers "People", "Problem" and "Process" as its main elements. Software engineering process

models such as "The Linear Sequential Model", "Prototyping Model", The RAD Model", "The Incremental Model", "The Spiral Model", "The Component Assembly Model", " The Concurrent Development Model" and "Formal Methods Model" discussed by Pressman are based under the concept of projects. IT acquisition can be based on this concept, but is not same since software is a subset of the whole IT conglomerate. But the basic steps involved in the software engineering projects are as shown in Figure 12.

Software development projects accomplish the task through distinct stages with setting the goal

Figure 12. Sample software acquisition process

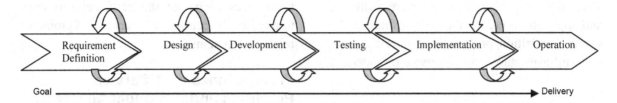

of the project in the initial stage through a series of activities (process based and could be iteratively organized standard procedures). These stages provide a scope to look back to its previous one in order to introspect and improve upon. The acquisition though is not generic, holds good for software development projects. Commercial Off The Shelf (COTS) or product based software also fall into these stages though treatment is little different. For example, ERP package purchased through a vendor also go through the same cycle as shown in Figure 12. However, design and development stages are taken care of by the product while shipped. Most of the requirements are defined well by the product. Unlike the software projects, IT projects encompass a group of ac-

tivities related to multiple components, multiple vendors (IT component/service providers). A typical IT acquisition scenario with the user as a stakeholder is shown in Figure 13. IT acquisition generates from the strategy for the CBIS formulated for the organization. In the IT acquisition processes the relationship among multiple stakeholders is quite complex and dynamic. Each stakeholder needs to be encouraged to involve in the process to make IT acquisition process successful. Role of IT-acquiring organization in the acquisition stage is as important as that of the IT service providers. As explained in Figure 13, IT acquisition in the organization creates infrastructure related to IS and IT. IS infrastructure creates information systems and relates to businesses in

Figure 13. IT acquisition process (Misra et al., 2004)

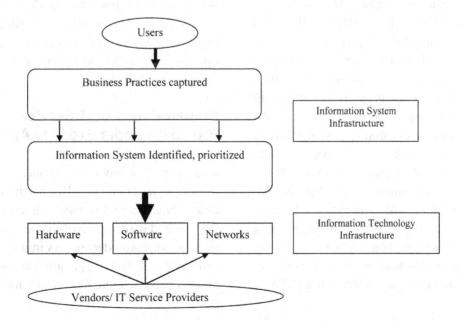

the organization. IT infrastructure provides hardware, software, networks, middleware, firmware and applications etc. for the organization. In the whole acquisition process users interface with these infrastructures and IT service providers.

IT ACQUISITION PREPAREDNESS: PERSPECTIVES OF IT SERVICE PROVIDERS

Preparedness of IT service providers can be assessed by a user through various indicators and one of the possible and immediate ways is through quality certification. This certification tests the credibility like any other technology acquisition. Various quality models ensure the acquiring organization to measure the capability of a supplier of product like operating system, hardware and networking, middleware and groupware; supplier of services like development of software for in-house requirement and business process outsourcing. Popular among these are Capability Maturity Model (CMM), International Standards Organization (ISO)-9000 etc. (Casper, and Ghassan, 2000; IEEE, 1994; Jalote, 2002; Mantel, and Teorey, 1989; Pressman, 1997). There are also product quality models like ISO 9126 (ISO, 1991) to evaluate components. Models like the CMM (Jalote, 2002) or ISO (9001) (IEEE, 1994) say something about a component developer's credibility. In addition, there are issues like process assessment and its improvement. However, in practice, they are not properly followed, and it is often the case that the management thinks about them after a decision has been taken to adopt IT to automate a business process. Users initially become enthusiastic since they only see the benefits of automation and not realizing the associated problems (like scalability, reliability etc) in advance. But when the system is operational such problems do appear one by one and then the gap between imagination and reality gradually becomes wider. Probably at this point the user

dissatisfaction may compel the top management to either reverse or alter the set of decisions made to acquire IT process which may lead of problems relating to cost and time.

Preparedness of IT Service Providers under Product Approach

Component driven technology has been flooding the market and application software is no exception today. Suppliers, oblivious of the requirements of organization specific requirements, try to incorporate their own knowledge base in the product they develop and attempt at customizing the product once installed at site. ERP is one of the products today which is very popular among the suppliers. However, due to lack of ability in the suppliers to understand the requirements of the acquiring organization, the product "fitness" remains as a major hurdle. Success of ERP implementation depends on organizational fit. They viewed that ERP has been looked at as a resource by an organization to proactively manage pressure due to dynamic changes in the external environment (Holland, and Light, 1999; Kumar and Hillegersberg, 2000). When we talk about introduction of IT in an organization, we are tempted to skew our approaches to acquisition of some software and put hardware in place. Generally speaking, one always is inclined to evaluate, and adopt make or buy options with cost benefit analyses. Many are even opposed to a product approach because of the fact that it might be a "misfit."

Preparedness of IT Service Providers under Process Approach

It is noted that buying a product is the initial activity in an IT project. But much needs to be done while tuning it to meet the requirement of the user and here, the capability and potential of the IT service provider are very important (Basili, and Boehm, 2001). Application software under process approach, are undertaken for respective client organizations. Software engineering as a discipline focuses on formal procedures for the development process, methods and tools (Pressman, 1997). Any software engineering based project calls for addressing certain issues such as problem definition (what needs to be solved), development of software (how) and its post implementation maintenance. These are called "stages" in the development scenario. Basically these models are aimed at solving the micro level issues through introduction of CBIS. The advent of Computer Aided Software Engineering (CASE) tools has also increased capability of organizations engaged in development of software and managing such development projects. Capability of an IT service provider however, brings in certain risks in terms of quality and standards. Basically project is managed by many popular software engineering models and one can always ascertain process capability of the developer. But it is difficult to say whether the product to be delivered would ensure the required quality (IFPUG, 2002). Therefore, process quality is also a major concern for a successful project.

IT ACQUISITION PREPAREDNESS: QUALITY PERSPECTIVES

Stages of IT acquisition in IT-acquiring organization can be as shown in Figure 14 (Eskelin, 2001; Evans, 2004).

It explains that "Initiation" stage begins with the business need. This need could be a part of the larger business plan formulated in the organization. In the "Planning" stage, the project team is formed or the IT team takes over the planning

process. Requirement determination and prioritization of the project delivery are formulated in this stage. Vendor relationship is developed in this stage as well. The third stage involves "Research" in the market, benchmarking similar projects in order to assess vendor credibility, product suitability, cost, time efficiency and effectiveness etc. of the project at hand. Tendering process and vendor evaluation for the product and/ or process takes place in "Evaluation" and "Negotiation" stages. "Implementation" and "Operation" stages are last stages of the acquisition process where delivered product (s) are assessed, evaluated and implemented with the help of users. Since mostly software is the central issue, it is treated as the driver for testing the IT infrastructure created. In each stage capability of the acquiring organization needs to be ensured for successful execution of the project.

As explained in Figure 14, IT acquisition is software centric, and quality in software acquisition is a concern in recent times. Software acquisition-CMM (SA-CMM) is one of the quality models associated with quality acquisition of software. It tries to understand the acquisition process through management plan for acquisition and software risk assessment. It involves the acquirer and the contractor. At times IT manager pushes an idea to introduce IT enabled services. As the acquisition begins to form, more requirements are identified and refined. This evolution precedes and the set of requirements continue to grow (Ferguson et al., 1997). By the time solicitation package is developed, a significant set of software technical and non-technical requirements exist. For the purpose of SA-CMM, these requirements must be base-lined (managed and controlled), not frozen.

Figure 14. Sample IT acquisition process

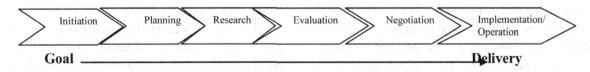

As software requirements further evolve (e.g. allocation, elaboration, and refinement) they are incorporated into the requirement baseline and managed and controlled. Management and control remain the acquirer's responsibility even though contractor may be involved during formalization of requirements. The SA-CMM is based on the expectation that a mature organization and its projects will do a thorough job of planning an acquisition. The SA-CMM accommodates the software that is acquired as a part of total system acquisition. It does not specifically address the system acquisition process; however, it is in harmony with that process. SA-CMM focuses on building the process capability of an organization.

"Evolutionary acquisition strategy" (Marple et al., 2001) develops and deploys core capability to understand stakeholder needs, expectations, constraints, and interface needs. One of the basic benefits of evolutionary acquisition is that a user's hands-on experience with the system generates potential new capabilities and requirements. Evolutionary acquisition strategy implies evolutionary development of requirements i.e. all of the detailed implementation requirements are not known. Though a good approach, it is suitable for large projects and iterative scenario where continuous proposals are assessed. GAO describes methodologies to understand the acquisition process in the organization. The GAO model having, three stages i.e. pre-solicitation, solicitation and award, and post-award, describes the acquisition process in the organization. This enables the acquiring organization to understand the acquisition process and decrease the risks in each stage. Pre-solicitation stage involves initialization, analysis of requirements, identify alternatives, and prepare acquisition plan specifications. The solicitation and award stage cover maintenance of project structure, proposal solicitation and evaluation and contractor selection. The post award stage describes the procedure adopted for contract management, monitor contract performance, testing and acceptance

of project delivered. It also tries to focus on the involvement of users at all levels including top management for a planned acquisition.

Users continue to become more demanding in terms of what they want from their systems and managers struggle to determine realistic expectations (Staples et al., 2002). Technological advances encouraged technologically competent persons to expect appropriate state of the art technology in their application whereas novice users demanded more user-friendly applications with simple interfaces. Systems usefulness, ease of use, information quality are three determinants of expectations. However, there is another school of thought that conflict would arise proportionately with the level of association/participation between end-user and systems developers during any Information System Development (ISD) project (Hartwick and Barki, 1999). Lack of trust and understanding, hostility, and frustration between IS developers and business managers are very much likely in any ISD project and an organization has to deal with the conflicts. Research on conflict suggests that a business organization's survival hinges on its ability to align IT capabilities with business goals (Yeh and Tsai, 2001). Even fear of computer dominance and distrust on computer professionals inhibits IT adoption and is a serious threat to IT acquisition process in an organization. Care should therefore, be taken to manage stakeholders' requirements appropriately at all levels and manage the conflicts which is rather natural in project between the users and project managers. This issue is organization centric and strategic users need to address this preparedness (Yetton et al., 2000). User participation should be termed as user involvement and it has six conditions; an opportunity to take important decisions, making a contribution to organization, self determination, freedom in work place, achievement and success (Barki and Hartwick, 1989).

IT acquiring organization assumes the role of a purchaser. It should remain equally responsible for providing details on its requirement, deliverables of the product and implementation process and the supplier should be responsible for delivering the product and/or IT components. The gap between the two must be bridged at any cost. The sooner in the acquisition process the gap is bridged, the better is the result. In order to bridge the "gap" and bring in a "strategic fit", capability of each stake-holder must be understood, and needs to be developed if not available.

Organizational Preparedness to Understand Product and Process Quality

The IT acquiring organization must deal with the hard issues involved in the IT acquisition process i.e. understanding the IT components, rightly identifying the requirements and mapping it to the acquisition process so as to properly acquire the components. This would happen only when the organization builds the capability to understand these issues. Perhaps by introducing an IT department and treating this as a function would provide the initiation in a right direction. Understanding the products and processes by the IT department and vice versa is the next issue that the acquisition process looks for (Luftman, 2000; Kappel, 2001). In order to understand the product and the process, the possible approach is to understand the quality system that organizes these issues properly and effectively (Anderson and Felici, 2001). Though there is no definite conclusion that a quality certified process would deliver a product that would fit

the requirement and/or deliver the desired result; it certainly provides a trust among the purchaser and the service provider that is essential in an acquiring process. It is essential that IT acquiring organization must look at the quality systems that are in place to recognize its process and product that its supplier can supply and the process under which the supplier either delivers its product. As regards the quality framework, CMM and ISO provide quality assurance certification (Pressman, 1997). Therefore, IT acquiring organizations use these as tools to test the credibility of the supplying organization. The CMM certifies for 1-5 levels and an organization can be certified with any level or all of these in order to enhance its credibility. Since software accounts for the major share in an IT acquisition process, this quality attribute should not be ignored.

Under the CMM framework SW-CMM, SA-CMM, CMM-I, PM-CMM, System Engineering-CMM (SE-CMM), Integrated Product Development (IPD-CMM), and IT services-CMM are mostly divided in five groups of quality assurance: product, process, integration, service and people (Eckes, 2001; Johnston and Carrico, 1998; Sheard, 1996; Curtis et al., 1995). Quality and Productivity (Q and P) triangle as shown in Figure 15 provides framework of how quality and productivity of a process is affected by process, technology and people (Jalote, 2002; Lee, Kang, Park, & Park, 2007). This triangle is the basis for the CMM, and the IT acquiring organization must look for the quality in all these groups in the IT-

Figure 15. Quality and productivity triangle

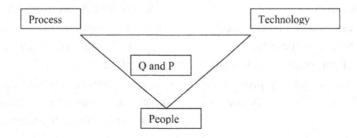

service provider during IT acquisitions. Even the IT-acquiring organization could establish an IT department where these process quality adherence tools could be deployed. However, the caveat is that this type of quality certification is necessary where the IT department in the organization is continuously loaded with projects for either internal use or for meeting external demand.

All these models under CMM organize the capability of user in assessing quality of the product/service by assessing the level of expertise/capability of the organization that delivers the product/service. Some of these models also touch upon as to how to organize the user' project management skills like SA-CMM. However, it does not hold true that all the organizations having assessed for the product delivery, process improvement, service delivery, project management shall eventually lead to managing the acquiring and installing good software driven information system. Therefore, User has to understand its own management dimensions before dwelling on these activities. Unfortunately each of these models is addressing the capabilities in isolation and leaves the user confused to appropriately apply depending on the organizational goals. An insight to the characteristics of the ISO and CMM reveals the following (ISO, 1991; Paulk, 1995; Jalote, 2002):

- CMM is a model directed to S/W development process while ISO-9001 emphasizes on product engineering and H/W.
- ISO-9001 does not explicitly emphasize a process improvement whereas CMM does.
- CMM is more focused on S/W while ISO-9001 focuses more on H/W, S/W, process materials, and services.
- Every Key Process area of CMM is weakly related to ISO-9001 in some way.
- ISO-9001 compliant organization would not necessarily satisfy all key process areas in level 2 of CMM, but satisfy goals of level 2 and 3.

- CMM seems to be focused on Key Performance Areas (KPA) and philosophies are different from any life-cycle models.

Therefore, in order for the IT acquiring organization to understand the credibility of the IT service provider (especially software and project related), it must look at the certifications the organization has. It is quite important for the acquiring organization to keep track of quality management issues, pursue implementation of quality models for process maturity, enforcing quality in service deliveries of service providers and inculcate the culture of providing user centric services (Zwikael and Globerson, 2004).

SUMMARY

This chapter focused on organizational issues related to IT acquisition. The chapter began with various generic scenarios that an organization can pursue for IT acquisitions. It was evident from the discussions that each of these scenarios offered various strengths and weaknesses in managing IT acquisition successfully leaving abundant scope for improvement especially in the areas of organizational preparedness. In order to ensure effectiveness in the organizational preparedness, a framework was presented with various components of preparedness that aim to improve upon the current scenarios in IT acquisition. The framework narrated the roles and preparedness of organization acquiring IT, IT service providers involved in the acquisition process and users who collaborate in the whole exercise as important stakeholders. Apart from recognizing involvement of these stakeholders the framework considered quality perspectives as an important input to the acquisition process.

This chapter posited that preparedness of IT acquiring organization is quite important in terms of creating abilities to understand product, process and quality attributes. It is also quite important to understand the process for integration of IT components with the information systems, to manage acquiring process, assess users' requirement and their preparedness to accept the CBIS. This preparedness needs to be organized before the whole process of IT acquisition commences and IT service providers are invited for the purpose. User capabilities were found to be the central issue that influences the preparedness in the acquiring organization and thus enough care has to be taken for supporting this process. In this context, contributions of quality management were posited to be quite important. This chapter concluded with the quality assessment models that are in use and can support the framework enhancing organizational capabilities.

REFERENCES

Anderson, S., & Felici, M. (2001). Requirements evolution: From process to product oriented management. In *Proceedings of the 3rd International Conference on Product Focused Software Profess Improvement* (LNCS), (vol. 2188, pp. 27-41). Kaiserslautern, Germany: Springer.

Arvanitis, S., & Louikis, E. (2009). A comparative study of the effect of the ICT, organizational and human capital on labour productivity in Greece and Switzerland. *Information Economics and Policy*, *21*, 43–61. doi:10.1016/j.infoecopol.2008.09.002.

Bacon, C. J. (1992, September). The use of decision criteria in selecting information systems/ technology investments. *Management Information Systems Quarterly*, 335–353. doi:10.2307/249532.

Bakopoulos, Y. J. (1985). Toward a more precise concept of information technology. In *Proceedings of International Conference on Information Systems*, (pp. 17-24). IEEE.

Barki, H., & Hartwick, J. (1989, March). Rethinking the concept of user involvement. *Management Information Systems Quarterly*, 53–63. doi:10.2307/248700.

Basili, V. R, & Boehm, B. (2001, May). COTS-based systems top 10 list. *Software Management*, 91-93.

Becerra-Fernandez, I., & Sabhewal, R. (2010). *Knowledge management: Systems and processes.* New Delhi: PHI Learning Pvt. Ltd..

Bharadwaj, A. S. (2000). A resource based perspective on IT capability and firm performance: An empirical investigation. *Management Information Systems Quarterly*, *24*(1), 169–196. doi:10.2307/3250983.

Broadbent, M., Weill, P., & O'Brien, T. (1996). Firm context and patterns of IT infrastructure capability. In *Proceedings of the 17th International Conference on Information Systems*, (pp. 174-194). Cleveland, OH: IEEE.

Broadbent, M., Weill, P., & St. Calir, D. (1999). The implications of information technology infrastructure for business process redesign. *Management Information Systems Quarterly*, *23*(2), 159–182. doi:10.2307/249750.

Casper, R., & Ghassan, A.-Q. (2000). *The orbital model: A methodology for development of interactive systems.* Melbourne, Australia: RMIT University. Retrieved from http://goanna.cs.rmit.edu.au/~ghasan/Orbital.doc

Chau, P. Y. C. (1994). Selection of packaged software in small business. *European Journal of Information Systems*, *3*(4), 292–302. doi:10.1057/ejis.1994.34.

Corbett, A. C. (2005). Experiential learning within the process of opportunity identification and exploitation. *Entrepreneurship Theory & Practice*, *29*, 473–491. doi:10.1111/j.1540-6520.2005.00094.x.

Cruz-Cunha, M. M. (2010). *Enterprise information systems for business integration in SMES, technological, organziational and social dimensions*. Hershey, PA: IGI Global Publications.

Curtis, B., Hefley, W. E., & Miller, S. (1995). *People capability maturity model*. Pittsburgh, PA: Software Engineering Institute, Carnegie Melon University.

Datnthanam, R., & Hartono, E. (2003). Issues in linking information technology capability to firm performance. *Management Information Systems Quarterly*, *27*(1), 125–153.

Davis, B. G., & Olson, M. H. (2000). *Management information systems: Conceptual foundations, structure and development* (2nd ed.). Singapore: McGraw-Hill.

Davis, F. D. (1989, September). Perceived usefulness, perceived ease of use, and user acceptance of information technology. *Management Information Systems Quarterly*, 319–340. doi:10.2307/249008.

Ditsa, G., & MacGregor, G. E. (1995). Models of user perceptions, expectations and acceptance of information systems. In *Proceedings of the Sixth International Conference of the Information Resource Management Association*, (pp. 221-229). IEEE.

Drucker, P. (1969). *The age of discontinuity: Guidelines to our changing society*. London: Heinemann.

Eckes, G. (2001). *Making six-sigma last: Managing the balance between cultural and technical change*. New York: John Wiley & Sons.

Eskelin, A. (2001). *Technology acquisition: Buying the future of your business*. Reading, MA: Addison-Wesley.

Evans, N. (2004). *Promoting fusion in the business-IT relationship*. Paper presented at the Issues in Informing Science and Information Technology Education Joint Conference. Rock Hampton, Australia.

Ferguson, J., Cooper, J., Falat, M., Fisher, M., Guido, A., & Marciniak, J. … Webster, R. (1997). Software acquisition process maturity questionnaire: The acquisition risk management initiative. Pittsburgh, PA: Software Engineering Institute, Carnegie Mellon University.

Flynn, J. D. (1998). *Information systems requirements: Determination and analysis* (2nd ed.). Berkshire, UK: The McGraw-Hill.

Fowler, F., Rice, D., Foemmel, M., Hieatt, E., Mee, R., & Stafford, R. (2003). *Patterns of enterprise application architecture*. Boston: Addison-Wesley.

Geraldi, J. G., Kutsch, E., & Turner, N. (2011). Towards a conceptualisation of quality in information technology projects. *International Journal of Project Management*, *29*, 557–567. doi:10.1016/j.ijproman.2010.06.004.

Gómez, J., & Vargas, P. (2009). The effect of financial constraints, absorptive capacity and complementarities on the adoption of multiple process technologies. *Research Policy*, *38*(1), 106–119. doi:10.1016/j.respol.2008.10.013.

Gómez, J., & Vargas, P. (2012). Intangible resources and technology adoption in manufacturing firms. *Research Policy*, *41*, 1607–1619. doi:10.1016/j.respol.2012.04.016.

Halle, B. V. (2002). *Business rules applied: Building better systems using the business rules approach*. New York: John Wiley & Sons, Inc..

Handy, C. (1989). *The age of unreason*. London: Business Books.

Hartwick, J., & Barki, H. (1999). Conflict management styles of users and analysts, and their impact on conflict resolution. In *Proceedings of 32nd Hawaii International Conference on Systems Sciences*. IEEE.

Hearst, M. A. (2009). *Search user interfaces*. New York: Cambridge University Press. doi:10.1017/CBO9781139644082.

Herron, D. (2002). *IT measurement: Practical advice from experts: International function point user group- Part-I*. Boston: Addison-Wesley Professional.

Holland, C. P., & Light, B. (1999, May/June). A critical success factors model for ERP implementation. *IEEE Software*, 30–36. doi:10.1109/52.765784.

Hoving, R. (2003). Executive response: Project management process maturity as a secret weapon. *MIS Quarterly Executive*, 2(1), 29–30.

Huff, S. L., & Munro, M. C. (1985, December). Information technology assessment and adoption: A field study. *Management Information Systems Quarterly*, 327–340. doi:10.2307/249233.

IEEE. (1994). How ISO 9001 fits into the software's world. *IEEE S/W, 11*.

IFMA. (2011). A framework for facilities lifecycle cost management. *International Facility Management Association*. Retrieved November 25, 2011 from http://www.ifma.org/tools/research/Asset_Lifecyle_Model.pdf

IFPUG. (2002). *IT measurement: Practical advice from experts: International function point users group*. Boston: Addison-Wesley.

ISO. (1991). *International organisation for standardization: ISO/IEC 9126*. Geneva: ISO.

Jalote, P. (2002). *CMM in practice: Process for executing software projects at infosys*. Delhi: Pearson Education.

Johnson, C. W. (2011). Identifying common problems in the acquisition and deployment of large-scale, safety–critical, software projects in the US and UK healthcare systems. *Safety Science*, 49, 735–745. doi:10.1016/j.ssci.2010.12.003.

Johnston, H. R., & Carrico, S. R. (1998, March). Developing capabilities to use information strategy. *Management Information Systems Quarterly*.

Kanter, R. M. (1983). *The change masters*. London: University of Chicago Press.

Kappel, T. A. (2001). Perspectives on roadmaps: How organizations talk about the future. *Journal of Product Innovation Management*, 18, 39–50. doi:10.1016/S0737-6782(00)00066-7.

Koellinger, P. (2008). The relationship between technology, innovation, and firm performance – Empirical evidence form e-business in Europe. *Research Policy*, 37, 1317–1328. doi:10.1016/j.respol.2008.04.024.

Kohli, R., & Devaraj, S. (2004). Realising business value of information technology investments: An organisational process. *MIS Quarterly Executive*, 3(1), 53–68.

Kumar, K., & Hillegersberg, J. (2000). ERP experiences and evolution. *Communications of the ACM, 43*(3), 22–26. doi:10.1145/332051.332063.

Ladley, J. (2010). *Making enterprise information management (EIM) work for business: A guide to understanding information as an asset*. London: Elsevier.

Lee, C. S. (2001). Modeling the business value of information technology. *Information & Management*, 39(3), 191–210. doi:10.1016/S0378-7206(01)00090-8.

Lee, S., Kang, S., Park, Y., & Park, Y. (2007). Technology roadmapping for R&D planning: The case of the Korean parts and materials industry. *Technovation*, 27, 433–445. doi:10.1016/j.technovation.2007.02.011.

Lewis, J. I. (2007). Technology acquisition and innovation in the developing world: Wind turbine development in China and India. *Studies in Comparative International Development, 42*(3–4), 208–232. doi:10.1007/s12116-007-9012-6.

Lichtenthaler, U. (2010). Technology exploitation in the context of open innovation: Finding the right 'job' for your technology. *Technovation*, 30, 429–435. doi:10.1016/j.technovation.2010.04.001.

Luftman, J. (2000). Assessing business – IT alignment maturity. *Communications of the AIS, 4*.

Luftman, J. (2003). Assessing IT/business alignment. *Information Systems Management, 20*(4), 9–21. doi:10.1201/1078/43647.20.4.20030901/77287.2.

Luftman, J. N., Papp, R., & Brier, T. (2002, September). Enablers and inhibitors of business-IT alignment. *ABInsight*.

Lycett, M., Macredie, R. D., Patel, C., & Paul, R. J. (2003). Migrating agile methods to standardised development practice. *IEEE Computer Magazine, 36*(6), 79–85. doi:10.1109/MC.2003.1204379.

Madhok, A., & Keyhani, M. (2012). Acquisitions as entrepreneurship: Asymmetries, opportunities, and the internationalization of multinationals from emerging economies. *Global Strategy Journal, 2*(1), 26–40. doi:10.1002/gsj.1023.

Mantel, M. M., & Teorey, T. J. (1989, September). Incorporating behavioural techniques into the systems development life cycle. *Management Information Systems Quarterly*.

Marino, J., & Rowley, M. (2010). Understanding SCA (service component architecture). Boston: Addison-Wesley. ISBN: 13: 978-0-321-51508

Marple, J., Clark, B., Jones, C., & Zubrow, D. (2001). *Measures in support of evolutionary acquisition*. Pittsburgh, PA: Software Engineering Institute, Carnegie Mellon University.

Miller, D., & Toulouse, J. M. (1986). Chief executive personality and corporate strategy and structure in small, firms. *Management Science, 32*(11), 1389–1409. doi:10.1287/mnsc.32.11.1389.

Misra, H., Satpathy, M., & Mohanty, B. (2003). A user centric IT-acquisition model. In *Proceedings of Sixth International Conference on Information Technology*, (pp. 439-445). IEEE.

Misra, H., Satpathy, M., & Mohanty, B. (2004). Organisation preparedness and information technology acquisition success: An assessment model. In *Proceedings of Tenth Americas Conference on Information Systems*, (pp. 3679-3692). New York: IEEE.

Monarch, I., Sisti, F., Ambrose, K., & Blanchette, S. (2004). *Why not network centric acquisition?* Paper presented at the Conference on Acquistion of Software Centric Systems. Pittsburgh, PA.

Ould, M. A. (1995). *Business processes modelling and analysis for re-engineering and improvement*. London: John Wiley & Sons.

Paulk, M. C. (1995). How ISO-9001 compares with the CMM. *IEEE Software, 12*(1), 74–83. doi:10.1109/52.363163.

Peppard, J. (2001). Bridging the gap between the IS organisation and the rest of the business: Plotting a route. *Information Systems Journal, 11*(3), 249. doi:10.1046/j.1365-2575.2001.00105.x.

Pervan, G. (1998). How the chief executive officers in large organisations view the management of their information systems. *Journal of Information Technology, 13*, 95–109. doi:10.1080/026839698344882.

Powell, T. C., & Dent-Micallef, A. (1997). Information technology as competitive advantage: The role of human, business and technology resources. *Strategic Management Journal, 18*(5), 375–405. doi:10.1002/(SICI)1097-0266(199705)18:5<375::AID-SMJ876>3.0.CO;2-7.

Pressman, R. S. (1997). *Software engineering: A practitioner's approach* (4th ed.). Singapore: McGraw-Hill.

Quinn, J. B., & Baily, M. B. (1994). Information technology: Increasing productivity in services. *The Academy of Management Executive, 8*, 28.

Rao, R. R., Eisenberg, J., & Schmitt, T. (Eds.). (2007). *Improving disaster management: The role of IT in mitigation, preparedness, response, and recovery*. Washington, DC: National Academy of Sciences.

Rastogi, P. N. (1995). *Management of technology and innovation: Competing through technological excellence*. New Delhi: Sage Publications India.

Ross, J. W., Beath, C. M., & Goodhue, D. (1996, Fall). Develop long-term competitiveness through IT assets. *Sloan Management Review*, 31–42.

Scarbrough, H. (1996). Perspectives on innovation in organizations. *Organization Studies, 17*(1), 107–129. doi:10.1177/017084069601700105.

Shang, S., & Seddon. (2002). Assessing and managing benefits of enterprise systems: The business manager's perspective. *Information Systems Journal, 12*(4), 271. doi:10.1046/j.1365-2575.2002.00132.x.

Sharma, S., & Rai, A. (2003). An assessment of the relationship between ISD leadership characteristics and IS innovation adoption in organizations. *Information & Management, 40*(5), 391–401. doi:10.1016/S0378-7206(02)00049-6.

Sheard, S. A. (1996). Twelve systems engineering roles. In *Proceedings of INCOSE*, (pp. 481-488). Minneapolis, MN: INCOSE.

Sinha, R. V., & Noble, S. H. (2008). The adoption of radical manufacturing technologies and firm survival. *Strategic Management Journal, 29*(9), 943–962. doi:10.1002/smj.687.

Sohal, A. S., & Ng, L. (1998). The role and impact of information technology in Australian business. *Journal of Information Technology, 13*, 201–217. doi:10.1080/026839698344846.

Staples, D. S., Wong, I., & Seddon, P. B. (2002). Having expectations of information systems benefits that match received benefits: Does it really matter? *Information & Management, 40*(2), 115–131. doi:10.1016/S0378-7206(01)00138-0.

Strong, D. M., & Volkoff, O. (2004, June). A roadmap for enterprise system implementation. *IEEE Computer*, 22-29.

Thomsen, M. (2010). *Procurement competence in procurement and development of IT - the skills-emergence in the shadow of knowledge fragmentation*. (PhD Thesis). Halmstad University, Sweden.

Torkzadeh, G., & Lee, J. (2003). Measures of perceived end-user computing skills. *Information & Management, 40*, 607–615. doi:10.1016/S0378-7206(02)00090-3.

Umanath, N. S. (2003). The concept of contingency beyond 'it depends': Illustrations from IS research stream. *Information & Management, 40*(6), 551–562. doi:10.1016/S0378-7206(02)00080-0.

Weill, P., & Vitale, M. (2002). What IT infrastructure capabilities are needed to implement e-business models?. *MIS Quarterly Executive, 1*(1).

Yap, C. S., Soh, C. P. P., & Raman, K. S. (1992). Information systems success factors in small business. *Omega: International Journal of Information Management, 20*(5/6), 597–609. doi:10.1016/0305-0483(92)90005-R.

Yeh, Q.-J., & Tsai, C.-L. (2001). Two conflict potentials during IS development. *Information & Management, 39*(2), 135–149. doi:10.1016/S0378-7206(01)00088-X.

Yetton, P., Martin, A., Sharma, R., & Johnston, K. (2000). A model of information systems development project performance. *Information Systems Journal, 10*(4), 263. doi:10.1046/j.1365-2575.2000.00088.x.

Zwikael, O., & Globerson, S. (2004). Evaluating the quality of project planning: A model and field results. *International Journal of Production Research, 42*(8), 1545–1556. doi:10.1080/00207540310001639955.

Chapter 4
Understanding IT Acquisitions:
Associated Models

ABSTRACT

IT acquisition processes are mostly organization specific and there is not enough evidence to establish that a successful acquisition process adopted in an organization would replicate the same scenario in another, but it is experienced that such predictability can be assured to a possible extent if organizations follow some best practices. Research in IT acquisition processes indicate varied results, and there are various models to address overarching issues related to IT acquisition processes showcasing IT preparedness in the organization. This chapter discusses various approaches pursued and models evolved in the area of IT acquisitions, processes to work on the preparedness of the organizations in managing IT infrastructure acquisitions, and their life cycles. This chapter includes discussions on models available for assessing the IT acquisition process, understanding organizational issues, capturing and analyzing user behaviour, and analyzing usability of the IT resources. Various models are also evaluated to understand their roles in capturing capability of the IT users in the organization, IT service providers, and component developers who participate in the acquisition process.

INTRODUCTION

IT acquisition is defined as an organizational activity and it needs to be viewed holistically. Investment in IT in organizations today is quite considerable in financial terms. But the intangible vales including risks, opportunity costs of not choosing the right components and ignoring overall preparedness of end users to accept the IT enabled services are quite phenomenal. It is

DOI: 10.4018/978-1-4666-4201-0.ch004

also quite complex to predict such organizational behavior during IT acquisitions. Thus there is a need to model the preparedness of all stakeholders in the acquisition process. In order to understand the roles and responsibilities of the stakeholders we embarked on defining preparedness of the organization so as to manage the IT acquisition process effectively. A framework was presented in this context to organize this preparedness exercise for IT acquisitions. Application of the framework to understand expected contributions of various stakeholders led to identification of areas of improvement. The areas of improvement included in the IT acquisition process are role of IT acquiring organization through its processes, structures, and systems; role of IT service providers in terms of capabilities to provide products and services; role of users in the context of IT adoption and internalization of IT enabled environment and role of quality management.

The framework used in the preceding chapter raised two important issues. One of the issues is related to examining feasibility of conducting any preparedness exercise. The second issue relates to explore whether there are any existing models that can be benchmarked to support the preparedness exercise. Thus this chapter extends the ambit of the framework discussed in chapter 3. It delves into the literature to identify and present various models related to the realm of the framework and find the necessary direction to conceptualize and develop a model to assess organizational capabilities in managing IT acquisitions. The literature review is taken up with the purviews of the framework and discusses various models available along with their deliverables. Initially models addressing organizational issues and to be more specific, IT acquiring organization's issues are presented. The next section includes identified models that are supporting the capabilities of IT service providers. The following section identifies models related to user centered services, their acceptance, satisfaction and usability of the systems developed with IT. The next section summarizes the deliverables of the models and identifies areas of improvement to support the feasibility of conceptualizing and development of an organizational preparedness assessment model.

MODELS ADDRESSING ORGANIZATIONAL ISSUES

In any IT acquisition process it is the responsibility of the IT service provider to display its credibility on providing required services to the acquiring organization as demanded. In some cases IT service providers guide IT acquiring organization to understand all the aspects of technology and various options. In business computing such credibility and competence are visible in terms of providing turnkey services for implementation of ERP, business intelligence applications and process automations like SCADA.

The acquisition model most often employed is the familiar "waterfall" development model in which well-defined increments of capability or technology are designed, developed, and implemented in a pre-specified order. The "flow" of releases is sequential and variations from the approved sequence are cause for a new baseline for the program. In extreme cases it may cause cancellation. However, as a new baseline generally triggers a complete top-to-bottom review of the program, delays are natural and often approvals at each step up the acquisition approval chain become more difficult to obtain (Melville, Kraemer and Gurbaxani, 2004; Defense Science Board, 2009).

There are various models which attempt to increase the level of understanding the issues and raise the level of expertise in approaching for this type of IT acquisition process. These categories of stakeholders are progressively adopting various quality models on enhancing their roles, and preparedness in acquisition process. Certifying organizations like ISO etc. have effectively worked on various models and also suggested guidelines, procedures that may be adopted by IT-Vendors. Most of these models have focused on process improvements. The reasoning behind developing these models is to effectively put in place a quality system, which can manage the process of acquisition. A standard and audited quality system underwrites three of the most important factors for any buyer which are to "understand the business process", "competence of the supplier to understand the buyer", and "mutual trust". The basic idea behind developing quality system (Humphrey, (1989) is to formalize a process of acquisition, which would be a tool for stakeholders to assess each other (Ramirez, Melville and Lawler, 2010). Besides, it would also enhance the understanding of the buyer while dealing with such processes. Obviously a big part of building trust rests on the vendor being able to guaranty that they can deliver on commitments. At the same time the vendor should also look at the intrinsic factors that could affect the quality of supply of IT components and/or implementation of the IT project in the acquiring organization. However, there is no single well-accepted conceptual model on service quality, nor any on generic operational aspects on how to measure it (Seth, Deshmukh and Vrat, 2005).

"Usability preparedness" of the product and/ or services is one such indicator that provides a better understanding on the credibility of the supplier, developer and organization. Credibility on this aspect with quality assurance is expected to bring encouraging results (Jokela, 2001). IT service providers should therefore, work towards achieving this preparedness. User Centered Design (UCD) methods of ISO 13407 can be used for development of software that might add to the credibility of software as well as the product quality. "Usability" is defined as one of the main software quality attributes in standard of ISO 9216 (Abrahamsson and Jokela, 2001; Jokela and Abrahamsson, 2000). ISO 9216 says that "The preparedness of the software product should be understood, learned, used and should also be attractive to the user, when used under specific conditions". Usability preparedness is a characteristic of software developing organization (contextually named as IT service provider/IT supplier) that could predict the level of usability. The concept behind the usability preparedness is

to understand "usability, user-centered design and usability-capability". As per quality standards ISO 13407 specifies usability as "the extent to which a product can be used by specified users to achieve their goals with effectiveness, efficiency and satisfaction in the desired context of use". Figure 1 tries to explain how the IT service provider can organize its usability capability so that user can use the product developed or supplied.

Usability capability models like Trillium, Philps, INUSE, INUSE HCS, and IBM profess some capability statements for the software development agencies. IT acquisition is apparently software centric and thus these models make sense to discuss about. However, their extent of applicability to the IT acquisition needs deliberations. For example Trillium is a process assessment model oriented towards telecommunication products, Philps refers to an assessment model aimed at Human-ware process assessment and INUSE is a process assessment model oriented for software processes defined in ISO15504. INUSE HRC (human centeredness) is based on IBM and that of ISO 13407, but looks at human dimension. These models suggest a possible support structure for the acquiring and service providing organizations to deliver "user acceptable software and services" through adherence to quality parameters. Some of the relevant models are discussed below in order to support the IT acquisition processes with organizational imperatives.

SISP Model

As discussed in chapter three, strategy formulation and providing direction to IT acquisition at organizational level should be one of the priorities

Figure 1. Usability capability actions (Abrahamsson & Jokela, 2001)

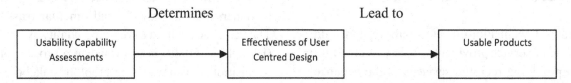

for strategic decision makers (Ward and Peppard, 2002). Model developed by Segars and Grover provides a framework to understand the role of strategic information system planning and its role in successful IT adoption as presented in Figure 2 (Segars and Grover, 1998). The model tries to understand four dimensions of success of SISP in an organization namely, "Alignment", "Analysis", "Cooperation" and "Improvement in Capabilities".

Payoff Measurement Model

Another relevant model related to organizational issues in IT acquisitions is Payoff Measurement Model. This model recognizes the issues concerning IT investments in the organization and argues in favour of IT alignment strategy for effective processes and related economics (Kohli and Sherer, 2002). Study on this issue revealed that often applications were implemented without good assessments of expected payoffs. It is argued here that deployment of IT without an effective strategy is considered a source of mixed results. It is also said that during acquisitions of IT components, the difference in competitive and economic gains is felt due to management of the technology involved, and strategic thinking for IT investments. In order to establish a framework, the researchers

supported the idea of layering of the organization in management principles to assess payoff on IT investments such as "operational", "tactical" and "strategic"; and recommended to assess the payoff on the grounds of "technical", "project" and "organizational" benefits and risks. It recommends using a four-stage process model mostly in line with a SDLC framework i.e. "Exploration", "Involvement", "Analysis" and "Communication", to implement IT payoff initiatives (Grehag, 2001). Each stage establishes a feedback mechanism so as to refine the next stage iteration. Besides, the framework also suggests that the IT payoff analysis should have stakeholder based evaluation process with defined authority based accountability. An activity analysis is proposed for the organization where all stakeholders help identify priorities and possible impact of IT investments through strategic documents.

Figure 3 explains the process for the IT acquisition in an organization which suggests it to be continuous process with a mechanism to understand the effects of change. This continuous process attempts to make "gap analysis" of "current work process" with that of "future work process" thereby understanding the impact of the IT investment planned and executed. This piece of work provides an impetuous for further research

Figure 2. SISP success model (Segars & Grover, 1998)

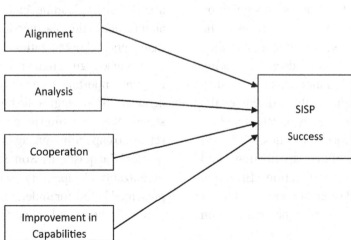

Figure 3. Value realization with activity analysis (Kohli & Sherer, 2002)

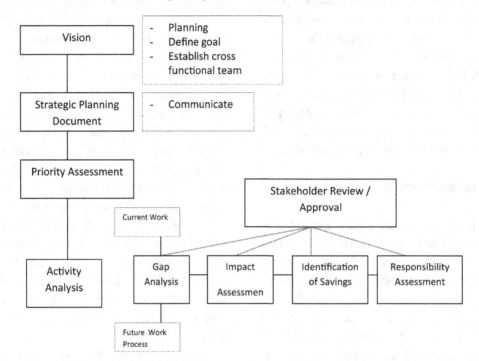

with a focus on strategic planning and evaluation of the IT payoff through stringent metrics at organizational level. The model encourages alignment exercises for the IT acquiring organization to ensure minimum gap between IS and IT deliverables.

Alignment refers to the "fit" between the strategies for business and IS formulated for the organization. It says that a linkage between these two strategic elements helps facilitate acquisition and deployment of IT which might fit in to the dynamic need of the organization rather than capturing existing patterns of decision making (Iivari, 1992). While alignment talks about strategic users' involvement, analysis discusses the "internal operations" in the organization and individual IS planning process. Besides, it refers to "architecture" of integrated applications and databases across the organization. Effective analysis should provide a clear understanding of how information is used within the organization

and uncover critical development areas. Cooperation refers to "conflict resolution" in the organization and should be built in to the strategy for IT acquisition. It involves all stakeholders working towards organizing priorities of the ISD projects. Besides, "standards" for development of applications and use of IT for the stakeholders need to be agreed among key coalitions in the organization. Improvement in capabilities involves assessment of planning, business process, associated technologies, partnership among functional managers and organizational changes.

It is also argued that post project management is quite important to analyze effectiveness and outcome of strategies formulated during early stage of the acquisition process. This phenomenon relates to capability management in the organization for IT acquisitions. Some of the closely related organizational capability assessment models are presented below for understanding the work done in this direction and scope for further work.

IS Assessment Model

The model in Figure 4 is based on a concept that includes studies on dimensions of planning systems to organizational contexts for effectiveness of IS planned. IS planning is described as a managerial process of providing an identity to all functions in the organization from information point of view. The attributes of the model are divided into three constructs i.e. "Organizational Contexts", "Planning System Dimensions", and "Planning System Effectiveness". Organizational context discusses issues related to formalization, future role of IS and decision making process in the organization (Zmud, 1982; Wang and Tai, 2003).

While future role of IS tries to capture and document a roadmap for the function it relates to, formalization and centralization advocates for understanding the process rules, procedures and capturing these in a form that is agreed by all in the organization. Organizational co-alignment refers to a status in the organization where the IS planning is accepted and this acceptance reflects the capability to execute projects with commitments from all the stakeholders. It also tries to capture an integration mechanism between planning of business and IS. It also tries to establish an implementation mechanism to introduce a control system. Environmental assessment represents the analysis of external events and trends in the economic, political, social, technological, regulatory and analysis of internal aspects of organizational weakness, strength etc. All these constructs lead to two outcomes in the planning process for the information systems i.e. "improvement in planning capability" and "fulfillment of planning objectives". These allow an examination of both process and outcome.

Information Technology Assessment and Adoption (ITAA) Model

ITAA model considers the IT acquisition issues to be that of the organization and not an isolated issue. Organizational behavior has a bearing on the IT adoption process and this is an important issue the organization needs to address in the pre-acquisition stage (Huff and Munro, 1985). ITAA tries to understand the prime mover for the IT acquisition process in the organization based on models like "issue-driven", "technology-driven", "opportunistic", and "normative" as shown in Figure 5.

Figure 4. IS planning model (Wang & Tai, 2003)

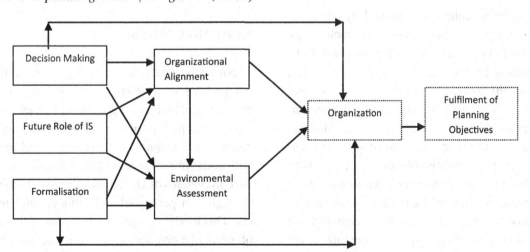

Figure 5. IT assessment and adoption model (Huff & Munro, 1985)

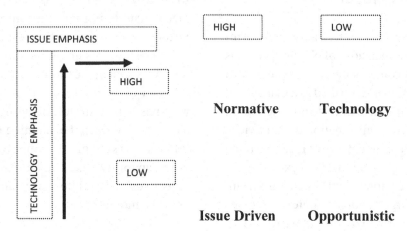

Issue-Driven Model

Issue-driven model talks about an environment in an organization which is closely geared to the corporate and systems planning processes where important issues are discussed and prioritized. Architecture (such as "centralized") can be conveniently attached to this type of organization where top-down approach is given for the planning process. This type of organization, it is observed, shows a sponsorship and leadership for new technology.

Technology-Driven Model

There are many technology centered organizations in which most of the activities are technology supported. For example, virtual organizations with strong Internet enabled support structures, and consulting organizations having professional bureaucracy have the potential to remain technology centered. In such organizations, technology managers lead the organization structure for rendering services. Other employees in the organization structure remain marginalized having fewer opportunities to contribute to the IT acquisitions. This model therefore, indicates less challenge for the IT service providers to manage organizational change to adopt IT which is considered intrinsic.

However, such types of organizations are not representative in nature to generalize and replicate IT acquisitions strategies adopted.

Opportunistic Model

This model recognizes unorganized approach that exists in some of the organizations for planning and prioritizing IT acquisition mandates. In such organizations, a particular component may take the lead among other components in IT. Occasionally a match occurs between the business issues and the technology. Organizational apathy is a major concern in such type of situations having least concern for organizational preparedness.

Normative Model

This model indicates that some organizations make comprehensive assessment of current services environment and future goals for IT acquisitions. This is mapped to the application level. Organizational and technological issues are addressed with equal importance. Organization is aware of the components of IT that encompasses hardware through user personnel and vendors and suppliers. This model recognizes strengths of this type of organizations for supporting organizational capability.

Change Readiness Capability Model

The model argues that IS preparedness shortens the development cycle for IT applications in an organization. It tries to capture design elements that can make an organization IS-change ready. Figure 6 explains the relationship of the attributes that lead to change-readiness.

This star model formulated (Clark et al., 1997) identifies the attributes to be "organization structure, processes, people-skill, reward system". In this star model, "strategy" is at the root of the exercise. It relates to a situation where an organization is capable of providing a strategy to build applications and provide IT leadership. "Structure" in the organization levels the responsibility among prospective users to group people, identify roles, relationship and tasks. "Process" concerns a mechanism to establish control, inform and direct individual and collective behavior. "People skill" relates to understanding technical competencies for understanding the issues related to IT. "Reward system" talks about the organizational mechanism to provide a system that encourages people to innovate either through a reward system or recognition system. In this star-model, three criteria have been chosen to test the congruence among the five elements. These three criteria are strategic-fit, strategies and internal fit that examine architectural element within the organization. These criteria are used for understanding wheth-

er strategy formulated fits in to the environment. This model is limited to testing of a case but thoroughly for a span of two years. However, it is implied that IT already exists in the organization and therefore, can be well used for understanding success in post acquisition stage.

Expectation Confirmation Model

This model examines the cognitive beliefs and effect influencing one's intention to continue using information systems (Bhattacharjee, 2001). It is mostly drawn from the consumer behavior literature. It reflects on the user behavior and suggests that users' continuance intention is determined by their satisfaction and perceived usefulness of continued IS use. It concludes that satisfaction derived from successful projects implemented earlier leads to an easy acceptance of the technology being implemented subsequently. It is almost in conformity with UTAUT models.

MODELS ADDRESSING IT SERVICE PROVIDER ISSUES

User Centered Design (UCD) is an approach to interactive system development that focuses specifically on making system usable. "Usability capability" is defined as capability of the IT-service providing organization that develops

Figure 6. Star model for IS-change readiness (Clark, et al., 1997)

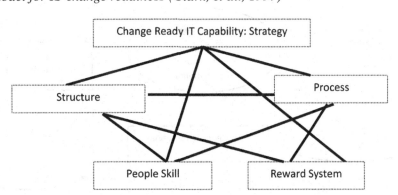

products to be utilized by the users. ISO 13407 says that effective user-centered design leads to usable products. There are three dimensions to the usability capability of an organization i.e., business management commitment, infrastructure (such as technology and skill) resources for implementation of UCD. UCD infrastructure determines the level how efficiently and effectively it can be potentially performed. It is also said that usability is quality characteristic of a product that is determined by the content and quality of UCD. Usability gives many benefits like increased productivity, enhanced quality of work, improved user satisfaction, reduction in support and training costs. ISO 13407 defines four processes for UCD:

- Understand and specify context of use: know the user, the environment of use.
- Understand what the tasks are.
- Specify the user and organizational requirements: how quickly the user is able to complete the task with the product.
- Produce designs against requirements. The designs are evaluated against user requirement.

ISO 13407 defines a set of principles aimed at allocating functions between systems and users, iteration of design solutions, active involvement of users and a multi-disciplinary teamwork. The activities are discussed in Figure 7. These activities should be performed seriously in order to produce valid data for the product design. This calls for skill sets, tools and methods to carry out the process well and therefore, determines and displays the capability of the product developer for evaluation by an IT acquirer and provides a scope to build trust.

It is opined that many products today in the market or systems that are in use represent poor usability (Jokela, 2001). A typical approach to start organizational improvement effort in any domain is to carry out current state analysis. Through current state analysis, one can identify strengths and weaknesses of an organization, and thus gets a good basis of planning and implementing process improvement techniques. Well known approaches for software process are CMM, Bootstrap and ISO 15504, also known as SPICE. But this does not guarantee success of IT acquisition as a whole. Each component of the infrastructure

Figure 7. User-centered design activities (Jokela, 2001)

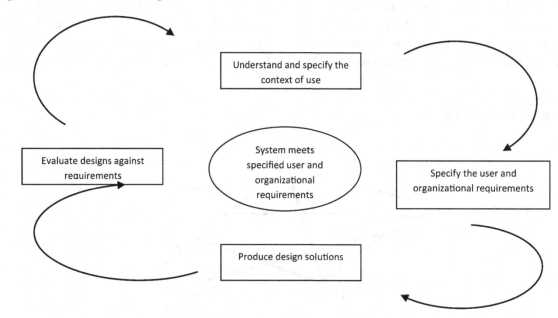

of IT has distinct issues and a holistic approach needs to be undertaken. CMM (Paulk et al., 1994) indicates the software developing organization's capability to organize its processes and technology along with its people, but it is not comprehensive.

There is a danger in adhering to the guiding principles of CMM and usability models that the project life cycle might linger unnecessarily. Besides, the problem is that, given the complexity of most IT projects it is difficult for any supplier or purchaser to provide that sort of guarantees (Ibrahim, 2000). But a quality model can be thought of or explored among various models available so as to make it fit for improvement of the process. Both supplier and purchaser (IEEE, 1994) should understand each other based on credibility and trust.

Two of the most ideal circumstances could be the awareness and comfort level in accepting each other. In any case the supplier must be demonstrably competent. And second, the buyer must be able to reliably identify a competent supplier. But at times history does not successfully repeat in the case a supplier to meet the requirements of a purchaser. However, if quality system modeling is done to ensure these two, it could be beneficial to both the stakeholders. Before proceeding further, a few HR acquisition models are being discussed next in relation to organizations using IT services. They are:

Just-In-Time (JIT) Model: A JIT acquisition model is largely based on company size and is predominantly found in small to mid-sized companies that have experienced growth and have a one-location, centralized IT department. As companies grow, so does the demand on the IT department (more support, more applications, more mobility, more security, and others). Increasingly complex environments create additional needs that existing internal resources cannot keep up with, causing an increased demand for both temporary and permanent IT professionals. In this model, in addition to meeting the internal service level agreements and project deliverables, IT management is also tasked with managing the recruitment process.

HR-Managed Model

In this model, a company introduces human resources into the buying process. The HR department often brings structure to the hiring process and tends to bring additional staffing providers to the table. Company size is a key characteristic to this model as it is typically employed by mid-sized companies who have outgrown the JIT model.

Preferred/Tiered Suppliers Model

This model builds off of the HR-Managed model where procurement is brought to the table to select a number of preferred suppliers, commonly four to six. Companies that employ this model are typically mid- to-large sized companies that find their IT department with HR needs dispersed amongst multiple geographies. In this model, procurement issues a formal Request for Proposal to External Service Providers (ESP) that may include a standard process for candidate submittals, on-boarding compliance information and a rate card. It may also typically have a governance process in place to ensure coverage and results once the contract is executed. The services provided can encompass a specific portion of the recruitment lifecycle such as sourcing, or the entire recruitment process for IT.

Managed Staffing Programs (MSP) Model

With this model, a company essentially outsources the full recruitment lifecycle to service provider who is then responsible for managing all other ESPs. Companies that employ this model are typically large companies with a high, ongoing volume of temporary staff. This is the most complex talent acquisition model as governance for such arrangements is the most important element. However, MSPs will utilize best practices, proven methodologies and technology to create customized recruitment programs for maximum operational efficiencies.

IT Service Provider's Preparedness under Product Approach

Under a product based acquisition many issues such as the delivery attributes and input characteristics are already addressed. Processes are also pre-determined and imposed on the acquirer. For example, an OS comes with directions from the manufacturer/intermediaries specifying details of deliverables. Unlike Linux as a product, most of OS manufacturers do not share the source codes with the users and these remain as a black box. Providing any further upgrades, updates and issues alike are left to the discretion of the manufacturer. Situation grows worse when the supplies are made through an intermediary trader who otherwise is not competent to address such issues. In this case it is manufacturer's credibility, competence that plays a vital role in accepting and using the product. Similar is the case with any middleware and firmware products.

Enterprise Resource Planning (ERP) on the other hand has a different story to tell. This product is built upon certain middleware products and compatible to various OS available in the market. But the serious problem arises in the acquiring organization during the process of implementation. Popular among the implementation strategies the manufacturers offer is the "modular" approach. Each module comes with specific product attributes. ERP, due to its inherent product attributes such as reduced cost, rapid implementation and high system quality provided a solution to IT industry's custom design problems. In 1980s warning was that though application packages have inherent advantages over custom designed applications developed in-house or otherwise, it has inherent acquisition risks like hidden costs and uncertainty (Gross and Ginzberg, 1984; Lynch, 1984). Despite growing popularity of ERP packages, this warning is still valid.

Survey results indicated that ERP systems are viewed to be the most strategic computing platform in an organization. But the alarming finding is that 60 percent of ERP projects have been judged unsuccessful by the ERP implementing firms (Handy, 1989). It is also attributed to the "mis-fit" in customer's desire for meeting their specific need for unique business solution and vendor's generic applications and "inflexible" module (Everdingen et al., 2000; Swan et al., 1999). Thus a product must qualify to meet the user's requirement. A product built somewhere else with generic attributes might not meet the specific requirement of the acquiring organization. Therefore, product tuning at site is a major issue for such products. Other IT components such as networks, middleware and firmware, though mostly are products, do not portray such problems. This is because of least common user interfaces. For example, US firms in 1996 invested around US $ 275 billion in software application and 53 percent of the projects failed not because of wrong codes, but their failure to understand the real organizational needs and systems required to solve the problems and meet the objectives (Palaniswamy, 2002). Therefore, IT service providers must be capable of portraying competence to understand the need of the IT acquiring organization and then prescribe IT components for selection and acquisition. It is also argued that failure of process approach for implementation of ERP is strongly related to social interaction of IT and organization (Markus and Robey, 1988).

Induction of a product into an organization demands "fit among "business strategy", "IT strategy", "IT infrastructure" and "processes" (Henderson and Venkatraman, 1993, Dvorak et al, 1997). Products are built in simulated environments with generic inputs from experts. It might therefore, at times demand a comprehensive change in business process. Inability of the acquiring firms to bring in changes in design and structure of their organization often prevents the organization to gain a competitive advantage that a product brings in. Many researchers also supported this finding as well (Grover et al, 1998; Lucas and Baroudi, J., 1994). This is a very important lesson to the organizations supporting the "product approach" and especially ERPs.

An important factor that influences a product life cycle is its acceptability in the market. Acceptance of the acquirer depends largely on product quality. While it is not necessary that a product adhering to the quality would lead to satisfactory use and sustainability as discussed above, it is essential that process through which product is made meets certain quality standards. COTS packages like any OS, databases, firmware and groupware and applications like Tally and ERPs should meet quality standards. Except for the applications which are intrinsic to the processes, other packages developed have generic use and product is seldom tuned to the requirements of the organization. Selection of these packages however, needs to be done at the macro level while dealing with large scale software applications where integration among OS, middleware and firmware is absolutely necessary. Capability of an IT service provider to meet the dynamic requirements for building and setting up IT support infrastructure would largely depend upon the capability of its employees in the service providing organization. This capability is however, just half of the entire story. This capability would be of no use if acquiring organization does not elaborate the structure of the organization, its future requirements and is not capable to understand the overall architecture in order to relate it to the IT architecture. This architectural "misfit" would lead to wrong alignment of IT components acquired at any stage. It is therefore, essential that IT service provider should develop its capability in bringing out the best from its client organization in this aspect.

It is interesting to note that application software constitutes 99 percent of CBS. However, more than half of the features in large COTS software products go unused having average product life cycles of eight to nine months. CBS development and post development efforts can scale as high as square the number of independently developed components targeted for integration. CBS post-deployment cost is higher than development costs (Basili and Boehm, 2001). It is further noted that organization's preparedness is absolutely essential during acquisition of CBS as it demands modification in technical and management processes and planning for non-developmental activities. It is observed that efforts to acquire and use CBS vary significantly across COTS products classes- OS, database, device drivers, groupware etc. Empirical tests suggested that the most determinant factor in successfully acquiring CBS is capability of personnel of CBS systems provider. As has been discussed in the case of ERPs where experiences are not encouraging, CBS (ERP is a class in CBS as well!) has been acquired with mixed responses. CBS is viewed to be a high risk activity for the IT service provider due to above reasons. CBS activities may lead to effort and schedule overruns, though there are many successful projects having cost reduction and early delivery. It is essential that IT service provider must provide inputs to the acquirer on cost and schedule estimates frequently during execution of projects in order to make a CBS to be effective. Capability of the IT service provider to foresee these indicators would contribute to the successful acquisition of the system. It is therefore, mandatory that an IT service provider should prepare its product with full knowledge on the attribute of the products, intrinsic dangers and strengths that each COTS based product and/or a CBS carries.

IT Service Provider's Preparedness under Process Approach

As discussed traditional approach for an organization to develop application software is based on SDLC. SDLC refers to the "staged approach" and is extensively viewed as a process model framework. Various models have been formulated and used extensively to manage software projects as discussed in appendix-1 (Hoffer et al., 2001). SDLC though is organization centric with strong bias to IS, it is not free from criticism due to some serious limitations. One of the criticisms is the way the SDLC is organized for freezing the milestones and then referring back after execution. The other criticism is the offshoot of the first one leading to high maintenance cost because of lack of time that SDLC provides for analysis and design. Structured analysis and Object Oriented Analysis and Design (OOAD) were then thought of providing a better solution to ensure good conduct of the projects under process approach. The third dimension of the limitation of SDLC is its suitability in project specific delivery. Most organizations use different life cycle models for different projects such as waterfall, spiral, COTS, incremental and evolutionary model to name a few. However, it is difficult to ascertain the survivability of the system thus developed for its life cycle with intended deliveries. (Mead et al., 2000). It is argued that most of the models popularly coming under SDLC have limitations in delivering good result in a complex scenario, but are successful in a tightly specified domain. All software models under SDLC can be characterized as a problem-solving loop, which may go through four distinct stages: Status quo, problem definition, solution integration and post-acquisition assessment. Status quo represents current status, problem definition identifies the specific problem to be solved, and technical development solves the problem through application of some technology.

The approach to understand the organization, its requirement from IT acquisition point view, vendor's approach and its capability is not new. There are various quality models available to assess vendor quality. As discussed in quality systems models above, many organizations are relentlessly working on this issue and some models are prescribed to address either independently for the

supplier or purchaser. Attempts are being made to bridge the gap between these two models. In order to have glance at the available models which are all inclusive but not exhaustive, possible quality models with the utilities are described below for the "software engineering approach" that talks about process by which products are built, implemented as per user's requirements. The other category called "Quality acquisition approach" describes model, standards and systems available for assessing capability or approaches made by supplier and purchaser for IT acquisition. Despite having limitations for "Reuse", and advent of CASE tools along with OOAD techniques, IT service providers adopted these skills set to develop, and manage software projects.

There are various formal methods that have evolved over the years such as "information engineering", "structured systems analysis and design", Jackson System Development (JSD)", Structure Systems Analysis and Design Method (SSADM)" and "Object oriented Modeling Technique (OMT)" (Flynn, 1998). These methods provide an insight to the IT service provider's capability ensuring a process to happen effectively. But these methods do not provide any guarantee to deliver a product that would suit the user's requirement since all these are in a project management mode. These methods could not provide support to manage change in user's requirement, allow the users to refine and reflect in the product delivered. User's knowledge is scantily represented through these methods.

In order to understand the capability of IT service providers, quality systems methodologies are also developed. These quality systems methodologies are based on three basic issues viz. "People", "Process" and "Product". The capability statement primarily depends on the capability of people to identify and manage user needs, management capabilities of IT service providing organization and its internal strength to handle the process and lastly capability of IT acquiring organization to conduct the process management.

As regards products, IT service providers need to have strengths to manage individual product (IT component) to bring out the final product and services. Similarly IT acquiring organization has to internalize the product specific services generated in the process of IT acquisition in post implementation scenario.

IT service providers are conscious of quality standards that a user looks for and making efforts to adopt such process and product quality frame works in order to remain competitive (Sheard, 1996). Software and system developers in particular and IT component providers in general should be aware of these frameworks to choose any or some as per the need. Various important quality frameworks are CMM, ISO, IEEE (1074, 1220), BOOT- STRAP, TRILLIUM, TickIT, IDEAL. All these frameworks fall under following six categories:

- Standards and Guidelines.
- Process improvement Models and Internal Appraisal Methods.
- Contractor selection.
- Quality Awards.
- Software Engineering Life-Cycle Models.
- Systems Engineering Models.

ISO 9000 series mostly satisfies standards and guidelines for any IT service provider and can be extensively used by the acquiring organization for verification. CMM and its family including Trillium try to satisfy the needs of process improvement models and internal appraisal methods. It is again applicable for both IT service provider as well as the acquiring organization. The family of CMM mostly includes CMM-SW, IPD-CMM, P-CMM and others. Two methods such as software Capability Evaluation (SCE) and offshoot of the CMM with Software Development Capability Evaluation (SDCE) largely constitute selection of IT service providers. Quality awards constituted by ISO, European Quality and Malcolm Baldridge national quality institutions are aimed

at ensuring that IT service providers confirm to certain standards for product and/or process these organizations market. It also provides a tool for the acquiring organization to select such quality certified organizations. While ISO/IEC 12207 (ISO, 1991) provides guidelines for software engineering life-cycle models; SE-CMM, INCOSE, systems engineering capability assessment model (SECAM), ISO 15288, IEEE 1220 provide guidelines for systems engineering. These also provide a basis for the IT acquiring organization to understand the capability of an IT service provider. These models aim at ensuring success in the IT acquisition. However, most of these models assume that acquiring organization has a project at hand for acquiring the technology and this implies existence of process specific goals.

CMMI model, in its acquisition module (Weber and Layman 2002; Team 2002), defines efficient and effective practices for government acquisition. These best practices are aimed at providing a foundation for acquisition process discipline and rigor that enable product and service development to be repeatedly executed with high level of ultimate acquisition success. This model aims to provide holistic approach to manage organizational capabilities. However, this is applicable for organizations involved in repeated and voluminous acquisition transactions with high value and large projects. Its applicability for organizations with less intensity and criticality with acquisition point of view, but having a larger impact due to process automation and competitiveness is not discussed.

However, CMMI acknowledges the concern that IT acquisition is a complex process because acquisition is bidirectional. In one direction focus if on acquiring products, systems, and services; and the other is inwardly directed towards conducting the acquisition process itself. It is also recognized that "lack of acquisition guidance" is a major concern for many organizations involved in acquisition and sustenance of systems, including software-intensive systems. Therefore, CMMI while taking the help of all the features available in SA-CMM, CMMI, FAA, iCMM, CMM-SW, CMM-IPD frameworks; advocates for timely collaboration of relevant stakeholders throughout the life of the product to better satisfy customer needs, expectations and requirements through the following concepts:

- Effective use of cross-functional or multi disciplinary teams.
- Commitment from leadership.
- Appropriate allocation and delegation of decision making.
- Definition of organization structures that reward performance.
- Design downstream processes.
- Focus on customer needs.
- Identification of risks.
- Focus on measurement and improvement of process.

Due to veracity of the problems discussed in IT acquisition process it is pertinent to examine the capabilities of the IT acquiring organization with much deeper understanding. It is also equally important to address concerns related to user management with much readiness.

MODELS ADDRESSING USER CENTERED ISSUES

Post acquisition success depends on the usefulness of the IT infrastructure acquired, user's intention to use, fit between task and technology delivery etc. There is serious research in this area in order to understand the success of IT acquisition and use delivering many models. Some relevant models are discussed here for the purpose.

Though not generic, it is a normal phenomenon that a project germinates with a requirement albeit at a higher level (Flynn, 1998). IS planning is a part of the strategic planning process and commitment of the strategic users is of paramount importance. Acquisition stage travels the difficult path to acquire the technology, product(s) and processes as well. During the post acquisition stage therefore, is essential to understand the outcome of the attempt made during the acquisition process. IT service providers enter into the "maintenance stage" whereas IT acquiring organization starts using the services rendered by the IT infrastructure developed. It is worth noting that it is not important how well the IS is planned or designed, it is of importance to understand how well these are used in the organizational context (Brynjolfsson and Hitt, 1998; Dewire, 2003; Lientz and Chen, 1981). Post acquisition stage just involves this exercise. In this context role of end users is quite critical in the IT acquisition which might pass through five stages: "initiation", "adoption", "adaptation", "acceptance", "routine use" (Cooper and Zmud, 1990). Though initiation stage is related to the pre-acquisition and acquisition stages, remaining stages are reflective of the post-acquisition stage. During system development mostly project is guided by the skilled users of IT till acceptance stage and after this end users (actual users) take over the IT enabled IS product. Success of the test depends on the actual use by the end users. Therefore, end users bear larger responsibilities to guide IT acquisition especially IS product being delivered and/or developed. It is argued that skill set of end users should be measured in terms of their interaction with application software developed, user's knowledge on and ability to use hardware, and procedures to manage applications in their domain. Besides, end users need to develop skills to interact effectively during analysis of information requirements, evaluation of application features, and influence designers to develop screens and output forms/reports (Torkzadeh and Lee, 2003). Enhanced skill set in end users is expected to influence quality design decisions for IS. This skill set may also prevent an organization from acquiring costly systems whose features might not ever be used by these set of users. After all, the caveat is that these users must be in the category of product designers, managers and may be domain analysts like finance, marketing and sales etc. and not as system analysts or system designers.

User's involvement is related to system success and it also can be measured through use of some variables as determinants of systems quality. Degree of user participation, user expertise, user/developer communication, user training, and user influence and user conflict are some of the variables organized for understanding user involvement (Tor et al., 2003). It is noted that importance of user participation, user training and user expertise are significant variables for system quality, user/developer communication, user influence and user conflict are found to have an indirect effect on system quality. Bad acquisition process leads to continued dissatisfaction of business managers over the gap between perceived value addition and what is derived out of IS investments (Peppard et al., 2000). Information should be viewed as "strategic asset" and strategic users in particular and the organization in general must acquire competency to leverage the information content. Longitudinal studies revealed the "gap" between IS and organization-business relationship that inhibits IT to contribute effectively and suggested the role of strategic users in playing active role to bridge the gap (Martins Keillermanns, 2001; Miller and Toulouse, 1986; McFarlan and McKenny, 1983; Peppard, 2001). This gap needs to be bridged during pre-acquisition stage. Study on Small and Medium-sized Enterprise (SME) to understand the inhibiting and enabling attributes of IS-IT alignment, suggested that top management's role and attitude plays a vital role in adopting IT in an organization and their preparedness is absolutely necessary (Flynn 1998; Franz and Robey, 1986; Galbraith, 1998; Gebauer, 1997) . Too often, assessment may be developed in terms of what is most easily measurable such as Return on Investment (RoI), budget variance etc. IS is a high risk issue and needs to be dealt with care. Poor performance of users and their disregard

to the learning process are major attributes for a system failure. Organization needs to address these issues as well and with care. On some occasions, failure on the part of lower ranks to the strategic decision makers to transmit the actual status of projects (failing or otherwise) leads to bad decisions and it is the prime responsibility of the strategic decision makers to establish the formal channel in the pre-acquisition scenario (Lyytinen and Robey, 1999; Smith and Keil, 2003). Though strategic decision makers make decisions on IT expenditure, they form a group who are incompetent in assessing IT usability and even in their own domain (Seeley and Targett, 1997). They need to know the way IT can be used for their own work well in advance and even before mooting the proposal for IT acquisition.

Assessing the post acquisition performance is not a new area of concern. Despite the innovations it is found in organizations where IT acquisition has taken place, many efforts have yielded advantage to the users and even sponsors (Johnston et al., 1998). Some efforts are abandoned prior to completion or fail to yield the expected advantages. The study reveals that successful deployment depends on the presence of a set of external environmental factors and mostly on developing a set of internal capabilities at tactical and operational levels that extends beyond the IS function. Internal capabilities include leadership, integration of IT, strategy functions in the organization, direct contact between IS function and line divisions and capability of IS function. Executives in the successful companies attributed their success to capabilities developed in the process of identifying opportunities to improve performance. Both line and IS executives believed that line leadership, integration of line and IS objectives are key to past success. It is also viewed that there are concerns about knowledge of IS employees, (though high on technology competence) on business which has affected the success. Computer users perceive a variety of skills needed to accomplish their work and that they experience freedom and independence associated with their jobs (Yaverbaum, 1988). Regular computer users characterized the motivating potential of their jobs in much the same way as employees who did not utilize computer regularly. It also revealed that the amount of course work completed was not linked to motivating potential. The study shows that efforts in work re-design must be concentrated in the areas where boredom and fear are producing motivational problems and job dissatisfaction. Managers and professional workers do not perceive their jobs as more meaningful as a result of technological innovation. Instead, anxiety and fear are often associated with the introduction of new technology. These issues needed a careful diagnosis during post-acquisition stage.

SERVQUAL Model

A way to understand the post-acquisition scenario is to understand how the service is provided to the users. IS and IT units normally are responsible for these activities and they also need support from all users. An IS unit can add value to systems by enhancing service quality as well as software quality. Clients determine the quality and effectiveness of an IS unit. Traditionally IS needs to look beyond systems building and install systems to improve organizational performance and organization's productivity. SERVQUAL is one of the procedures adopted for the purpose (Yap et al., 1992). This largely depended on the comparison between what customer feels should be offered and what is provided. Therefore, the onus lies with customer, not with the supplier and this demands preparedness of the customer to organize itself in order to improve quality of IS. Quality is determined by the users and SERVQUAL has five dimensions that enables customer to evaluate service quality. These are tangibles, reliability, responsiveness, assurance and empathy. These are measured with scores corresponding to perception and expectations.

This is a customer-enabling and auditing technique that tries to measure the gap at each of the five attributes. They also recommended some steps to improve quality of service like linking IT strategy to business strategy, communicating with clients, designing service quality processes, training and reward system and lastly building service quality in to IS at the strategic, tactical and operational levels. It emphasized that delivery of QoS requires action at all these three levels of management. At strategic level it should be ensured that IS delivers as per client need. A tactical level need to assure that IS delivers service and at operational level there is empathy in providing reliable service to client expectations. All these activities require capability of the users to understand their role to collaborate with IT service providers. Therefore, it is essential that organization's IT acquisition is based on assessing success at all these levels.

User Acceptance Models

Apart from the model discussed above detailing all the users at the organizational level, there are quite good number of models examining the user acceptance behavior. The basic concept of the underlying user acceptance models is as described in Figure 8.

UTAUT Model

Among various models, the most relevant we discuss here is the Unified Theory of Acceptance and Use of Technology (UTAUT) (Venkatesh et al. 2003) and DeLone and McLean Models (Rai et al., 2002). It is based on Technology Acceptance Model (TAM and TAM2) (Dewire, 2003). UTAUT model comprehensively discusses user management issues as presented in Table 1. User management issues are captured through eight prominent models which constitute UTAUT. These eight models are:

Theory of reasoned action:

Figure 8. Concept of user acceptance models (Venkatesh et al., 2003)

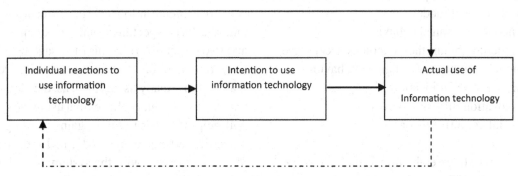

Table 1. Technology acceptance models and user's role

User's Attribute	Model	Remarks
User's Attitude	Theory of Reasoned Action (TRA)	It relates the biased attitude of a person positively/negatively towards use of computers/IT. It does not indicate in which stage of acquisition we need to capture.
User's Perceived Usefulness of Technology	Technology Acceptance Model (TAM)	It indicates high reliability of these two variables to user acceptance of technology. But it is silent on choosing a stage of acquisition where testing is appropriate.
User's Perceived ease of Use		
Motivation	Motivation Model	Captures extrinsic and Intrinsic motivation with relation to improved job performance. Here also it is not clear as when this model needs to be applied to understand its usefulness.
Attitude toward Behavior	Theory of planned behavior (TPB)	An extension of TRA with addition of behavior control. But do not explicitly suggest its applicability in the IT acquisition process
Behavior Control		
Combination of usefulness, behavior, attitude	Combined TAM and TPB	It is a hybrid model. It combines the prediction of TPB with perceived usefulness form TAM.
Job-fit, Complexity, Long term consequence, Inclination to use	Model of PC Utilization	This talks of post acquisition scenario, but does not reflect the preparedness of users to accept PC based environment.
Social Factors, Facilitating conditions (Extra services at no cost)		
Relative Advantage	Innovation Diffusion Theory (IDT)	This model in use since 1960s is used for information systems as well. It is said to be predictive model to study individual acceptance.
Ease of Use		
Image, Visibility, compatibility		
Demonstrable Result		
Voluntary ness of Use		
Outcome Expectations: Performance and Personal	Social Cognitive Theory (SCT)	Mostly used for social research has been used for information systems research as well. Talks about the intentions to use and can be termed as a pre-acquisition user preparedness.
Self-confidence		
Anxiousness		
Affinity		

1. Technology acceptance model.
2. Motivational model.
3. Theory of planned behavior.
4. Model combining the technology acceptance model and theory of planned behavior.
5. Model of PC utilization.
6. Innovation diffusion theory.
7. Social cognitive theory.

Analyses of these eight models indicate scope for linking UTAUT to the preparedness of the users in managing the acquisition process. The UTAUT is claimed to have provided the managers a tool that need to assess the likelihood of success for new technology adoption and helps them understand the drivers of acceptance in order to proactively design interventions targeted at populations of users that may be less inclined to adopt and use new systems. It also recommends for future research to refine measurements of core constructs used in UTAUT, and understanding the organizational outcomes associated with new technology use. The research model at Figure 9 provides the base for further research and the indicators for the user preparedness.

These indicators are based on three determinants of "intention to use" (performance expectancy, effort expectancy, and social influence) and two direct determinants of "usage behavior" (intention and facilitating conditions). Performance expectancy is defined as the degree to which an individual believes that using the system will help him/ her to attain gains in job performance. Effort expectancy is defined as the degree of ease associated with the system. Social influence is defined as a measure of perceived capabilities of users to use new system. Facilitating condition is defined as the degree to which an individual believes that an organizational and technical infrastructure exists to support use of the system. These lead to behavioral intention and in turn to use behavior. UTAUT is a predictive that considers realities in user acceptance. It should be noted that performance expectancy appears to be a determinant of perceived user involvement in IT acquisition process.

The effect of effort expectancy is perceived to be influenced by gender and age. Age has received little attention to technology acceptance in literature, yet UTAUT indicates some relationship.

Figure 9. UTAUT model (Venkatesh et al., 2003)

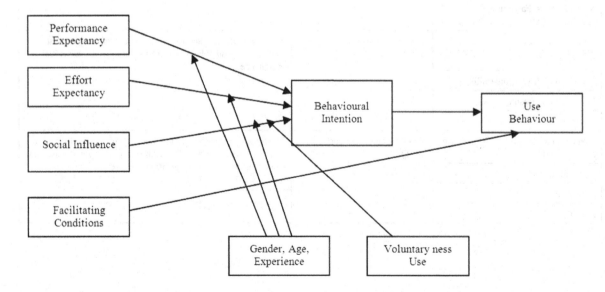

Results suggest that social influence does matter; however, they are more likely to be salient to older workers, particularly women, and even during early stages of experience/adoption. This pattern mirrors that for effort expectancy with added caveat that social influence is more likely to be important in mandatory usage settings. Studies on UTAUT indicate existence of scope for addressing challenges related to user acceptance leading to enhancement in organizational effectiveness. It is often assumed that actual usage of IT enabled services would result in positive outcomes. However, this effect still remains to be tested.

UTAUT provides a base for the managers to assess the likelihood of success for new technology adoption and helps them understand the drivers of acceptance. The key determinants are "user's intention to use" and "usage behavior". This model extensively organizes user expectations, but is limited to the software-centric efforts. But there is a need for capturing and analyzing organizational capabilities. Some of the attributes to understand organizational capabilities are strategy, structure, size, environment, technology, task and individual characteristics Weill and Olson, 1989. It is therefore relevant to comprehensively consider organizational capability issues and capture them early in the IT acquisition process. This approach is likely to provide better results in IS-IT alignment (Wang and Tai, 2003).

Technology Acceptance Model

TAM adapted from the Theory of Reasoned Action (TRA), assumes that an individual's IS acceptance is determined by two major variables: Perceived Usefulness (PU) and Perceived Ease of Use (PEOU) (Lee et al., 2003). After introducing IS into organization, it was found that user technology acceptance could receive fairly extensive attention (Rogers, 1983; Cooper and Zmud, 1990; Swanson, 1988; Grady, 1992); Grady and Caswell, 1987). TAM evolved to provide an explanation to determinants of computer acceptance in general, and capable of explaining user behavior technologies. However, actual usage may not be a direct or immediate consequence of such attitudes and intentions. TAM suggests that when users are presented with a new software package, a number of factors come into their decision about how and when they will use it. Although TAM has aided the understanding of IS acceptance, it was concluded that a deeper understanding of factors contributing to ease of use and usefulness it needed. One neglected area is examining different IS and environments. TAM stresses to examine the relationship between actual usage and objective outcome measures. Structure of TAM is as shown in Figure 10.

TAM has been extensively applied during research spanning across communication systems (E-mail, V-mail), general purpose systems (like

Figure 10. Technology acceptance model (Lee et al., 2003)

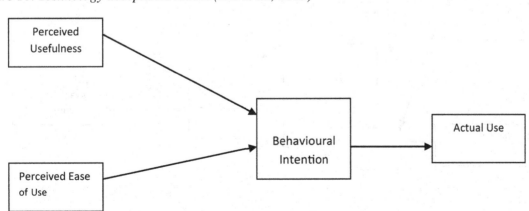

windows, PCs, Internet etc.), office systems (word processors, spreadsheets etc.) and specialized business systems (i.e. CASE tools, MRP/ERP, Decision Support Systems (DSS), Expert Systems etc.). Researches converge to a common finding that relationship between perceived usefulness and intention to use. It means that users willingly use the system that has been functionally useful to them. TAM studies assume that relationship between IS usage and satisfaction, productivity, and quality is positive. IS implementation is costly and has a relatively low success rate (Orlikowski and Barley, 2001). Many IS research studies including TAM have contributed towards understanding this process and its outcomes.

A study in 1998 revealed that only 26 percent of all MIS projects, and less than 23.6 percent of large company projects, are completed on time, and within budget, with all requirements fulfilled, 46 percent of projects were over budget, late and with fewer features and functions than originally planned. Almost 28 percent of projects were cancelled. Use of TAM proved successful in predicting system's use in 40 percent of cases (Riemenschneider et al., 2003). In this context, it is argued that organizational preparedness is part of strategic choices, as opposed to personal choices and this would bolster the importance of user capabilities in influencing IT acquisitions (Henderson and Venkatraman, 1993).

DeLone and McLean Model

Many of the models discussed so far converged on user acceptance and its impact in post-acquisition stage. There are many other models that try to address some issues at organizational level during this stage. DeLone and McLean Model is one of the prominent models and widely used. It says that IS successes depends on Systems Quality, Information Quality, IS Use, User Satisfaction, Individual Impact and Organizational Impact as shown in Figure 11. It narrates the situation where individual satisfaction leads to organizational IS success.

In this model quality system belongs to technical level, and information quality belongs to semantic level. IS use, User Satisfaction and individual impact belong to effectiveness-influence level. In this model, the relationship between perceived use and user satisfaction is found to be weakly linked (Rai et al., 2002).

Seddon Model

Seddon Model described in Figure 12 includes all the components of DeLone and McLean Model with an additional component called perceived usefulness. It is argued that IS use is a consequence of IS success, rather than being an inherent characteristic of IS success. Accordingly, IS use as a

Figure 11. DeLone and McLean model

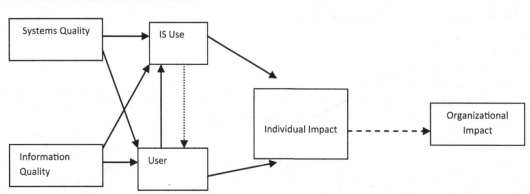

Figure 12. Seddon's IS success model

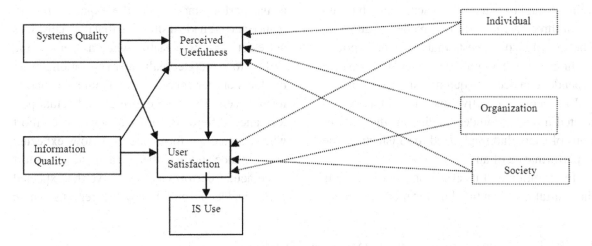

behavior is separated from the IS success model, and IS related behavior is modeled as caused by IS success. This leads to three classes of interrelated variables. The first two classes of variables- information and system quality and perceptions of net benefits of IS use- constitute the IS success model, while a third class of variables focus on IS use as a behavior and constitutes the partial behavior model of IS use.

- **IS Use:** depends on IS dependence. Higher the scale, greater is the dependence.
- **User Satisfaction:** It has been indirectly measured through information quality, system quality, and other variables used by both DeLone and McLean Model and Seddon Model.
- **Perceived Usefulness:** It is defined in Seddon's model. It suggests that effects of information quality on system dependence,

the measure of IS use and User Satisfaction are greater than the effects of ease of use. Perceived usefulness is an additional measure of net benefits and is impacted by satisfaction and IS use.

- **Cognitive Dissonance Theory:** Proposed in 1957, the theory states that when an individual has two cognitive structures (ideas) which are contradicting each other, the individual attempts to attain a state of consonance by changing one of the structures and the model is explained in Figure 13 and Figure 14.

Figure 13 explains a model of user expectations in development and implementations of an information system. User expectations are positioned between pre-implementation factors and two indicators of IS success. The model suggests pre-implementation factors for user satisfaction

Figure 13. User satisfaction and expectation (Rai et al., 2002)

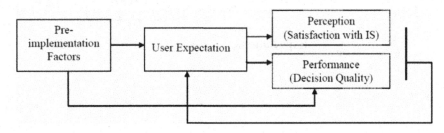

are "user involvement, management support, user training" and tries to scale the expectation of users in three categories: high, moderate and low. The model also suggests that "user perceptions leading to satisfaction" and "user performance dependent on decision quality" are two measures of IS success. Cognitive dissonance theory is a related model for understanding on the perceptions of users that might lead to satisfaction due to performance of an IS.

Expectation and its effect on performance is the central issue captured in this model. Catego-

ry A as shown in Figure 14 is a situation where actual performance meets the expected performance and is an ideal situation that normally does not exist. This is possible when a user has the ability to generate realistic expectations from products and/or services. Areas under B and C form a scenario where expected and actual performance differs. B forms a negative comfort where actual performance is below expected performance and in C there is a positive comfort since actual performance is above the expected performance. D and E are the regions where

Figure 14. Cognitive dissonance theory (Szajna & Scamell, 1993)

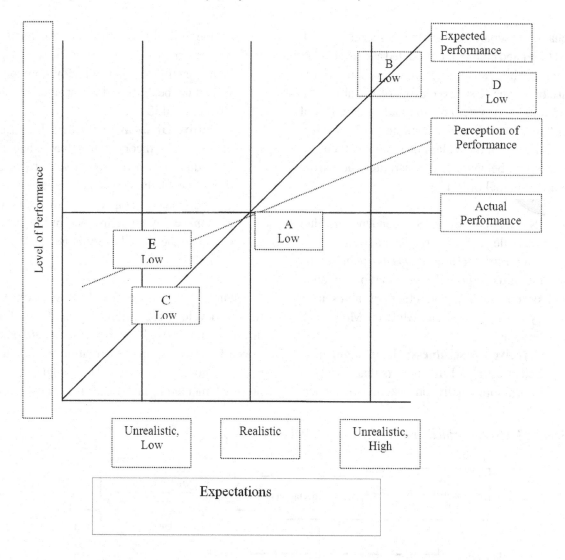

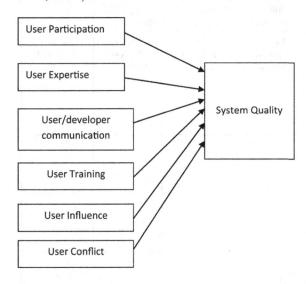

Figure 15. Systems quality prediction (Guimaraes et al., 2003)

perceptions are created and predictions of performance are done by the users for a project/product/service.

User-Related Factors for Systems Development Quality

User's involvement in making a systems development project successful is a much researched area. The model discussed in Figure 15 tries to capture the importance of user involvement through certain variables for predicting systems success.

The variables chosen are "user participation, user expertise, communication, training, user influence and user conflict" which are earlier used by researchers to conduct similar studies. It predicted that a positive attempt to address these variables has a positive effect on the systems quality and success.

SUMMARY

This chapter posited that IT acquisition in an organization is a complex issue. The IT acquisition can be made in stages. However, with regard to the number of stages in the process, various authors have suggested different approaches. Further, it is noted that there are various stakeholders including IT users and IT service providers who contribute to the acquisition process in addition to organizational strategies.

This chapter discussed various models available for assessing the IT acquisition process, understanding organizational issues, capturing and analyzing user behaviour, analyzing usability of the IT resources in order to appreciate the acquisition holistically. Various models are presented to understand the capability of the IT users in the organization, IT service providers, and component developers who participate in the acquisition process.

Table 2 suggests that most of the models address generic acquisition processes and are aimed at assessing capability of IT service providers to deliver quality products and engage in managing quality processes. These models support acquisition processes where requirement is frozen. Many models also tend to independently assess the post acquisition scenario using various metrics such as IS success, user satisfaction, IT assessment and adoption, change readiness among users, expectation confirmation, pay-off assessment and value realization. It therefore, indicates that there are various methods through which acquiring process can be evaluated.

As regards organizational preparedness, review on the models suggested that readiness of the stakeholders in the acquiring organization to manage the acquisition is a weak area and assessing this readiness prior to the initiation of acquisition process is the least addressed issue. If these issues are not taken care of in the pre-acquisition stage it is quite likely that IT acquisition will not deliver the result as expected. Review has indicated that many projects fail not because of the technology, but because of lack of preparedness among various

Table 2. Models supporting stages of IT acquisition

Sl. No.	Model Description	Areas of Concern	Acquiring Organization's Capability Assessment		Service Provider's Capability Assessment		User Centered Services
			Under Product Approach	Under Process Approach	Under Product Approach	Under Process Approach	
1	Strategic Alignment Model (Ward and Peppard 2002)	IS-IT Alignment	✓	✓			✓
2	Nolan's Stage Theory Ward and Peppard 2002	IT Acquisition					
3	Alignment Maturity Model; Luftman (2000); (2003)	Aligning Business and IT Strategies	✓	✓			✓
4	Activity Analysis (Kohli and Sherer, 2002)		✓	✓			✓
5	SW-CMM, P-CMM, SE-CMM, CMMI, IPD-CMM	Understanding capability of IT Service Providers			✓	✓	
6	SA-CMM, CMMI, CMMI-AM	IT-Acquiring Organization's Process	✓	✓			
7	ISO 13407	Development of S/W			✓	✓	
8	ISO 9216/ 15504/ SPICE	User Centered S/W	✓		✓	✓	
9	UCD Model, (Jokela and Abramson,2000)				✓		
10	Trillium, INUSE, Profess (Sheard, 1996)	User Centered Design for products			✓		
11	GAO Model (Carlone, Grossshans, 1992)	Managing Acquisition Process	✓	✓			
12	SERVQUAL; Watson et al., 1998	To assess IT Acquired		✓			
13	TRA	Mapping User's Attitude		✓			
14	TAM	User's Perceived Usefulness of Technology and Perceived Ease of Use		✓			
15	TPB	User Behavior		✓			
16	IDT	Predict individual acceptance		✓			

continued on following page

Table 2. Continued

| Sl. No. | Model Description | Areas of Concern | Acquiring Organization's Capability Assessment | | Service Provider's Capability Assessment | | User Centered Services |
			Under Product Approach	Under Process Approach	Under Product Approach	Under Process Approach	
17	SCT	Capturing User Intention		✓			
18	DeLone and McLean Model (Rai et al.,2002)	User Acceptance		✓			
19	Seddon Model; (Rai et al.,2002)	IS Success Measure		✓			
20	Cognitive Dissonance Theory; (Szajna and Scamell, 1993)	Capturing User's Satisfaction		✓			
21	SISP Model; (Segars and Grover, 1998)	Provide direction to IT acquisition		✓			
22	IS Planning Model; (Wang and Tai, 2003)	IS assessment Model		✓			
23	Systems Quality Prediction Model; (Guimaraes et al., 2003)	To predict systems quality		✓			
24	IT Assess and Adoption Model; (Huff and Munro,1985)	Organizational Assessment on IT adoption		✓			
25	Star Model; (Clark et al., 1997)	Organizational IS Change Readiness		✓			
26	Expectation Confirmation Model (Bhattacherjee, 2001)	User Behavior and attitude to IT acceptance		✓			

stakeholders to appreciate the business processes, understand inter-process linkages etc. and these are the larger organizational issues. Strategic alignment models including CMMI provide leads for establishing focus on assessment of organizational IT acquisition capabilities. However, there is scope for using these models and developing a comprehensive model to converge organizational competencies with IT mediated competencies. This chapter summarizes the scopes for development of a suitable assessment model that can be used for organizational capabilities to manage the acquisition process. This capability is assumed to be a facilitating factors establishment of better information system planning, IT policies, and project management policies in the IT acquiring organization.

REFERENCES

Abrahamsson, P., & Jokela, T. (2001). *Implementing user-centred design in to a software development organsiation- a subcultural analysis.* Paper presented at the 24th Information Systems Research Seminar. Scandinavia, Norway.

Basili, V. R., & Boehm, B. (2001, May). COTS-based systems top 10 list. *Software Management,* 91-93.

Bhattacherjee, A. (2001). Understanding information systems continuance: An expectation- confirmation model. *Management Information Systems Quarterly, 25*(3), 351–370. doi:10.2307/3250921.

Brynjolfsson, E., & Hitt, M. (1998). Beyond the productivity paradox computers are the catalyst for bigger changes. *Communications of the ACM, 41,* 49. doi:10.1145/280324.280332.

Carlone, R.V., & Grosshans, W. (1992). Information technology: An audit guide for assessing acquisition risks. *GAO/IMTEC-8.1.6.*

Clark, C. E., Cavanaugh, N. C., Brown, C. V., & Sambamurthy, V. (1997, December). Building readiness capabilities in the organisation: Insights from the Bell Atlantic experience. *Management Information Systems Quarterly,* 425–454. doi:10.2307/249722.

Cooper, R. B., & Zmud, R. W. (1990). Information technology implementation research: A technology diffusion approach. *Management Science, 34*(2), 123–139. doi:10.1287/mnsc.36.2.123.

Davis, F. D. (1989, September). Perceived usefulness, perceived ease of use, and user acceptance of information technology. *Management Information Systems Quarterly,* 319–340. doi:10.2307/249008.

Defence Science Board. (2009). *Report of the task force on defense science board.* Washington, DC: Department of Defense Policies and Procedures for the Acquisition of Information Technology.

Dewire, T. D. (2003). From the editor. *Information Systems Management, 20*(4), 5–8. doi:10.1201/1078/43647.20.4.20030901/77286.1.

Dvorak, R., Holen, E. E., Mark, D., & Meehan, W. F. (1997). Six principles of high-performance IT. *The McKinsey Quarterly, 3,* 164–177.

Everdingen, Y., Hillergersberg, J., & Waarts, E. (2000). ERP adoption by European midsize companies. *Communications of the ACM, 43*(3), 27–31. doi:10.1145/332051.332064.

Flynn, J. D. (1998). *Information systems requirements: Determination and analysis* (2nd ed.). Berkshire, UK: The McGraw-Hill.

Franz, C. R., & Robey, D. (1986). Organizational context, user involvement and the usefulness of information systems. *Decision Sciences, 17*(4), 329–356. doi:10.1111/j.1540-5915.1986.tb00230.x.

Galbraith, J. R. (1998). *Strategy implementation: The role of structure and process.* St. Paul, MN. MN: West.

Gebauer, J. (1997). Modeling the IT-infrastructure of inter-organisational processes-automation vs. flexibility. In *Proceedings of Conference of International Society for Decision Support(IDSS).* Lausanne, Switzerland: IDSS.

Grady, R. B. (1992). *Practical software metrics for project management and process improvement.* Upper Saddle River, NJ: Prentice Hall.

Grady, R. B., & Caswell, D. L. (1987). *Software metrics: Establishing company-wide programme.* Upper Saddle River, NJ: Prentice Hall.

Grehag, A. (2001). *Requirements management in a life cycle perspective- A position paper.* Paper presented at the 7th International Workshop on Requirement Engineering: Foundation for Software Quality (REFSQ:2001). Interlaken, Switzerland.

Gross, P. H. B., & Ginzberg, M. J. (1984). Barriers to the adaptation of application software packages. *Systems, Objectives. Solutions*, *4*(4), 211–226.

Grover, V., Teng, J., Segars, A., & Fiedler, K. (1998). The influence of information technology and business process changes in perceived productivity: The IS executive's perspective. *Information & Management*, *34*(3), 141. doi:10.1016/S0378-7206(98)00054-8.

Handy, C. (1989). *The age of unreason*. London: Business Books.

Henderson, J. C., & Venkatraman, N. (1993). Strategic alignment: Leveraging information technology for transforming organisations. *IBM Systems Journal*, *32*(1), 4–16. doi:10.1147/sj.382.0472.

Hoffer, J. A., George, J. F., & Valacich, J. S. (2001). *Modern systems analysis and design* (2nd ed.). Singapore: Addison Wesley Longman.

Huff, S. L., & Munro, M. C. (1985, December). Information technology assessment and adoption: A field study. *Management Information Systems Quarterly*, 327–340. doi:10.2307/249233.

Humphrey, W. S. (1989). *Managing the software process*. Englewood Cliffs, NJ: Addison Wesley.

Ibrahim, L. (2000). Using an integrated capability maturity model - The FAA experience. In *Proceedings of the Tenth Annual International Symposium of the International Council on Systems Engineering (INCOSE)*, (pp. 643-648). INCOSE.

IEEE. (1994). How ISO 9001 fits into the software's world. *IEEE S/W, 11*.

Iivari, J. (1992). The organisational fit of information systems. *Journal of Information Systems*, *2*, 3–29. doi:10.1111/j.1365-2575.1992.tb00064.x.

ISO. (1991). *International organisation for standardisation: ISO/IEC 9126*. Geneva: ISO.

Jalote, P. (2002). *CMM in practice: Process for executing software projects at infosys*. Delhi: Pearson Education.

Johnston, H. R., & Carrico, S. R. (1998, March). Developing capabilities to use information strategy. *Management Information Systems Quarterly*.

Jokela, T. (2001). *Review of usability capability assessment approaches*. Paper presented at the 24th Information Systems Research Seminar. Scandinavia, Norway.

Jokela, T., & Abrahamsson, P. (2000). Modelling usability capability-Introducing the dimensions. In *Proceedings of PROFES 2000*. Oulu, Finland: PROFES.

Kohli, R., & Sherer, S. A. (2002). Measuring payoff information technology investments: Research issues and guidelines. *Communications of AIS, 9*.

Lee, Y., Kozar, K. A., & Larsen, K. R. T. (2003). The technology acceptance model: Past, present and future. *Communications of AIS*, *12*, 750–780.

Lientz, B. P., & Chen, M. (1981). Assessing impact of new technology in information systems. *Long Range Planning*, *14*(6), 44–50. doi:10.1016/0024-6301(81)90059-5.

Lucas, H., & Baroudi, J. (1994, Spring). The role of information technology in organisation design. *Journal of Management Information Systems*, 9.

Luftman, J. (2000). Assessing business – IT alignment maturity. *Communications of the AIS, 4*.

Luftman, J. (2003). Assessing IT/business alignment. *Information Systems Management*, *20*(4), 9–21. doi:10.1201/1078/43647.20.4.20030901/77287.2.

Lynch, R. K. (1984). Implementing packaged application software: Hidden costs and new challenges. *Systems, Objectives. Solution*, *4*(4), 227–234.

Lyytinen, K., & Robey, D. (1999). Learning failure in information systems development. *Information Systems Journal, 9*(2), 85. doi:10.1046/j.1365-2575.1999.00051.x.

Markus, M. L., & Robey, D. (1988). Information technology and organisational change: causal structure in theory and research. *Management Science, 34*(5), 583–598. doi:10.1287/mnsc.34.5.583.

Martins, L., & Keillermanns, F. W. (2001). User acceptance of a web-based information system in a non-voluntary context. In *Proceedings of the 22nd International Conference on Information Systems (ICIS)*, (pp. 607-612). New Orleans, LA: ICIS.

McFarlan, F. W., & McKenny, J. L. (1983). *Corporate information systems management: The issues facing senior executives*. Homewood, IL: Irwin.

Mead, N. R., Ellison, R., Linger, R. C., Lipson, H. F., & McHugh, J. (2000). Life cycle models for survivable systems. In *Proceedings of Third Information Survivability Workshop, ISW-2000*. Boston: ISW.

Melville, N., Kraemer, K., & Gurbaxani, V. (2004). Review: Information technology and organizational performance: An integrative model of IT business value. *Management Information Systems Quarterly, 28*(2), 283–322.

Miller, D., & Toulouse, J. M. (1986). Chief executive personality and corporate strategy and structure in small, firms. *Management Science, 32*(11), 1389–1409. doi:10.1287/mnsc.32.11.1389.

Orlikowski, W. J., & Barley, S. R. (2001). Technology and institutions: What can research on information technology and research on organisations learn from each other? *Management Information Systems Quarterly, 25*(2), 145–146. doi:10.2307/3250927.

Palaniswamy, R. (2002). An innovation–diffusion view of implementation of enterprise resource planning (ERP) systems and development of a research model. *Information & Management, 40*, 87–114. doi:10.1016/S0378-7206(01)00135-5.

Paulk, M. C., Weber, C. V., & Curtis, B. (1994). *The capability maturity model for software: Guidelines for improving the software process*. Reading, MA: Addison-Wesley.

Peppard, J. (2001). Bridging the gap between the IS organisation and the rest of the business: Plotting a route. *Information Systems Journal, 11*(3), 249. doi:10.1046/j.1365-2575.2001.00105.x.

Peppard, J., Lambart, R., & Edwards, C. (2000). Whose job is it anyway? Organisational competencies for value creation. *Information Systems Journal, 10*(4), 291. doi:10.1046/j.1365-2575.2000.00089.x.

Rai, A., Lang, S. S., & Welker, R. B. (2002). Assessing the validity of IS success models: An empirical test and theoretical analysis. *Information Systems Research, 13*(1), 50–69. doi:10.1287/isre.13.1.50.96.

Ramirez, R., Melville, N., & Lawler, E. (2010). Information technology infrastructure, organizational process redesign, and business value: An empirical analysis. *Decision Support Systems, 49*, 417–429. doi:10.1016/j.dss.2010.05.003.

Riemenschneider, C. K., Harrison, D. A., & Mykytyn, P. P. Jr. (2003). Understanding it adoption decisions in small business: Integrating current theories. *Information & Management, 40*(4), 269–285. doi:10.1016/S0378-7206(02)00010-1.

Rogers, D. M. (1983). *Diffusion of innovations*. New York: The Free Press.

Seeley, M. E., & Targett, D. (1997). A senior executive end-user framework. *Information Systems Journal, 7*(4), 289. doi:10.1046/j.1365-2575.1997.00019.x.

Seeley, M. E., & Targett, D. (1997). A senior executive end-user framework. *Information Systems Journal, 7*(4), 289. doi:10.1046/j.1365-2575.1997.00019.x.

Segars, A. H., & Grover, V. (1998, June). Strategic information systems planning: An investigation of the construct and its measurement. *Management Information Systems Quarterly*, 139–163. doi:10.2307/249393.

Seth, N., Deshmukh, S., & Vrat, P. (2005). Service quality models: A review. *International Journal of Quality & Reliability Management, 22*(9), 913–949. doi:10.1108/02656710510625211.

Sheard, S. A. (1996). The frameworks quagmire: A brief look. *Software Productivity Consortium*. Retrieved from http://www.software.org/quagmire/frampapr/FRAMPAPR.HTML

Smith, J. H., & Keil, M. (2003). The reluctance to report bad news on troubled software projects: A theoretical model. *Information Systems Journal, 13*(1), 69. doi:10.1046/j.1365-2575.2003.00139.x.

Swan, J., Newell, S., & Robertson, M. (1999). The illusion of 'best practice' in information systems for operations management. *European Journal of Information Systems, 8*, 284–293. doi:10.1057/palgrave.ejis.3000336.

Swanson, E. B. (1988). *Information system implementation bridging the gap between design and utilization.* Homewood, IL: Irwin.

Szajna, B., & Scamell, R. W. (1993, December). The effects of information system user expectations on their performance and perceptions. *Management Information Systems Quarterly*, 493–516. doi:10.2307/249589.

Team, C. P. (2002). *CMMI for systems engineering/software engineering, version 1.1- Staged representation (CMU/SEI–2002-TR-02, ADA339224).* Pittsburgh, PA: Software Engineering Institute, Carnegie Mellon University.

Tor, G. M., Staples, D. S., & Mckeen, J. D. (2003). Emprically testing some main user-related factors for systems development quality. *American Society for Quality Journal, 10*(4), 39–54.

Torkzadeh, G., & Lee, J. (2003). Measures of perceived end-user computing skills. *Information & Management, 40*, 607–615. doi:10.1016/S0378-7206(02)00090-3.

Venkatesh, V., Morris, M. G., Davis, G. B., & Davis, F. D. (2003). User acceptance of information technology: Toward a unified view. *Management Information Systems Quarterly, 27*(3), 425–478.

Wang, E. T. G., & Tai, J. C. F. (2003). Factors affecting information systems planning effectiveness: Organizational contexts and planning systems dimensions. *Information & Management, 40*(4), 287–303. doi:10.1016/S0378-7206(02)00011-3.

Ward, J., & Peppard, J. (2002). *Strategic planning for information systems.* London: John Wiley and Sons.

Watson, R. T., Pitt, L. F., & Kavan, B. C. (1998, March). Measuring information systems service quality: Lessons from two longitudinal case studies. *Management Information Systems Quarterly*, 61–79. doi:10.2307/249678.

Weber, C., & Layman, B. (2002). Measurement maturity and the CMM: How measurement practices evolve as processes mature. *Soft Qual Pract, 4*(3).

Weill, P., & Olson, M. H. (1989). An assessment of the contingency theory of management information systems. *Journal of Management Information Systems, 6*(1), 59–85.

Yap, C. S., Soh, C. P. P., & Raman, K. S. (1992). Information systems success factors in small business. *Omega: International Journal of Information Management, 20*(5/6), 597–609. doi:10.1016/0305-0483(92)90005-R.

Yaverbaum, G. J. (1988, March). Critical factors in the user environment: An experimental study of users, organisation and tasks. *Management Information Systems Quarterly*, 75–88. doi:10.2307/248807.

Zmud, R. W. (1982). Diffusion of modern software practices: Influence of centralization and formalisation. *Management Science*, *28*(12), 1421–1431. doi:10.1287/mnsc.28.12.1421.

Chapter 5
Conceptualization of IT Acquisition Life Cycle Management Model

ABSTRACT

Models are expected to present near real life situations and possible effects on the deliverables based on given input environment. However, models do not necessarily indicate the true solutions and provide scope to work on them incrementally. As discussed earlier, organizations may not follow similar paths to acquire IT and may not even derive desired results despite adopting one. This chapter considers it important to include IS as critical input to managing IT acquisition life cycles and delves further into the IT life cycle management principles to conceptualize a model to specific contributions to assess organizational preparedness for IT acquisitions. This model largely includes discussions on IS centric models and argues in favour of assessing the preparedness across three phases, pre-acquisition, acquisition, and post-acquisition. Each phase considers specific inputs with expected deliverables for successful assessment of the preparedness of the organization in that phase.

INTRODUCTION

It is important to note that role of IS is quite critical input to managing IT acquisition life cycles. Purviews of systems are founded on IS management and it reflects systemic and systematic behaviors in the organization. With this perspective, the chapter delves further into the IT life cycle management principles followed by model specific contributions in this area to prepare the foundations for organizational preparedness assessment. In the following section, the framework is presented in detail with the support of related works done so far. The framework posits that whole exercise for assessment of organizational preparedness to manage IT acquisition life cycle is conducted in three phases having distinct roles to contribute. These three phases are pre-acquisition, acquisition, and post-acquisition. These are subsequently discussed

DOI: 10.4018/978-1-4666-4201-0.ch005

in detail to support the framework conceptualized for overall assessment. Each phase of the framework is supported with various models discussed in previous chapters to build on the strengths.

IT ACQUISITION LIFE CYCLE

The best practices for managing, budgeting, and funding IT solutions persist to evolve. Organizations have realized that IT is a consumable asset, unlike a commercial vehicle. As a particular IT asset ages, it generally requires more maintenance and support, because of its age and more importantly due to relentless progression in technology innovations. Hence, alike other consumable assets, IT assets need to be renewed regularly. In this context creation of a technology life-cycle management plan that produces a framework to fund, renew, and retire IT equipment is rapidly emerging as an industry best practice. Moreover, higher levels of funding that is required to sustain the IT infrastructure, combined with the need to regularly renew assets, has led many organizations to utilize a range of leasing and financing options.

IT infrastructure has emerged as the critical communication, collaboration, and information facilitator of the modern enterprise, broadly enabling most business processes, decision making, practices, and innovation initiatives. To deliver these capabilities, organizations have evolved their roles beyond supporting a collection of servers and software into managing a well-defined and comprehensive suite of equipment, technologies, and services, such as the modern IT infrastructure. A major component of the modern organization's expanded technology management role is an expanding requirement to effectively balance financial requirements of acquiring an IT infrastructure, as well as deliver and sustain it in a capable and secured way. Experienced professionals understand well that carefully evaluating and optimizing financial options when acquiring,

purchasing, financing, or leasing IT equipment and services has become more important for sustaining an optimum IT environment. Furthermore, the best practices for managing, budgeting, and funding IT acquisitions continue to evolve. Many organizations have realized that IT is a consumable asset, not unlike a profit-making vehicle. As a particular IT asset ages, it generally requires more maintenance and support, due to its age and more importantly due to technology's inexorable progression. Like other consumable assets, IT assets need to be rehabilitated regularly. Creating a technology life-cycle management plan that produces a framework to fund, renew, and retire IT acquisition is rapidly emerging as an industry best practice. The higher levels of funding required to sustain the IT infrastructure, combined with the need to regularly renew assets has led many organizations to utilize a range of leasing and financing options (Pucciarelli and Waxman, 2008).

The challenge for every organization is to provide an appropriately robust IT infrastructure that facilitates business processes and recommends effective tools for communicating and collaborating while minimizing total cost. It is noted that optimum solution to this complex situation is for organizations to focus on maximizing the value of their IT resources collectively, as a portfolio, rather than attempting to optimize each piece of equipment separately. In this aspect, the first and most important step in this process is to establish a life-cycle model for each major category of equipment, which provides a method to establish a planned useful life; incorporate actual performance and repair information, and establish criteria regarding when equipment should be refreshed or upgraded. However, the challenge is to establish a life-cycle planning model that looks across two or three equipment cycles and minimizes the total cost for the portfolio across multiple cycles (for example, conducting portfolio analysis). By doing so, planners are challenged to consider the interaction of individual assets, the differing requirements of specific aspects of the portfolio, and the opportunities to optimize strategies for the differing technology requirements. Furthermore, to minimize the total cost of ownership for both current and future generations of networking and communications equipment, organizations should strive to establish policies and practices to systematically measure obsolescence and proactively refresh. Alike any other consumable assets, there are significant opportunities for organizations to enhance their IT management approaches by investing in technology life-cycle management practices. This practice may include life-cycle investment and retirement models based on operational inputs, and other strategies.

Critical challenges of current acquisition processes have been observed as time consuming, which may lead the system to be ineffective, over-burdened and overly bureaucratic. Therefore, the IT acquisition processes should support acquisition practices that enable, not hinder, by capturing technology opportunities before they become useless or outdated. The acquisition process should also recognize and make efficient and cost-effective accommodations for shared IT infrastructure under a framework of effective, collaborative governance and a set of well-defined, rapidly responsive acquisition processes, whereby deployed applications are encouraged to leverage that shared infrastructure (MIEA Review, 2011). Furthermore, the conceptual model should also be able to operationalize any link between cooperation, constructive vs. destructive conflict, distributor's entrepreneurial orientation (EO), international entrepreneurship (IE) and manufacturer's knowledge acquisition (MKA) holistically to provide successful IT acquisition (Li, Liu and Liu, 2011; Reuber and Fischer, 2011).

When organizations would like to establish a technology life-cycle management practice, they may:

- **Establish a Planned Useful Life:** Organizations should consider the acquisition cost, the cost to support and maintain the equipment, and the impact of new labor cost saving configuration and management features. The basis of competition between many IT providers is the new rapid configuration and streamlined management features. Organizations should factor these features into the life-cycle plan.

- **Incorporate Maintenance and Support Experience:** Most organizations capture support, maintenance, and upgrade information within the support center. They should factor this information into evaluation and technology migration planning and including disposition of end-of-life products planning. Virtually every IT operations team needs to prepare a list of equipment for excessive maintenance and support. Organizations should factor this information into an annual life-cycle management review.

- **Flexibility with Rapid Technology Cycles:** Leasing and financing is used by many organizations to achieve a three- to four-year IT equipment refresh life cycle instead of being locked into a five-year depreciation schedule that is longer than the equipment's useful life;

- **Scheduled Review Cycle and Asset Update:** With a lease in place, network and communication technology planners are better equipped to perform systematic reviews of their technology portfolios and plan for migrations and replacements.

- **Additional IT Capital Management Options:** With increasing demand in expanding infrastructure and communication needs and constrained budgets IT managers are often burdened on exploring options for acquisitions. In this context, many IT professionals embrace financing as a means to systematically renew their technology assets and maintain predictable budgets. Financing enables IT professionals to balance the capital and expense budget conundrum.

- **Define Thresholds:** The opportunity for organizations is to fairly and fully explore the thresholds for adopting strategies to own or outsource infrastructure and services. It needs analytical framework to justify acquisitions and use of business.

Lastly, it is critical to remember that the true value of a technology life-cycle management process and a more thorough review process for funding options depends upon the use of those adapted practices, not just by IT staff but also by business and IT managers. However, when moving forward with a new approach in IT operation management, organizations can find potential shortcomings or flaws with new practices relatively easily. The existence of these shortcomings can readily be translated into reasons not to try and attempt change. Foremost, when evaluating and implementing new options, organizations should strive for excellence, not perfection (Pucciarelli & Waxman, 2008; Cragg, Caldeira & Ward, 2011).

IT acquisition initiatives lead to an investment that requires the expenditure of funds for IT. Furthermore, an IT acquisition initiative could address a single acquisition; a logical grouping of hardware, software, telecommunications, and support services that will involve multiple acquisitions; or a project that will take place either within a particular fiscal year or over a longer life cycle and involve multiple acquisitions. An initiative might be a proposal for new funding within the budget process or it might be a new proposal for a major IT acquisition for an ongoing project.

It is a common perception that IT acquisition in an organization revolves around acquisition of IT hardware, application software and alignment of business processes. Once the software is in place

it should be able to drive the business processes successfully. However, researchers have found that even though these aspects are adequately taken care of, still the IT acquisition process does not become successful as expected. There are other factors, which are not addressed properly and therefore, the success of IT acquisition process is affected adversely (Gibson and Nolan, 1974). It is therefore, pertinent to understand those other factors that might affect the success of IT acquisition process in an organization. These factors are enumerated in the proposed framework with support of the findings from previous chapters.

In an organization, business processes vary in nature and their delivery. These processes have to be aligned with the IT projects and eventually are to be managed and supported by the IT service provider. This leads to a situation where the business process owners interact with the IT service provider. For example, if an organization plans for automating its accounting processes to manage transactions of its creditors as well as debtors, the need for acquisition of IT components stems from the requirements raised by concerned process owners in the accounting department. In the process of acquisition, this software becomes the central issue and necessary infrastructure such as networks, computers and communication infrastructure are acquired as demanded by this software.

Eliciting requirement of the process owner and the users is a daunting task and the responsibility should be jointly shared by the IT service provider as well as the process owner. This requirement should match with the organization's larger interest since investment will be made in this acquisition. Therefore, any acquisition should display "fit" among organization, processes as well as users. It is empirically argued and verified by researchers that irrespective of the approach of the organization to acquire COTS system or develop the system in-house, success of acquisition is influenced by "organizational fit", "user's fit" and "process-fit" (Hong and Kim, 2002; Palaniswamy, 2002).

But in actual practice it is difficult to have a total agreement because of diverse view points and dynamic requirements at the organizational, user and process levels.

Figure 1 describes the situation in which IS development takes place in an organization. In the extreme cases Information System Development (ISD) could be either "User-led" or "IT people led". The advantages of user-led ISD projects are impressive. The advantages and risks of a user-led ISD project are as shown in Table 1. IT-aligned systems demand a mix of both the IT-service providers and the end-users for its successful alignment. But getting the right or optimized mix of the two is a matter of concern. Users normally have limited scope to detail the technology related issues whereas IT-service providers know less about the organization specific process rules and logics because restrictive access to each other's domain.

It is a daunting task for the strategic planner to get the right mix of the involvement of users and IT professionals in an IT acquisition process. Mostly an organization develops complexity with growth and IS is influenced by this factor. Dynamic ambient conditions such as market, policy of the government and requirements of the customers do impose limitations on the business processes as discussed in Chapters 1 and 2. These in turn influence the application software and alignment of the business processes. Therefore, capability of the service provider to understand the business processes

Table 1. Advantages and risks of user-led ISD projects (Hong & Kim, 2002; Palaniswamy, 2002)

Advantages	Risks
• Make analysts and programmers more productive • Use of systems would be easy • Transfer of application software development work to the users. It might reduces the problem of requirement determination • Transfer of ISD projects completely to the users	• Loss of a technology oriented and "outside of the process" view of the application • Loss of an opportunity to evaluate alternate approaches and Software engineering models • Loss of an opportunity to elicit complete requirement • Lack of quality assurance for applications • Unstable systems • Risk from encouraging closed information systems

before the IT project is planned is of paramount importance in designing and supporting the IT acquisition process effectively.

It is evident from the discussions in chapter 4 that preparedness of the organization is a primary contributor to successful IT acquisition process. However, other elements of the acquisition process such as suppliers' credibility assessment, understanding acquisition process on project mode and even assessing user's involvement with respect to IT acquisition success are also the influencing factors. Therefore, in the proposed framework, it is considered important to address following objectives:

1. Understand various associated models available in software engineering.

Figure 1. Information system development projects (Davis & Olson, 2000)

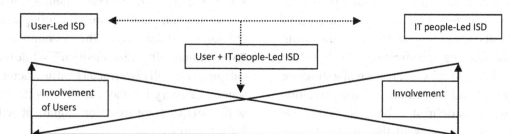

2. Ascertain rationale for phasing the acquisition process.

3. Understand various phases of the acquisition process.

4. Identify the influencers which affect the pre-acquisition process.

5. Relate influencers through an a priori understanding of cause and effect relationship in pre-acquisition phase.

6. Identify the possible effects of pre-acquisition phase on the acquisition and post acquisition phase.

7. Develop an overall model to explain such relationship.

ASSOCIATED IT ACQUISITION LIFE CYCLE MODELLING PRINCIPLES

Acquisition of IT by an organization has an element of risk, since it not only demands process re-engineering but asks for overall acceptance across all the levels of users. Mostly IT end-users, planners, and service providers constitute these users and act as stakeholders. Understanding these users and their attitude as well as behavior is critical in an IT acquisition process. Realizing this risk of acquiring IT in an organization, General Accounting Office (GAO) of the United States came up with a procedure to audit the acquisition process and its outcome. It said that the important phases of IT acquisition are "Pre-solicitation", "solicitation and award", and "post-award" (Casper and Ghassan, 2000). Such individual phases need to be understood in detail in order to reduce the risk of acquisition. In pre-solicitation phase, the GAO has prescribed procedures for analysis of requirements, identifying alternatives, preparing a plan and freezing specifications. "Solicitation and Award" phase calls for creation of a structure of the project and evaluation of the contractors. "Post Award" is defined to be execution phase and involves monitoring of the project, testing

and acceptance of the delivered product. Basically, it suggests and tries to audit the involvement of users across all these phases. However, this is project specific and is essentially applicable for an organization where projects are taken up iteratively. Besides, it does not define the overall requirements of the organization. An acquisition process involves two major stakeholders "Acquiring Organization" and "Supplying Organization". It is to be noted here that though there is a relationship between IT acquiring and supplying organizations, the responsible stakeholders are the users of the technology.

IT refers to various categories of products such as hardware (computers and communications), operating systems, middleware in the form of databases and front-end, groupware in the forms of office automation applications like lotus notes and other vendor specific products. These are aimed at extensive and purposeful use by the acquirer. However, selection of such products depends on the acquirer. Normally, IT is perceived as a conglomerate of high profile technology oriented products which are used through an interface of software driven systems. Though it is not easy to apportion the expenditure incurred in different components of IT implementation process, it is experienced that substantial amount or effort is made for software acquisition. This is an important component in the acquisition process. This process necessitates coordinated effort to ensure success in acquiring IT components in a holistic way. IT acquisitions follow selection of components, vendors and the tools for ISD project management. The selection process can be categorized in two broad areas for an acquirer viz. "IT component acquisition" (hardware and middleware and groupware acquisition) and the second (the most important) is "Application software acquisition". While the first category normally is termed IT infrastructure, the second category is conceptualized as IS coupled with tools that are used for alignment with IT infrastructures.

UNDERSTANDING ORGANIZATIONAL ISSUES AND NEEDS FOR IT ACQUISITION

In an organization, acquisition of IT components rather starts spontaneously than through a systematic analysis on its requirements at the macro level. IT acquisition needs to be based on a strategy (Earl, 1993). It is viewed that strategy for an IS planning process tries to address three broad areas in an organization: (1) aligning investment in IS with business goals, (2) exploiting IT for competitive advantage, directing efficient and effective management of IS resources and (3) developing technology policies and architectures. It is also said that organizations use five different methods for Strategic Information Systems Planning (SISP); business-led, method-driven, administrative, technological and organizational approach. Three concerns are used to determine the success of SISP; "method concerns", "process concerns", "implementation concerns". "Method concerns" are centered on the SISP technique, procedure or methodology employed and this strategy needs to exist in an organization before initiating an IT acquisition process.

It is often experienced that an organization starts IT acquisition process mostly for immediate benefits (Grady, 1992). Contemporary methods suggest IT acquisitions with strategies for alignment among organization, systems and technologies. The IS acquisition refers to systems that aim at capturing process knowledge in an organization and understanding the parameters for organizing, monitoring and evaluating input/output attributes of the process. Therefore, regardless of the organization it operates in, process knowledge and IS acquisition would provide not only the product advantage (the outcome of the process) but also the production advantage in terms of optimizing process costs (Rangan and Adner, 2001). IT has over the years become inextricably intertwined with business systems (Rockart, 1988). Today many organizations want to develop a strategy to manage IS / IT. Many also like to re-do whatever they have done. Most of the organizations have also learnt the capability of IT by experimenting, implementing, learning incrementally and not appreciating the challenges till they faced them (Earl, 1992). It is generally viewed that most organizations fail to realize benefits from their investment in IT because investments are made in IT without understanding or realizing the nature of the activities that IT should support (Ward and Peppard, 2002). It is understood by many that IT has no inherent value – but adds value to the organization if utilized properly. Failure at IS level will affect badly on the investments on IT acquisition (Szajna and Scamell, 1993). Being able to predict the IS failure before implementation of a system could facilitate changes in the IS that can lead to system success. The realism of user expectation has been suggested as one of the possible means of assessing eventual success or failure of an IS (Barua, Konana, Whinston & Yin, 2004; Chandra & Coviello, 2010).

It is not an easy task to understand the acquisition process in an organization though there are some models that try to explain the evolution process. One of such models is "Four Phase Growth Model" (Gibson and Nolan, 1974). This is based on the explanation that IS in an organization is based on strategic planning, management control and operational control. The four- phase model describes (1) rate of IT expenditure, (2) technological configuration, (3) application portfolio (Antony's model), and (4) data processing issues to be the phases of growth in an organization (Anthony, 1965; Ward and Peppard, 2002). Later, two more phases are added i.e. (5) control approaches and (6) user awareness (later named as initiation, contagion, control, integration, data management and maturity and known as Nolan's Phase Theory) (Kanter, 1983; Ward and Peppard, 2002).

Nolan Phase Theory

In 1973, Richard Nolan discussed a stage theory for describing the intensification of IS within organizations, which had a profound impact on the information systems community. Characterized as an evolutionary theory, Nolan´s hypothesis itself developed among papers written during the following years to conclude in 1979 with the final form of his hypothesis. Nolan postulated the existence of six stages through which an original IS passes, in the course of its evolution to effective and efficient support of an organization's information requirements. The stages are initiation, contagion, control, integration, data administration and maturity. These stages represent, in the theory of Nolan, as unavoidable phases of growth that are driven by technology. His theory provides benchmarks for diagnosing a firm´s existing standing within its progress through the stages and describes guidelines for managing that growth to maturity, in a way which will diminish the occurrence of crisis situations and lost opportunities (Marble, 1992).

Furthermore, as per the theory, in the "initiation phase" batch processing efforts are made in an organization when transactions grow voluminous, users demand automation and with no serious involvement of management, this phase grows. The "contagion phase" accelerates the automation growth based on the high expectations of benefits and might lead to online transactions. No control is exercised at this phase, but due to growth in user's demands, a drive is initiated for centralized monitoring. These two phases lead to high expenditures for fulfilling transactions and management feels to exercise cost control in the "control phase" and all attempts to justify the expenditure is made. It is expected that organization seeks adherence to standards for better controls with user performance and accountability. Involvement of the management is gradually visible in a planned way and effort to integrate the automated processes is envisaged. User accountability is expected at this phase. "Data management phase" becomes an obvious outcome of the "integration phase" because of bringing a methodical approach to avoid redundancy due to integration approach. Organization with the active support from the management understands the value of a database and that of information. This leads to "maturity phase" where a closed coordination is managed. Figure 2 explains these phases.

Criticism of Nolan's Phase Theory

Though this model resembles many real examples in the industry, reviews and empirical research done by many researchers found this theory to

Figure 2. Nolan's phase theory (Marble, 1992)

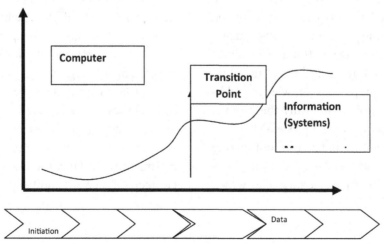

be weak and inconclusive (Benbasat et al., 1987). By beginning 1990, empirical research indicated that the model provided little help to the CIO or IT director to create a successful IS unit in the organization. Wiseman (Wiseman, 1985) stated that Nolan's general-purpose approach to IS (based on Antony's three tier model) has the scope to include strategic issues. It was observed that Nolan's model is a useful starting point, but has undue emphasis on "expenditure" in each phase (Kind, and Kraemer, 1984). It was further viewed that six phases of the model can be separated into two "eras" from a larger perspective: separated by a transition point between phases 3 and 4 (control and integration). It provided a pointer towards renewed thinking on how IS and IT resources are managed in an organization and how role of IS and IT should be evaluated. This approach is presented in Figure 3.

Strategic Alignment Model

The Strategic Alignment Model is composed of four quadrants that comprise of three components each. These twelve components identify what each quadrant is as far as alignment is concerned. All of the components working together determine the extent of alignment for the company that is

being assessed. The model is divided into two distinct areas, business and information technology. Furthermore, each area has two quadrants providing details on relevant aspects in business (see Figure 4) (Coleman & Papp, 2006). The IT Alignment model is a good framework for comparing, analyzing the goals and objectives (Henderson & Venkatraman, 1992). The power of the model lies in the parsimonious delineation of the dimensions and the conceptual separation of IT strategy from the internal issues related to IT infrastructure and processes (Henderson & Venkatraman, 1990).

The thinking process converged to a strategic approach where a roadmap for IT acquisition was seriously contemplated. During early phase of IT acquisition, it was seen that managing IT activities relating to operation, programming and data collection were the major areas of concern. In later phases focus was on establishing a unit to look after various types of applications over an extended lifecycle, despite change in technology. However, review of IS/IT has been occasional in the organizational areas (Bowen et al., 2002). Two areas of concern which emerged in an organization in early 1970s were "data processing (DP)" and "Management Information System (MIS)" (Ward and Peppard, 2002). In early 1980s a third area

Figure 3. Management of IS and IT resource (Ward & Peppard, 2002)

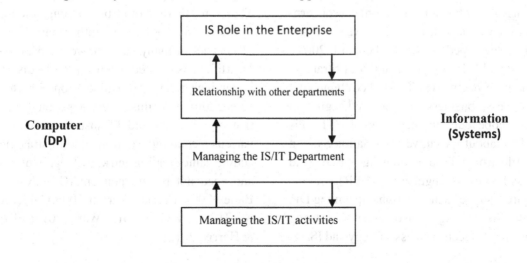

Figure 4. The strategic alignment model (adapted from Henderson & Venkatraman, 1990)

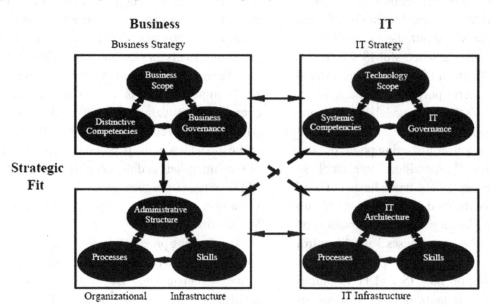

of concern evolved i.e., strategy for leveraging lessons learned from DP and MIS (Ward and Peppard, 2002). DP approach was focused to ensure automation through IS/IT of the processes to achieve required efficiency. Most IT departments started involving users and their roles were specified ensuring responsibilities. But MIS could not be integrated with DP developed. Frequently MIS applications got divorced from DP systems resulting in use of different sources of data from different MIS applications. The third era concerning a strategy to provide the link between DP and MIS thus developed (Ward and Peppard, 2002). Thus, DP and MIS became a subset of Strategic Information System (SIS). This talked about business process, business network redesign and business scope redefinition, all using IS / IT. This also talked about Executive Information System (EIS), Electronic Data Interchange (EDI) and Business Process Reengineering (BPR).

Figure 5 suggests the relationship among DP, MIS and SIS. The figure also describes a strong relationship between business strategy and IS/IT.

It was also felt that systems design should start at the fag-end of the strategic planning process and should be on project mode. But normally the project cycle starts immediately after some requirements are set for the organization and vendor embarks on executing the project, thus bypassing the necessary phases that should have been taken care of. Researchers argue that IS need not be IT centric, but efficient and /or effective operation of IS depends on the use of IT (Alter, 2003). Therefore, there should be a strong orientation of IS towards work-system rather than becoming IT-centric. In many cases however, presence of IT artifacts is noticed wherever the IS discipline is genuinely relevant providing scope for effective value additions. In this context it is strongly viewed that organization and IT just co-exist through various technology sourcing and IS strategies in adding value creation and knowledge acquisition, and need not be independent (Orlikowski and Barley, 2001; Currie & Parikh, 2006; Gable, 2010; Xu, Huang & Gao, 2012, Ward, 2012; Fletcher & Harris, 2012).

Figure 5. Systems relationship (adapted from Ward & Peppard, 2002)

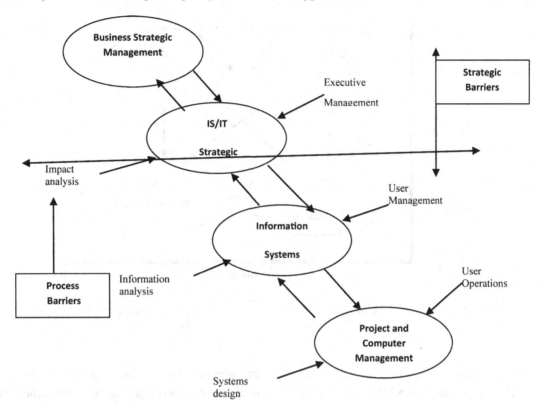

Venkatraman and Henderson Alignment Model

In order to make an application or IT acquisition successful, focusing on technology itself will not help, but there should be clear guiding principles to understand the IS and IT required for the organization and a clear understanding on the distinction between "IS" and "IT" strategies should be formulated (Earl, 1987). In reality organizations grow to be complex with pervasive use of IT acquired (Shayo et al., 1999; Ward and Peppard, 2002). This leads to a phenomenon called "IS demand" and "IT supply."

An alignment between these two elements is necessary for an organization. Massachusetts Institute of Technology (MIT) in a research project (Morton, 1991) indicated that organization's inability to realize the value of investment in IS and IT is due to lack of alignment and bridging

the gap. They developed a model that provided integration between "functional" and "strategic" building blocks. Alignment of IS and IT can happen at four levels, i.e., (1) business strategy, (2) organizational process and Infrastructure, (3) IT strategy, and (4) IS infrastructure (Henderson and Venkatraman, 1993) as shown in Figure 6.

This model suggests two clear domains i.e. "Business domain" and "IT domain" and there should be a strategy to link these two at certain phase in the acquisition process (Figure 6). Strategic thinking to this integration should be reflected in the acquisition process in order to provide a right dimension to it. It is still fresh to realize the consequences of ".com companies" who were engaged in Web-enabled services such as e-business, business-to-business (B2B), business-to-customer (B2C), e-market places, and e-hubs etc. This situation provides enough reasons to have scrupulous introspection to such misad-

Figure 6. Strategic alignment model (Ward & Peppard, 2002)

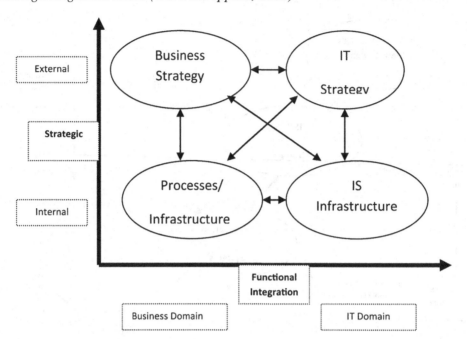

ventures. Advent of standard application packages (ERP packages such as SAP, BaaN, ID Edwards etc.) has also prompted organizations to gain in short term. Researches show that these do not provide a long term and sustainable solution though these are very cost-intensive (Volkoff, 1999; Clemons and Row, 1991). It is noted that one of the major reasons behind such failures was appropriateness of the planning specific to a particular circumstance and was not dynamic! Even feasibility of such planning was not assessed in depth prior to launching any such activity. Therefore, linking to external environment was a major problem. The model as discussed in Figure 6 provided a serious limitation to organize IT acquisition strategy for the organization in a dynamic environment (Weill and Vitale, 2002; Ward and Peppard, 2002). Another school of thought in this context was to value the organization structure and its "fit" with the IS/IT strategy. Mere adopting best technologies would not help the

organization to streamline processes. Strategic decision makers rather need to examine the fitness (Venkatraman, et al., 1993; Broadbent and Weill, 1993). While there has been growing acceptance of IT, there are concerns about sustenance of IT acquired. This "fitness' plays a major role since the users form a critical factor in establishing this link. These users not only use the infrastructure developed, but also implement the strategy formulated through the technology acquired, irrespective of whether it is "external" or "internal" to the organization. This behavior of the users provides an opportunity to effectively utilize the business effectiveness. IT domain suggests that IT gradually is treated as a function and this should strategically link to the IS, thereby allowing co-evolution of IS and IT (Agarwal and Sambamurthy, 2002). Success in functional areas in an organization is related to involvement of the entire organization, but not just the IT function (Kohli and Devaraj, 2004).

Luftman's Strategic Alignment Maturity Assessment Model

Alignment of IS and IT in an organization is a known phenomenon. However, the phase in which this alignment is to be done in the acquisition life cycle needs utmost attention of the strategic planners. While discussing the alignment in depth Luftman (Luftman, 2000) provided "twelve indicators" indicating "five levels" leading to a Strategic Alignment Maturity (SAM) assessment instrument. The model provided "four phases" and "six criteria" for assessing the maturity. His assessment model is tested with 25 fortune-500 companies. In this exercise he concluded that strategic managers' strong support is one of the major criteria in IT acquisition process. Alignment maturity needs a relationship that should evolve in the organization where function of IT and other business functions adapt their strategies

together as indicated by Henderson and Ventka-traman's model. As regards levels of maturity of an organization Luftman prescribed six criteria as detailed below:

1. Communications Maturity.
2. Competence/Value Measurement Maturity.
3. Governance Maturity.
4. Partnership Maturity.
5. Scope and Architecture Maturity.
6. Skill Maturity.

The illustrations of these six criteria are shown in Figure 7. Based on applications of these criteria in an organization, it is evaluated and mapped into one of the five levels such as: Initial / Ad Hoc Process, Committed Process, Established Focussed Process, Improved / Managed Process and Optimized Process. Luftman in his research indicated the importance of alignment of IS and

Figure 7. Twelve indicators of alignment maturity (Luftman, 2000)

PHASE 1: BUSINESS STRATEGY

1. **Business Scope**: Includes market where organization operates
2. **Distinctive Competencies**: Organization's strengths
3. **Governance**: The way organization manages internal resources and liaises with external stakeholders

PHASE 2: ORGANIZATION INFRASTRUCTURE and PROCESSES

4. **Administrative Structure**: The way organization conducts its business
5. **Processes**: Process flow, ownership and issues relating to improvement
6. **Skills**: Employee's profile and their competencies, motivation level

PHASE 3: IT STRATEGY

7. **Technology Scope**: The important information applications existing and scope of having one
8. **Systemic Competencies**: Capabilities to have access to information
9. Governance: How IT is used by all the stakeholders

STAGE 4: IT INFRASTRUCTURE and PROCESSES

10. **Architecture**: Priorities on technology, choices that allow application and other IT components and integration issues
11. **Processes**: Practices adopted to acquire IT

IT in an organization in order to bring success to the acquisition process. Since there is no clear and definite process to effect an alignment and make it sustainable, identifying an alignment maturity indicator will certainly provide an excellent vehicle for understanding the IS-IT relationship (Papp and Luftman, 1995). It is viewed that competitive advantage could be attained through IS / IT provided the organization is prepared to link its infrastructure with strategies (Kettinger, Grover, Guha, & Segars, 1994).

Researchers observed that the IT acquisition alone is not enough and IS preparedness is mandatory for the organization. Less focus on IT and more on process of organizing and managing IS would benefit the organization and for this IS capability needs to be organized (Bharadwaj, 2000). In this pre-acquisition phase one therefore, needs to understand the IS-IT alignment issues involving strategic planners. Thus it is essential that all the stakeholders are capacitated enough to deal with such a risky proposition (Figure 8).

Figure 8. Alignment maturity criteria (Luftman, 2000)

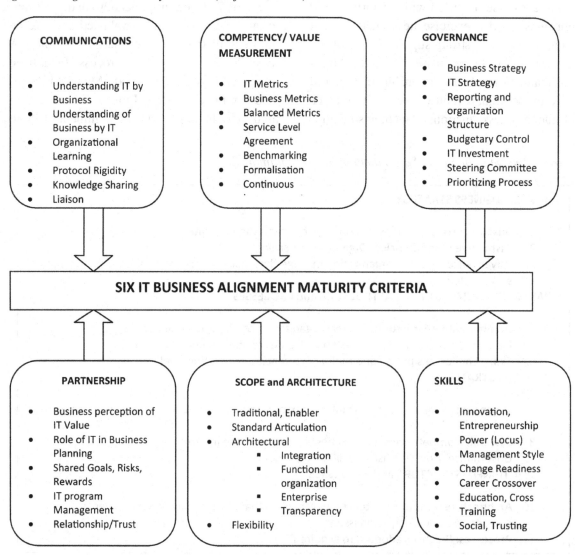

CONCEPTUALIZATION AND DEVELOPMENT OF A FRAMEWORK

Organizational preparedness to understand the situation early is expected to be an area of concern. The framework proposed recognizes various layers in an organization in the context of decision making process, managing resources and discharging their responsibilities. These layers are strategic, tactical and operational.

This framework considers operational users to be having limitations to understand the process of acquisition and involve themselves with devotion whereas strategic and tactical users may be able to provide a direction to the whole process by preparing themselves early. Figure 9 describes the phases of the acquisition process. The whole acquisition process is divided into three phases i.e. pre-acquisition, acquisition and post acquisition. The Figure 9 suggests that these three phases are to be sequentially handled in the organization. Each phase is described with various influencers and their relationship in the acquisition process. This framework aims to measure the IT acquisition scenario through a process that assesses each of the three phases of the acquisition process. The first phase i.e., the pre-acquisition phase, measures the pre-acquisition process preparedness and the pre-acquisition climate in the organization. The pre-acquisition process preparedness involves

Figure 9. Phases in the IT acquisition process

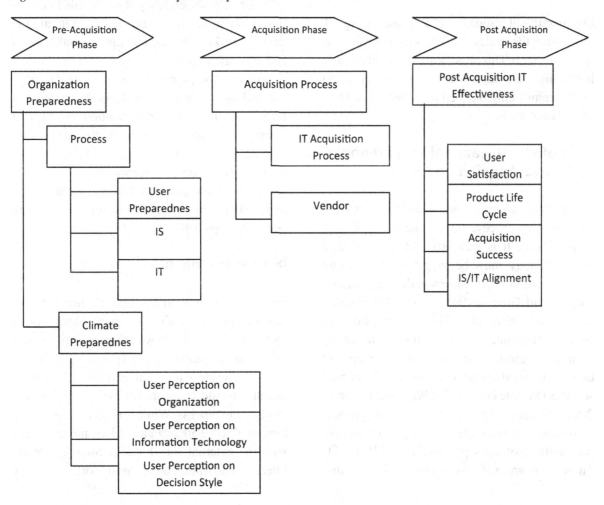

assessment of preparedness of users, information systems, and technology. The climate preparedness is similarly assessed through user perceptions on the decision style, perception on technology use and organization's policy to support the acquisition process. The second phase is the acquisition phase. The project management capabilities of the IT cell and IT vendor determine the preparedness at this phase. In the third phase which is called as post-acquisition phase, the aim is to understand user satisfaction, success in component as well as product acquisition, the life cycle of the components, and above all the successful IS-IT alignment.

PREPAREDNESS IN THE PRE-ACQUISITION PHASE

Organizational preparedness in managing IT acquisition life cycles originates from the pre-acquisition phase. This phase is quite critical because it examines the preparedness of the organization and systems being planned for adoption of IT in appropriate areas.

Role of Organizational Preparedness in the Pre-Acquisition Phase

As discussed in Figure 9, pre-acquisition preparedness involves process preparedness and climate preparedness. It is well articulated in research that a strategy must be in place for adequate pre-acquisition preparedness in the organization (Segars and Grover, 1998; Jokela and Abrahamsson, 2000; Earl, 1993; Huang et al., 2004). In course of the strategy determination there is need for tasks definition, stakeholder involvement and taking informed decision for better IT enabled services (Marple et al., 2001; Ward and Peppard, 2002; Luftman, 2003). Pre-acquisition process preparedness consists of three components namely preparedness of users, preparedness of IS and IT. These issues are explained progressively hereafter.

Preparedness of Users Influencing IS and Technology

Users' involvement in IS and IT acquisition success is quite important. In order to understand the role of the users in the planning process there stratification in the organization is essential. The stratification of users in an organization means the layers that MIS principles largely accept and these are "Strategic Users", "Tactical Users" and "Operational Users" (Kohli and Sherer, 2002; Davis and Olson, 2000). Requirement of these stratified users is different since their involvement in decision making process is quite different in nature. Though models like TAM, UTAUT; De-Lone and McLean model provide insight to the role of user in making the system successful. It also discusses dependency of user in his/her position in the hierarchy in the organization and the decision making process (i.e. operational, tactical and strategic users).

Further, the preparedness of strategic, tactical and operational users depends on process awareness. There is varied requirement of skill among users to collaborate in the acquisition process. Users in the strategic level need to have desired skill in strategy formulation, tactical users in functional planning and operational users in transaction awareness. These dependencies are shown in Figure 10.

IS Preparedness

Strategic Information Systems Planning (SISP) demands readiness of information systems (Ward and Peppard, 2002). SAM discusses the issues related to information systems planning (Luftman, 2000). Layering of the organization's stakeholders and understanding business processes initiate the IS planning process. While this exercise is mostly "internal" to the organization it demands interfaces with the external stakeholders. Strategy for IS, interface and transactions are supported by many

Figure 10. User-preparedness framework (Source: Rai, et al., 2002; Segars & Grover, 1998; Lee, et al., 2003; Venkatesh, et al., 2003; Luftman, et al., 2002)

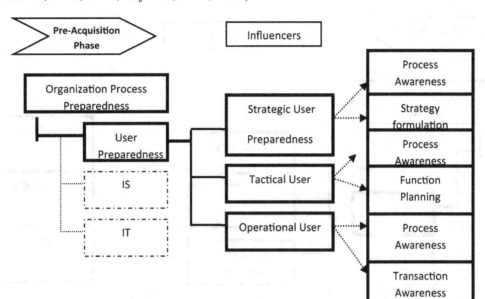

models to understand and prepare for comprehensiveness, formalization, focus, flow, participation, consistency and also suggests internal alignment of these elements with the processes. IS strategy is the responsibility of the strategic and tactical users. These users deal with information systems and their overall relationships with the organizational objectives. Transaction strategy is to be formulated by the operational users as well as the tactical users in order to streamline the procedure. "Wang and Tai model" describes some of these attributes as well but again devoid of these layering. SAM also talks about the process of preparing the planning process for an information system.

IS preparedness has been seen as organization's preparedness to harness IT. IS is an important component of the organizations environment for building interfaces (Seddon, et al., 1999), and integration (Broadbent, et al. 1999). It is experienced that strong orientation of IS towards business processes rather than becoming IT centric would provide better results and better use of IT

artifacts (Alter, 2003). IS preparedness is proposed to understand existence of any strategy for establishing systems orientation to information, a MIS framework for successful transactions (Lamb and Kling, 2003; Seagars and Grover, 1998; Lee, Kozar and Larsen, 2003). Figure 11 describes this IS preparedness and its dependency on IS strategy, interface strategy for inter functional communication and transaction strategy for conducting processes. These depend on system planning, functional IS planning and transaction readiness respectively in the organization.

IT Preparedness

This component in the model would assess Organization's strategy to organize IT (Broadbent et al., 1996). Drawing up the "Business maxim" and "deriving the IT maxim" are the major deliverables of an acquiring organization in the pre-IT acquisition scenario. IT comes with relevant components (networks, databases, applications

Figure 11. IS-preparedness framework (Source: Segars & Grover, 1998; Wang & Tai, 2003; Ward & Peppard, 2002)

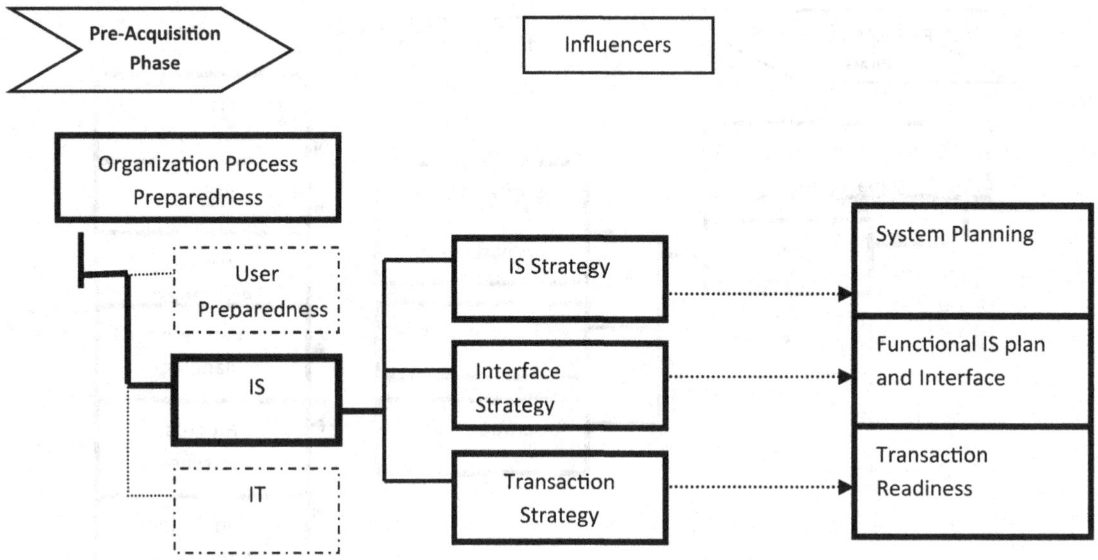

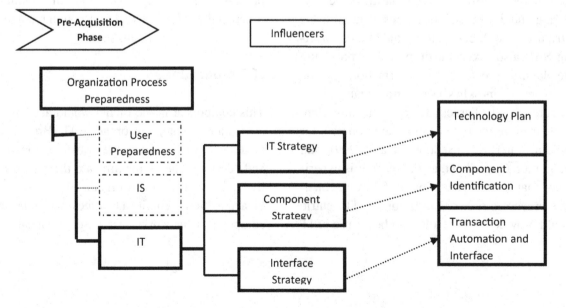

and expertise etc.) and a strategy must be formulated for acquisition of each component in order to provide a better alignment strategy to the IS (Huang and Hu, 2004).

Effecting control over the IS driven IT infrastructure for meeting the business needs is an indicator of IS preparedness (Datnthanam and Hortono, 2003, Lamb and Kling, 2003, Jokela, 2001). Empirical research supports the technological acceptance model (TAM) for adoption of IT (Karahanna et al., 1999). Mapping the readiness of IT cell and its employees to gain control over technologies and understand business processes is the deliverable for this component. Figure 12

Figure 12. IT-preparedness framework (Source: Lee, et al., 2003; Venkatesh, et al., 2003 ; Ward & Peppard, 2002)

describes the dependency of IT preparedness on strategies related to IT components and their interfaces. These are indicated by suitable plan for IT component identification and transactions through technology in the form of reports and forms etc.

Role of Climate Preparedness in the Pre-Acquisition Phase

Here the proposed framework tries to recognize the importance of the Organizational climate that affects the IT-acquisition process. Organization's climate often is termed as a catalyst to change (Olson, 1982). Organization culture is one of the important factors of the climate in an organization that could play a vital role in accepting IT. A culture that encourages users to accept innovative ideas will eventually accelerate the pace of its absorption in the organization. Culture devoid of such ambience will not derive better absorption and benefits despite much investment. User' perception on the organization especially strategic user's consistency in the decision making style, provides a formal ambience. This formalization helps in imbibing a good work culture and matured processes and formal transactions. It is often found that managers and professional workers are averse to IT because of fear and anxiety to deal with new technology (Grover et al., 1998; Yaverbaum, 1988, Karahanna et al., 1999). It is also interesting to note that in some cases business professionals perceive IT professionals as "bad elements" in the business process. Therefore, opinion of IT professionals does not get support from these ultimate users. This impression also works negatively in absorbing IT in an organization (Evans, 2004).

IT in an organization should not be considered as a technical problem only. It has all the potential to affect the culture of the organization. Therefore, participatory approach should be adopted for IT acquisition wherein all the stakeholders may actively involve as per the need. An ambience needs to be created much before initiating the very proposal of acquisition (Janssen et al. 1999). Using IT wisely can bring in a positive effect and a right type of culture can hasten the process of acceptance of IT in the organization. It is also found that though the technology as such is neutral, and the way the technology is accepted determines the success in an organization (Page, 1996).

Various models like TAM, UTAUT, Seddon describe how acceptance of technology spreads in the organization and therefore, in turn reflects change in organization's culture. Along with TAM, ITAA model provides some indications to predict the future acceptance through understanding the phase of the organization as discussed in chapter 2. UTAUT model while attempting to capture motivation among the users in an Organization helps relate to the culture as well. Luftman framework also discusses organizational issues in relation to technology adoption.

Organization's decision making style plays a vital role in understanding the pre-acquisition preparedness. Architecture (Shaw and Garlan, 1996) displays the decision making behaviour and capturing it early to provide an opportunity to display the behaviour of all the stakeholders and therefore would ease the component identification in the process as well as finding a way to understand the integration issues. Table 2 explains the influencers identified for the evaluation of pre-acquisition preparedness in the organization as a summary. Figure 13 describes this dependency. The identified influencers described in the table are provided with notations for using these during validation of the relationship among influencers and construction of model in subsequent chapters.

PREPAREDNESS IN IT-ACQUISITION PHASE

This phase, subsequent to the pre-acquisition phase in the acquisition process assumes that proper IS planning is in place and priorities are

Table 2. Influencers used in the pre-acquisition phase

Dependent Influencer	Aggregated Independent Influencer		Independent Influencers
Pre Acquisition Organization Preparedness (O)	Pre-acquisition Process Preparedness (P)	User Preparedness (U)	Strategic User Preparedness (U1)
			Tactical User Preparedness (U2)
			Operational User Preparedness (U3)
		IS Preparedness (I)	IS Strategy (I1)
			Interface Strategy (I2)
			Transactions Strategy (I3)
		Technology Preparedness (T)	IT Strategy (T1)
			Component Strategy (T2)
			Interface Strategy (T3)
	Pre Acquisition Climate Preparedness (C)	User Perception on Organization (C1)	Strategic User Perception
			Tactical User Perception
			Operational User Perception
		User Perception on IT (C2)	Strategic User Perception
			Tactical User Perception
			Operational User Perception
		User Perception Decision Style (C3)	Strategic User Perception
			Tactical User Perception
			Operational User Perception

Figure 13. Models associated for climate-preparedness framework (Source: Lee, et al., 2003; Venkatesh, et al., 2003; Rai, et al., 2002; Luftman, 2003; Huff & Munro, 1985)

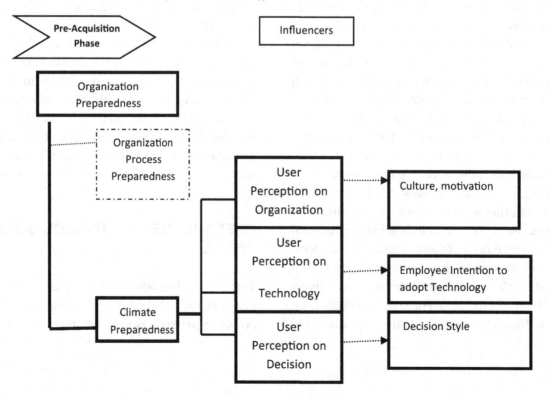

set for adopting technology. Roles of the acquiring organization and the vendors/suppliers are critical to this phase.

IT Acquisition Management Capability

Mostly user's role in this phase is to prepare for outlining requirement specific to the project taken up by the IT department. At the same time it is the capability of the IT department that enables identification of proper vendor/supplier assuming the role of "partner" and organizing the project well. Determining the delivery as well as requirements for the projects is a major challenge for the IT cell.

In today's environment, diffusion of IT has been pervasive, though it is difficult to measure its effectiveness. It is therefore, essential to understand the acquisition process in an Organization and usefulness of the acquired IT assets. The model tries to capture the role of users in acquisition process, its involvement in evaluation, monitoring IT projects and vendors' understanding on the business processes (Figure 14). "Quality assurance" on the part of acquirer is major indicator for successfully predicting a project success. CMM/

ISO and Seddon's Models describe the quality assurances of the vendor as well as acquirer to manage a project effectively. Component acquisition in this phase is an important activity. The project becomes successful with a strategic approach to acquisition of hard and soft assets in its entirety. Even during the project execution, project managers' success relates positively to the IS planning maturity and also outcome of the project largely depends on it (Jiang, Klein and Shephard, 2001; Schimtt and Kozar, 1978). Project management is a skill that needs to be acquired by the acquiring organization and this needs to be an indicator for success of a project.

Vendor Management

Supplier/vendor needs to be seriously evaluated during acquisition process. Vendor supplying a product as a component or developing an application which would later be used as a component needs to understand the process it tries to enable with the component. This "fit" could be the result of a close "coordination" between the acquirer and supplier (Papp et al., 1996). Quality assurance from the vendor is probably one of the most

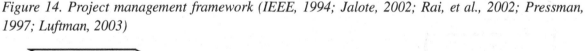

Figure 14. Project management framework (IEEE, 1994; Jalote, 2002; Rai, et al., 2002; Pressman, 1997; Luftman, 2003)

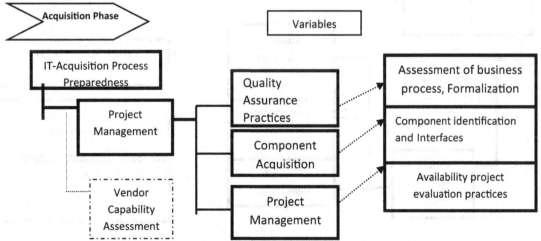

useful indicators that acquirer could ascertain during evaluation as well as during execution of the project. Acquirer's quality consciousness would benefit the process and vendors would be forced to carry out the process and adopt methods with quality assurance. Displaying quality certification from the agencies also enhances credibility of the supplier/vendor; despite the fact that quality certification does not necessarily lead to producing quality products. SW-CMM, ISO family provide enough scope for the vendor to practice and adopt quality assurance methods. Process quality assurance enhances possibility of developing a component and a vendor may specialize producing, developing and/or providing matured processes for the acquirer. For example Microsoft, SCO, IBM supplying OS would not require any contest from the user's end. Similarly, Oracle, SYBASE supplying database technology would not require any debate for its quality. However, user must have a methodology to understand the "fit" between the product being chosen and requirement of the

Organization. Therefore, vendors must display this strength to get accepted by the acquirer. Figure 15 explains the framework.

As regards project management, IT cell of the acquiring Organization must display its strength in managing a project related to IT acquisition since it involves different component based vendors. Software engineering methodologies along with CMM/ISO family describe in detail the procedures and related issues that acquiring Organization must address in this phase in order to expect a successful project.

PREPAREDNESS IN POST-ACQUISITION PHASE

Post-acquisition phase is the most extensively researched area where the facts are gathered, assessed and analyzed. Products and processes are also examined. In this phase, research is focused on usability of the product delivered, user

Figure 15. Framework for vendor capability (Ryan & Al-Qaimari, 2000; IEEE, 1994; Jalote, 2002; Rai, et al., 2002; Pressman, 1997; Luftman, 2003)

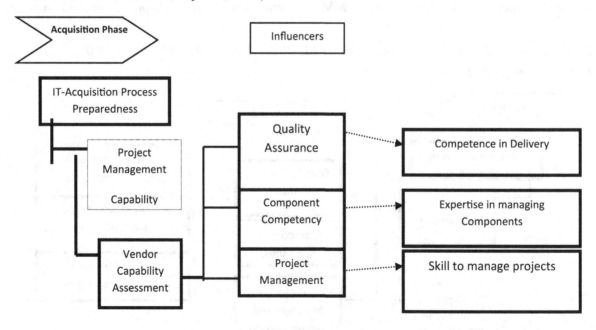

satisfaction, project success, performance of the vendors, economic and financial assessments of the investments etc. IS and IT alignment issues as existing are also center of research for many. In this framework it is tried to bring some useful indicators in order to assess the "fit" that IT has brought in with the IS. This phase has some influencers which can be used for assessment mostly drawn from the models used extensively in this area, but with a motive to provide a scope of assessment. These influencers are "Life Cycle", "Successful Acquisition", "User satisfaction" and "IS and IT Alignment".

Life Cycle

Life cycle determines the system usability for a time period and it is a major area of concern for any Organization. IS preparedness though provides a scope to provide systems orientation to the functions in an Organization (Flynn, 1998), verifying its usability is a daunting task. This is just because of the fact that organizing indicators for all the stakeholders is not an easy task and in a dynamic scenario it becomes more difficult to organize (Papp et al.,1996). However, life cycle of the IS developed with or without the influence of IT and its "effective use" could be two indicators that might throw some light to understand the behaviour of the IS. Urge to computerize an IS in a function or generation of "IT demand" by the end-users might be an indicator for IS preparedness. Seddon and UCD models try to understand the "quality of systems" and "usability capability" respectively. But while Seddon model restrict it to the users, UCD models refer mostly to the ISO standards and then try to predict the usability behaviour. Life cycle of the IS as indicator is not served completely by these two models (Irani, 2002). This indicator talks about the frequency of revamping the system for the function in order to stabilize the system. This largely depends on the processes that the system tries to manage and the dynamics involved at the Organizational level (Figure 16).

Figure 16. Framework life cycle (Rai, et al., 2002; Jokela, 2001)

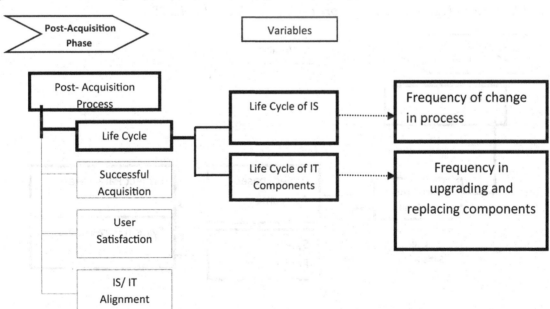

Successful Acquisition

IT is seen as having many components as already discussed above (Huff and Munro, 1985). IT acquisition involves hard components as well as soft components (Broadbent et al., 1996). Success of IT acquisition also depends on how successfully the components are planned, acquired and used (Figure 17). One of the measurable indicators for understanding success of IT infrastructure created is to assess on generic project performance indicators such as physical and financial performance (Rai et al., 2002). Besides, system performance indicators can also be used for the purpose which includes predefined delivery of the automated business processes such as mode of transactions, latency in communication and processing the transactions as well as mean time between failures.

User Satisfaction

End-user computing has received attention of the researchers and it is an indicator that tries to provide the realistic assessment of IT infrastructure management. Seddon, Luftman, and UCD models bring most of the user's concern in effectively using IT infrastructure.

These also provide major contribution to the user's involvement in acquisition phase. Figure 18 describes the scope of assessing user satisfaction. End-users through this model are divided in two categories, one segment of users are those who are ignorant of the technology and IT infrastructure, but use the technology for the business purposes and the other segment of users are the core-IT professionals who use the technology and infrastructure to render services to the business-centric users. Satisfaction of these users has an effect on the business and IT productivity (Ward et al., 1990; Sohal and Ng, 1998). Technology imposed on IT-service providers might lead to dissatisfaction and services rendered might be unproductive. Training, IT-professional's exposure lead to acceptance of a technology and once comfort level is attained, productive and usability increases. However, none of the models try to differentiate these two categories and the model proposed tries to capture these elements.

Figure 17. Successful acquisition framework (Rai, et al., 2002; Jokela, 2001)

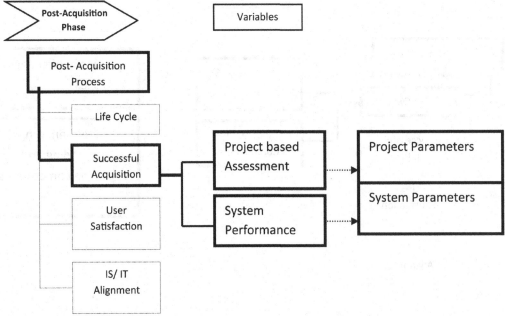

Figure 18. User satisfaction framework (Rai, et al., 2002; Jokela, 2001; Luftman, 2003)

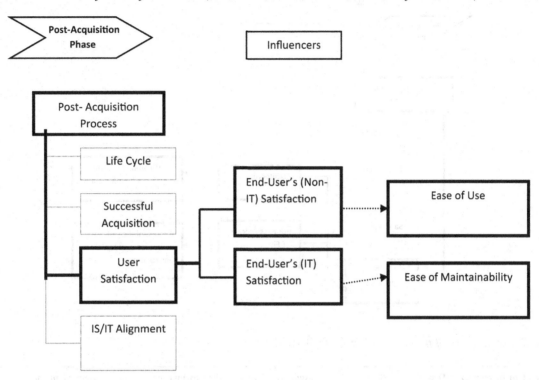

IS-IT Alignment

IT, when acquired, does not only bring in technology at component level, it spreads across the entire organization having effect on its culture and process.

IT cannot be viewed with perspective of technology used for process-improvement tool. It needs a strategy as explained by SAM. Figure 19 explains the approach to understand the "fit" that IT and business have provided. This fitness largely depends on the strategy formulated during the phases of acquisition. Architectural fit determines how well the business process architecture has aligned with that of the IT architecture (Papp and Luftman,1995; Luftman 2000). However, one needs to understand the layers of the organization's decision making process as discussed earlier. Fit across all layers (strategic, tactical and operational) are necessary in order to establish organizational fit of the technology adopted.

Business and IT maxims (Broadbent and Weill, 1996) can be obtained if all these layers are taken care of individually as well as collectively at the Organizational level. Many researchers have provided indicators (Luftman, 2003; Luftman, 2000) to assess an Organization and its "fit" between business and IT acquired. The relationship among influencers of all the three phases of acquisition process is described in Table 3.

It is noted that preparedness in pre-acquisition phase will have a cascading effect for the acquiring phase as well as in the performance IT resources acquired in the process.

SUMMARY

This chapter discussed strategic alignment exercises for the IT acquisition organization and conceptualized the need for establishing a framework for assessment of organizational preparedness.

Figure 19. IS and IT alignment framework (Ward & Peppard, 2002; Huff & Munro, 1985; Luftman, 2003)

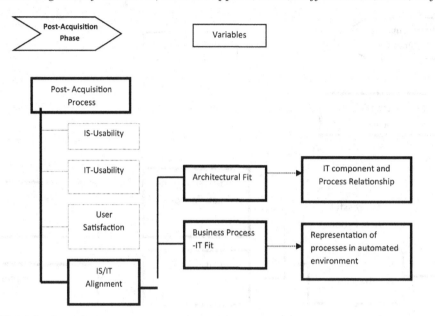

Table 3. Influencers of the IT acquisition framework

Dependent Influencer	Dependent Influencer	Aggregated Independent Influencer		Independent Influencers
Tier III	(Tier III)	(Tier II)		Tier I
IT Acquisition IT (G)	Pre Acquisition Organization Preparedness (O)	Process Preparedness (P)	User Preparedness (U)	Strategic User Preparedness (U1)
				Tactical User Preparedness (U2)
				Operational User Preparedness (U3)
			IS Preparedness (I)	IS Strategy (I1)
				Interface Strategy (I2)
				Transactions Strategy (I3)
			Technology Preparedness (T)	IT Strategy (T1)
				Component Strategy (T2)
				Interface Strategy (T3)
		Climate Preparedness (C)	User Perception on Organization (C1)	Strategic User Perception
				Tactical User Perception
				Operational User Perception
			User Perception on IT (C2)	Strategic User Perception
				Tactical User Perception
				Operational User Perception
			User Perception Decision Style (C3)	Strategic User Perception
				Tactical User Perception
				Operational User Perception
	Acquisition Process (AQ)		IT Project Management (AT)	
			Vendor Preparedness (VC)	

The chapter built on the strengths of various life cycle approaches discussed in chapters 1, 2, and 3 and reflected their behaviour in the assessment framework. The framework also included strengths of various model for assessment of quality and user capabilities. The conceptual foundations for the assessment framework are based on the premises that IT acquisitions in organization have various life cycles including products, processes, organization structures and systems and IT acquisitions can learn from these organizational life cycles. The framework included assessment of barriers and preparedness of the organization to overcome them in the IT acquisition life cycle. These barriers include human resources and other stakeholders like suppliers, customers, and technology providers.

The framework built on the scope for improvement in involving many other stakeholders, especially in the areas of organizational preparedness in addition to IT service providers. In this chapter it was considered important to understand the process for integration of IT components with the information systems, to manage acquiring process, assess users' requirement and their preparedness to accept the CBIS. User capabilities were found to be the central issue that influences the preparedness in the acquiring organization and thus enough care has to be taken for supporting this process. In this context, contributions of quality management were posited to be quite important in the assessment framework. The framework used various models to capture organizational imperatives holistically and bind them with user capabilities to support acquisition life cycle. Another founding dimension of the framework is the phasing of the IT acquisition life cycle having three distinct phases. These three phases are pre-acquisition, acquisition and post-acquisition. These are subsequently discussed in detail to support the framework conceptualized for overall assessment. Each phase of the framework is supported with various models discussed in previous chapters to build on the strengths.

REFERENCES

Abdul-Gader, A. H., & Kozar, K. A. (1995, December). The impact of computer alienation on information technology investment decisions: An exploratory cross-national analysis. *Management Information Systems Quarterly*, 535–559. doi:10.2307/249632.

Agarwal, R., & Sambamurthy, V. (2002). Principles and models for organising the IT function. *MIS Quarterly Executive*, *1*(1), 1–16.

Alter, S. (2003). 18 reasons why IT-related work systems should replace: The IT artifact as the core subject matter of the field. *Communications of the Association for Information Systems*, *12*, 365–394.

Anthony, R. N. (1965). *Planning and control: A framework for analysis*. Boston: Harvard University Press.

Barua, A., Konana, P., Whinston, A., & Yin, F. (2004). An empirical investigation of net-enabled business value. *Management Information Systems Quarterly*, *28*(4), 585–620.

Benbasat, I., Goldstein, D. K., & Mead, M. (1987, September). The case research strategy in studies of information systems. *Management Information Systems Quarterly*, 369–386. doi:10.2307/248684.

Bharadwaj, A. (2000). A resource-based perspective on information technology and firm performance: An empirical investigation. *Management Information Systems Quarterly*, *24*(1), 169–196. doi:10.2307/3250983.

Bowen, P. L., Heales, J., & Vongphakdi, M. T. (2002). Reliability factors in business software: Volatility, requirements and end-users. *Information Systems Journal*, *12*(3), 18. doi:10.1046/j.1365-2575.2002.00128.x.

Broadbent, M., & Weill, P. (1993). Improving business and information strategy alignment: Learning from the banking industry. *IBM Systems Journal*, *32*(1), 162–179. doi:10.1147/sj.321.0162.

Broadbent, M., Weill, P., & O'Brien, T. (1996). Firm context and patterns of IT infrastructure capability. In *Proceedings of the 17th International Conference on Information Systems,* (pp. 174-194). IEEE.

Broadbent, M., Weill, P., & St. Calir, D. (1999). The implications of information technology infrastructure for business process redesign. *Management Information Systems Quarterly, 23*(2), 159–182. doi:10.2307/249750.

Casper, R., & Ghassan, A. (2000). *The orbital model: A methodology for development of interactive systems.* Melbourne, Australia: RMIT University. Retrieved from http://goanna.cs.rmit.edu.au/~ghasan/Orbital.doc

Chandra, Y., & Coviello, N. (2010). Broadening the concept of international entrepreneurship: Consumers as international entrepreneurs. *Journal of World Business, 45*(3), 228–236. doi:10.1016/j.jwb.2009.09.006.

Clemons, E. K., & Row, M. C. (1991). Sustaining IT advantage: The role of structural difference. *Management Information Systems Quarterly, 15*(3), 275–292. doi:10.2307/249639.

Coleman, P., & Papp, R. (2006). Strategic alignment: Analysis of perspectives. In *Proceedings of the 2006 Southern Association for Information Systems Conference,* (pp. 242 – 250). AISC.

Cragg, P., Caldeira, M., & Ward, J. (2011). Organizational information systems competences in small and medium-sized enterprises. *Information & Management, 48,* 353–363. doi:10.1016/j.im.2011.08.003.

Datnthanam, R., & Hartono, E. (2003). Issues in linking information technology capability to firm performance. *Management Information Systems Quarterly, 27*(1), 125–153.

Davis, B. G., & Olson, M. H. (2000). *Management information systems: Conceptual foundations, structure and development* (2nd ed.). Singapore: McGraw-Hill.

Earl, M. (1993, March). Experiences in strategic information systems planning. *Management Information Systems Quarterly.* doi:10.2307/249507.

Earl, M. J. (1987). Information systems strategy formulation. In Boland, R. J., & Hirschheim, R. A. (Eds.), *Critical Issues in Information Systems Research.* Chichester, UK: John Wiley & Sons.

Earl, M. J. (1992). Putting IT in its place: A polemic for the nineties. *Journal of Information Technology, 7,* 100–108. doi:10.1057/jit.1992.15.

Evans, N. (2004). *Promoting fusion in the business-IT relationship.* Paper presented at the Issues in Informing Science and Information Technology Education Joint Conference. Rock Hampton, Australia.

Fletcher, M., & Harris, S. (2012). Knowledge acquisition for the internationalization of the smaller firm: Content and sources. *International Business Review, 21,* 631–647. doi:10.1016/j.ibusrev.2011.07.008.

Flynn, J. D. (1998). *Information systems requirements: Determination and analysis* (2nd ed.). Berkshire, UK: The McGraw-Hill.

Gable, G. (2010). Strategic information systems research: An archival analysis. *The Journal of Strategic Information Systems, 19,* 3–16. doi:10.1016/j.jsis.2010.02.003.

Gibson, C. F., & Nolan, R. L. (1974, January/February). Managing the four stages of EDP growth. *Harvard Business Review,* 76–88.

Grady, R. B. (1992). *Practical software metrics for project management and process improvement.* Upper Saddle River, NJ: Prentice Hall.

Grover, V., Teng, J., Segars, A., & Fiedler, K. (1998). The influence of information technology and business process changes in perceived productivity: The IS executive's perspective. *Information & Management, 34*(3), 141. doi:10.1016/S0378-7206(98)00054-8.

Henderson, J., & Venkatraman, N. (1990). *Strategic alignment: A model for organizational transformation via information technology* (Working Paper 3223-90). Cambridge, MA: Sloan School of Management, Massachusetts Institute of Technology.

Henderson, J., & Venkatraman, N. (1992). Strategic alignment: A model for organizational transformation through information technology. In Kochan, T., & Unseem, M. (Eds.), *Transforming Organisations*. New York: Oxford University Press.

Henderson, J. C., & Venkatraman, N. (1993). Strategic alignment: Leveraging information technology for transforming organisations. *IBM Systems Journal, 32*(1), 4–16. doi:10.1147/sj.382.0472.

Hong, K., & Kim, Y. (2002). The critical success factors for ERP implementation: An organizational fit perspective. *Information & Management, 40*(1), 25–40. doi:10.1016/S0378-7206(01)00134-3.

Huang, C., Derrick, C., & Hu, O. (2004). Integrating web services with competitive strategies: The balance scorecard approach. *Communications of AIS, 13*.

Huff, S. L., & Munro, M. C. (1985, December). Information technology assessment and adoption: A field study. *Management Information Systems Quarterly*, 327–340. doi:10.2307/249233.

IEEE. (1994). How ISO 9001 fits into the software's world. *IEEE S/W, 11*.

Irani, Z. (2002). Information systems evaluation: Navigating through problem domain. *Information & Management, 40*(1), 11–24. doi:10.1016/S0378-7206(01)00128-8.

Jalote, P. (2002). *CMM in practice: Process for executing software projects at infosys*. Delhi: Pearson Education.

Janssen, P., Ikaheimo, S., & Malinen, P. (1999). Capital formation in Kenyan farmer-owned cooperatives: A case study. Turku, Finland. ISBN 92-5-104330-2

Jiang, J. J., Klein, G., & Shepherd, M. (2001). The materiality of information system planning to project performance. *Journal of the Association for Information Systems, 2*(5).

Jokela, T. (2001). *Review of usability capability assessment approaches*. Paper presented in the 24th Information Systems Research Seminar. Scandinavia, Norway.

Jokela, T., & Abrahamsson, P. (2000). Modelling usability capability-introducing the dimensions. In *Proceedings of PROFES 2000*. Oulu, Finland: PROFES.

Kanter, R. M. (1983). *The change masters*. London: University of Chicago Press.

Karahanna, E., Straub, D. W., & Chervany, N. L. (1999). Information technology adoption across time: A cross-sectional comparison of pre-adoption and post-adoption beliefs. *Management Information Systems Quarterly, 23*(2), 183–213. doi:10.2307/249751.

Kettinger, W.V, & Grover, S. G., & Segars. (1994). Strategic information systems revisited: A study in sustainability and performance. *Management Information Systems Quarterly, 18*(1), 31–33. doi:10.2307/249609.

Kind, J. L., & Kraemer. (1984). Evolution and organisational information systems: An assessment of Nolan's stage model. *Communications of the ACM, 27*(5), 466–470. doi:10.1145/358189.358074.

Kohli, R., & Devaraj, S. (2004). Realising business value of information technology investments: An organisational process. *MIS Quarterly Executive, 3*(1), 53–68.

Kohli, R., & Sherer, S. A. (2002). Measuring payoff information technology investments: Research issues and guidelines. *Communications of AIS, 9.*

Lamb, R., & Kling, R. (2003). Re-conceptualising users as social actors in information systems research. *Management Information Systems Quarterly, 27*(2), 197–235.

Lee, Y., Kozar, K. A., & Larsen, K. R. T. (2003). The technology acceptance model: Past, present and future. *Communications of AIS, 12,* 750–780.

Li, Y., Liu, Y., & Liu, H. (2011). Co-opetition, distributor's entrepreneurial orientation and manufacturer's knowledge acquisition: Evidence from China. *Journal of Operations Management, 29,* 128–142. doi:10.1016/j.jom.2010.07.006.

Luftman, J. (2000). Assessing business – IT alignment maturity. *Communications of the AIS, 4.*

Luftman, J. (2003). Assessing IT/business alignment. *Information Systems Management, 20*(4), 9–21. doi:10.1201/1078/43647.20.4.20030901/77287.2.

Luftman, J. N., Papp, R., & Brier, T. (2002, September). Enablers and inhibitors of business-IT alignment. *AB Insight.*

Marble, R. P. (1992). A stage – theoretic approach to information systems planning in existing business entities of recently established market economies. In *Proceedings of the 10th International Conference of the System Dynamics Society 1992,* (pp. 405-414). Utrecht, Netherlands: IEEE.

Marple, J., Clark, B., Jones, C., & Zubrow, D. (2001). *Measures in support of evolutionary acquisition.* Pittsburgh, PA: Software Engineering Institute, Carnegie Mellon University.

Morton, M., & Scott, S. (1991). *The corporation of the 1990s.* New York: Oxford University Press.

Olson, M. H. (1982). New information technology and organsiational culture. *Management Information Systems Quarterly,* 71–92. doi:10.2307/248992.

Orlikowski, W. J., & Barley, S. R. (2001). Technology and institutions: What can research on information technology and research on organisations learn from each other? *Management Information Systems Quarterly, 25*(2), 145–146. doi:10.2307/3250927.

Page, S. M. (1996). Organisational culture & information systems. In *Proceedings of the United Kingdom Academy for Information Systems, 1ˢᵗ Annual Conference.* AIS.

Palaniswamy, R. (2002). An innovation – diffusion view of implementation of enterprise resource planning (ERP) systems and development of a research model. *Information & Management, 40,* 87–114. doi:10.1016/S0378-7206(01)00135-5.

Papp, R., & Luftman, J. (1995). Business and IT strategic alignment: New perspectives and assessments. In *Proceedings of the Association for Information Systems, Inaugural Americas Conference on Information Systems.* Pittsburgh, PA: AIS.

Papp, R., Luftman, J., & Brier, T. (1996). Business and IT in harmony: Enables and inhibitors to alignment. In *Proceedings of AMCIS.* Phoenix, AZ: AMCIS.

Pressman, R. S. (1997). *Software engineering: A practitioner's approach* (4th ed.). Singapore: McGraw-Hill.

Pucciarelli, J. C., & Waxman, J. (2008). *Financing options to improve IT acquisition and long-term management strategies* (White Paper). New York: IDC Corporate.

Pucciarelli, J. C., & Waxman, J. (2008). *Financing options to improve IT acquisition and long-term management strategies* (White Paper). New York: International Data Corporation (IDC).

Rai, A., Lang, S. S., & Welker, R. B. (2002). Assessing the validity of IS success models: An empirical test and theoretical analysis. *Information Systems Research, 13*(1), 50–69. doi:10.1287/isre.13.1.50.96.

Rangan, S., & Adner, R. (2001). *Profitable growth in internet-related business: Strategy tales and truths* (Working Paper, 2001/11/SM). Fontainebleau, France: INSEAD.

Reuber, A. R., & Fischer, E. (2011). International entrepreneurship in Internet-enabled markets. *Journal of Business Venturing, 26*, 660–679. doi:10.1016/j.jbusvent.2011.05.002.

Review, M. I. E. A. (2011). *Maritime intelligence, surveillance, and reconnaissance enterprise acquisition (MIEA) review*. Washington, DC: Department of Defence.

Rockart, J. (1988, Summer). The line takes leadership – IS management in a wired society. *Sloan Management Review*, 57–64.

Schimtt, J. W., & Kozar, K. A. (1978). Management's role in information system development failures: A case study. *Management Information Systems Quarterly*, 7–16. doi:10.2307/248937.

Seddon, P. B., Staples, S., Patnayakuni, R., & Bowtell, M. (1999). Dimensions of information systems success. *Communications of AIS Volume, 2*(20).

Segars, A. H., & Grover, V. (1998, June). Strategic information systems planning: An investigation of the construct and its measurement. *Management Information Systems Quarterly*, 139–163. doi:10.2307/249393.

Shaw, M., & Garlan, D. (1996). *Software architecture: Perspectives on an emerging discipline*. Upper Saddle River, NJ: Prentice Hall.

Shayo, C., Olfman, L., & Teitrlroit, R. (1999). An exploratory study of the value of pre-training end-user participation. *Information Systems Journal, 9*(1). doi:10.1046/j.1365-2575.1999.00049.x.

Sohal, A. S., & Ng, L. (1998). The role and impact of information technology in Australian business. *Journal of Information Technology, 13*, 201–217. doi:10.1080/026839698344846.

Szajna, B., & Scamell, R. W. (1993, December). The effects of information system user expectations on their performance and perceptions. *Management Information Systems Quarterly*, 493–516. doi:10.2307/249589.

Venkatesh, V., Morris, M. G., Davis, G. B., & Davis, F. D. (2003). User acceptance of information technology: Toward a unified view. *Management Information Systems Quarterly, 27*(3), 425–478.

Venkatraman, N., Henderson, J. C., & Oldash, S. (1993). Continuous strategic alignment: Exploiting information technology capabilities for competitive success. *European Management Journal, 11*(2), 139–149. doi:10.1016/0263-2373(93)90037-I.

Volkoff, O. (1999). Using the structurational model of technology of analyse an ERP implementation. In Proceedings of Academy of Management '99 Conference. AM.

Wang, E. T. G., & Tai, J. C. F. (2003). Factors affecting information systems planning effectiveness: Organizational contexts and planning systems dimensions. *Information & Management, 40*(4), 287–303. doi:10.1016/S0378-7206(02)00011-3.

Ward, J., Griffiths, P., & Peppard, W. (1990). *Strategic planning for information systems*. Chichester, UK: John Wiely and Sons Ltd..

Ward, J., & Peppard, J. (2002). *Strategic planning for information systems*. London: John Wiley and Sons.

Ward, J. M. (2012). Information systems strategy: Quo vadis? *The Journal of Strategic Information Systems, 21*, 165–171. doi:10.1016/j.jsis.2012.05.002.

Weill, P., & Vitale, M. (2002). What IT infrastructure capabilities are needed to implement e-business models?. *MIS Quarterly Executive, 1*(1).

Wiseman, C. (1985). *Strategy and computers*. Homewood, IL: Dow Jones-Irwin.

Xu, K., Huang, K., & Gao, S. (2012). Technology sourcing, appropriability regimes, and new product development. *Journal of Engineering and Technology Management, 29*, 265–280. doi:10.1016/j.jengtecman.2012.03.003.

Yaverbaum, G. J. (1988, March). Critical factors in the user environment: An experimental study of users, organisation and tasks. *Management Information Systems Quarterly*, 75–88. doi:10.2307/248807.

Section 3
Modeling Process

Chapter 6
Development of IT Acquisition Life Cycle Management Model

ABSTRACT

It is noted that modeling techniques envisage capturing the inputs, processes, and the deliverables in an agreed environment. The modeling process argues in favour of measurements and establishing certain standards to validate the outcomes. Therefore, it is important to establish methods for validation of the model. This chapter discusses a framework for the assessment of preparedness in each phase of the model with support from various existing models associated. It includes broad understanding of the whole gamut of the challenges related to IT acquisition preparedness exercise across all the phases. Goal-Question-Metrics (GQM) principles are adopted to validate various hypotheses developed to assess phase specific deliverables. This process is described in detail to appreciate the cyclic behavior of the assessment model conceptualized for an IT acquiring organization. It is also indicated that this framework can be used at any point in the acquisition life cycle.

INTRODUCTION

In this chapter the conceptualized framework is used for development of a suitable model. In the process, architectural issues are discussed for binding different phases of the IT acquisition life cycle to the overall organizational set up for continuity. In this chapter architectural framework discussed in chapter five is modeled with formulation of hypotheses and measurement systems through Goal-Question-Metrics (GQM) techniques. The model is thereafter subjected to

DOI: 10.4018/978-1-4666-4201-0.ch006

validations, generalizations, and fitness exercise. Development of this model draws inspirations from software engineering process modeling techniques incorporating architectural principles to capture organizational imperatives.

ROLE OF MODELING TECHNIQUES IN SOFTWARE ENGINEERING

Historically, the introduction of IT has been characterized by a series of major deployments occurring at intervals often measured in years or even decades. These long cycles of times reflect in part the traditional waterfall acquisition process. This form of acquisition model presumes a linear development process that proceeds in stages from development of a comprehensive requirement specification to design, implementation and integration, next to testing, installation and maintenance. Furthermore, modified versions of the model acknowledge some role for feedback between each of these stages (Boehm, 1981).

The Software Engineering field has been primarily focused in information systems development improving the reliability and efficiency of data services. However, the current users of these services are being increasingly interested in deeper functions integrated in the information systems supported by the knowledge related with the data conceptual domains (Cuena and Molina, 2000).

It is evident from contemporary literature review that preparedness of an organisation is least addressed during IT acquisition process at macro level while each element in the organisation such as suppliers' credibility assessment, understanding acquisition process on project mode and even assessing user's involvement with respect to IT acquisition success are discussed in isolation (Misra, Satpathy & Mohanty, 2007). Furthermore, the discipline of IT architecture and engineering (especially, software architecture and engineering) is relatively immature in comparison to other disciplines (AFEI, 2010).

In recent years, a wide variety of non-standard software solutions are in use. This sort of approach limits effectiveness and increases cumulative costs in deploying IT resources. In order to address this type of situations, various software engineering models have argued in favour of analyzing the need for deliberative IT acquisition processes that include requirements gathering, strategic mission alignment, cost benefit and alternatives analyses (Robillard & Sambrook, 2008; Brown, 2010). It is often argued that best practices for IT acquisitions should include an emphasis on iterative development, increased opportunities to test and evaluate technology in practice, and

capture realistic concepts of operations. The best practices also look for organized processes for design and evaluation of systems that provides scope for strong coupling among practitioners, researchers, and industry (National Research Council, 2007). However, due to long IT acquisition cycles, it is considered difficult to incorporate rapid technological changes while ensuring the tight coupling of the stakeholders' views. Due to rapid technological changes, IT acquisition life cycles are shortened though organizations are tempted to acquire new technologies because of the premium in value added benefits. But this form of linear IT acquisition process often fails to deliver the expected IT capabilities in the organization. Furthermore, requirement elicitation crawl may end up making the ultimate design overly cumbersome, complex, or costly to implement, leading to cost overruns, delays, and even program cancellation. Additionally, users, who not only have input to the front end of the process, may find that the IT process capabilities delivered do not meet their needs. In circular reference, new process capabilities, new technology opportunities and ever increase in requirements make the systems developed unsustainable. Thus systems developed become difficult and expensive to manage changes dynamically. Though many artifacts of a system grow organically, reality is that large systems emerge from incremental additions in ways entirely unanticipated by the designers of the original systems. If the original system is successful, users will almost certainly want to add new functionality.

Undeniably, it is essentially impossible in practice for even the most operationally experienced IT systems developers to be able to predict in detail and in advance of all system´s requirements and specifications. Often users change their minds about the features they want, or even more difficult to deal with when they want to introduce contradictory features, and certainly, it is difficult to foresee all potential users. Thus, system requirements and specifications are inherently incomplete, even though they underlie and drive the relationships among various components of the system. In other words, the paradox is that successful system development requires non-trivial understanding of the entire system in its ultimate form before the system can be successfully developed. Hence, system designers need experience to understand the implications of their design choices. But experience can only be gained by making mistakes, learning from them, and having a mechanism to modify and evolve systems over time. It requires understanding of both users and designers of the systems being developed. In this aspect, it is often argued that following an experimentally verified model would minimize the mistuning or misguidance. Therefore, development methodologies may presume an iterative approach in building systems. An iterative process has multiple, short acquisition cycles, which over time deliver and improve on system capabilities as the system grows. Such a process encourages feedback from users and allows them to play a constructive and central role in a system´s progression. However, an iterative process requires, among other things mechanism for users to provide feedback to technology innovators and providers.

With the iterative development, systems that initially include limited functionality are often introduced. Furthermore, as users adopt the technology, they have a mechanism for identifying improvements to that functionality. They also participate in identifying desirable new or additional features that technology providers can incorporate during maintenance phases or design of new product versions. One example which can be cited is the programs for smart phone or android functionalities. These functionalities incrementally include greater performance and a wider range of features in order to market the devices in better ways.

An iterative acquisition process may have other advantages. Often requirements thought to be essential at the beginning may turn out to be relatively unimportant or little used once deployed.

The functionality supporting those requirements can be dropped from future product versions, thus helping minimize complexity hitch. Hence, essential feature frequently go unidentified until the system begins to be widely used. Therefore, these features can be added in a more orderly fashion, evolving the system with continuing feedback from users. Incremental introduction of technology also allow one to exploit the current technology preferences, where the costs of components such as microprocessors are lowest, thus keeping down costs and making more frequent IT acquisition cycles possible (National Research Council, 2007).

MODELLING TECHNIQUES: SOFTWARE ENGINEERING PERSPECTIVES

Eliciting user requirements is important in software process models and in the context of Information Technology (IT) acquisition (Misra, Satpathy & Mohanty, 2007). Requirements analysis is an essential component of software design and engineering. It involves descriptions of how a proposed system should behave along with its attributes and other relevant properties (Sommerville & Sawyer, 1997).

Explicit models of software evolution go back to the earliest projects developing large software systems in the 1950's and 1960's (Hosier, 1961; Royce, 1970). However, the apparent purpose of these early software life cycle models was to provide a conceptual scheme for rationally managing the development of software systems. Such a scheme could serve as a basis for planning, organizing, staffing, coordinating, budgeting, and directing software development activities. In this context, a software life cycle model is either a descriptive or prescriptive characterization of how software is or should be developed. A descriptive model describes the history of how a particular software system was developed. Descriptive models may be used as the basis for understanding and improving software development processes, or for building empirically grounded prescriptive models (Curtis et al., 1988). On the other hand, a prescriptive model prescribes how a new software system should be developed. Prescriptive models are used as guidelines or frameworks to organize and structure how software development activities should be performed, and in what order. In contrast to software life cycle models, software process models often represent a networked sequence of activities, objects, transformations, and events that embody strategies for accomplishing software evolution. Such models can be used to develop more precise and formalized descriptions of software life cycle activities. Their power emerges from their utilization of a sufficiently rich notation, syntax, or semantics, often suitable for computational processing (Scacchi, 2001).

MODELLING TECHNIQUES: ARCHITECTURAL PERSPECTIVES

As described in Figure 1, Management Information System (MIS) is a federation of information systems in an organization and it describes certain components that are to be in place for its effective implementation. MIS is also closely attached to the functioning of an organization and MIS is

considered as a tool for decision making for the managers. It also provides scope to build further into decision support system as well. Therefore, MIS looks for a strategy that would work for longer period. MIS encompasses all the processes in an organization and effectively manages all transactions and information systems as well.

It is viewed that MIS provides a base for federating the IS developed for the organization and an MIS plan should be the first step towards organizing as well as planning IT components (Davis and Olson, 2000). Integration of IT components especially functional information systems is one of the major deliverables of the MIS plan. MIS plan originating from the mission of the organization traverses a path thus providing a road map for integration leading to formalized documentation for integration. Involvement of strategic decision makers provide a definite strategy to IT planning as well. This also provides an ambience to create internal and organizational preparedness for IT acquisition as IT plan is an offshoot of the MIS plan. IT acquiring organization should therefore, understand the urgency of MIS plan for the organization to reflect on its preparedness. It is not always true that organizations do not acquire IT components without having an MIS plan. In most of the cases this approach is either lacking or even not organized (Kanter, 2000). In such cases it becomes rather difficult to leverage the

Figure 1. Development of MIS plan under traditional approach

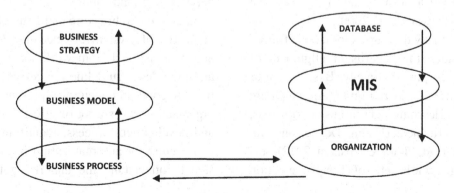

investments already made while considering for integration at enterprise level (Linthicum, 2004). MIS plan along with a strategy for Enterprise Application Integration (EAI) would rather consolidate the strategy for the organization. Understanding the issues of integration prior to IT acquisition process increases capability of the organization to identify products and/or processes with better "fit". For example, acquiring an ERP which is based on integration of functional information systems needs an extensive exercise (Preston and Karahanna,2009).

"Information islands" formed by the organization with induction of automation technologies forces the business manager to think of integration because of availability of tools, technology and products. Any information system devoid of integration/interface capability will affect the productivity in the long run. It is noted that around 35 percent of time is devoted for creating and implementing interface and integration rules for existing applications (Linthicum, 2004). Organization's preparedness is therefore, essential to understand the implications. Interfaces challenge integration projects at enterprise level and they are very much critical to packaged applications. Unless properly planned, packaged applications and ERPs in particular would pose serious threat to the integration projects (Brown and Vessey, 2003). An ERP implementation is a significant intervention in organization's life. Preparedness or lack of it in the context of organization's culture, user involvement and leadership practices affect success of ERP acquisition and it needs to be ascertained (Stewart et al., 2000).

There are many discourses for having frameworks to match the benefits of alignment of IT with the corporate strategy. Basically, four dimensions are considered important which are innovation and learning, internal business process, customer and financial (Huang, Derrick and Hu, 2004; Rampersad, Plewa & Troshani, 2012). It is argued that strategic benefits of IT implementation can be realized if the IT initiatives are planned and implemented within a framework of an IT strategy that is designed to support the business strategy of a firm. Many of the initiatives are strategic in nature and it is expected that all the four dimensions as mentioned above are taken into considerations for effective IT acquisitions in an organization. Generically however, organizations concentrate on the operational aspects of IT projects ignoring strategic implications of the investment decision in IT acquisitions. Lack of appropriate methodologies to integrate technologies with a firm's competitive strategy often forces the decision on IT acquisitions as an act of faith and may hamper the development and acceptance of technologies strategically such as Web services. The significance of aligning IT with corporate strategy is well noted by academics, but the lack of rigorous methodologies prevented practitioners from integrating IT projects effectively with competitive strategies. As a result, a new and promising technology such as Web services may be deployed based on "gut feelings" or "act of faith" without appropriate strategic management tools, and the outcome may be marginal or even undesirable.

Addressing Architectural Issues

An important aspect of IT acquiring organization's capabilities is "preparedness on architectural issues" and it is important from integration point of view. IT architecture has distinct architectural styles for its components (software, hardware, networks etc) and should be a part of enterprise architecture. Architecture is the fundamental organization of a system reflected in its components and establishes a framework for relationships and provides a guideline for design and evolution. A good architectural representation in an organization saves a lot of effort during design and development process. Identifying software architecture for an organization is an important step to understand the underlying technology

Figure 2. Systems development life cycle

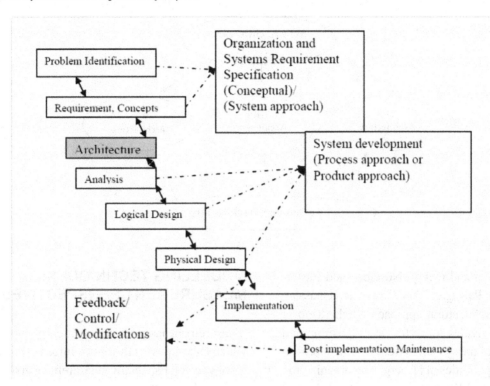

architecture, business architecture (Kown and Zmud,1987; Garland and Anthony, 2003) . Architecture fits in to the system development life cycle (SDLC) as shown in Figure 2. An analogy can be drawn between the architect of a city and that of a MIS planner. Role of architect for a city is to gather environmental issues, infrastructure issues, user's requirements, user's views and then with right abstraction the architect models the city for further examination. Similar methodology can be adopted while preparing MIS plan for an organization. An MIS planner goes through the SDLC stage while planning information systems. But the architecture part of it would describe the subsystems in detail as well as its relationships. Integration of all the processes and providing a systemic approach to the integration is the responsibility of the IT acquiring organization (Lee, 2001).

SDLC related models rest on the very fact that a system is in place and user requires developing software for automation of the system. Normal SDLC starts therefore, from the user requirement analyses and ends after handing over of product thus developed. The models under this SDLC format generally fail to recognize complex system architectural issues and therefore ignore organization architecture. Various models however, approach different methodologies to accomplish this task. Despite their variation in approaching the process of SDLC, these tend to address only specific problems of the organization. But these models are building blocks for larger software and cannot be undermined while thinking of larger enterprise modeling software systems. In general, user's involvement is merely on freezing requirements for the viewpoint of software developers, which rather provide a monolithic view of the entire process. There remains at times, a gap between

Figure 3. Integrative feature of enterprise MIS

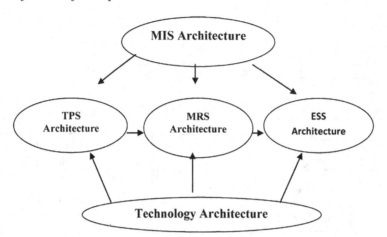

the perception and reality (Nuseibeh and Easter-brook, 2000; Palyagar, 2004; Casper and Ghassan, 2000).An architectural approach (Richardson et al., 1990) provides scope for decomposition and integration of the systems. Architectural approach looks for capabilities of IT-acquiring organization to formulate an MIS plan integrating all the desired services across all levels in the organization as shown in Figure 3.

These levels are Transaction Process System (TPS), Management of Reporting Structure (MRS) and Executive Support System (ESS). Processes and technology (if any) architectures should also match with that of the MIS. Need for integration has been felt since long and Federal Aviation Administration (FAA) considered it seriously with development of integrated capability maturity model (FAA-iCMM); (Ibrahim, 2000). FAA developed this in order to provide guidance to acquiring organization for improvement in engineering, management process. Despite difficulty in implementing, FAA recommends that FAA-iCMM could be used as a learning tool at the organizational level spread across processes and disciplines in the organization. Similarly, CMM- Integrated (CMM-I) aims at providing a framework for the acquiring organizations to improve processes in an integrated environment (Ahen et al., 2001).

MODELLING TECHNIQUES: MEASUREMENT PERSPECTIVES

Measurement has remained a critical phenomenon which encompasses the entire Information Technology sector. Especially measurement in software engineering has gained much importance despite the maturity the IT sector has claimed over the years. There is a growing need for continuous evaluation on impact of technology, methodology and effective use of organizational resources during software development and acquisition process. Various metrics and measurement criteria have emerged for measurement of methods, tools and technology used in software engineering. Organizations irrespective of their size are adopting various quality models, performance measurement metrics and tools to showcase their maturity levels to gain confidence of the market they work in. However, market dynamics influence the very measurement criteria used and thus there is a latent pressure on the organizations to continuously stay engaged in the measurement process. It is argued that gaining maturity in establishing measurement standards in an organization is complex. Thus "measure what is measurable" principles need to evolve in the organization for better clarity (Díaz-Ley et al., 2010).

Software engineering process models often prescribe for use of measurement techniques to quantify and objectively verify intended deliverables (IFPUG, 2002). The validation principle discussed above suggested three stages of validation process. The validation processes capture quantitative attributes of the variables and then measure them to assess the status of each stage in the acquisition process. Three Tiers of variables discussed above therefore needs certain measurement methods. This method is dependent on the type of variables used for measurement and what to measure. Certain metrics are used to assess the measurement done in the process. Quantitative as well as qualitative assessment can be done through formulation of metrics. In software engineering measurement, metrics are used to measure the attributes and one of the measurements methods is Goal-Question-Metrics method (GQM) (Basili, 1994; Wohlin et al., 2000), Goal-Driven Software Measurement, GQ(I)M, PSM and ISO/IEC 15939 etc. (Díaz-Ley et al., 2010). Despite having adequate methodologies and approaches to measurements linking to software centric performances, there is a scope to take it forward to cover the interfaces between organizational objectives and IT infrastructure acquisitions in the organizations in which software is a component. Architectural deliveries in managing such interfaces are quite important in order to minimize the risks of failures in implementing IT acquisition strategies in the organizations. Architectural deliveries remain as an important issue in the entire life cycle of the IT acquisition in the organization. Architecture and its component specific measurements should be reflected in any IT acquisition related project that comes up for consideration in the organization. The model discussed in this book captures many aspects of architectural components related to organizations and IT infrastructure acquisitions to measure the success in the entire life cycle.

MODEL FOR IT ACQUISITION LIFE CYCLE MANAGEMENT

In this modeling, techniques use formalization of layers as per MIS architecture discussed above followed by incorporation of measurement systems with GQM methods. GQM measurement method is supported by various variables representing various Tiers in consonance with organizational architectures. These different Tiers of influencers used for all the phases of the acquisition process are indicated in Figure 4.

Tier I influencers represent the basic tenets of MIS deliverables. It considers operational, tactical and strategic layers in the organization as important influencers of the acquisition process and the proposed model captures their contributions. Tier II influencers provides the deliverables that can be measured with the help of a series of SDLC or any other software engineering process model driven attributes for measurement of the acquisition process. Measurements in Tier III are strategic in nature and relate to overall design objectives of the IT acquisition model. These variables indicate overall performance of the resources used in the acquisition process and provide insights to areas of improvement.

THE PROPOSED MODEL

Based on the framework described in chapter 5 and the influencers identified for three phases of the acquiring process, a model has been developed as shown in Figure 5 that captures the user-preparedness in the IT-acquisition process and relationships among the phases as well respective influencers are indicated.

The model developed and presented is based on Tier-II and Tier-III influencers explained in Figure 4. Tier-I influencers are not indicated here for simplification purpose and will be discussed during validation. This model is supported by the framework and the proposed relationships among

Figure 4. Influencer and its relationships in the model

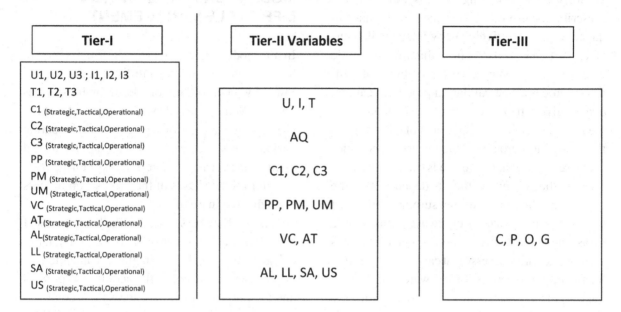

the influencers identified for assessment of three phases of the acquisition process.

Construction of the Model

Construction of the model is based on the phases as discussed earlier in Chapter Five, i.e., "Pre-Acquisition Phase", "Acquisition Phase" and "Post-Acquisition Phase". In the pre-acquisition phase preparedness of the Organization is ascertained by taking into consideration the preparedness of Users, IS, IT followed by Climate preparedness. Each component has been discussed in detail in the fore-going section supported by existing models and its limitations that this proposed model tries to address. The Organizational preparedness in this model depends on two major components i.e. "Pre-Acquisition preparedness" based on Users, IS and IT preparedness and "Climate preparedness. It means that pre-acquisition preparedness is a mandatory process that every acquiring Organization needs to exercise in order to bring in necessary level of preparedness in the Organization.

Each influencer in the model has specific objective to assess in the acquisition process.

Nomenclature for each influencer is also provided. The table explains the aggregate behaviour of the independent influencers (Tier-II) U1, U2, U3; I1, I2, I3; T1,T2,T3; C1, C2, C3, VC and AT. These independent influencers are the attributes of the respective second order influencers abstracted for the model. "U" representing the "user preparedness" is the aggregated representation of three influencers U1, U2, and U3. Similarly "I", "T", and "C" are the aggregated forms of respective influencers I1, I2, I3; T1,T2,T3; C1, C2, C3. VC and AT contribute for aggregating AQ whereas P and C contribute to measure O. Progressively, O and AQ contribute to measure the overall IT acquisition scenario in the organization. These influencers are qualitative in nature and thus their measures are dependent on collective predictability of each of the influencers defined. However, these influencers form the basis of understanding behaviour of an IT acquisition process in the Organization. Interrelationship among these second order influencers is defined to understand Organization's pre-acquisition process preparedness "P", its climate preparedness "C" and in turn predicting the preparedness of the Organization

Figure 5. The proposed model

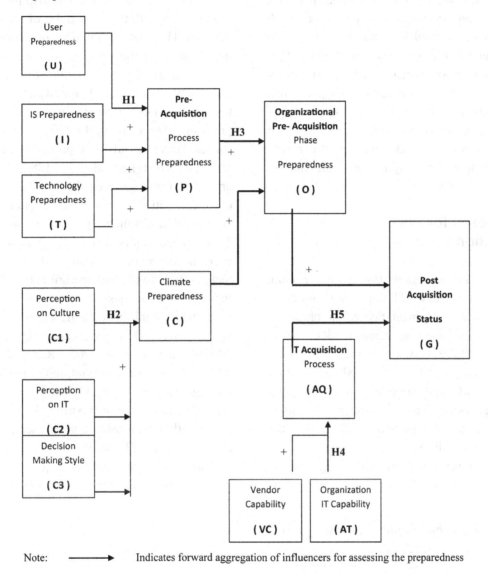

Note: ───▶ Indicates forward aggregation of influencers for assessing the preparedness

during the planning phase of the IT acquisition "O". Post acquisition phase "G" is the measure of the Organization's success in IT acquisition and is grossly influenced by the preparedness of the Organization in pre-acquisition phase "P" coupled with the way IT acquisition process is handled "AQ". AQ is an aggregation of influencers "VC" that describes vendor's capacity while "AT" discusses the Organization's capability to manage a vendor and/or the project. These influencers are termed as Tier-III influencers.

Formulation of Hypothesis

Development of models for systems aims to design procedures, validate the expected behaviour of the processes and relate them so as to proactively predict the systems behaviour in dynamic situations. Modeling in software engineering practices is largely accepted for its intrinsic benefits of decomposed behavioral analyses coupled with large scale integration without losing the benefits of individual modules (Niu and Atlee, 2003). In this modeling similar approach is taken with a view to capture organizational dynamics through a controlled and simulated environment with the help of quantifiable and measured variables. This simulated behaviour is managed through relationships and thus there is a necessity to hypothesize. Hypotheses, as per facet theory, provide a systematic approach to theory construction, research design, data analyses and validation of complex theories proposed for any model (Guttman and Greenbaum, 1998).

Hypotheses for Pre-Acquisition Phase

Preparedness of an organisation to initiate, plan, control and monitor the IT acquisition process is the centre of the study in this phase. This phase has been discussed based on various models associated with it. There are two attributes in this phase. These are "pre-acquisition preparedness" dealing with users, information systems and technology in the organisation and "climate preparedness" dealing with the culture and architecture of the organisation are discussed in this phase.

In this exercise it is intended to organise the capability of the stakeholders to not only under- stand the IT relates issues, but also prepare the organisation with the view point of information systems. The relationship of preparedness of the organisation in the pre-acquisition phase with "user preparedness" is a concern. Predicting success of system and its quality is a daunting task. Understanding user's involvement in the pre-acquisition phase and relating this role with successful IT acquisition process is also not well researched (Baroudi et al., 1986). It is often argued that user involvement in the early phases of IT acquisition improves the system usage and successful dissemination of information (Tait, 1988). Besides, it is also debated that stratifying users in an organisation in to three (strategic, tactical/ functional, and operational) and assessing their preparedness in pre-acquisition phase have made significant contributions to the IT acquisition process in the organization (Lee et al., 2003; Venkatesh et al. 2003 ; Rai et al., 2002). Thus there is a need for comprehensive study on user involvement in the IT acquisition process, especially in the pre-acquisition phase. Figure 6 presents the relationship among users, information systems and IT with specific relation to their preparedness in managing IT acquisition process in the pre-acquisition phase. In order to discuss

Figure 6. Hypotheses in pre-acquisition phase

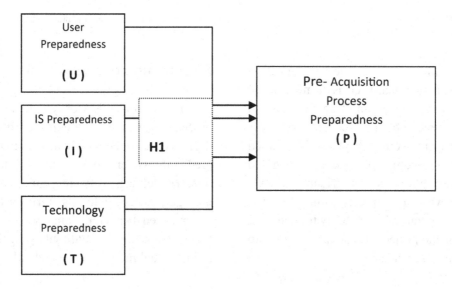

with certain clarity hypotheses in "null" form as well as its alternate hypothesis are postulated hereunder.

- **Hypothesis $H1_0$:** Pre-acquisition preparedness is not positively associated with users' preparedness, IS preparedness and Technology preparedness in the organisation.
- **Hypothesis $H1_A$:** Pre-acquisition preparedness is positively associated with users' preparedness, IS preparedness and Technology preparedness in the organisation.

Climate Preparedness

The attribute "climate preparedness" is believed to influence the organisational preparedness in the pre-acquisition phase. This preparedness addresses two issues regarding the culture and architecture of the organisation.

Attitude and behaviour of users displayed historically during any acquisition can be related to the case of IT acquisition. The relationship is explained in Figure 7.

Hypothesis H2

It refers to three constituents. The first is user perception on the organisation. It displays some ambient conditions that a user has perceived such as the decision making process, attitude of management and adoption of new ideas. The second is aimed at capturing perceived attitude of user in particular and organisation in general in accepting IT. The third is decision making style in the organisation which might influence the information systems. These three collectively might affect the climate in the organisation while adopting IT. The relationship is explained in Figure 8.

- **Hypothesis (Null) $H2_0$:** Perception of Users on the Organisation, Perception of users towards IT and Perception of Users on the Decision making Style do not affect positively the IT acquisition process preparedness in the pre-acquisition phase.
- **Hypothesis (Alternate) $H2_A$:** Perception of Users on the Organisation, Perception of users towards IT and Perception of Users on the Decision making Style do affect

Figure 7. Climate preparedness in pre-acquisition phase

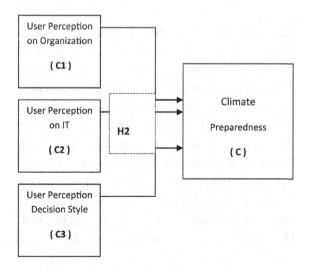

Figure 8. Prediction of organisational preparedness in pre-acquisition phase

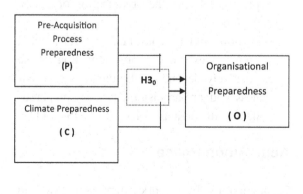

positively the IT acquisition process pre-paredness in the pre-acquisition phase.

Pre-Acquisition Preparedness of the Organisation

The proposed model describes the "prepared-ness of acquiring organisation" as an important attribute to assess successful IT-acquisition in the organisation. In this model it is tried to relate to pre-acquisition preparedness of the users, systems and technology as well as the climate in the organisation. Climate preparedness and pre-acquisition preparedness are considered two independent attributes since many acquisitions do take place irrespective of whether there is a climate to absorb and /or there is a preparedness to man-age it. It refers to two constituents. The first being pre-acquisition preparedness of the organisation it displays ambient conditions in which organisation prepares itself for the users, IS and IT. The second is aimed at capturing the climate. "O" indicates the constituent of organisation preparedness in the pre-acquisition scenario. Figure 8 explains the relationship among the elements.

- **Hypothesis (Null) H3$_0$:** Organisational preparedness in the pre-acquisition phase do not positively depend on the climate preparedness and pre-acquisition process preparedness of the organisation on users, IS and IT.
- **Hypothesis (Alternate) H3$_A$:** Organisational preparedness in the pre-acquisition phase positively depend on the climate prepared-ness and pre-acquisition process prepared-ness of the organisation on users, IS and IT.

Acquisition Phase

IT acquisition framework suggests relying on internal capability of the organisation to not only manage its resources, but also understand the

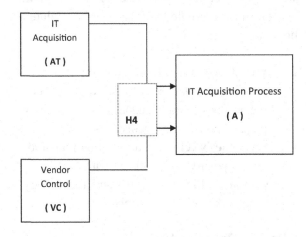

Figure 9. IT acquisition process

vendor assessment issues. Therefore, it has two components to depend on, one is to "organise its internal processes" and "organisational prepared-ness to manage vendors and acquisition process". Figure 9 explains the relationship.

- **Hypothesis (Null) H4$_0$:** Capability of ven-dors and capability of IT-Cell of acquiring organisation do not have positive effect on IT acquisition process.
- **Hypothesis (Alternate) H4$_A$:** Capability of vendors and capability of IT-Cell of ac-quiring organisation have positive effect on IT acquisition process.

Post-Acquisition Phase

Post acquisition phase determines the success of IT acquired. Delivery in an IT acquisition process can be assessed by many models prescribed by researchers who have taken keen interest in this area (Lee et al.,(2003); (Venkatesh et al., 2003); (Rai et al.,2002); (Luftman, 2003). This model attempts to capture some indicators developed by researchers earlier and tries to trace through the causal effects on it. Figure 10 explains the de-pendency of the delivery in an acquisition process and organisational preparedness. It is argued that IT acquisition process though must depend on

Figure 10. Delivery of the IT-acquisition process

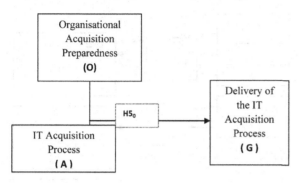

the organisation preparedness, is not necessarily followed by the acquiring organisation and might acquire IT without assessing the preparedness. The hypothesis proposed therefore, is as follows.

- **Hypothesis (Null) $H5_0$:** Delivery of IT in post-acquisition phase does not get influenced positively with the preparedness of the organisation in pre-acquisition phase and proper IT acquisition process.
- **Hypothesis (Alternate) $H5_A$:** Delivery of IT in post-acquisition phase gets influenced positively with the preparedness of the organisation and proper IT acquisition process.

HYPOTHESES FOR TIER-I INFLUENCERS

In addition to the above relationships, another set of hypotheses are proposed to support the influencers considered in the model in Figure 5. The set of influencers used for assessing each phase of the acquisition processes need to be measured independently in order to establish an effective relationship. The influencers which are to be validated are user preparedness (U), IS preparedness(I), technology preparedness (T), perception on organization (C1), perception on technology (C2) and perception on decision style (C3) in pre-acquisition phase; organization

preparedness in pre-acquisition phase (O); IT acquisition management capability (AT), Vendor capability (VC) in acquisition phase; IT acquisition status in the organization (G) in post acquisition phase. These are discussed below.

Pre-Acquisition Process Preparedness

Figure 11 discusses the relationship. Hypothesis in "null" form as well as its alternate hypothesis is postulated hereunder. These are aimed to provide an aggregated relationship among independent influencers considered for the model.

The stratification principle used for the model requires a collaborative participation from strategic, tactical and operational users. Each element contributing to the hypothesis is supported by respective hypotheses in *"null"* form as described hereunder. Besides, its alternate hypothesis is also postulated for the purpose of testing.

- **Hypothesis (Null) $H1_{U0}$:** Strategic, Tactical/Functional, Operational users do not

Figure 11. Hypotheses for user, IS, and IT preparedness

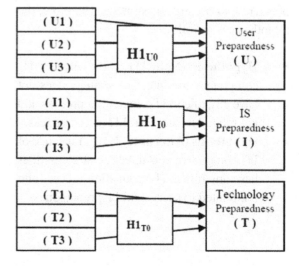

contribute collectively to successful user-preparedness.

- **Hypothesis (Alternate) H1$_{UA}$:** Strategic, Tactical/Functional, Operational users do contribute collectively to successful user-preparedness.

Information system preparedness depends on the IS strategy that exists in the organization. It is therefore, useful to understand the availability of IS strategy, IS integration and transaction strategy. Therefore, the hypothesis postulated for the purpose takes the form as follows:

- **Hypothesis (Null) H1I0:** Presence of IS strategy, integration strategy, transaction strategy do not collectively have any effect in IT-acquisition process and not related to successful IS-preparedness.
- **Hypothesis (Alternate) H1IA:** Presence of IS strategy, integration strategy, transaction strategy do collectively have any effect in IT-acquisition process and not related to successful IS-preparedness.

Technology preparedness is dependent on how well the existing IT infrastructure is planned. This availability will depend on availability of IT strategy, component strategy, and interface strategy. Strategic, tactical and operational users play a role to capture this strategy. Therefore, the hypothesis is as follows.

- **Hypothesis (Null) H1$_{T0}$:** Presence of IT, component and Interface strategy does not have any role in IT-acquisition process and not related to successful IT-preparedness.
- **Hypothesis (Alternate) H1$_{TA}$:** Presence of IT, component and Interface strategy does have any role in IT-acquisition process and not related to successful IT-preparedness.

Figure 12. Hypotheses for user perception

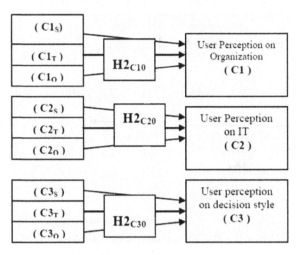

Climate Preparedness

In order to appreciate the feasibility of climate preparedness, inputs from "layered subjects" as discussed above in Figure 12 and preceding chapters, following hypotheses are formulated. This is aimed at establishing the predictive behaviour of subject-respondents for the influencers.

- **Hypothesis (Null) H2$_{C10}$:** Strategic, Tactical and Operational Users do not collectively contribute to the organisation culture.
- **Hypothesis (Alternate) H2$_{C1A}$:** Strategic, Tactical and Operational Users collectively contribute to the organisation culture.
- **Hypothesis (Null) H2$_{C20}$:** Strategic, Tactical and Operational Users do not collectively contribute to the perception on IT adoption.
- **Hypothesis (Alternate) H2$_{C2A}$:** Strategic, Tactical and Operational Users collectively contribute to the perception on IT adoption.
- **Hypothesis (Null) H2$_{C30}$:** Strategic, Tactical and Operational Users do not collectively contribute to the decision making style in the organisation.
- **Hypothesis (Alternate) H2$_{C3A}$:** Strategic, Tactical and Operational Users collectively

contribute to the decision making style in the organisation.

ACQUISITION PHASE

In order to appreciate the feasibility of understanding climate preparedness, inputs from "layered subjects" as discussed above and preceding chapters following hypotheses are formulated. The relationship is shown in Figure 13.

- **Hypothesis (Null) H4$_{AT0}$:** Appropriate skill set of Strategic, Tactical and Operational employees of IT-Cell do not collectively contribute to the successful control over IT acquisition.
- **Hypothesis (Alternate) H4$_{ATA}$:** Appropriate skill set of Strategic, Tactical and Operational employees of IT-Cell collectively contribute to the successful control over IT acquisition.
- **Hypothesis (Null) H4$_{VC0}$:** Appropriate skill set of IT-Vendors engaged by IT acquiring organisation do not contribute to effective vendor management during IT acquisition.

Figure 13. IT acquisition process

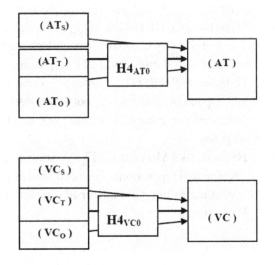

- **Hypothesis (Alternate) H4$_{VCA}$:** Appropriate skill set of IT-Vendors engaged by IT acquiring organisation collectively contribute to effective vendor management during IT acquisition.

Organization Preparedness

It refers to three attributes as shown in the Figure 14. These attributes capture pre-acquisition preparedness of the organisation at macro level which could be verified through availability of planning and policy, project management preparedness and user motivation. These influencers need to be validated through the stratified users in the organization. Therefore, the hypotheses are as stated.

- **Hypothesis (Null) H6$_0$:** Policy of the organisation on users, Planning of technology, User Motivation and Project Management Capability do not positively relate to organisational preparedness in the pre-acquisition phase.
- **Hypothesis (Alternate) H6$_A$:** Policy of the organisation on users, User Motivation and Project Planning Management positively relate to organisational preparedness in the pre-acquisition phase.
- **Hypothesis (Null) H6$_{PP0}$:** Strategic, Tactical and Operational Users do not collectively contribute to the Planning and Policy for IT acquisition.
- **Hypothesis (Alternate) H6$_{PPA}$:** Strategic, Tactical and Operational Users collectively contribute to the Planning and Policy for IT acquisition.
- **Hypothesis (Null) H6$_{PM0}$:** Strategic, Tactical and Operational Users do not collectively contribute to the Project Management Preparedness.
- **Hypothesis (Alternate) H6$_{PMA}$:** Strategic, Tactical and Operational Users collective-

Figure 14. Assessment of organisational preparedness

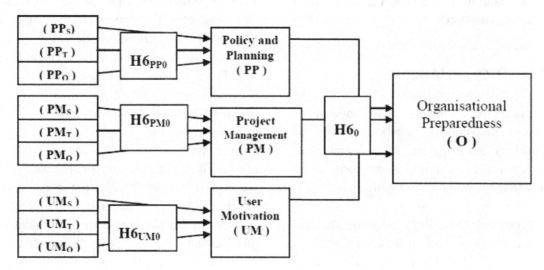

ly contribute to the Project Management Preparedness.

- **Hypothesis (Null) H6$_{UM0}$:** Strategic, Tactical and Operational Users do not collectively contribute to the User Motivation for IT acquisition.
- **Hypothesis (Alternate) H6$_{UMA}$:** Strategic, Tactical and Operational Users collectively contribute to the User Motivation for IT acquisition.

Post-Acquisition Phase

Post acquisition phase determines the success of IT acquired. Delivery in an IT acquisition process can be assessed by many models prescribed by researchers who have taken keen interest in this area (Lee et al.,2003; Venkatesh et al. 2003; Rai et al.,2002; Luftman, 2003). This model attempts to capture some indicators developed by researchers earlier and tries to trace through the causal effects on it Figure 15. The hypotheses proposed are as follows.

- **Hypothesis (Null) H7$_0$:** Success of IT acquired in post-acquisition phase does not depend positively on technology acquisi-

tion, user satisfaction, longer life cycle, IS-IT alignment.
- **Hypothesis (Alternate) H7$_A$:** Success of IT acquired in post-acquisition phase depends positively on technology acquisition, user satisfaction, longer life cycle, IS-IT alignment.

In order to appreciate the success of the acquisition process, following hypotheses are formulated to establish the predictive behaviour of subject-respondents.

- **Hypothesis (Null) H7$_{SA0}$:** Strategic, Tactical and Operational Users do not collectively contribute to the successful IT acquisition.
- **Hypothesis (Alternate) H7$_{SA0}$:** Strategic, Tactical and Operational Users collectively contribute to the successful IT acquisition.
- **Hypothesis (Null) H7$_{LL0}$:** Strategic, Tactical and Operational Users do not collectively contribute to pursue a longer life cycle for IT acquired.
- **Hypothesis (Alternate) H7$_{LLA}$:** Strategic, Tactical and Operational Users collectively contribute to pursue a longer life cycle for IT acquired.

Figure 15. Delivery of the IT-acquisition process

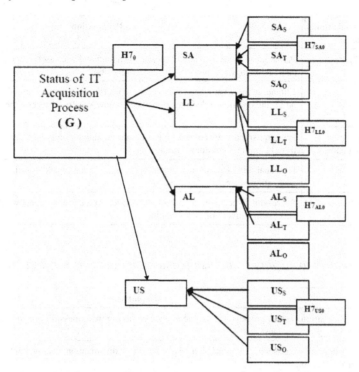

- **Hypothesis (Null) H7$_{ALA}$:** Strategic, Tactical and Operational Users do not collectively contribute to pursue an effective IS-IT alignment.

- **Hypothesis (Alternate) H7$_{ALA}$:** Strategic, Tactical and Operational Users collectively contribute to pursue an effective IS-IT alignment.

- **Hypothesis (Null) H7$_{US0}$:** Strategic, Tactical and Operational Users do not collectively contribute to IT user satisfaction in the organisation.

- **Hypothesis (Alternate) H7$_{USA}$:** Strategic, Tactical and Operational Users collectively contribute to IT user satisfaction in the organisation.

SUMMARY OF HYPOTHESES AND DEPENDENCY

As mentioned earlier in this chapter, there are two groups of hypotheses. First group of hypotheses are H1, H2, H3, H4, H5, whose validity would support each phase of the acquisition process and are based on Tier-II and Tier-III influencers. These are summarized in Table 1.

As regards understanding their relationships, it is noted that "Dependency" and "relationship" are two major attributes of a model (Rumbaugh et al., 2004). A dependency indicates a semantic relationship among elements in the model. Therefore, dependency is the prime concern that needs to be proved by testing the hypotheses. This dependency will also be used for supporting the model proposed. The "dependency" is explained in Table 2.

The second group of hypotheses are formulated to support the influencers used in the various phases of the acquisition model based on predictor influencers Tier-I. The dependency among

Table 1. Hypothesis formulated for IT acquisition process

Sl. No.	Phase of The Acquisition Process	Proposition
H1	Pre-Acquisition: Process Preparedness	Pre-acquisition preparedness is positively associated with users' preparedness, IS preparedness and Technology preparedness in the organisation.
H2	Pre-Acquisition: Climate Preparedness	Climate in the organisation with regard to users' perception on organization, users' perception on IT and decision style in the organization have positive effect on the Organisation's preparedness.
H3	Pre-Acquisition: Organisation Preparedness	Pre-acquisition preparedness on its climate Preparedness in the organisation would have a positive effect on successful IT acquisition
H4	IT Acquisition: Process Preparedness	IT- Capability of Acquiring Organisation and Vendor capability will have an effect on IT acquisition process.
H5	Post-Acquisition: Phase	Successful IT acquisition process and organisational preparedness would effect positively on successful delivery of IT acquisition.

Table 2. Dependency matrix to display relationship among influencers for first group

Dependency	Explanation
$P= d*$ (U, I, T)	Pre acquisition process preparedness would *depend* on user preparedness, IS preparedness and technology preparedness
$C= d*$ (C1, C2, C3)	Climate preparedness would *depend* on user perception on organization, user perception on IT and user perception on decision style
$O= d*$ (P, C)	Pre acquisition organization preparedness would *depend* on pre acquisition process preparedness and climate preparedness
$AQ= d*$ (AT, VC)	Acquisition phase would *depend* on the capability of the IT cell and vendor capability to manage projects
$G= d*$ (O,AQ)	IT acquisition status in the acquiring organization would *depend* on organization's preparedness to acquire IT and the IT acquisition process

* "*d*" denotes "Predictive Dependency";

these influencers is shown in Table 3 along with the respective hypothesis.

THE MODEL RESTATED

Proposed model aims to assess the preparedness of the acquiring organization in the pre-acquisition stage. In other words the organization will be assessed to display its preparedness for the information systems planning, information technology plan and existence of a congenial atmosphere for the use of IT resources etc. This research model uses variables listed in pre-acquisition stage of the acquiring process. Besides, the proposed model also aims to assess the preparedness of the

acquiring organization to manage the subsequent two stages of the acquisition process and assess the effect of the pre-acquisition preparedness on these two stages. This proposed model exhibits relationships among these three stages in the form of hypotheses and the model is represented in Figure 16.

METHODOLOGY

Validations of the model through its influencers across various Tiers need appropriate measurement tools. For this model, the appropriate measurement tools used are the metrics. The mythology helps prepare metrics (what

Table 3. Dependency matrix to display relationship among influencers for second group

Relationship	Explanation	Hypothesis
$U = d* (U1, U2, U3)$	User preparedness "U" *depends* on strategic, tactical and operational users	$H1_U$
$I = d* (I1, I2, I3)$	IS preparedness "I" *depends* on IS strategy, interfaces and transactions	$H1_I$
$T = d* (T1, T2, T3)$	Technology preparedness "T" *depends* on IT strategy, component strategy and interface strategy	$H1_T$
$C1 = d* (C1_S, C1_T, C1_O)$	Understanding of User perception on organisation "C1" *depends* on perception of strategic ($C1_S$), tactical ($C1_T$) and operational users($C1_O$)	$H2_{C1}$
$C2 = d* (C2_S, C2_T, C2_O)$	Understanding of User perception on IT "C2" *depends* on perception of strategic($C2_S$), tactical($C2_T$) and operational users($C2_O$)	$H2_{C2}$
$C3 = d* (C3_S, C3_T, C3_O)$	Understanding of decision making style in the organisation "C3" *depends* on clarity of strategic($C3_S$), tactical($C3_T$) and operational users($C3_O$)	$H2_{C3}$
$O = d* (PP, PM, UM)$	Organization preparedness *depends* on Availability of planning and policy for IT acquisition (PP), Project management principles (PM) and User Motivation (UM)	$H6_O$
$PP = d* (PP_S, PP_T, PP_O)$	Understanding on availability of planning and policy in the organisation "PP" *depends* on clarity of strategic(PP_S), tactical(PP_T) and operational users(PP_O)	$H6_{PP}$
$PM = d* (PM_S, PM_T, PM_O)$	Understanding on availability of project Management capability in the organisation "PM" *depends* on clarity of strategic(PM_S), tactical(PM_T) and operational users(PM_O)	$H6_{PM}$
$UM = d* (UM_S, UM_T, UM_O)$	Understanding on availability of User Motivation in the organisation "UM" *depends* on clarity of strategic(UM_S), tactical(UM_T) and operational users(UM_O)	$H6_{UM}$
$VC = d* (VC_S, VC_T, VC_O)$	Understanding on availability of vendor control capability in the organisation "VC" *depends* on clarity of strategic(VC_S), tactical(VC_T) and operational users(VC_O)	$H4_{VC}$
$AT = d* (AT_S, AT_T, AT_O)$	Understanding on availability of IT acquisition process capability in the organisation "AT" *depends* on clarity of strategic(AT_S), tactical(AT_T) and operational users(AT_O)	$H4_{AT}$
$G = d* (LL, SA, US, AL)$	IT acquisition status in an organization *depends* on life cycle of the IT infrastructure (LL), Acquisition success (SA), User satisfaction (US) and alignment of IS and IT (AL)	$H7_G$
$LL = d* (LL_S, LL_T, LL_O)$	Understanding on availability of better life cycle of IT acquired in the organisation "LL" *depends* on clarity of strategic(LL_S), tactical(LL_T) and operational users(LL_O)	$H7_{LL}$
$SA = d* (SA_S, SA_T, SA_O)$	Understanding on successful IT acquisition in the organisation "SA" *depends* on clarity of strategic(SA_S), tactical(SA_T) and operational users(SA_O)	$H7_{SA}$
$US = d* (US_S, US_T, US_O)$	Understanding on availability of user satisfaction on IT use in the organisation "US" *depends* on clarity of strategic(US_S), tactical(US_T) and operational users(US_O)	$H7_{US}$
$AL = d* (AL_S, AL_T, AL_O)$	Understanding on availability of alignment of IS and IT in the organisation "AL" *depends* on clarity of strategic(AL_S), tactical(AL_T) and operational users(AL_O)	$H7_{AL}$

"*d*" denotes "Predictive Dependency"

to measure) and the measurements (who to measure and how to measure). While metrics are designed through the model developed, measurement criteria will be framed through this Goal Question Metrics (GQM) method. Since each Tier of variable is expected to play a specific role for validating the model and there are three Tiers of variables, there will be four stages to accomplish this task of assessment of metrics and validation. The first stage is to apply the GQM methodology to understand the metrics and relate these metrics to questions to

Figure 16. The proposed model

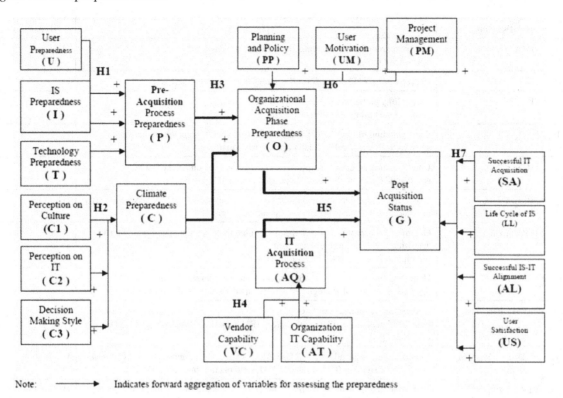

Note: ———▶ Indicates forward aggregation of variables for assessing the preparedness

prepare survey instruments. These instruments will be administered to respondents to build the foundation for the measurement process. In the second stage, assessment of Tier-I variables will be assessed. In the third stage, assessment of Tier-II variables will be done through suitable aggregation of Tier-I variables. The third stage will utilize the tire-II variables to ascertain the relationships among Tier-III variables. In the fourth stage, the model will be assessed for its overall fitness through an appropriate methodology which will use each Tier of the variables.

APPLICATION OF GOAL-QUESTION-METRICS (GQM) PRINCIPLES

Understanding an abstracted variable quite meaningfully is a difficult proposition. In this research however, these abstract variables are used extensively to capture the behaviour of users, technology, culture etc in the organization. In this chapter it is attempted to understand what each item of the variable is expected to assess and deliver in the process. These are explained in next few tables that follow. These tables are generated based on the Goal-Metric Questions Model (GQM) (Basili et al.,1994; Wohlin et al., 2000) usually followed for software engineering processes. The basic understanding behind choosing the GQM approach is to relate indicated components (Variables) of the model to gross the requirement for the output measures of the model. Figure 17 explains the process of GQM.

Goal/Question/Metric paradigm provides a useful framework and it is intended to measure certain attributes in an organization. This model is successfully used in software developing organizations which adopt software engi-

Figure 17. Structure of goal question metric model (Basili et al., 1994)

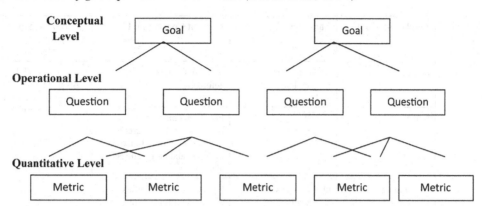

neering practices and organize software development projects very often. Since software is a vital component and its effective use is dependent on various other supporting IT infrastructure (hard as well as soft), GQM methodology is adopted for the study. The characteristics of the model are based on the understanding that

- A goal needs to be specified for each component.
- Trace the goal to certain data elements to define goal operationally.
- Provide a framework to interpret data acquired.

A set of issues is framed to measure these data elements and to predict/verify the result. The measurement can be done at three levels with a hierarchy as shown in Figure 17 above (Conceptual, Operational and Quantitative levels). At conceptual Level a goal is defined for an item. This item could be traced through its next level to understand the necessity of measuring the goal. At operational level a set of questions is used to understand the process that traces through the goals set. Questions try to characterize the attribute of a goal through measurement. A set of data is then associated at the quantitative level and provide metrics for understanding the measured values (Grady,1992; Fenton and Pfleeger, 2002).

PRE-ACQUISITION PROCESS PREPAREDNESS OF THE ORGANIZATION (P)

Conceptual Level (Goal)

Pre-acquisition preparedness aims to understand the issues related to the pre-acquisition phase. In this phase organization needs to take up macro level issues leading to increasing awareness of the effects of IT in the organization, understanding strength and weaknesses of the IT manpower to undertake the task ahead. It needs to capture users' limitations to stipulate their requirement in advance and their ability/ inclination to involve themselves in the projects for effecting a successful technology acceptance.

Table 4 describes overall goal that a metric would expect from the variables supporting it as presented in Figure 18. User preparedness (U), a metric, is dependent on variables used for strategic user (U1), functional user (U2), and operational user (U3). The goal is to measure user involvement in pre-acquisition phase of the IT acquisition process. This can be achieved if all the categories of the users defined in the model. Goal for each of the metric is different since these distinct layers are expected to perform with specific goals. A strategic user dictates a strategy for IT acquisition for the organization with stated delivery. Similarly

Table 4. User-preparedness components

Organization Preparedness Components	Level of Attributes	Variables	Goals at Conceptual Level	Overall Goal of the Component
HR Preparedness (User) (U)	Strategic	Strategic User Preparedness (U1)	Strategy for system automation	(U) {Awareness on IT acquisition Process, Support to strategy Formulation}
	Functional	Functional User Preparedness (U2)	Functional manager's business process awareness, inclination to have functional planning and preparedness for automation	
	Operational	Operational User Preparedness (U3)	Operational Users' process awareness, Preparedness for automated transactions	
IS Preparedness (I)	Strategic	IS strategy Preparedness (I1)	Existence of IS planning	(I) {Ability to Prepare IS Plan }
	Integrative	Interface Preparedness (I2)	Existence of interface plan.	
	Transactional	Transaction Preparedness (I3)	Existence of effective transactions	
Technology Preparedness (T)	Strategic	IT strategy Preparedness (T1)	Existence of IT road map.	(T) {Ability to identify technology, Components; Ability to manage Users and IS-IT alignment}
	Systemic	Technology Component Preparedness (T2)	Existence of knowledge base on identifying tools, IT components.	
	Transactional	Interface Preparedness (T3)	Availability component level links for transactions	

Figure 18. Variable for pre-acquisition preparedness

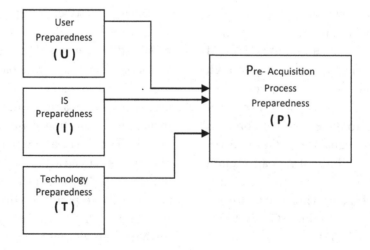

a functional manager needs to prepare a strategy at the functional level where the defined processes are well documented with stated inputs, outputs and laid down process rules and logics. An operational manager needs to understand and take the ownership of routine transactions, monitoring of the transactions and have a mechanism to verify, rollback erroneous interactions with processes. Documentation at this level would also entail fulfilment of goals.

As regards IS preparedness (I), it is a metric based on the variables IS strategy (I1), Interface strategy (I2) and Transaction strategy (I3). These variables aggregate to meet the goal set for IS preparedness. I1 sets a goal for providing an IS plan that ensures identification of information systems in the organization and inclusion of possible processes and rules under it. I2 therefore, is the subsequent approach to interface all the information systems planned. This strategy calls for a plan and prioritization of interfaces among the information systems. I3, the last in the IS planning process, formalizes all the possible transactions across all information systems and depends upon a formalized interface plan and the information systems. Overall goal for "I" therefore, is to establish an IS plan for the organization and should be made available in the pre-acquisition phase. Technology preparedness (T) in the model demands preparedness of the

IT cell in the organization. Even existence of IT cell confirms a good step during pre-acquisition phase. This preparedness calls for a concerted effort to prepare an IT plan (T1), attempt to identify the components that would be procured component strategy (T2) and effort to provide a road map to provide IS –IT alignment (T3). IT Cell's capability is enforced here with right exposure to the components being planned for acquisition.

Questions and Metrics for "P"

This section attempts to frame questions to capture and reflect the goals set for the variables. These questions are independent items for the variables or called as "Predictors". Metrics are also attached to appreciate these questions. Tables below explain questions along with the metrics generated for the purpose.

PRE-ACQUISITION CLIMATE PREPAREDNESS OF THE ORGANIZATION (C)

Conceptual Level (Goal)

Model emphasizes that culture, user perception, decision making style of the acquiring organization

Table 5. U1: Strategic user preparedness. Question-metric matrix for strategic user preparedness.

Question	Metrics	Elements in Questionnaire	Questions (Reference)
What is Strategic User's View on IT-Acquisition?	Process Awareness	MIS plan is an absolute requirement for IT acquisition	U101
		Style of capturing information planning does not change too often in the organization and IT can help in meeting these changes.	U102
	Strategy Formulation	IT acquisition needs a strategy and should follow IS strategy.	U103
		Investment in IT needs justification in the organization	U104
		Organization has in-house capability to acquire IT.	U105
		Organization has an IT strategy	U106

Table 6. U2: Functional user preparedness. Question-metric matrix for functional user preparedness.

Question	Metrics	Elements in Questionnaire	Questions (Reference)
What is Functional User's View on IT-Acquisition?	Process Awareness	IT will reduce the burden of routine decisions and routine decisions are identified	U201
		IT helps maintain a formal communication link with other departments	U202
	Function Planning	Process manuals are available	U203
		Functional IS strategy is needed	U204
		Strategy for IT acquisition for your department exists	U205
		Employees handle processes well	U206

Table 7. U3: Operational user preparedness. Question-metric matrix for operational user preparedness.

Question	Metrics	Elements in Questionnaire	Questions (Reference)
What is the Level of Awareness sand Involvement of operational User for IT-Acquisition?	Process Awareness, Transaction Awareness	IT can help you in routine work	U301
		IT can help in providing information	U302
		Training is necessary before introducing IT	U303
		IT can release some burden	U304
		IT should be there in the organization.	U305

Table 8. I1: IS Strategy. Question-metric matrix for IS strategy.

Question	Metrics	Elements in Questionnaire	Questions (Reference)
What is User's View on Information System Strategy?	System Planning	Employees are capable of absorbing change due to a systemic approach.	I101
		There is no exist frequent change in reports/forms	I102
		There is systemic approach to completing transactions in your organization?	I103
		Information is received in need	I104
		There is capability to outline requirement to IT vendor/ IT department to align the process	I105
		In-house capability exists to suggest an IS strategy in the organization.	I106

Table 9. I2: IS interface strategy. Question-metric matrix for IS interface strategy.

Question	Sub-Metrics	Elements in Questionnaire	Questions (Reference)
What is the User's View on Interface Strategy for Information Systems?	Functional IS Plan and Interfaces	Most of time is spent in arranging resources and support from peers.	I201
		There should have been otherwise taken care of without your intervention	I202
		There is a system that provides interface with peer functions for routine works	I203
		Interfaces for the function are identifiable	I204

Table 10. I3: Transaction strategy. Question-metric matrix for transaction strategy.

Question	Metrics	Elements in Questionnaire	Questions (Reference)
What is the User's View on Transactional Readiness?	Transaction Readiness	Routine transactions are proven to be effective	I301
		Iteratively reports are generated daily	I302
		Transactions are completed in time	I303
		Transactions can be prioritized	I304

Table 11. T1: IT strategy. Question-metric matrix for IT strategy.

Question	Metrics	Elements in Questionnaire	Questions (Reference)
What is User's Role in Information Technology Strategy?	IT Plan	IT department has the capability to provide you suitable services/ products as required.	T101
		IT department has the expertise needed	T102
		Training is planned before any IT acquisition.	T103
		There is a plan to retain IT professionals.	T104
		IT employees have knowledge on domains in the organization other than IT.	T105
		Employees from other domains are encouraged to work in IT projects	T106
		IT Vendors are selected based on quality certifications	T107

Table 12. T2: IT component strategy. Question-metric matrix for IT component strategy.

Question	Metrics	Elements in Questionnaire	Questions (Reference)
What is the User's View on Components in IT Acquisition?	Components Identification Strategy	IT Managers, employees in IT Cell are updated on their skill regularly	T201
		IT applications are product specific	T202
		IT applications are quality certified	T203
		IT vendors are quality certified	T204
		IT Service providers attend to problems well	T205
		IT department has a good set up to meet the demand of users	T206
		IT managers, Solution providers understand the process well.	T207
		IT managers, Solution providers provide training regularly.	T208

Table 13. T3: interface strategy. Question-metric matrix for interface strategy.

Question	Metrics	Elements in Questionnaire	Questions (Reference)
What is User's view on Transactions?	Transaction Automation and Interface	There is adequacy in completing a transaction because of peer incapability, non-cooperation	T301
		Transaction waiting time is proper	T302
		IT can improve productivity through automation of transactions	T303
		Quality certified products will provide better interface	T304
		Interface is well planned as required	T305
		Interface is not affected due to IT	T306

play a vital role in making acquisition successful. Goal of each of the variables is as explained in Table 14.

Pre-Acquisition Organization Preparedness of the Organization (O)

This variable called Organizational Preparedness (O) depends on Pre-acquisition Process Preparedness (P) and Climate Preparedness (C) as shown in Figure 19. Measurement of organizational preparedness is expected to display a commanding behaviour for planning, monitoring and executing IT projects in the organization and should display a user-led vendor management scenario. Organizational preparedness (O) is a gross indicator for (P) and (C) as already discussed.

Table 18 describes the metrics for understanding Organizational Preparedness. Table 19 below explains the metrics and questions generated for the

purpose of evaluation. These questions are independent manifestation of "O" though this preparedness is a predicted variable and dependent on climate (C) and pre-acquisition process preparedness (P).

IT Acquisition Process in the Organization (AQ)

IT acquisition process is the phase subsequent to pre-acquisition process preparedness and it is essential to successfully execute the project where IT cell of the acquiring organization and vendors engaged discharge their responsibilities as per agreed terms. Model proposed expected a harmony between the capabilities of supplier and acquirer in order to bring the synergy. Table 20 below explained the conceptual goal for a purposeful acquisition.

Table 14. Organization climate preparedness

Organization Preparedness Components	Variable	Goals at Conceptual Level	Overall Goal of the Component
Organization Climate Preparedness (C)	User Perception on Organization (C1)	Understand User perception on Culture of the organization	(C) {Organization Culture, motivation; User intention to use technology; Decision making style}
	User Perception on IT (C2)	Understand attitude of Users on IT	
	Organization Architecture (C3)	Effect of technology on architectural style	

Table 15. C1: User perception on organization. Question-metric matrix for user perception on organization (C1).

Question	Metrics	Elements in Questionnaire	Questions (Reference)
What is User's View on Climate in Organization?	Culture, Motivation	Employee role is defined in the organization	C101
		Most of time is lost to track routine events leaving little scope to work with a strategy.	C102
		People in the organization wait for instructions to do certain job.	C103
		It would be possible to bring in change in people if organization needs to change in strategy.	C104
		Top management is not difficult to change in the organization and they take all routine decisions.	C105
		Organization has formalized process manuals	C106
		Manuals are followed	C107

Table 16. C2: User perception on it. Question-metric matrix for user perception on IT (C2).

Question	Metrics	Elements in Questionnaire	Questions (Reference)
What is User's View on Accepting IT?	Inclination to accept Technology	IT is treated as a technology and is not treated differently.	C201
		Employees support introduction of new technologies.	C202
		Organization supports introduction of IT.	C203
		IT if introduced would not pose problems in working style	C204
		Areas for IT alignment identified	C205
		IT if introduced would not pose a threat to your competency, presence in your organization.	C206
		There is a priority in the organization to bring in IT.	C207
		Employee can prioritize areas that can be aligned to IT	C208

Table 17. C3: User perception on decision style. Question-metric matrix for user perception on decision style (C3).

Question	Sub-Metrics	Elements in Questionnaire	Questions (Reference)
What is User's View on Decision Style in the Organization?	Decision Style	There is definite and formal decision making procedure	C301
		Organization does not change the style too often	C302
		Formalization is the strength of the organization	C303
		Strategic decision makers support formalization	C304
		IT will not affect decision making style	C305
		Employees follow the procedure diligently	C306
		IT will not affect Procedures	C307

Figure 19. Organizational preparedness in pre-acquisition phase

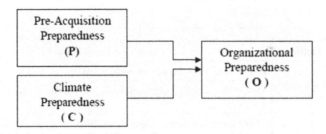

Table 18. Organizational preparedness components (O)

Overall Goal of the Component	Goal of the Item at Conceptual Level (O)
(P) {IS leadership, IT leadership}	{IS leadership, IT leadership, Project Management, User Motivation}
(C) {Understand User perception on Culture of the organization, Understand attitude of Users on IT and Decision making style}	

Table 19. Question-metric matrix for assessment of organizational preparedness components (O)

Question	Metrics	Elements in Questionnaire	Questions (Reference)
What is User's View on Preparedness in the organization for Information Technology Acquisition?	Clarity in definition of Policy, Project Management Skill, User Motivation	Organization has a written policy for conduct any acquisition and IT in particular	PP01
		Organization supports the entire IT acquisition Cycle	PP02
		There is a policy on training Acquisition Management Personnel before acquisition commences	PP03
		Organization has a planning, monitoring, reviewing policy for IT acquisition	PP04
		Organization believes in formalising IS plan before IT planning is done	PP05
		Acquisition management personnel are experienced to take up the activity	PM01
		Organization has understood the risks in IT acquisition and there is a plan to address	PM02
		Project evaluation standards and metrics are developed for IT projects	PM03
		There is documentation policy for IT components	PM04
		Project management team is encouraged to benchmark before solicitation	PM05
		There is policy to evaluate vendor and its management	PM06
		End user groups are motivated to be a part of solicitation activity and planning process	UM01
		Incentive policy is in force to attract end-users to accept and use IT	UM02
		Project team attaches importance to process requirements	UM03
		There is a policy to train end-user groups	UM04
		There is a strong reward system for employees	UM05

Table 20. IT acquisition process (AQ)

Component	Items	Identification	Goals at Conceptual Level	Overall Goal of the Component
IT-Acquisition Process (A)	Organization Capability IS-IT Alignment	AT	Capture relationship among IT components and automated information systems	(AQ) {Quality Assurance Policies, Component Identification Policies, Project Evaluation Practices}
	Vendor Capability	VC	Capture understanding of Vendors on organization and Vendor's quality	

Table 21. AT: User view on acquisition of information technology acquisition. Question-metric matrix (AT).

Question	Metrics	Elements in Questionnaire	Questions (Reference)
User's View on Information Technology Management in the organization	Clarity in definition of delivery, clarity in Interrelationship among Components, Project Management Skills	IT components are upgraded frequently	AT01
		IT applications are implemented smoothly	AT02
		Automation is taken care of incrementally	AT03
		Computerization plan exists	AT04
		Inter Module Communication does exist	AT05
		Process Clarity is available through manuals	AT06

Table 22. VC: Vendor's role in it acquisition process. Question-metric matrix (VC).

Question	Metrics	Elements in Questionnaire	Questions (Reference)
User's View on Vendor's Role in Information Technology Acquisition Process	Clarity in definition of delivery, ability to provide services	Vendors selected know business processes well	VC01
		Vendors delivery ensures time, money as planned	VC02
		Vendors are urged to submit documentation on processes taken up for IT alignment	VC03
		System and application documentation are available on demand	VC04
		Documents are user-friendly and frequently updated	VC05
		IT audit is carried out periodically and seriously	VC06

IT ACQUISITION STATUS IN THE ORGANIZATION (G)

"G" refers to the IT acquisition process delivery that has taken place in the organization. It needs to be compared with a set of variables that normally is expected of an acquisition process. These expectations are enumerated in Figure 20. These variables are adopted from the research done in the context of organizational review on the IT acquisition process and mainly drawn from recent works done (Luftman, 2003; Papp et al., 1996). The 'gap' between the 'stated' objectives/delivery and 'actual delivery' (measured through manifested variables as shown in Table 23) determines the situation in the organization on the success of IT acquisition process adopted (Evans, 2004). Gap among the stated and expected variables provide

Figure 20. Delivery of the IT-acquisition process

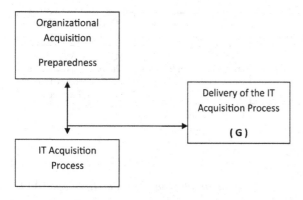

an insight by tracing through the items in the model thereby providing a scope to introspect the strength and weaknesses of the IT acquisition process adopted.

EXPECTED IT ACQUISITION IN AN ORGANIZATION (G)

Stated delivery from an IT acquisition process is a complex phenomenon. It needs a holistic view in terms of creation and use of IT infrastructure. Understanding this complexity through hypothesized preparedness exercises of various stakeholders, appropriateness of components of IT infrastructure in an organization has remained a grey area for the researchers. Recent studies stress on understanding successful use of IT acquired in the organization and analyzing the attributes to the success in using IT infrastructure (Luftman, 2003; Papp et al., 1996; Evans, 2004). There are stipulations from SEI, CMM, ISO families

Table 23. IT-acquisition quality indicators for the organization

Component	Items	Identification	Goals at Conceptual Level	Overall Goal of the Component
IT-Acquisition Quality Attributes (G)	Successful IT Acquisition	SA	Assess perception on success of IT acquired in the organization.	(G) {Process alignment, User satisfaction, Project performance, Systems Performance}
	Life-Cycle of IS	LL	Assess life cycle of IS developed/automated.	
	Successful IS-IT Alignment	AT	Assess success of IS-IT alignment.	
	User Satisfaction	US	Assess satisfaction of end-users.	

Table 24. SA: User's view on it acquisition. Question-metric matrix for user's view on IT acquisition (SA).

Question	Metrics	Elements in Questionnaire	Questions (Reference)
User's View on IT Acquired	Project Assessment, Systems Assessment	Project does not have time and cost overrun	SA01
		Project is executed as per IT Plan	SA02
		IT Acquisition is managed by IT professionals	SA03
		Mean time between failures is not high	SA04
		Current status of IT intervention is as expected	SA05
		User department is involved during IT project proposal	SA06

Table 25. LL: User's view on life cycle of it acquired. Question-metric matrix user's view on life cycle of IT acquired (LL).

Question	Metrics	Elements in Questionnaire	Questions (Reference)
User's View on Life Cycle of IT Acquired	Frequency in changing Processes, Frequency in Component Upgradation	IS planning exists	LL01
		IS planning does not change very often	LL02
		IT department is involved in IS planning	LL03
		IT planning does not change very often	LL04
		IT Component (Database) has not been upgraded frequently	LL05
		IT Component (H/W) has not been upgraded frequently	LL06
		IT Component (applications) has not been upgraded / abandoned frequently	LL07

Table 26. AL: User's view on is-it alignment. Question-metric matrix for user's view on IS-IT alignment (AL).

Question	Metrics	Elements in Questionnaire	Questions (Reference)
User's View on IS-IT alignment	IT and IS components Relationship, Reflection of IS in IT	Formalized business activities are IT enabled	AL01
		There is high dependency on IT-enabled activities	AL02
		A single activity translates to multiple functions to support without much interference	AL03
		Developed systems have made reference to the manuals	AL04
		Decision making style is not affected due to IT-enabled processes	AL05
		Role clarity is well reflected in the new IT-aligned processes	AL06
		All transactions are well managed in the IT-enabled environment	AL07

Table 27. US: User's satisfaction on using it aligned is. Question-metric matrix for user's satisfaction on using IT aligned IS (US).

Question	Sub-Metrics	Elements in Questionnaire	Questions (Reference)
User's satisfaction on IT aligned IS	Ease of Use, Ease of Maintainability	IT enabled processes are reflective of process manuals	US01
		Timely access to data is possible	US 02
		Timely generation of reports is possible as required	US 03
		There is ease of use of applications and ease in navigation of applications	US 04
		System is available on demand	US 05
		Dynamic report generation is possible	US 06
		Service of IT department is available on demand	US07
		Service of IT infrastructure is available on demand	US08
		System debugging is infrequent	US09

Table 28. Metrics for the proposed model (G)

Indicators of the Model Proposed	Metrics used in the proposed Model	Measures Designed for the posed Model
Pre-acquisition Preparedness (P)	HR Preparedness	Process awareness, Strategy Formulation, Function Planning, Transaction awareness
	IS Preparedness	System Planning, Functional IS plan, Interface Plan, Transaction Readiness
	Technology Preparedness	IT Plan, Component identification, Transaction automation and Interface
Climate Preparedness (C)	Organization Culture	Culture to adapt to agility
	Perception on IT	Attitude to use IT
	Decision Style	Decision making process of the organization
Acquisition Process (A)	IT Acquisition	User's knowledge on processes, Capability to identify tools/ components/ managing projects and specifying delivery Quality Assurance
	Vendor Capability	Quality assurance, Component competency and Project management
Post Acquisition (G)	Successful IT Acquisition	Project evaluation, System Availability
	Life-Cycle of IS	Determining life of the IS and IT projects
	IS-IT Alignment	Architectural fit and Representation of processes in IT enables IS
	User Satisfaction	Ease of Use and Ease of Maintainability

engaged in quality assurance who profess for listing these attributes for IT acquisition success (Marple et al., 2001; Ferguson et al., 1997; Lee et al., 2003; Venkatesh et al., 2003). The models that closely discuss these attributes are Strategic Alignment Model (SAM) (Ward & Peppard, 2002; Henderson & Venkatraman, 1993), Luftman Model (Luftman, 2003), and CMMI (Marple et al., 2001). attempt to posit the organization's alignment and acceptance issue in the context of information technology. 'G' denoting the stated indicators for assessing an organization is rather an ideal approach. This is explained in Table 28.

SUMMARY

In this chapter model is developed based on the framework discussed in the Chapter 5. Developed model is supported with suitably formulated hypotheses, variables enumerated to support the measurements of the output of the model with a formal method. It is essential to note that the model developed can be used for the entire life cycle of the IT acquisition that emerge in an organization and thus can be dynamically used.

REFERENCES

AFEI. (2010). Industry perspective on the future of DoD IT acquisition (Industry Task Force Report). Arlington, VA: The Association of Enterprise Information (AFEI).

Ahen, D. M., Clouse, A., & Turner, R. (2001). *CMMI distilled: A practical introduction to integrated process improvement*. Boston: Addison-Wesley.

Baroudi, J. J., Olson, M. H., & Ives, B. (1986). An empirical study of the impact of user involvement on system usage and information satisfaction. *Communications of the ACM, 29*(3), 232–238. doi:10.1145/5666.5669.

Basili, V. R., Caldiera, G., & Rombach, H. D. (1994). Goal question metrics paradigm. In *Encyclopedia of Software Engineering (Vol. 1*, pp. 528–532). New York: Wiley.

Boehm, B. W. (1981). *Software engineering economics*. Hoboken, NJ: Prentice Hall.

Brown, I. (2010). *Strategic information systems planning: Comparing espoused beliefs with practice*. Paper presented at the 18th European Conference on Information Systems. Pretoria, South Africa.

Cuena, J., & Molina, M. (2000). The role of knowledge modeling techniques in software development: A general approach based on a knowledge management tool. *International Journal of Human-Computer Studies, 52*, 385–421. doi:10.1006/ijhc.1999.0232.

Curtis, B., Krasner, H., & Iscoe, N. (1988). A field study of the software design process for large systems. *Communications of the ACM, 31*(11), 1268–1287. doi:10.1145/50087.50089.

Davis, B. G., & Olson, M. H. (2000). *Management information systems: Conceptual foundations, structure and development* (2nd ed.). Singapore: McGraw-Hill.

Díaz-Ley, M., García, F., & Piattini, M. (2010). MIS-PyME- Software measurement capability maturity model – Supporting the definition of software measurement programs and capability determination. *Advances in Engineering Software, 41*, 1223–1237. doi:10.1016/j.advengsoft.2010.06.007.

Evans, N. (2004). *Promoting fusion in the business-IT relationship*. Paper presented at Issues in Informing Science and Information Technology Education Joint Conference. Rock Hampton, Australia.

Fenton, N. E., & Pfleeger, S. L. (2002). *Software metrics: A rigorous & practical approach* (2nd ed.). Singapore: Thomson Asia Pte. Ltd..

Ferguson, J., Cooper, J., Falat, M., Fisher, M., Guido, A., & Marciniak, J. … Webster, R. (1997). Software acquisition process maturity questionnaire: The acquisition risk management initiative. Pittsburgh, PA: Software Engineering Institute, Carnegie Mellon University.

Garlan, J., & Anthony, R. (2003). *Large-scale software architecture: A practical guide using UML*. New Delhi: Wiley Dreamtech India.

Grady, R. B. (1992). *Practical software metrics for project management and process improvement*. Upper Saddle River, NJ: Prentice Hall.

Guttman, R., & Greenbaum, C. W. (1998). Facet theory: Its development and current status. *European Psychologist, 3*(1), 13–36. doi:10.1027/1016-9040.3.1.13.

Henderson, J. C., & Venkatraman, N. (1993). Strategic alignment: Leveraging information technology for transforming organisations. *IBM Systems Journal, 32*(1). doi:10.1147/sj.382.0472.

Hosier, W. A. (1961). Pitfalls and safeguards in real-time digital systems with emphasis on programming. *IRE Transactions on Engineering Management, 8*.

Ibrahim, L. (2000). Using an integrated capability maturity model - The FAA experience. In *Proceedings of the Tenth Annual International Symposium of the International Council on Systems Engineering (INCOSE)*, (pp. 643-648). Minneapolis, MN: INCOSE.

International Function Point Users Group (IF-PUG). (2002). *IT measurement: Practical advice from experts*. Reading, MA: Addison-Wesley.

Kanter, J. (2000). *Managing with information* (4th ed.). New Delhi: Prentice Hall.

Kown, T. H., & Zmud, R. W. (1987). Unifying the fragmented models of information systems implementation. In *Critical Issues in Information Systems Research*. New York, NY: John Wiley and Sons.

Lee, C. S. (2001). Modeling the business value of information technology. *Information & Management, 39*(3), 191–210. doi:10.1016/S0378-7206(01)00090-8.

Lee, Y., Kozar, K. A., & Larsen, K. R. T. (2003). The technology acceptance model: Past, present and future. *Communications of AIS, 12*, 750–780.

Linthicum, D. S. (2004). *Enterprise application integration*. New Delhi: Pearson Education.

Luftman, J. (2003). Assessing IT/business alignment. *Information Systems Management, 20*(4), 9–21. doi:10.1201/1078/43647.20.4.20030901/77287.2.

Marple, J., Clark, B., Jones, C., & Zubrow, D. (2001). *Measures in support of evolutionary acquisition*. Pittsburgh, PA: Software Engineering Institute, Carnegie Mellon University.

Misra, H., Satpathy, M., & Mohanty, B. (2005). Stratified users and organisation preparedness for information technology acquisition: A causal model. *Vilakshan XIMB Journal of Management, 2*(1), 1–21.

Misra, H., Satpathy, M., & Mohanty, B. (2007). Measuring user's role to assess organisation preparedness in a systems acquisition life cycle: A cognitive framework. *International Journal of Information and Communication Technology, 1*(1), 50–61. doi:10.1504/IJICT.2007.013277.

National Research Council. (2007). *Improving disaster management: The role of IT in mitigation, preparedness, response, and recovery*. Washington, DC: National Academies Press.

Niu, J., & Atlee, J. M. (2003). Template semantics for model-based notations. *IEEE Transactions on Software Engineering, 29*(10).

Nuseibeh, B., & Easterbrook, S. (2000). Requirements engineering: A roadmap. In *Proceedings of International Conference on Software Engineering (ICSE-2000)*. Limerick, Ireland: ICSE.

Papp, R., Luftman, J., & Brier, T. (1996). *Business and IT in harmony: Enables and inhibitors to alignment*. Paper presented at AMCIS. Phoenix, AZ.

Preston, K., & Karahanna, E. (2009). The antecedents of IS strategic alignment: A nomological network. *Information Systems Research, 20*(2), 159–179. doi:10.1287/isre.1070.0159.

Rai, A., Lang, S. S., & Welker, R. B. (2002). Assessing the validity of IS success models: An empirical test and theoretical analysis. *Information Systems Research, 13*(1), 50–69. doi:10.1287/isre.13.1.50.96.

Rampersad, G., Plewa, C., & Troshani, I. (2012). Investigating the use of information technology in managing innovation: A case study from a university technology transfer office. *Journal of Engineering and Technology Management, 29*, 3–21. doi:10.1016/j.jengtecman.2011.09.002.

Richardson, G. L., Jackson, B. M., & Dickson, G. W. (1990, December). A principles-based enterprise architecture: Lessons from texaco and star enterprise. *Management Information Systems Quarterly*, 380–403.

Robillard, J., & Sambrook, R. (2008). USAF emergency and incident management systems: A systematic analysis of functional requirements. *EIM Requirements Study*, 1-13.

Royce, W. W. (1970). Managing the development of large software systems. In *Proceedings of the 9th International Conference on Software Engineering*, (pp. 328-338). IEEE Computer Society.

Rumbaugh, J., Booch, G., & Jacobson, I. (2004). *The unified modeling language reference manual* (2nd ed.). Reading, MA: Addison-Wesley.

Scacchi, W. (2001). Process models in software engineering. In Marciniak, J. J. (Ed.), *Encyclopedia of Software Engineering* (2nd ed.). New York: John Wiley and Sons.

Sommerville, I., & Sawyer, P. (1997). *Requirements engineering: A good practice guide*. New York: Wiley.

Tait, P. (1988, March). The effect of user involvement on systems success: A contingency approach. *Management Information Systems Quarterly*, 91–108. doi:10.2307/248809.

Venkatesh, V., Morris, M. G., Davis, G. B., & Davis, F. D. (2003). User acceptance of information technology: Toward a unified view. *Management Information Systems Quarterly*, 27(3), 425–478.

Ward, J., & Peppard, J. (2002). *Strategic planning for information systems*. London: John Wiley and Sons.

Wohlin, C., Runeson, P., Host, M., Ohlsson, M. C., Regnell, B., & Wesslen, A. (2000). *Experimentation in software engineering: An introduction*. London: Kluwer Academic Publishers. doi:10.1007/978-1-4615-4625-2.

Chapter 7
Validation of Model:
The Process

ABSTRACT

The validation process for the model largely depends on the behavior of influencers (variables), which are used for measurement of the inputs, processes, and the outputs. In order to indicate the utility of the framework supporting the model conceptualized, this chapter includes detailed discussions on the method adopted. It includes the sampling plan adopted to help the reader appreciate the management principles in categorizing stakeholders and their contributions to overall IT acquisition preparedness in the organization. A three-tier approach is considered important with the grounding theory that every organization displays general hierarchies across three layers, and roles of stakeholders are governed by the expected layer-specific strategies. It is argued that despite layer-specific contributions, overall preparedness in the organization needs convergence among these layers in terms of their roles, tasks, and other deliverables.

INTRODUCTION

The validation process for the model largely depends on the behaviour of influencers (variables) which are used for measurement of the responses received to understand overall behaviour of the model. The measurement is used for assessment of certain metrics developed which are already presented in Chapter 6. This stage involves application of methods which will prepare the survey instruments, and sampling plan testing these instruments. "Likert-scaling" has been used for eliciting responses for influencers. The proposed model tries to estimate the preparedness of various stakeholders in the acquisition process. Since the "stimuli" are aimed at the stakeholders and a "summation" is needed to understand the overall preparedness of the organization Likert scaling method is adopted to conduct the survey and analysis (Mcliver and Camines, 1994). Likert scaling has been adopted in order to accomplish the task of testing hypotheses formulated and the model in turn. Technology selectors, implement-

DOI: 10.4018/978-1-4666-4201-0.ch007

ers and users form the basic respondents who scale the questions (stimuli) administered. The study spanned for a year during which an organization tried to implement the action planned. The test was organization specific and thus mostly all the employees were involved in the exercise. In the beginning of the study we did not initiate any orientation plan since we wanted to observe the process and study the behaviour. The strategic users and IT managers found it helpful to use this model as an exercise to identify the strength and weaknesses in the acquisition process and assess the current preparedness of the organization. Summative feature and the multi-item scaling property of Likert scaling are deployed to understand the predictors as well the dependent influencers developed for the measurement (Nunnally, 1978). Workshops were held in the organization in the end of the observations.

Three interrelated tasks were taken up for Likert scaling approach as described below.

- Item Variable
- Item Scoring
- Item Selection

As explained in Figure 1, the stages of the process are considered in this research for adopting the methodology. The questionnaire for the items, variable developed (Basili et al., 1994) is developed based on on GQM principles. The questionnaires thus developed were administered in the organizations. Besides, the questionnaires were discussed among the academicians and practitioners pursuing IS related research as well as implementing the IS methodologies.

Item Scoring

Likert scale with range 1-7 (Mcliver and Camines, 1994); (1: Strongly Disagree, 2: Disagree, 3: Somewhat Disagree, 4: Un-Decided, 5: Somewhat Agree, 6: Agree, 7: Strongly Agree) has been used for eliciting response. The model demands an in depth study on the Organizations. Work Locus of Control Scale (WLCS) (Spector,1988) method which supports Likert's summative scaling, has been adopted for scoring as a) it supports writing of items in a straight forward manner, b) it requires a sample size of around 200 subjects and c) it is not complicated to administer.

Scoring in a summative scale does bring in an "error" to the measurement and describing items plays a vital role in scoring these. A negatively stated item needs to be treated by the respondent differently as compared to that of a positively stated item. Therefore, appropriately worded and described items have been used in the questionnaire for this research survey in order to avoid "polarity" (Mcliver and Camines, 1994). Besides the structured approach to receive responses from the subjects, semi-structured interview process were largely adopted in order to provide qualitative stimuli. Since IT acquisition needs a strategy, qualitative analysis is quite important for having a holistic view on the process.

Figure 1. Steps for developing summative scale (Mcliver & Camines, 1994)

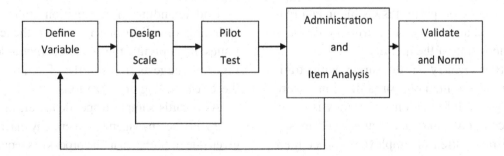

Item Selection

Items generated on the basis of GQM approach were administered among some sample respondents in an organization for testing. This was intended to understand the "difficulty" level and also the "polarity" that might have occurred. Besides, questionnaires were also discussed among practitioners and academicians involved in IS implementation and research, in order to capture un-biased view of the respondents. The items are also mostly adapted from the research done in this area and are selected to suit the need of the model proposed.

Sampling Plan

The model demands assessment of involvement of the acquiring organization in all the stages in the acquisition process with specific attention to the pre-acquisition stage. One of the difficult propositions in preparing a sampling plan in order to assess the involvement is the "unequal distribution" of the subjects in the organization. Layers (Strategic, Tactical, and Operational) are mostly hierarchical in nature and therefore, sampling plan also follows the pattern in the sample organization. "Stratified sampling" technique is adopted since it is essential to capture the subjects at all these layers in an organization (Minieak and Kurzeja, 2001). This sampling technique justifies its application since it attempts at targeting all sections of the population by dividing into a number of groups. It also advocates for a predetermined sample size proportional to the size of the stratum. While in this case, though not known, the proportion is visible in an organization and an organization structure displays the composition of the hierarchy.

In order to carry out the survey with stratified sampling method, organizations were chosen where information technology is being introduced and/or has been introduced in any form. Stratification of employees as per their roles and responsibilities are well discoursed and mostly defined in an organization (Nonaka, 1988; Mintzberg and Lampel, 1988; Pearce and Robinson,1996). Strategy gets formulated, implemented through the layers of the employees who rather act differently as per their role. Top managers (strategic) strategically provide directions; middle managers carry forward the strategic issues objectively and deploy resources for the operational managers/employees to carry out the tasks thus prioritised (Nonaka, 1988; Mintzberg and Lampel, 1988; Pearce and Robinson, 1996) and therefore, largely depend on the organization structure and processes. It is assumed that organization structure normally follows a strategic pyramid (Kanter, 2000).

Questionnaires were administered following a workshop which was largely attended by the strategic as well as middle level managers. However, there was a good response from the operational level employees while soliciting response. As discussed earlier, actual survey was based on following steps: a) choosing organizations, b) determining sample size, c) collecting responses. It has been planned to understand the applicability of the model in a heterogeneous environment. Therefore, it was aimed to cover organizations with different core processes and conduct in depth study (both qualitative and quantitative studies. Twenty organizations were contacted personally where IT acquisition has been in different stages and the researcher had access. Thirteen of them responded to this exercise confirming participation. Demography of the responding organizations is described Figure 2.

Understanding IT acquisition status in responding organizations is one of the critical issues in applying the research methodology. Figure 3 suggests status of the IT acquisition in these responding organizations.

As regards sample respondents, all the three layers in the management hierarchy have been given due importance in the process as required in

Figure 2. Demography of responding organizations

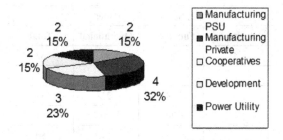

the "stratified sampling" methodology. Table 1 and Figure 4, and figure 5 describe the sampling plan.

Table 1 indicates that overall response rate was around 21 percent. The response rate in organization 1 and 2 was high. In the remaining eleven, though there were visits to these organizations for qualitative analyses, filled-in questionnaires were solicited by post at a later stage. Analysis shows that in strategic respondent's category the response was 32 percent whereas in the category of functional and operational the response rates were 36 percent and 16 percent respectively. It revealed that in the category of operational respondents, the inquisitiveness was low where as in other two categories; there was awareness on the issue.

VALIDATION OF TIER-I INFLUENCERS

These predictors are in summative scale form generated from the responses received. Likert (Nunnally,1978; Mcliver and Camines, 1994) scaling is used under the premise that a group of items predict a single phenomenon through scoring in a scale adopted for the purpose. Another assumption is that these items correlate each other. While it is difficult to conclusively determine the predictability of a phenomenon, this procedure in conjunction with other methods is chosen to substantiate. These are as follows:

1. Cronbach Alpha.
2. Alpha-if-Item-deleted.
3. Item-to-Total Correlation.
4. Varimax Factor Analysis (Factor loadings).
5. Communality and Eigenvalues.

Reliability and validation are two major issues that these four methods would try to address collectively because no individual tool is adequate. While reliability is an empirical issue, validity raises theoretical orientation of the issue. Reliability of variable and its validity are central to the discussion here and thus

Figure 3. IT acquisition scenario in responding organizations

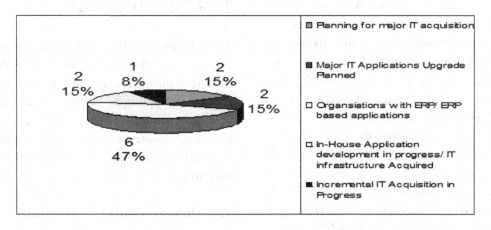

Table 1. Composition of the sample employees in respondent organizations

Organization	Sample Size Targeted				Subjects Responded			
	Strategic	Functional	Operational	Total	Strategic	Functional	Operational	Total
1	10	36	130	176	4	19	39	62
2	18	50	180	248	7	24	45	76
3	18	50	180	248	5	18	25	48
4	18	50	180	248	4	20	30	54
5	18	50	180	248	6	23	21	50
6	18	50	180	248	5	12	20	37
7	18	50	180	248	5	18	19	42
8	18	50	180	248	6	16	21	43
9	18	50	180	248	7	11	17	35
10	18	50	180	248	6	8	15	29
11	18	50	180	248	5	14	18	37
12	18	50	180	248	6	15	19	40
13	18	50	180	248	8	12	31	51
Total	226	636	2290	3152	74	210	320	604

Figure 4. Composition of sample respondents

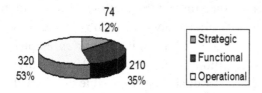

summative scaling is important to support (Carmines and Zeller,1994). While Cronbach Alpha determines the reliability, other methods are used to understand the multi-dimensionality of items thus grouped to predict a phenomenon, which Cronbach Alpha does not display. Choosing between "exploratory Factor Analysis (FA)" and "Principal Component Analysis (PCA)" is a tricky job since these two provide inherent limitations and advantages as well. It is often argued to use FA for identification of latent influencers (as is in this case) and PCA for weighted linear combinations (Fabrigar et al.,1999). Some advocate that FA is little

complicated and conservative in comparison to PCA. Besides, some feel that solutions generated from PCA differ little from those derived from FA and this difference deceases with number of influencers (Rietveld & Van Hout, 1993; Field, 2000). Considering these aspects PCA has been used for analysis in this case.

VALIDATION OF TIER-II INFLUENCERS

These influencers rely on the first Tier influencers for its prediction and its relationships are described through proposed hypotheses. In most cases the sampling is "stratified", and sampling size is "unequal". These groups as discussed earlier are "strategic", "tactical/functional", and "operational". Validation of these influencers is therefore, done through methods as noted below:

1. **Dummy Coding:** Since there are three distinct groups having distinct responsi-

Figure 5. Stratified sample respondents

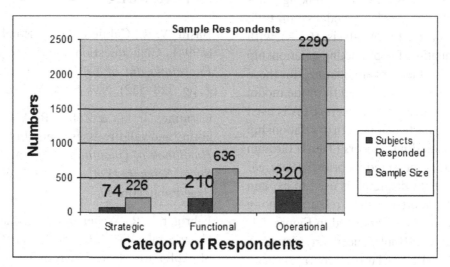

bility and role in the acquisition process, these become independent of each other. However, collectively these groups need to predict the success of the phenomenon as designed in the model. For instance U1, U2, U3 represent strategic, tactical and operational subject groups who respond to the user preparedness in their respective groups. However, these groups predict user preparedness U in Tier-II. This prediction is done through regression and categorical influencers (Pedhazur, 1997). Categorical influencers need coding and while there are three coding methods to do the task, "Dummy Coding" is adopted here. The other two coding methods i.e. "Effect Coding" and "Orthogonal Coding" provide the same result and therefore, it is not of importance to choose among. It is to be noted here that though dummy coding needs a control group to compare the behaviour of the comparison groups in this case no group is considered to be a control group. This is justified since we are expecting all the users to collectively contribute to the success of the acquisition process.

2. **Hypothesis:** Hypotheses present a positive relationship between the Tier-I and Tier-II influencers. Multiple regression analysis methods are used for validation of the hypotheses formulated (Pedhazur, 1997).

VALIDATION OF TIER-III INFLUENCERS

Tier-III influencers are dependent influencers which are predicted by latent influencers detailed in Tier-II hypothesized through items in Tier-I. Structural Equation Modeling (SEM) method which uses "path analysis" and is quite similar to regression analysis has been adopted to validate these latent influencers. "Prediction" and "Explanations" are two central issues since the model tries to predict "the success" of IT acquired in the organization as well "the preparedness" of the organization though not in any order / sequence. Explanation is powerful means for predictions and use of regression analysis is of relevance (Pedhazur, 1997). Predictive features are well discoursed through the "causal analysis" and SEM provides the scope just to do that. Since multiple regressions are used for causal analysis, causal thinking plays a central role for SEM. "Goodness of Fit"; "Confirmatory Factor Analysis (CFA)"with structural equation for predicting relationship among latent influencers are obtained for these Tier-III influencers and overall fit of the model is assessed in subsequent chapters. CFA is used here to capture particular pattern of relationship between measured influencers (Tier-I) through common factors measured "a priori" (Fabrigar et al.,1999). "Path diagram" is used to explain hypothesized pattern of causal relations among a set of influencers as explained in Figure-4.1. In this model Tier-II influencers are termed as "exogenous" and Tier-III influencers are termed as "endogenous influencers". This model assumes that relationships among influencers are linear, additive and causal, and thus use of SEM methodology is considered appropriate (Pedhazur, 1997).

CONCLUSION

In this chapter, the process of validating variables is presented. It is noted that binding organizational issues to the IT acquisition process needs careful considerations involving all stratified layers in the organization as discussed in chapters one and two. Besides, it is also important to note that overall validations need convergence among all variables despite having different measurement criteria. This multi-Tier validation process is discussed in subsequent three chapters before examining overall fitness of the developed model.

REFERENCES

Basili, V. R., Caldiera, G., & Rombach, H. D. (1994). Goal question metrics paradigm. In *Encyclopaedia of Software Engineering* (*Vol. 1*, pp. 528–532). New York: Wiley.

Carmines, E. G., & Zeller, R. A. (1994). Reliability and validity assessment. In *International Handbook of Quantitative Applications in the Social Sciences* (*Vol. 4*, pp. 154–160). London: Sage Publications.

Fabrigar, L. R., Wegener, D. T., MacCallum, R. C., & Strahan, E. J. (1999). Evaluating the use of exploratory factor analysis in psychological research. *Psychological Methods*, *3*, 272–299. doi:10.1037/1082-989X.4.3.272.

Field, A. (2000). *Discovering statistics using SPSS for windows*. Thousand Oaks, CA: Sage Publications.

Kanter, J. (2000). *Managing with information* (4th ed.). New Delhi: Prentice Hall.

Mcliver, J. P., & Carmines, E. G. (1994). Unidimensional scaling. In *International Handbook of Quantitative Applications in the Social Sciences* (*Vol. 4*, pp. 154–160). London: Sage Publications.

Minieak, E., & Kurzeja, Z. D. (2001). *Statistics for business with computer applications*. Cincinnati, OH: Thomson Learning.

Mintzberg, H., Ahlstrand, B., & Lampel, J. (1988). *Startegy safri*. New York: The Free Press.

Nonaka, I. (1988). Toward middle-up-down management: Accelerating information creation. *Sloan Management Review*, *29*(3), 9–18.

Nunnally, J. C. (1978). *Psychometric theory*. New York: McGraw-Hill.

Pearce, J. A., & Robinson, R. B. (1996). *Strategic management: Formulation, implementation and control*. Burr Ridge, IL: Irwin.

Pedhazur, E. J. (1997). *Multiple regression in behavioral research* (3rd ed.). New York: Harcourt Brace College Publishers.

Rietveld, T., & Van Hout, R. (1993). *Statistical techniques for the study of language and language behaviour*. Berlin: Mouton de Gruyter. doi:10.1515/9783110871609.

Spector, P. E. (1988). Development of the work locus of control scale. *Journal of Operational Psychology, 61*, 335–340.

Chapter 8
Validation of Model:
The Process for Tier-I Variables

ABSTRACT

Tier-I influencers form the baseline for the modeling process. These influencers aim to capture and measure collective orientation of organizational preparedness for IT acquisitions. This approach includes all the management principles (one of the two frontiers of the model, i.e., management science and computing science). Tier-I influencers include stakeholders in operational, tactical, and strategic layers in the organization as important influencers of the acquisition process, and the proposed model captures their contributions. The model considers it important to capture perceived benefits of IT acquisitions, climate in the organization for taking collective decisions in planning and policy driven issues, capabilities in managing IT projects and IT vendors, motivation of users in the organizational hierarchy, user contributions in reflecting organizational deliverables in IT enabled processes, and mapping expected contributors of successful IT acquisitions. In this chapter, quantitative methods are used for measuring and validating collective contributions of all the stakeholders.

RELIABILITY TEST OF TIER-I VARIABLES

As explained earlier the model argues in favour of having overall and proactive engagement of all stakeholders in the acquisition process. In pre-acquisition phase of the acquisition process, the model expects involvement of employees of the acquiring organization across all the three layers (Strategic, Tactical, and Operational) to coordinate, collaborate and arrive at a common point of agenda in terms of establishing better ambience for IT acquisitions, display and pursue standards in managing internal processes and formulating overall strategy for accepting a new scenario that is likely to emerge during and post-acquisition phases (Nonaka, 1988; Pearce & Robinson, 1996). It is however, important to note that organizations being generally hierarchical in nature, the scales used for measurements need to

DOI: 10.4018/978-1-4666-4201-0.ch008

be carefully chosen because of overall goals that employees ion different layers pursue (Kanter, 2000; Basili et al., 1994; Mintzberg & Lampel, 1988). Despite these inequalities in goals and aspirations, organizational priorities need to be given the priority through appropriate methods and thus various scales need to be use to assess the scope for improvement and establish overall preparedness in the organization to bring positive changes in the climate, instill motivations among all employees and prepare them for IT acquisitions. This process needs use of carefully chosen measurement tools for assessment of reliabilities of the results obtained since stratifies samples (in this model all the samples are employees at various levels) are expected to holistically contribute to the organization's overall pre-acquisition preparedness (Nunnally, 1978; Pedhazur, 1997; Rietveld & Van Hout, 1993; Spector, 1988; Carmines et al., 1999; Field, 2000; Mcliver & Carmines, 1994; Minieak, et al, 2001). In this chapter various tools and methods are used to assess the reliabilities data captured through the sampling process discussed earlier.

Table 1 provides the details of reliability-test of the variables done through "Cronbach alpha" and SPSS-10.1 has been used for the purpose.

It may be noted that Cronbach alpha coefficient (α) for the variables that provides for internal consistency, lies between 0.65 and 0.89. It is noted that alpha of around 0.7 could be taken as an acceptable figure for further Validation. In only two cases reliability has been found to be below 0.7, but is close to it. Other validation tests are conducted for tier-I variables progressively in this chapter.

VALIDATION OF PREDICTORS

Since correlation matrices are important for understanding multi-dimensionality (even if Cronbach alpha shows high reliability), these are made available for Validation as below.

Strategic User Preparedness (U1)

Table 2 records "Pearson correlation coefficient" uniformly and approximately in the same range for all the variables. This recommends that all the variables do not display multi-dimensionality.

Question U102 has the lowest communality, least corrected question-total correlation and is the weakest question. It is verifiable through alpha-if-question-deleted value which shows highest reliability of 0.8669. This is followed by the scree-plot as shown in Figure 1 and eignvalues in Table 3. It is noted to have single factor for these questions (63.315 percent). However, since Cronbach alpha does not improve much by deleting U102, and there is no multi-dimensionality; all the questions were retained for the purpose.

As regards sampling plan, Kaiser-Meyer-Olkin (KMO) and Bartlett's test measures were used to confirm question validity for U1. Since value of KMO is 0.860 (expected value to be > 0.5) and Bartlett's test of specificity is significant (i.e. associated probability should be <0.05), U1 is found to be in conformity with requirements.

Tactical User Preparedness (U2)

Table 4 records "Pearson correlation coefficient" uniformly and approximately in the same range for all the variables. This recommends that all the variables do not display multi-dimensionality and are in conformity with reliability Validation.

Reliability of U2 variable is of 0.83. Question U202 displays the least communality followed by question U206 vide Table 5. Varimax method of rotation showed that there is one component (vide Table 6) and the eigenvalues along with scree plot (Figure 2) supported this finding. Corrected-Question-Total correlation values indicated U206 having the least followed by U205 and U204. Since there was no improvement in reliability by factoring and supported by alpha-if-question-deleted, none of the questions were extracted. This is supported by Pearson's correlation analysis

Table 1. Reliability of questions of the questions administered

Sl. No.	Variable Identification	Variable Description	Number of Questions	Sample Size	Cronbach Alpha
1	U1	Strategic User Preparedness	6	74	0.87
2	U2	Tactical User Preparedness	6	210	0.83
3	U3	Operational User Preparedness	5	320	0.72
4	I1	IS Strategy	6	74	0.88
5	I2	Interface Strategy	4	210	0.79
6	I3	Transaction Strategy	4	320	0.77
7	T1	IT Strategy	7	74	0.89
8	T2	Component Strategy	8	210	0.86
9	T3	Interface Strategy	6	320	0.86
10	C1 (Strategic) C1 (Tactical) C1 (Operational)	User perception on Organisation	7	604	0.71
11	C2 (Strategic) C2 (Tactical) C2 (Operational)	User Perception on IT	8	604	0.69
12	C3 (Strategic) C3 (Tactical) C3 (Operational)	Decision Making Style	7	604	0.78
13	PP (Strategic) PP (Tactical) PP (Operational)	Planning and Policy	5	604	0.65
14	PM (Strategic) PM (Tactical) PM (Operational)	Project Management	6	604	0.82

continued on following page

Table 1. Continued

Sl. No.	Variable Identification	Variable Description	Number of Questions	Sample Size	Cronbach Alpha
15	UM (Strategic)	User Motivation	5	604	0.75
	UM (Tactical)				
	UM (Operational)				
16	VC (Strategic)	Vendor Management	6	604	0.75
	VC (Tactical)				
	VC (Operational)				
17	AT (Strategic)	IT Acquisition	6	604	0.71
	AT (Tactical)				
	AT (Operational)				
18	LL (Strategic)	Life Cycle	7	604	0.81
	LL (Tactical)				
	LL (Operational)				
19	SA (Strategic)	Acquisition Success	6	604	0.82
	SA (Tactical)				
	SA (Operational)				
20	US (Strategic)	User Satisfaction	9	604	0.71
	US (Tactical)				
	US (Operational)				
21	AL (Strategic)	Alignment	7	604	0.82
	AL (Tactical)				
	AL (Operational)				

Table 2. Correlations for strategic user preparedness (U1)

QUESTION		U101	U102	U103	U104	U105	U106
U101	Pearson Correlation	1	.559**	.599**	.604**	.614**	.615**
	Sig. (2-tailed)	.	.000	.000	.000	.000	.000
U102	Pearson Correlation	.559**	1	.495**	.424**	.409**	.431**
	Sig. (2-tailed)	.000	.	.000	.003	.001	.000
U103	Pearson Correlation	.599**	.495**	1	.510**	.441**	.471**
	Sig. (2-tailed)	.000	.000	.	.000	.000	.001
U104	Pearson Correlation	.604**	.424**	.510**	1	.627**	.500**
	Sig. (2-tailed)	.000	.003	.000	.	.000	.000
U105	Pearson Correlation	.614**	.409**	.441**	.627**	1	.681**
	Sig. (2-tailed)	.000	.001	.000	.000	.	.000
	N	74	74	74	74	74**	74
U106	Pearson Correlation	.615**	.431**	.471**	.500**	.681	1
	Sig. (2-tailed)	.000	.000	.001	.000	.000	.

** Correlation is significant at the 0.01 level (2-tailed).
N=74

Table 3. Reliability of questions (predictors) for strategic user preparedness (U1)

Question	Communality (Extraction)	Eigenvalue % Variance	Corrected Question-Total Correlation	Alpha if Question Deleted	Alpha	Sampling Adequacy (KMO and Bartlett's Test)	
U101	.747	61.450	.7815	.8321	.8726	Kaiser-Meyer-Olkin Measure of Sampling Adequacy = 0. 860	
U102	.479	12.040	.5737	.8669		Bartlett's Test of Sphericity	Chi-Square =200.71
U103	.551	853	.6267	.8607			Df=15
U104	.627	7.844	.6850	.8492			Sig=0.00
U105	.656	5.346	.7041	.8456			
U106	.626	4.466	.6840	.8491			

Figure 1. Scree plot for strategic user preparedness (U1)

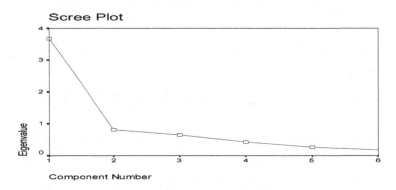

172

Table 4. Correlations for predictors for tactical user preparedness (U2)

QUESTION		U201	U202	U203	U204	U205	U206
U201	Pearson Correlation	1	.446**	.513**	.550**	.492**	.464**
	Sig. (2-tailed)	.	.000	.000	.000	.000	.000
U202	Pearson Correlation	.446**	1	.337**	.441**	.464**	.375**
	Sig. (2-tailed)	.000	.	.001	.000	.000	.000
U203	Pearson Correlation	.513**	.337**	1	.436**	.476*	.404**
	Sig. (2-tailed)	.000	.001	.	.000	.010	.037
U204	Pearson Correlation	.550**	.441**	.436**	1	.402**	.452**
	Sig. (2-tailed)	.000	.000	.000	.	.000	.000
U205	Pearson Correlation	.492**	.464**	.476*	.402**	1	.437**
	Sig. (2-tailed)	.000	.000	.010	.000	.	.000
U206	Pearson Correlation	.464**	.375**	.404**	.452**	.437**	1
	Sig. (2-tailed)	.000	.000	.037	.000	.000	.

** Correlation is significant at the 0.01 level (2-tailed).
N=210

shown in Table 4 and these variable do not display multi-dimensionality. As regards sampling plan, Kaiser-Meyer-Olkin (KMO) and Bartlett's test measures are examined for U2 and found to be in conformity with requirements; KMO being 0.865 (expected value to be > 0.5) and Bartlett's test of specificity being significant (i.e. associated probability should be <0.05).

Operational User Preparedness (U3)

Table 7 records "Pearson correlation coefficient" non-uniformly and except in one question U303, all the four variables approximately in the same range for all the variables. This recommends that all the variables do not display multi-dimensionality and are in conformity with reliability Validation.

In the case of U3 variable, the questions displayed a single factor with reliability is of 0.72. Though question U302 displays the least communality vide Table 8, communality of other questions are in proximity. Varimax method of rotation showed that there is one component (vide Table 9)

and the eigenvalues (461%) along with scree plot (Figure 5.3) supported this finding. Corrected-Question-Total correlation values indicated U302 having the least followed by U305 and U304. Since there was no improvement in reliability, there was a single factor and supported by alpha-if-question-deleted, and display of uni-dimensionality; none of the questions was extracted.

As regards sampling plan, Kaiser-Meyer-Olkin (KMO) and Bartlett's test measures are examined for U3 and found to be in conformity with requirements; KMO being 0.744 (expected value to be > 0.5) and Bartlett's test of specificity being significant (i.e. associated probability should be <0.05).

Information Systems Preparedness (I1)

Table 10 records "Pearson correlation coefficient" uniformly and approximately in the same range for all the variables. This recommends that all

Table 5. Reliability of questions (predictors) for tactical user preparedness (U2)

Question	Communality (Extraction)	Eigenvalue % Variance	Corrected Question-Total Correlation	Alpha if Question Deleted	Alpha	Sampling Adequacy (KMO and Bartlett's Test)	
U201	.634	53.295	.6725	.7848	.8285	Kaiser-Meyer-Olkin Measure of Sampling Adequacy = 0. 865	
U202	.473	11.202	.5455	.8117		Bartlett's Test of Sphericity	Chi-Square =385
U203	.516	10.395	.3571	.8053			Df=15
U204	.560	9.814	.3970	.7977			Sig=0.00
U205	.553	7.596	.3870	.7984			
U206	.500	7.069	.3260	.8072			

N=210

Figure 2. Scree plot for tactical user preparedness (U2)

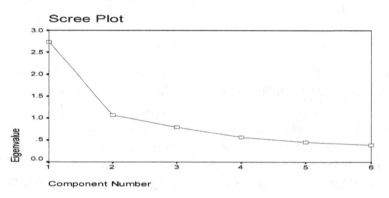

Table 6. Component matrix ^{a} for U2

QUESTION	Component
U201	.796
U202	.688
U203	.718
U204	.748
U205	.743
U206	.707

- **Extraction Method:** Principal Component Analysis:
- **Rotated Component Matrix:** Extraction Method: Principal Component Analysis.
- **Rotation Method:** Varimax with Kaiser Normalization. Rotation converged in 3 iterations. Could not be rotated.

the variables do not display multi-dimensionality and are in conformity with reliability Validation.

In the case of I1 variable, the questions displayed a single factor with reliability is of 0.883. Though question I103 displays the least communality vide Table 11, communality of other questions are in proximity. Varimax method of rotation showed that there is one component (vide Table 12) and the eigenvalues (55.79%) along with scree plot (Figure 4) supported this finding. Corrected-Question-Total correlation values indicated I103 having the least. Since there was a single factor and supported by alpha-if-question-deleted had not shown

Table 7. Correlations for operational user preparedness (U3)

QUESTION		U301	U302	U303	U304	U305
U301	Pearson Correlation	1	.284**	.525**	.353**	.231**
	Sig. (2-tailed)	.	.000	.000	.000	.000
U302	Pearson Correlation	.284**	1	.287**	.320**	.283**
	Sig. (2-tailed)	.000	.	.000	.000	.000
U303	Pearson Correlation	.525**	.287**	1	.349**	.338**
	Sig. (2-tailed)	.000	.000	.	.000	.000
U304	Pearson Correlation	.353**	.320**	.349**	1	.369**
	Sig. (2-tailed)	.000	.000	.000	.	.000
U305	Pearson Correlation	.231**	.283**	.338**	.369**	1
	Sig. (2-tailed)	.000	.000	.000	.000	.

** Correlation is significant at the 0.01 level (2-tailed).
N=320

Table 8. Reliability of questions (predictors) for operational user preparedness (U3)

Question	Communality (Extraction)	Eigenvalue % Variance	Corrected Question-Total Correlation	Alpha if Question Deleted	Alpha	Sampling Adequacy (KMO and Bartlett's Test)	
U301	.512	46.894	.5060	.6549	0.716	Kaiser-Meyer-Olkin Measure of Sampling Adequacy = 0.744	
U302	.375	16.865	.4044	.6944		Bartlett's Test of Sphericity	Chi-Square =281
U303	.565	14.613	.5494	.6350			Df=10
U304	.493	12.549	.4914	.6613			Sig=0.000
U305	.401	9.078	.4212	.6880			

N=320

Figure 3. Scree plot for operational user preparedness (U3)

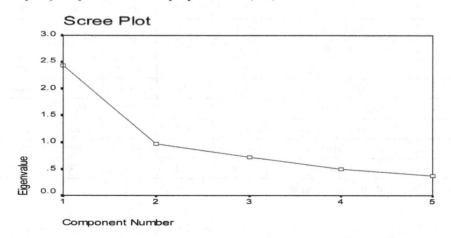

175

Table 9. Component matrix ª for U3

QUESTION	Component	
	1	**2**
U301	.716	-
U302	.612	-
U303	.751	-
U304	.702	-
U305	.633	-

- **Extraction Method:** Principal Component Analysis: 1 component extracted.
- **Rotated Component Matrix:** Extraction Method: Principal Component Analysis. Rotation Method: Varimax with Kaiser Normalization. Solution could not be rotated.

a comparable increase by deleting, besides having uni-dimensionality through Pearson correlation (Table 10) no question was extracted for the purpose.

As regards sampling plan, Kaiser-Meyer-Olkin (KMO) and Bartlett's test measures are examined for I1 and found to be in conformity with requirements; KMO being 0.852 (expected value to be > 0.5) and Bartlett's test of specific-

ity being significant (i.e. associated probability should be <0.05).

System Interface Strategy (I2)

Table 13 above records "Pearson correlation coefficient" uniformly and approximately in the same range for all the variables. This recommends that all the variables do not display multi-dimensionality and are in conformity with reliability Validation.

In the case of I2 variable, the questions displayed a single factor with reliability is of 0.79. Though question I202 displays the least communality vide Table 14, communality of other questions are mostly in proximity. Varimax method of rotation showed that there is one component and the eigenvalues (61.39%) along with scree plot (Figure 5) supported this finding. Corrected-Question-Total correlation values indicated I202 having the least. Since there was a single factor; there is no multi-dimensionality and alpha-if-question-deleted did not show any com-

Table 10. Correlations for information systems preparedness I1

QUESTION		I101	I102	I103	I104	I105	I106
I101	Pearson Correlation	1	.410**	.471**	.593**	.682**	.495**
	Sig. (2-tailed)	.	.000	.000	.000	.000	.000
I102	Pearson Correlation	.410**	1	.408**	.603**	.572**	.602**
	Sig. (2-tailed)	.000	.	.000	.000	.000	.000
I103	Pearson Correlation	.471**	.408**	1	.571**	.602**	.481**
	Sig. (2-tailed)	.000	.000	.	.000	.000	.000
I104	Pearson Correlation	.593**	.603**	.571**	1	.609**	.660**
	Sig. (2-tailed)	.000	.000	.000	.	.000	.000
I105	Pearson Correlation	.682**	.572**	.602**	.609**	1	.570**
	Sig. (2-tailed)	.000	.000	.000	.000	.	.000
I106	Pearson Correlation	.495**	.602**	.481**	.660**	.570**	1
	Sig. (2-tailed)	.000	.000	.000	.000	.000	.

** Correlation is significant at the 0.01 level (2-tailed).
N=74

Table 11. Reliability of questions (predictors) for information systems preparedness (I1)

Question	Communality (Extraction)	Eigenvalue % Variance	Corrected Question-Total Correlation	Alpha if Question Deleted	Alpha	Sampling Adequacy (KMO and Bartlett's Test)	
I101	.588	63.131	.6614	.8676	0.883	Kaiser-Meyer-Olkin Measure of Sampling Adequacy = 0.852	
I102	.566	11.310	.6046	.8706		Bartlett's Test of Sphericity	Chi-Square =215
I103	.542	949	.6250	.8729			Df=15
I104	.726	7.041	.7661	.8495			Sig=0.000
I105	.724	5.596	.7687	.8491			
I106	.642	3.973	.7013	.8614			

N=74

Figure 4. Scree plot for information system preparedness (I1)

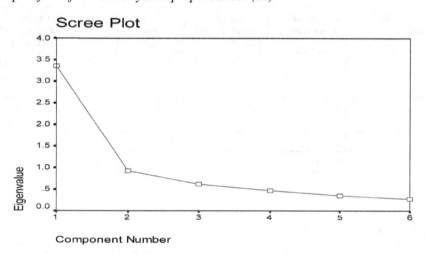

Table 12. Component matrix ^{a} for I1

QUESTION	Component	
	1	2
I101	.767	-
I102	.752	-
I103	.736	-
I104	.852	-
I105	.851	-
I106	.801	-

- **Extraction Method:** Principal Component Analysis: 1 component extracted.
- **Rotated Component Matrix:** Extraction Method: Principal Component Analysis.
- **Rotation Method:** Varimax with Kaiser Normalization. Solution could not be rotated.

parable increase in reliability, no question was extracted for the purpose.

As regards sampling plan, Kaiser-Meyer-Olkin (KMO) and Bartlett's test measures are examined for I2 and found to be in conformity with requirements; KMO being 0.750 (expected value to be > 0.5) and Bartlett's test of specificity being significant (i.e. associated probability should be <0.05).

Transaction Preparedness (I3)

Table 16 records "Pearson correlation coefficient" uniformly and approximately in the same range

Table 13. Correlations for system interface strategy (I2)

QUESTION		I201	I202	I203	I204
I201	Pearson Correlation	1	.407**	.583**	.537**
	Sig. (2-tailed)	.	.000	.000	.000
I202	Pearson Correlation	.407**	1	.389**	.536**
	Sig. (2-tailed)	.000	.	.002	.000
I203	Pearson Correlation	.583**	.389**	1	.452**
	Sig. (2-tailed)	.000	.000	.	.000
I204	Pearson Correlation	.537**	.536**	.452**	1
	Sig. (2-tailed)	.000	.000	.000	.

** Correlation is significant at the 0.01 level (2-tailed).
N=210

Table 14. Reliability of questions (predictors) for system interface strategy (I2)

Question	Communality (Extraction)	Eigenvalue % Variance	Corrected Question-Total Correlation	Alpha if Question Deleted	Alpha	Sampling Adequacy (KMO and Bartlett's Test)	
I201	.663	61.391	.6380	.7166	.790	Kaiser-Meyer-Olkin Measure of Sampling Adequacy = 0.750	
I202	.537	17.219	.5352	.7681		Bartlett's Test of Sphericity	Chi-Square =244.68
I203	.598	11.780	.5852	.7440			Df=6
I204	.657	9.610	.6348	.7195			Sig=0.000

N=210

Table 15. Component matrix ^{a} for I2

QUESTION	Component	
	1	2
I201	.814	-
I202	.733	-
I203	.774	-
I204	.811	-

- **Extraction Method:** Principal Component Analysis: 1 component extracted.
- **Rotated Component Matrix:** Extraction Method: Principal Component Analysis.
- **Rotation Method:** Varimax with Kaiser Normalization. Solution could not be rotated.

Figure 5. Scree plot for system interface strategies (I2)

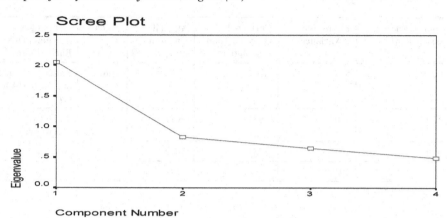

Table 16. Correlations for transaction preparedness (I3)

QUESTION		I301	I302	I303	I304
I301	Pearson Correlation	1	.371**	.557**	.512**
	Sig. (2-tailed)	.	.000	.000	.000
I302	Pearson Correlation	.371**	1	.321**	.455**
	Sig. (2-tailed)	.000	.	.000	.000
I303	Pearson Correlation	.557**	.321**	1	.475**
	Sig. (2-tailed)	.000	.000	.	.000
I304	Pearson Correlation	.512**	.455**	.475**	1
	Sig. (2-tailed)	.000	.000	.000	.

** Correlation is significant at the 0.01 level (2-tailed).
N=320

for all the variables. This recommends that all the variables do not display multi-dimensionality and are in conformity with reliability Validation.

In the case of I3 variable, the questions displayed a single factor with reliability is of 0.766. Though question I303 displays the least communality vide Table 17, communality of other questions are mostly in proximity. Varimax method of rotation showed that there is one component (vide Table 18) and the eigenvalues (586%) along with scree plot (Figure 6) supported this finding. Corrected-Question-Total correlation values indicated I303 having the least. Since there was a single factor, variables do not display multi-dimensionality and alpha-if-question-deleted did not show a comparable increase in reliability, no question was extracted for the purpose.

As regards sampling plan, Kaiser-Meyer-Olkin (KMO) and Bartlett's test measures are examined for I3 and found to be in conformity with requirements; KMO being 0.753 (expected value to be > 0.5) and Bartlett's test of specificity being significant (i.e. associated probability should be <0.05).

Table 17. Reliability of questions (predictors) for transaction preparedness (I3)

Question	Communality (Extraction)	Eigenvalue % Variance	Corrected Question-Total Correlation	Alpha if Question Deleted	Alpha	Sampling Adequacy (KMO and Bartlett's Test)	
I301	.652	5866	.6163	.6822	.766	Kaiser-Meyer-Olkin Measure of Sampling Adequacy = 0.753	
I302	.456	1107	.4635	.7611		Bartlett's Test of Sphericity	Chi-Square = 323
I303	.600	12.093	.5733	.7062			Df=6
I304	.647	10.935	.6151	.6845			Sig=0.000

N=320

Table 18. Component matrix ᵃ for I3

QUESTION	Component	
	1	2
I301	.808	-
I302	.675	-
I303	.774	-
I304	.804	-

- **Extraction Method:** Principal Component Analysis: 1 component extracted.
- **Rotated Component Matrix:** Extraction Method: Principal Component Analysis.
- **Rotation Method:** Varimax with Kaiser Normalization. Could not be rotated.

IT Strategy (T1)

Table 19 records "Pearson correlation coefficient" uniformly and approximately in the same range for all the variables. This recommends that all the variables do not display multi-dimensionality and are in conformity with reliability Validation.

In the case of T1 variable, the questions displayed two factor with reliability is of 0.895. Though question T103 displayed the least communality Table 20, communality of other questions are mostly in proximity. Varimax method of rotation

Figure 6. Scree plot for transaction preparedness (I3)

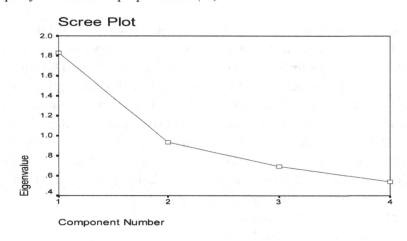

Table 19. Correlations for IT strategy (T1)

QUESTION		T101	T102	T103	T104	T105	T106	T107
T101	Pearson Correlation	1	.521**	.570**	.533**	.673**	.573*	.610*
	Sig. (2-tailed)	.	.000	.000	.000	.000	.000	.000
T102	Pearson Correlation	.521**	1	.456**	.541**	.532**	.615**	.523
	Sig. (2-tailed)	.000	.	.000	.000	.000	.000	.000
T103	Pearson Correlation	.570**	.456**	1	.411**	.567**	.568**	465**
	Sig. (2-tailed)	.000	.000	.	.000	.000	.000	.000
T104	Pearson Correlation	.533**	.541**	.411**	1	.449**	.720**	.547**
	Sig. (2-tailed)	.000	.000	.000	.	.000	.000	.000
T105	Pearson Correlation	.673**	.532**	.567**	.449**	1	.560**	.565**
	Sig. (2-tailed)	.000	.000	.000	.000	.	.000	.000
T106	Pearson Correlation	.573**	.615**	.568**	.720**	.560**	1	.510**
	Sig. (2-tailed)	.000	.000	.000	.000	.000	.	.000
T107	Pearson Correlation	.610**	.523**	.465**	.547**	.565**	.510**	1
	Sig. (2-tailed)	.000	.000	.000	.000	.000	.000	.

** Correlation is significant at the 0.01 level (2-tailed).
N=74

Table 20. Reliability of questions (predictors) for IT strategy (T1)

Question	Communality (Extraction)	Eigenvalue % Variance	Corrected Question-Total Correlation	Alpha if Question Deleted	Alpha	Sampling Adequacy (KMO and Bartlett's Test)	
T101	.674	61.36	.741	.874	0.895	Kaiser-Meyer-Olkin Measure of Sampling Adequacy = 0.881	
T102	.581	1.25	.671	.882		Bartlett's Test of Sphericity	Chi-Square = 260
T103	.536	7.97	.635	.886			Df=21
T104	.589	6.85	.676	.882			Sig=0.000
T105	.632	5.78	.708	.878			
T106	.694	4.51	.755	.872			
T107	.591	3.28	.677	.882			

N=74

showed that there are two components (Table 21) and the eigenvalues (61.36%) along with scree plot (Figure 7) supported this finding. Corrected-Question-Total correlation values indicated T103 having the least. Since components could not be rotated, there is no multi-dimensionality and alpha-if-question-deleted did not show a comparable increase in reliability, no question was extracted. As regards sampling plan, Kaiser-Meyer-Olkin (KMO) and Bartlett's test measures are examined for T1 and found to be in conformity with requirements; KMO being 0.881 (expected value to be > 0.5) and Bartlett's test of specificity being significant (i.e. associated probability should be <0.05).

Table 21. Component matrix ª for T1

QUESTION	Component	
	1	2
T101	.821	-
T102	.762	-
T103	.732	-
T104	.767	-
T105	.795	-
T106	.833	-
T107	.769	-

- **Extraction Method:** Principal Component Analysis: One components extracted.
- **Rotated Component Matrix:** Extraction Method: Principal Component Analysis. Rotation Method: Varimax with Kaiser Normalization: could not be rotated.

Component Strategy (T2)

Table 22 records "Pearson correlation coefficient" uniformly and approximately in the same range for all the variables. This recommends that all the variables do not display multi-dimensionality and are in conformity with reliability Validation.

In the case of T2 variable, the questions displayed two factor with reliability is of 0.859. Though question T202 displayed the least communality Table 23, communality barring that of other questions are mostly in proximity. Varimax method of rotation showed that there are two components and the eigenvalues (50.46%) along with scree plot (Figure 8) supported this finding. Corrected-Question-Total correlation values indicated T202 having the least. Since there was a single factor which could not be rotated, there is no multi-dimensionality and alpha-if-question-deleted did not show a comparable increase in reliability, no question was extracted. As regards sampling plan, Kaiser-Meyer-Olkin (KMO) and Bartlett's test measures are examined for T2 and found to be in conformity with requirements; KMO being 0.893 (expected value to be > 0.5) and Bartlett's test of specificity being significant (i.e. associated probability should be <0.05).

Interface Strategy (T3)

Table 25 records "Pearson correlation coefficient" uniformly and approximately in the same range for all the variables. This recommends that all the variables do not display multi-dimensionality and are in conformity with reliability Validation.

In the case of T3 variable, the questions displayed two factor with reliability is of 0.864.

Figure 7. Scree plot for IT strategy (T1)

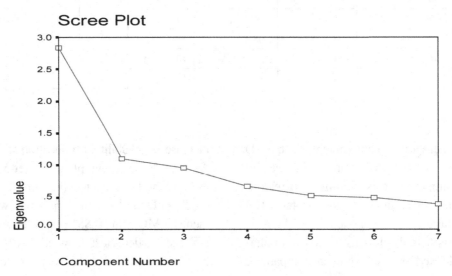

Table 22. Correlations for component strategy (T2)

		T201	T202	T203	T204	T205	T206	T207	T208
T201	Pearson Correlation	1	.373**	.597**	.420**	.461**	.485**	.404**	.449**
	Sig. (2-tailed)	.	.000	.000	.000	.000	.000	.000	.000
T202	Pearson Correlation	.373**	1	.342**	.383**	.449**	.363**	.496**	.371**
	Sig. (2-tailed)	.000	.	.000	.000	.000	.000	.000	.000
T203	Pearson Correlation	.597**	.342**	1	.390**	.426**	.536**	.451**	.501**
	Sig. (2-tailed)	.000	.000	.	.000	.000	.000	.000	.000
T204	Pearson Correlation	.420**	.383**	.390**	1	.469**	.429**	.465**	.386**
	Sig. (2-tailed)	.000	.000	.000	.	.000	.000	.000	.000
T205	Pearson Correlation	.461**	.449**	.426**	.469**	1	.379**	.426**	.445**
	Sig. (2-tailed)	.000	.000	.000	.000	.	.000	.000	.000
T206	Pearson Correlation	.485**	.363**	.536**	.429**	.379**	1	.370**	.468**
	Sig. (2-tailed)	.000	.000	.000	.000	.000	.	.000	.000
T207	Pearson Correlation	.404**	.496**	.451**	.465**	.426**	.370**	1	.390*
	Sig. (2-tailed)	.000	.000	.000	.000	.000	.000	.	.000
T208	Pearson Correlation	.449**	.371**	.501**	.386**	.445**	.468**	.390**	1
	Sig. (2-tailed)	.000	.000	.000	.000	.000	.000	.000	.

** Correlation is significant at the 0.01 level (2-tailed).

N=210

Table 23. Reliability of questions (predictors) for component strategy (T2)

Question	Communality (Extraction)	Eigenvalue % Variance	Corrected Question-Total Correlation	Alpha if Question Deleted	Alpha	Sampling Adequacy (KMO and Bartlett's Test)	
T201	.554	50.46	.6386	.838	0.859	Kaiser-Meyer-Olkin Measure of Sampling Adequacy = 0.893	
T202	..429	10.65	.548	.848		Bartlett's Test of Sphericity	Chi-Square = 576
T203	.570	7.72	.654	.837			Df=28
T204	.477	7.45	.585	.844			Sig=0.000
T205	.509	7.08	.609	.842			
T206	.506	6.61	.603	.842			
T207	.492	5.46	.595	.843			
T208	.500	4.55	.599	.843			

N=210

Table 24. Component matrix ^{a} for T2

QUESTION	Component	
	1	**2**
T201	.744	-
T202	.655	-
T203	.755	-
T204	.691	-
T205	.714	-
T206	.711	-
T207	.701	-
T208	.707	-

- **Extraction Method:** Principal Component Analysis: 1 component extracted.
- **Rotated Component Matrix:** Extraction Method: Principal Component Analysis.
- **Rotation Method:** Varimax with Kaiser Normalization. Could not be rotated.

Though question T305 displayed the least communality (Table 26), communality of other questions are mostly in proximity. Varimax method of rotation showed that there is one component (Table 27) and the eigenvalues (59.50%) along with scree plot (Figure 9) supported this finding. Corrected-Question-Total correlation values indicated T305 having the least. Since there is one

factor, there is no multi-dimensionality, and alpha-if-question-deleted did not show a comparable increase in reliability, no question was extracted. As regards sampling plan, Kaiser-Meyer-Olkin (KMO) and Bartlett's test measures are examined for T3 and found to be in conformity with requirements; KMO being 0.873 (expected value to be > 0.5) and Bartlett's test of specificity being significant (i.e. associated probability should be <0.05).

Perception on Organisation (C1)

Table 28 records "Pearson correlation coefficient" uniformly and approximately in the same range for all the variables. This recommends that all the variables do not display multi-dimensionality and are in conformity with reliability Validation.

In the case of C1 variable, the questions displayed single factor with reliability is of 0.706. These questions remain same for all the three layers of subjects (C1-strategic, C1-tactical, and C1-operational) and therefore, responses are analysed with a single variable. Though question C103 displayed the least communality (Table 29), communality of questions is mostly in proximity. Varimax method of rotation showed that there is

Figure 8. Scree plot for component strategy (T2)

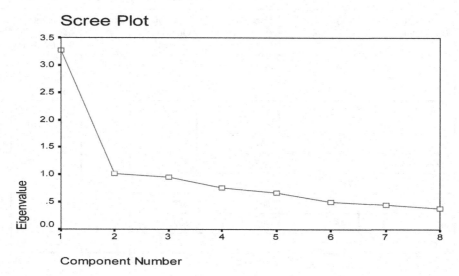

Table 25. Correlations for interface strategy (T3)

QUESTION		T301	T302	T303	T304	T305	T306
T301	Pearson Correlation	1	.482**	.593**	.541**	.521**	.510**
	Sig. (2-tailed)	.	.000	.000	.000	.000	.000
T302	Pearson Correlation	.482**	1	.407**	.621**	.475**	.541**
	Sig. (2-tailed)	.000	.	.000	.000	.000	.000
T303	Pearson Correlation	.593**	-.131*	1	.108	.167**	.173**
	Sig. (2-tailed)	.000	.000	.	.000	.000	.000
T304	Pearson Correlation	.541**	.621**	.453**	1	.487**	.575**
	Sig. (2-tailed)	.000	.000	.000	.	.000	.000
T305	Pearson Correlation	.521**	.475**	.544**	.487**	1	.461**
	Sig. (2-tailed)	.000	.000	.000	.000	.	.000
T306	Pearson Correlation	.510**	.541**	.494**	.575**	.461**	1
	Sig. (2-tailed)	.000	.000	.000	.000	.000	.

** Correlation is significant at the 0.01 level (2-tailed).
N=320

Table 26. Reliability of questions (predictors) for interface strategy (T3)

Question	Communality (Extraction)	Eigenvalue % Variance	Corrected Question-Total Correlation	Alpha if Question Deleted	Alpha	Sampling Adequacy (KMO and Bartlett's Test)	
T301	.624	59.50	.680	.836	0.864	Kaiser-Meyer-Olkin Measure of Sampling Adequacy = 0.873	
T302	.580	11.93	.645	.843		Bartlett's Test of Sphericity	Chi-Square = 786
T303	.565	53	.636	.844			Df=15
T304	.637	7.59	.689	.835			Sig=0.000
T305	.563	6.41	.632	.840			
T306	.600	6.05	.660	.840			

N=320

a single component (Table 30) and the eigenvalues (36.22%) along with scree plot (Figure 10) supported this finding. Since alpha-if-question-deleted did not show a comparable increase in reliability, there is no multi-dimensionality, no question was extracted.

As regards sampling plan, Kaiser-Meyer-Olkin (KMO) and Bartlett's test measures are examined for C1 and found to be in conformity with requirements; KMO being 0.804 (expected value to be > 0.5) and Bartlett's test of specificity being significant (i.e. associated probability should be <0.05).

Perception on IT (C2)

Table 31 records "Pearson correlation coefficient" uniformly and approximately in the same range for all the variables. This recommends that all

Table 27. Component matrix ª for T3

QUESTION	Component	
	1	**2**
T301	.790	-
T302	.762	-
T303	.752	-
T304	.798	-
T305	.750	-
T306	.775	-

- **Extraction Method:** Principal Component Analysis: 1 component extracted.
- **Rotated Component Matrix:** Extraction Method: Principal Component Analysis.
- **Rotation Method:** Varimax with Kaiser Normalization. Could not be rotated.

the variables do not display multi-dimensionality and are in conformity with reliability Validation.

In the case of C2 variable, the questions displayed single factor with reliability is of 0.724. These questions remain same for all the three layers of subjects (C2-strategic, C2-tactical, and C2-operational) and therefore, responses are analysed with a single variable. Though question C205 displayed the least communality (Table 32), communality of questions is mostly in proximity. Varimax method of rotation showed that there are two components (Table 33) and the eigenvalues (32.50% and 12.55%) along with scree plot (Figure 11) supported this finding. Corrected-Question-Total correlation values indicated C202 having the least, alpha-if-question-deleted having not shown a comparable increase in reliability, and there could be no pattern traceable from the extracted and rotated components, unrotated components were verified. Besides, there is no multi-dimensionality displayed by Pearson correlation coefficients and therefore, all the questions were retained for the purpose.

As regards sampling plan, Kaiser-Meyer-Olkin (KMO) and Bartlett's test measures are examined for C2 and found to be in conformity with requirements; KMO being 0.776 (expected value to be > 0.5) and Bartlett's test of specificity being significant (i.e. associated probability should be <0.05).

Decision Making Style (C3)

Table 34 records "Pearson correlation coefficient" uniformly and approximately in the same range for all the variables. This recommends that all the variables do not display multi-dimensionality and are in conformity with reliability validation.

Figure 9. Scree plot for interface strategy (T3)

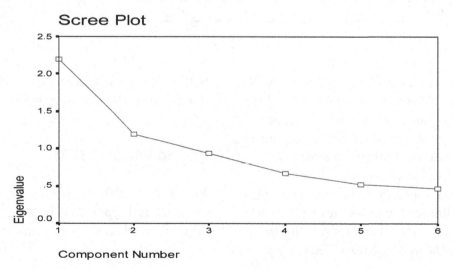

Table 28. Correlations for perception on organisation (C1)

QUESTION		C101	C102	C103	C104	C105	C106	C107
C101	Pearson Correlation	1	.245**	.285**	.266**	.264**	.217**	.200**
	Sig. (2-tailed)	.	.000	.000	.000	.000	.000	.000
C102	Pearson Correlation	.245**	1	.230**	.333**	.330**	.315**	.228**
	Sig. (2-tailed)	.000	.	.000	.000	.000	.000	.000
C103	Pearson Correlation	.285**	.230**	1	.268**	.222**	.236**	.236**
	Sig. (2-tailed)	.000	.000	.	.000	.000	.000	.000
C104	Pearson Correlation	.266**	.333**	.268**	1	.188**	.255**	.226**
	Sig. (2-tailed)	.000	.000	.000	.	.000	.000	.000
C105	Pearson Correlation	.264**	.330**	.222**	.188**	1	.225**	.295**
	Sig. (2-tailed)	.000	.000	.000	.000	.	.000	.000
C106	Pearson Correlation	.217**	.315**	.236**	.255**	.225**	1	.303**
	Sig. (2-tailed)	.000	.000	.000	.000	.000	.	.000
C107	Pearson Correlation	.200**	.228**	.236**	.226**	.295**	.303**	1
	Sig. (2-tailed)	.000	.000	.000	.000	.000	.000	.

** Correlation is significant at the 0.01 level (2-tailed). N=604

Table 29. Reliability of questions (predictors) for perception on organisation (C1)

Question	Communality (Extraction)	Eigenvalue % Variance	Corrected Question-Total Correlation	Alpha if Question Deleted	Alpha	Sampling Adequacy (KMO and Bartlett's Test)	
C101	.338	36.22	.396	.678	0.706	Kaiser-Meyer-Olkin Measure of Sampling Adequacy = 0.804	
C102	.424	12.47	.458	.661		Bartlett's Test of Sphericity	Chi Square = 540
C103	.337	11.76	.397	.677			Df=21
C104	.365	11.44	.418	.672			Sig=0.000
C105	.359	10.03	.413	.674			
C106	.370	9.88	.422	.671			
C107	.342	17	.399	.677			

N=604

In the case of C3 variable, the questions displayed single factor with reliability is of 0.777. These questions remain same for all the three layers of subjects (C3-strategic, C3-tactical, and C3-operational) and therefore, responses are analysed with a single variable. Though question C302 displayed the least communality (Table 35), communality of questions is mostly in proximity. Varimax method of rotation showed one component (Table 36) and the eigenvalues (43.15%) along with scree plot (Figure 12) supported this finding. Corrected-Question-Total correlation

Table 30. Component matrix ᵃ for C1

QUESTION	Component	
	1	**2**
C101	.582	-
C102	.651	-
C103	.580	-
C104	.604	-
C105	.599	-
C106	.608	-
C107	.585	-

- **Extraction Method:** Principal Component Analysis:1 component extracted.
- **Rotated Component Matrix:** Extraction Method: Principal Component Analysis.
- **Rotation Method:** Varimax with Kaiser Normalization. Could not be rotated.

values indicated C302 having the least, there being no multi-dimensionality and alpha-if-question-deleted having not shown a comparable increase in reliability, and there being only one component all the questions were retained for the purpose.

As regards sampling plan, Kaiser-Meyer-Olkin (KMO) and Bartlett's test measures are examined for C3 and found to be in conformity with requirements; KMO being 0.822 (expected value to be > 0.5) and Bartlett's test of specificity being significant (i.e. associated probability should be <0.05).

Planning and Policy (PP)

Table 37 records "Pearson correlation coefficient" uniformly and approximately in the same range for all the variables. This recommends that all the variables do not display multi-dimensionality and are in conformity with reliability Validation.

In the case of PP variable, the questions displayed single factor with reliability is of 0.649 which though moderately low, is acceptable. These questions remain same for all the three layers of subjects (PP-strategic, PP-tactical, and PP-operational) and therefore, responses are analysed with a single variable. Though question PP02 displayed the least communality (Table 38), communality of questions is mostly in proximity. Varimax method of rotation showed two components (Table 39) and the eigenvalues (42.06% and > 1) along with scree plot (Figure 13) supported this finding. Since there is no variation in Corrected-Question-Total correlation values (PP02 having indicated the least), alpha-if-question-deleted did not show a comparable increase in reliability for any of the questions, there being no multi-dimensionality and there being one components extracted and all the components could not be rotated, no question was deleted for the purpose.

As regards sampling plan, Kaiser-Meyer-Olkin (KMO) and Bartlett's test measures are examined

Figure 10. Scree plot for user perception of organization (C1)

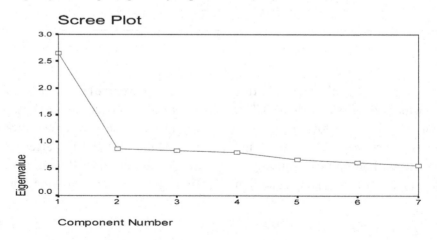

Table 31. Correlations for perception on IT (C2)

QUESTION		C201	C202	C203	C204	C205	C206	C207	C208
C201	Pearson Correlation	1	.233**	.275**	.235**	.229**	.214**	.119**	.163**
	Sig. (2-tailed)	.	.000	.000	.000	.000	.000	.003	.000
C202	Pearson Correlation	.233**	1	.100*	.257**	.207**	.166**	.145**	.195**
	Sig. (2-tailed)	.000	.	.014	.000	.000	.000	.000	.000
C203	Pearson Correlation	.275**	.100*	1	.236**	.258**	.246**	.149**	.252**
	Sig. (2-tailed)	.000	.014	.	.003	.000	.000	.000	.000
C204	Pearson Correlation	.235**	.257**	.236**	1	.197**	.296**	.210**	.229**
	Sig. (2-tailed)	.000	.000	.000	.	.000	.000	.000	.000
C205	Pearson Correlation	.229**	.207**	.258**	.197**	1	.194**	.257**	.220**
	Sig. (2-tailed)	.000	.000	.000	.000	.	.000	.000	.000
C206	Pearson Correlation	.214**	.166**	.246**	.296**	.194**	1	.188**	.393**
	Sig. (2-tailed)	.000	.000	.000	.000	.000	.	.000	.000
C207	Pearson Correlation	.119**	.145**	.149**	.210**	.257**	.188**	1	.341**
	Sig. (2-tailed)	.009	.000	.000	.000	.000	.000	.	.000
C208	Pearson Correlation	.163**	.195**	.252**	.229**	.220**	.393**	.341**	1
	Sig. (2-tailed)	.000	.000	.000	.000	.000	.000	.000	.

** Correlation is significant at the 0.01 level (2-tailed).

* Correlation is significant at the 0.05 level (2-tailed).

N=604

Table 32. Reliability of questions (predictors) for perception on IT (C2)

Question	Communality (Extraction)	Eigenvalue % Variance	Corrected Question-Total Correlation	Alpha if Question Deleted	Alpha	Sampling Adequacy (KMO and Bartlett's Test)	
C201	.586	32.05	.362	.670	0.694	Kaiser-Meyer-Olkin Measure of Sampling Adequacy = 0.776	
C202	.359	12.56	.318	.680		Bartlett's Test of Sphericity	Chi-Square = 581
C203	.337	11.49	.375	.667			Df=28
C204	.379	11.03	.414	.658			Sig=0.000
C205	.321	9.17	.387	.664			
C206	.422	76	.425	.656			
C207	.540	28	.345	.674			
C208	.625	6.67	.448	.650			

N=604

Table 33. Component matrix ᵃ for C2

QUESTION	Component		Component (Rotated)	
	1	**2**	**1**	**2**
C201	.533	.550	.765	-3.543E-02
C202	.481	.357	.595	6.968E-02
C203	.557	.164	.518	.262
C204	.595	.157	.542	.293
C205	.562	7.373E-02	.459	.332
C206	.618	-.200	.313	.569
C207	.525	-.514	3.012E-02	.734
C208	.641	-.462	.151	.776

- **Extraction Method:** Principal Component Analysis: 2 components extracted.
- **Rotated Component Matrix:** Extraction Method: Principal Component Analysis.
- **Rotation Method:** Varimax with Kaiser Normalization. Rotation converged after 3 iterations.

Figure 11. Scree plot for user perception of IT (C2)

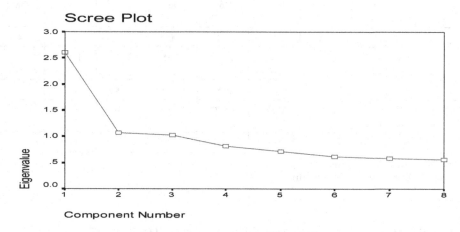

for PP and found to be in conformity with requirements; KMO being 0.751 (expected value to be > 0.5) and Bartlett's test of specificity being significant (i.e. associated probability should be <0.05).

Project Management Capability (PM)

Table 40 records "Pearson correlation coefficient" uniformly and approximately in the same range for all the variables. This recommends that all the variables do not display multi-dimensionality and are in conformity with reliability Validation.

In the case of PM variable, the questions displayed single factor with reliability is of 0.816 which is acceptable. These questions remain same for all the three layers of subjects (PM-strategic, PM-tactical, and PM-operational) and therefore, responses are analysed with a single variable. Though question PM06 displayed the least communality (Table 41), communality of questions is mostly in proximity. Varimax method of rotation showed one components (Table 42) and the eigenvalues (52.20% and > 1) along with scree plot (Figure 14) supported this finding. Though Corrected-Question-Total correlation values in-

Table 34. Correlations for decision making style (C3)

QUESTION		C301	C302	C303	C304	C305	C306	C307
C301	Pearson Correlation	1	.293**	.506**	.320**	.375**	.279**	.331**
	Sig. (2-tailed)	.	.000	.000	.000	.000	.000	.000
C302	Pearson Correlation	.293**	1	.180**	.409**	.354**	.307**	.248**
	Sig. (2-tailed)	.000	.	.000	.000	.000	.000	.000
C303	Pearson Correlation	.506**	.180**	1	.295**	.322**	.270**	.269**
	Sig. (2-tailed)	.000	.000	.	.000	.000	.000	.000
C304	Pearson Correlation	.320**	.409**	.295**	1	.406**	.378**	.295**
	Sig. (2-tailed)	.000	.000	.000	.	.000	.000	.000
C305	Pearson Correlation	.375**	.354**	.322**	.406**	1	.414**	.366**
	Sig. (2-tailed)	.000	.000	.000	.000	.	.000	.000
C306	Pearson Correlation	.279**	.307**	.270**	.378**	.414**	1	.422**
	Sig. (2-tailed)	.000	.000	.000	.000	.000	.	.000
C307	Pearson Correlation	.331**	.248**	.269**	.295**	.366**	.422**	1
	Sig. (2-tailed)	.000	.000	.000	.000	.000	.000	.

** Correlation is significant at the 0.01 level (2-tailed). N=604

Table 35. Reliability of questions (predictors) for decision making style (C3)

Question	Communality (Extraction)	Eigenvalue % Variance	Corrected Question-Total Correlation	Alpha if Question Deleted	Alpha	Sampling Adequacy (KMO and Bartlett's Test)	
C301	.459	43.15	.533	.744	0.777	Kaiser-Meyer-Olkin Measure of Sampling Adequacy = .822	
C302	.356	13.71	.442	.762		Bartlett's Test of Sphericity	Chi-Square = 926
C303	.373	11.60	.451	.760			Df=21
C304	.462	86	.530	.743			Sig=0.000
C305	.514	26	.565	.736			
C306	.453	7.79	.516	.746			
C307	.403	6.61	.477	.754			

N=604

Table 36. Component matrix ᵃ for C3

QUESTION	Component	
	1	2
C301	.677	-
C302	.596	-
C303	.611	-
C304	.680	-
C305	.717	-
C306	.673	-
C307	.635	-

- **Extraction Method:** Principal Component Analysis: 1 component extracted.
- **Rotated Component Matrix:** Extraction Method: Principal Component Analysis.
- **Rotation Method:** Varimax with Kaiser Normalization. Could not be rotated.

dicated PM02 having the least, alpha-if-question-deleted having not shown a comparable increase in reliability, there being no multi-dimensionality and there being one component all questions were retained for the purpose.

As regards sampling plan, Kaiser-Meyer-Olkin (KMO) and Bartlett's test measures are examined for PM and found to be in conformity with requirements; KMO being 0.867 (expected value to be > 0.5) and Bartlett's test of specificity being significant (i.e. associated probability should be <0.05).

Existence of User Motivation (UM)

Table 43 records "Pearson correlation coefficient" uniformly and approximately in the same range for all the variables. This recommends that all the variables do not display multi-dimensionality and are in conformity with reliability validation.

In the case of UM variable, the questions displayed single factor with reliability is of 0.749 which is acceptable. These questions remain same for all the three layers of subjects (UM-strategic, UM-tactical, and UM-operational) and therefore, responses are analysed with a single variable. Though question UM04 displayed the least communality (Table 44), communality of questions is mostly in proximity. Varimax method of rotation showed one components (Table 45) and the eigenvalues (50.13% and > 1) along with scree plot (Figure 15) supported this finding. Though Corrected-Question-Total correlation values indicated UM04 having the least, alpha-if-question-deleted having not shown a comparable increase in reliability, there being no multi-dimensionality and there being one component all questions were retained for the purpose.

As regards sampling plan, Kaiser-Meyer-Olkin (KMO) and Bartlett's test measures are examined for UM and found to be in conformity with requirements; KMO being 0.800 (expected value

Figure 12. Scree plot for user perception of decision making style (C3)

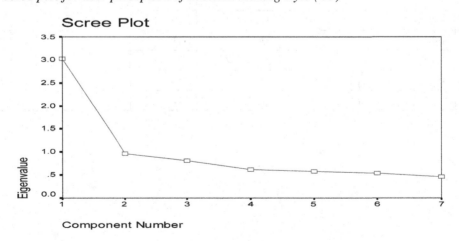

Table 37. Correlations for planning and policy (PP)

QUESTION		PP01	PP02	PP03	PP04	PP05
PP01	Pearson Correlation	1	.274**	.302**	.346**	.278**
	Sig. (2-tailed)	.	.000	.000	.000	.000
PP02	Pearson Correlation	.274**	1	.197**	.271**	.268**
	Sig. (2-tailed)	.000	.	.000	.000	.000
PP03	Pearson Correlation	.302**	.197**	1	.228**	.315**
	Sig. (2-tailed)	.000	.000	.	.000	.000
PP04	Pearson Correlation	.346**	.271**	.228**	1	.271**
	Sig. (2-tailed)	.000	.000	.000	.	.000
PP05	Pearson Correlation	.278**	.268**	.315**	.271**	1
	Sig. (2-tailed)	.000	.000	.000	.000	.

** Correlation is significant at the 0.01 level (2-tailed).
N=604

Table 38. Reliability of questions (predictors) for planning and policy (PP)

Question	Communality (Extraction)	Eigenvalue % Variance	Corrected Question-Total Correlation	Alpha if Question Deleted	Alpha	Sampling Adequacy (KMO and Bartlett's Test)	
PP01	.481	42.07	.448	.577	0.649	Kaiser-Meyer-Olkin Measure of Sampling Adequacy = 0.751	
PP02	.367	16.52	.369	.619		Bartlett's Test of Sphericity	Chi-Square = 341
PP03	.387	15.16	.378	.608			Df=10
PP04	.432	13.71	.412	.593			Sig=0.000
PP05	.436	12.52	.419	.589			

N=604

Table 39. Component matrix ^{a} for planning and policy (PP)

QUESTION	Component	
	1	2
PP01	.694	-
PP02	.606	-
PP03	.622	-
PP04	.657	-
PP05	.661	-

- **Extraction Method:** Principal Component Analysis. 1 component extracted.
- **Extraction Method:** Principal Component Analysis. Rotation Method: Varimax with Kaiser Normalization. Could not be rotated.

to be > 0.5) and Bartlett's test of specificity being significant (i.e. associated probability should be <0.05).

Capability for Vendor Control (VC)

Table 46 records "Pearson correlation coefficient" uniformly and approximately in the same range for all the variables. This recommends that all the variables do not display multi-dimensionality and are in conformity with reliability Validation.

In the case of VC variable, the questions displayed two factors with reliability is of 0.745 which is acceptable. These questions remain same

Figure 13. Scree plot for planning and policy (PP)

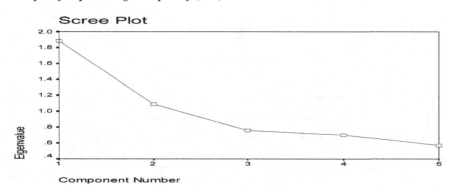

Table 40. Correlations for project management capability (PM)

QUESTION		PM01	PM02	PM03	PM04	PM05	PM06
PM01	Pearson Correlation	1	.423**	.528**	.439**	.445**	.383**
	Sig. (2-tailed)	.	.000	.000	.000	.000	.000
PM02	Pearson Correlation	.423**	1	.433**	.431**	.396**	.364**
	Sig. (2-tailed)	.000	.	.000	.000	.000	.000
PM03	Pearson Correlation	.528**	.433**	1	.393**	.496**	.419**
	Sig. (2-tailed)	.000	.000	.	.000	.000	.000
PM04	Pearson Correlation	.439**	.431**	.393**	1	.413**	.411**
	Sig. (2-tailed)	.000	.000	.000	.	.000	.000
PM05	Pearson Correlation	.445**	.396**	.496**	.413**	1	.411**
	Sig. (2-tailed)	.000	.000	.000	.000	.	.000
PM06	Pearson Correlation	.383**	.364**	.419**	.411**	.411**	1
	Sig. (2-tailed)	.000	.000	.000	.000	.000	.

** Correlation is significant at the 0.01 level (2-tailed).
N=604

for all the three layers of subjects (VC-strategic, VC-tactical, and VC-operational) and therefore, responses are analysed with a single variable. Though questions VC02 and VC05 displayed the least communality (Table 47), communality of questions is mostly in proximity. Varimax method of rotation showed one component (Table 48) and the eigenvalues (44%) along with scree plot (Figure 16) supported this finding. Since there was only one factor, alpha-if-question-deleted did not show a comparable increase in reliability through extraction, there being no multi-dimensionality and there being a single factor having no scope to rotate, all the variables were retained despite VC02 and VC05 showing least Corrected Question-Total Correlation.

Table 41. Reliability of questions (predictors) for project management capability (PM)

Question	Communality (Extraction)	Eigenvalue % Variance	Corrected Question-Total Correlation	Alpha if Question Deleted	Alpha	Sampling Adequacy (KMO and Bartlett's Test)	
PM01	.482	52.20	.606	.780	0.815	Kaiser-Meyer-Olkin Measure of Sampling Adequacy =0.831	
PM02	.392	10.97	.552	.792		Bartlett's Test of Sphericity	Chi-Square = 726
PM03	.445	10.77	.623	.776			Df=15
PM04	.430	9.45	.566	.788			Sig=0.000
PM05	.540	9.15	.588	.783			
PM06	.467	7.45	.534	.795			

N=604

Table 42. Component matrix ᵃ for PM

QUESTION	Component	
	1	2
PM01	.748	-
PM02	.699	
PM03	.762	-
PM04	.709	-
PM05	.732	-
PM06	.681	-

- **Extraction Method:** Principal Component Analysis. 1 component extracted.
- **Extraction Method:** Principal Component Analysis. Rotation Method. Varimax with Kaiser Normalization. Could not be rotated.

As regards sampling plan, Kaiser-Meyer-Olkin (KMO) and Bartlett's test measures are examined for VC and found to be in conformity with requirements; KMO being 0.829 (expected value to be > 0.5) and Bartlett's test of specificity being significant (i.e. associated probability should be <0.05).

Validation of Predictors for Capability of IT Cell (AT)

Table 49 records "Pearson correlation coefficient" uniformly and approximately in the same range for all the variables. This recommends that all

Figure 14. Scree plot for project management capability (PM)

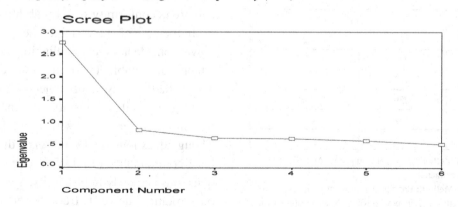

Table 43. Correlations for existence of user motivation (UM)

QUESTION		UM01	UM02	UM03	UM04	UM05
UM01	Pearson Correlation	1	.480**	.407**	.355**	.366**
	Sig. (2-tailed)	.	.000	.000	.000	.000
UM02	Pearson Correlation	.480**	1	.425**	.287**	.341**
	Sig. (2-tailed)	.000	.	.000	.000	.000
UM03	Pearson Correlation	.407**	.425**	1	.385**	.373**
	Sig. (2-tailed)	.000	.000	.	.000	.000
UM04	Pearson Correlation	.355**	.287**	.385**	1	.336**
	Sig. (2-tailed)	.000	.000	.000	.	.000
UM05	Pearson Correlation	.366**	.341**	.373**	.336**	1
	Sig. (2-tailed)	.000	.000	.000	.000	.

** Correlation is significant at the 0.01 level (2-tailed).
N=604

Table 44. Reliability of questions (predictors) for existence of user motivation (UM)

Question	Communality (Extraction)	Eigenvalue % Variance	Corrected Question-Total Correlation	Alpha if Question Deleted	Alpha	Sampling Adequacy (KMO and Bartlett's Test)	
UM01	.558	50.13	.558	.689	0.749	Kaiser-Meyer-Olkin Measure of Sampling Adequacy =0.800	
UM02	.523	14.88	.525	.700		Bartlett's Test of Sphericity	Chi-Square = 608
UM03	.546	13.22	.550	.692			Df=10
UM04	.426	11.74	.460	.725			Sig=0.000
UM05	.453	1.03	.480	.718			

N=604

Table 45. Component matrix ^{a} for UM

QUESTION	Component	
	1	2
UM01	.747	-
UM02	.723	-
UM03	.739	-
UM04	.652	-
UM05	.673	-

- **Extraction Method:** Principal Component Analysis. 1 component extracted.
- **Extraction Method:** Principal Component Analysis. Rotation Method: Varimax with Kaiser Normalization. Could not be rotated.

the variables do not display multi-dimensionality and are in conformity with reliability validation.

In the case of AT variable, the questions displayed one factors with reliability is of 0.708 which is acceptable. These questions remain same for all the three layers of subjects (AT-strategic, AT-tactical, and AT-operational) and therefore, responses are analysed with a single variable. Though questions AT03 and AT04 displayed the least communality (Table 50), communality of questions is mostly in proximity. Varimax method of rotation showed two components (Table 51) and the eigenvalues (40.88%) along with scree

Figure 15. Scree plot for existence of user motivation (UM)

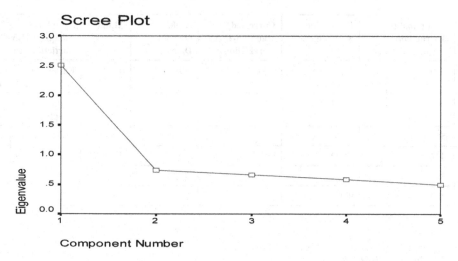

Table 46. Correlations for capability for vendor control (VC)

QUESTION		VC01	VC02	VC03	VC04	VC05	VC06
VC01	Pearson Correlation	1	.337**	.447**	.335**	.268**	.394**
	Sig. (2-tailed)	.	.000	.000	.000	.000	.000
VC02	Pearson Correlation	.337**	1	.289**	.294**	.254**	.291**
	Sig. (2-tailed)	.000	.	.000	.000	.000	.000
VC03	Pearson Correlation	.477**	.289**	1	.346**	.271**	.417**
	Sig. (2-tailed)	.000	.000	.	.000	.000	.000
VC04	Pearson Correlation	.335**	.294**	.346**	1	.300**	.370**
	Sig. (2-tailed)	.000	.000	.000	.	.000	.000
VC05	Pearson Correlation	.268**	.254**	.271**	.300**	1	.285**
	Sig. (2-tailed)	.000	.000	.000	.000	.	.000
VC06	Pearson Correlation	.394**	.291**	.417**	.370**	.285**	1
	Sig. (2-tailed)	.000	.000	.000	.000	.000	.

** Correlation is significant at the 0.01 level (2-tailed).
N=604

plot (Figure 17) supported this finding. Since there was only one factor, alpha-if-question-deleted did not show a comparable increase in reliability through extraction, there being no multi-dimensionality and there being a single factor having no scope to rotate, all the variables were retained despite AT03 and AT04 showing least Corrected Question-Total Correlation. As regards

Table 47. Reliability of questions (predictors) for capability for vendor control (VC)

Question	Communality (Extraction)	Eigenvalue % Variance	Corrected Question-Total Correlation	Alpha if Question Deleted	Alpha	Sampling Adequacy (KMO and Bartlett's Test)	
VC01	.510	44.09	.534	.693	0.745	Kaiser-Meyer-Olkin Measure of Sampling Adequacy =0.829	
VC02	.363	13.22	.425	.724		Bartlett's Test of Sphericity	Chi-Square = 642
VC03	.507	12.44	.534	.694			Df=15
VC04	.442	11.22	.487	.708			Sig=0.000
VC05	.325	9.93	.396	.731			
VC06	.499	9.07	.527	.697			

N=604

Table 48. Component matrix [a] for VC

QUESTION	Component	
	1	2
VC01	.714	-
VC02	.603	-
VC03	.712	-
VC04	.665	-
VC05	.570	-
VC06	.706	-

- **Extraction Method:** Principal Component Analysis. 1 component extracted.
- **Rotation Method:** Varimax with Kaiser Normalization. Could not be rotated.

sampling plan, Kaiser-Meyer-Olkin (KMO) and Bartlett's test measures are examined for AT and found to be in conformity with requirements; KMO being 0.794 (expected value to be > 0.5) and Bartlett's test of specificity being significant (i.e. associated probability should be <0.05).

Longer Life Cycle (LL)

Table 52 records "Pearson correlation coefficient" uniformly and approximately in the same range for all the variables. This recommends that all

Figure 16. Scree plot for vendor control (VC)

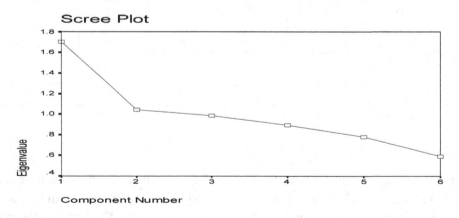

Table 49. Correlations for capability of IT cell (AT)

QUESTION		AT01	AT02	AT03	AT04	AT05	AT06
AT01	Pearson Correlation	1	.289**	.357**	.204**	.316**	.334*
	Sig. (2-tailed)	.	.000	.000	.000	.000	.000
AT02	Pearson Correlation	.289**	1	.234**	.213*	.311**	.290**
	Sig. (2-tailed)	.000	.	.000	.000	.000	.000
AT03	Pearson Correlation	.357**	.234**	1	.213**	.311**	.290**
	Sig. (2-tailed)	.000	.000	.	.000	.000	.000
AT04	Pearson Correlation	.204**	.277**	.213**	1	.161**	.326**
	Sig. (2-tailed)	.000	.000	.000	.	.000	.000
AT05	Pearson Correlation	.316**	.320**	.311**	.161**	1	.357**
	Sig. (2-tailed)	.000	.000	.000	.000	.	.000
AT06	Pearson Correlation	.334**	.336**	.290**	.326**	.357**	1
	Sig. (2-tailed)	.000	.000	.000	.000	.000	.

** Correlation is significant at the 0.01 level (2-tailed).N=604

Table 50. Reliability of questions (predictors) for capability of IT cell (AT)

Question	Communality (Extraction)	Eigenvalue % Variance	Corrected Question-Total Correlation	Alpha if Question Deleted	Alpha	Sampling Adequacy (KMO and Bartlett's Test)	
AT01	.437	40.87	.462	.665	0.708	Kaiser-Meyer-Olkin Measure of Sampling Adequacy =0.794	
AT02	.412	14.87	.445	.668		Bartlett's Test of Sphericity	Chi-Square = 526
AT03	.391	12.81	.424	.674			Df=15
AT04	.289	11.13	.355	.694			Sig=0.000
AT05	.425	10.74	.453	.666			
AT06	.499	9.58	.510	.647			

N=604

the variables do not display multi-dimensionality and are in conformity with reliability validation.

In the case of LL variable, the questions displayed two factors with reliability is of 0.814 which is acceptable. These questions remain same for all the three layers of subjects (LL-strategic, LL-tactical, and LL-operational) and therefore, responses are analysed with a single variable. Though question LL06 displayed the least communality (Table 53), communality of questions

Table 51. Component matrix ^{a} AT

QUESTION	Component	
	1	**2**
AT01	.661	-
AT02	.642	-
AT03	.625	-
AT04	.538	-
AT05	.652	-
AT06	.706	-

- **Extraction Method:** Principal Component Analysis. 1 component extracted.
- **Rotation Method:** Varimax with Kaiser Normalization. Rotation converged in 3 iterations. Could not be rotated.

is mostly in proximity. Varimax method of rotation showed one components (Table 54) and the eigenvalues (47.418% and > 1) along with scree plot (Figure 18) supported this finding. Corrected-Question-Total correlation values indicated LL05 to be least, alpha-if-question-deleted not having shown a comparable increase in reliability, there being no multi-dimensionality and there being one component all variables were retained for the purpose. As regards sampling plan, Kaiser-Meyer-Olkin (KMO) and Bartlett's test measures are examined for LL and found to be in confor-

mity with requirements; KMO being 0.881 (expected value to be > 0.5) and Bartlett's test of specificity being significant (i.e. associated probability should be <0.05).

Software Acquisition Success (SA)

Table 55 records "Pearson correlation coefficient" uniformly and approximately in the same range for all the variables. This recommends that all the variables do not display multi-dimensionality and are in conformity with reliability validation.

In the case of SA variable, the questions displayed two factors with reliability is of 0.815 which is acceptable. These questions remain same for all the three layers of subjects (SA-strategic, SA-tactical and SA-operational) and therefore, responses are analysed with a single variable. Though question SA03 displayed the least communality (Table 56), communality of questions is mostly in proximity. Varimax method of rotation showed one components (Table 57) and the eigenvalues (52.188% and > 1) along with scree plot (Figure 19) supported this finding. Corrected-Question-Total correlation values indicated SA03 to be least, alpha-if-question-deleted not having shown a comparable increase in reliabil-

Figure 17. Scree plot for acquisition of technology (AT)

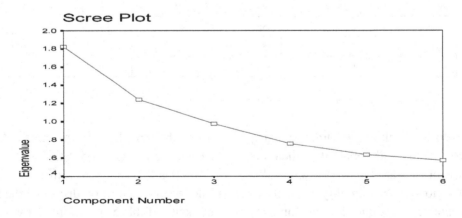

Table 52. Correlations for longer life cycle (LL)

QUESTION		LL01	LL02	LL03	LL04	LL05	LL06	LL07
LL01	Pearson Correlation	1	.365**	.418**	.406**	.343**	.355**	.385**
	Sig. (2-tailed)	.	.000	.000	.000	.000	.003	.000
LL02	Pearson Correlation	.365**	1	.421**	.453**	.323**	.365**	.439**
	Sig. (2-tailed)	.000	.	.000	.000	.000	.000	.000
LL03	Pearson Correlation	.418**	.421**	1	.404**	.360**	.413**	.409**
	Sig. (2-tailed)	.000	.000	.	.000	.000	.000	.000
LL04	Pearson Correlation	.406**	.453**	.404**	1	.360**	.413**	.409**
	Sig. (2-tailed)	.000	.000	.000	.	.000	.000	.000
LL05	Pearson Correlation	.343**	.323**	.360**	.334**	1	.322**	.454**
	Sig. (2-tailed)	.000	.000	.000	.000	.	.000	.000
LL06	Pearson Correlation	.355**	.365**	.413**	.377**	.322**	1	.338**
	Sig. (2-tailed)	.003	.000	.000	.000	.000	.	.000
LL07	Pearson Correlation	.385**	.439**	.409**	.416**	.454**	.338**	1
	Sig. (2-tailed)	.000	.000	.000	.000	.000	.000	.

** Correlation is significant at the 0.01 level (2-tailed).
N=604

Table 53. Reliability of questions (predictors) for longer life cycle (LL)

Question	Communality (Extraction)	Eigenvalue % Variance	Corrected Question-Total Correlation	Alpha if Question Deleted	Alpha	Sampling Adequacy (KMO and Bartlett's Test)	
LL01	.459	47.42	.541	.791	0.814	Kaiser-Meyer-Olkin Measure of Sampling Adequacy =.881	
LL02	.494	10.68	.565	.787		Bartlett's Test of Sphericity	Chi-Square = 1073
LL03	.512	9.69	.582	.784			Df=21
LL04	.501	9.15	.572	.786			Sig=0.000
LL05	.413	25	.505	.797			
LL06	.423	7.58	.513	.796			
LL07	.517	7.20	.585	.783			

N=604

Table 54. Component matrix ᵃ LL

QUESTION	Component	
	1	**2**
LL01	.677	-
LL02	.703	-
LL03	.715	-
LL04	.708	-
LL05	.642	-
LL06	.650	-
LL07	.719	-

- **Extraction Method:** Principal Component Analysis. 1 component extracted.
- **Rotation Method:** Varimax with Kaiser Normalization. Could not be rotated.

ity, there being no multi-dimensionality and there being one component all variables were retained for the purpose.

As regards sampling plan, Kaiser-Meyer-Olkin (KMO) and Bartlett's test measures are examined for SA and found to be in conformity with requirements; KMO being 0.819 (expected value to be > 0.5) and Bartlett's test of specificity being significant (i.e. associated probability should be <0.05).

User Satisfaction (US)

Table 58 records "Pearson correlation coefficient" uniformly and approximately in the same range for all the variables. This recommends that all the variables do not display multi-dimensionality and are in conformity with reliability Validation.

In the case of US variable, the questions displayed three factors with reliability is of 0.712 which is acceptable. These questions remain same for all the three layers of subjects (US-strategic, US-tactical, and US-operational) and therefore, responses are analysed with a single variable. Though question US08 displayed the least communality (Table 59), communality of questions is mostly in proximity. Varimax method of rotation showed three components (Table 60) and the eigenvalues (30.87% and > 1) along with scree plot (Figure 20) supported this finding. Corrected-Question-Total correlation values indicated SA04 to be least, alpha-if-question-deleted not having shown a comparable increase in reliability, there being no multi-dimensionality and three components (including rotated) did not showing any pattern, all variables were retained for the purpose. As regards sampling plan, Kaiser-

Table 55. Correlations for software acquisition success (SA)

QUESTION		SA01	SA02	SA03	SA04	SA05	SA06
SA01	Pearson Correlation	1	.484**	.366**	.450**	.414**	.436**
	Sig. (2-tailed)	.	.000	.000	.000	.000	.000
SA02	Pearson Correlation	.484**	1	.456**	.501**	.409**	.459**
	Sig. (2-tailed)	.000	.	.000	.000	.000	.000
SA03	Pearson Correlation	.366**	.456**	1	.352**	.403**	.341**
	Sig. (2-tailed)	.000	.000	.	.000	.000	.000
SA04	Pearson Correlation	.450**	.501**	.352**	1	.428**	.451**
	Sig. (2-tailed)	.000	.000	.000	.	.000	.000
SA05	Pearson Correlation	.414**	.409**	.403**	.428**	1	.428**
	Sig. (2-tailed)	.000	.000	.000	.000	.	.000
SA06	Pearson Correlation	.436**	.459**	.341**	.451**	.428**	1
	Sig. (2-tailed)	.000	.000	.000	.000	.000	.

** Correlation is significant at the 0.01 level (2-tailed).
N=604

Figure 18. Scree plot for longer life cycle (LL)

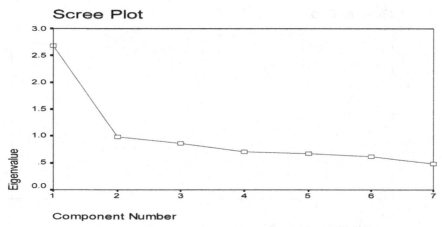

Table 56. Reliability of questions (predictors) for software acquisition success (SA)

Question	Communality (Extraction)	Eigenvalue % Variance	Corrected Question-Total Correlation	Alpha if Question Deleted	Alpha	Sampling Adequacy (KMO and Bartlett's Test)	
SA01	.532	52.18	.587	.784	0.815	Kaiser-Meyer-Olkin Measure of Sampling Adequacy =0.867	
SA02	.596	11.59	.637	.773		Bartlett's Test of Sphericity	Chi-Square = 1010
SA03	.438	10.23	.512	.799			Df=15
SA04	.546	9.26	.598	.783			Sig=0.000
SA05	.501	9.11	.563	.789			
SA06	.518	7.61	.577	.786			

N=604

Table 57. Component matrix ᵃ for SA

QUESTION	Component	
	1	2
SA01	.730	-
SA02	.772	-
SA03	.662	-
SA04	.739	-
SA05	.708	-
SA06	.720	-

- **Extraction Method:** Principal Component Analysis. 1 component extracted.
- **Rotation Method:** Varimax with Kaiser Normalization. Could not be rotated.

Meyer-Olkin (KMO) and Bartlett's test measures are examined for US and found to be in conformity with requirements; KMO being 0.782 (expected value to be > 0.5) and Bartlett's test of specificity being significant (i.e. associated probability should be <0.05).

Successful is-IT Alignment (AL)

Table 61 records "Pearson correlation coefficient" uniformly and approximately in the same range for all the variables. This recommends that all the variables do not display multi-dimensionality and are in conformity with reliability validation.

Figure 19. Scree plot for software acquisition success (SA)

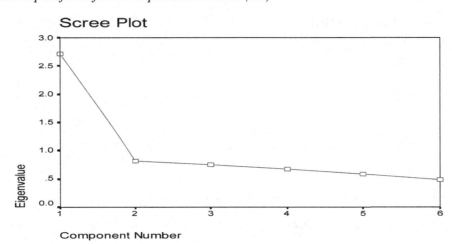

Table 58. Correlations for user satisfaction (US)

QUESTION		US01	US02	US03	US04	US05	US06	US07	US08	US09
US01	Pearson Correlation	1	.423**	.397**	.288**	.189**	.283**	.206**	.285**	.136**
	Sig. (2-tailed)	.	.000	.000	.000	.000	.000	.000	.000	.001
US02	Pearson Correlation	.423**	1	.404**	.270**	.209**	.175**	.226**	.178**	.139**
	Sig. (2-tailed)	.000	.	.000	.000	.000	.000	.000	.000	.001
US03	Pearson Correlation	.397**	.404**	1	.240**	.141**	.107**	.163**	.234**	.102*
	Sig. (2-tailed)	.000	.000	.	.000	.001	.008	.000	.000	.012
US04	Pearson Correlation	.288**	.270**	.240**	1	.233**	.243**	.250**	.221**	.181**
	Sig. (2-tailed)	.000	.000	.000	.	.000	.000	.000	.000	.000
US05	Pearson Correlation	.189**	.209**	.141**	.233**	1	.426**	.215**	.187**	.117**
	Sig. (2-tailed)	.000	.000	.001	.000	.	.000	.000	.000	.004
US06	Pearson Correlation	.283**	.175**	.107**	.243**	.426**	1	.160**	.178**	.087*
	Sig. (2-tailed)	.000	.000	.008	.000	.000	.	.000	.000	.033
US07	Pearson Correlation	.206**	.226**	.163**	.250**	.215**	.160**	1	.122**	.241**
	Sig. (2-tailed)	.000	.000	.000	.000	.000	.000	.	.003	.000
US08	Pearson Correlation	.285**	.178**	.234**	.221**	.187**	.178**	.122**	1	.133**
	Sig. (2-tailed)	.000	.000	.000	.000	.000	.000	.003	.	.001
US09	Pearson Correlation	.136**	.139**	.102*	.181**	.117*	.087*	.241**	.133**	1
	Sig. (2-tailed)	.001	.001	.012	.000	.004	.033	.000	.001	.

** Correlation is significant at the 0.01 level (2-tailed).
* Correlation is significant at the 0.05 level (2-tailed).
N=604

Table 59. Reliability of questions (predictors) for user satisfaction (US)

Question	Communality (Extraction)	Eigenvalue % Variance	Corrected Question-Total Correlation	Alpha if Question Deleted	Alpha	Sampling Adequacy (KMO and Bartlett's Test)	
US01	.583	30.87	.505	.663	0.712	Kaiser-Meyer-Olkin Measure of Sampling Adequacy =0.782	
US02	.544	12.80	.457	.673		Bartlett's Test of Sphericity	Chi-Square = 768
US03	.624	11.55	.405	.684			Df=36
US04	.377	9.59	.433	.679			Sig=0.000
US05	.658	26	.379	.688			
US06	.705	7.93	.367	.690			
US07	.533	7.13	.350	.693			
US08	.267	6.39	.340	.696			
US09	.678	5.48	.245	.713			

N=604

Table 60. Component matrix [a] for US

QUESTION	Component			Component (Rotated)		
	1	2	3	1	2	3
US01	.687	-.281	-.180	.732	.201	7.903E-02
US02	.644	-.356	-5.946E-02	.718	7.482E-02	.154
US03	.586	-.516	-.124	.787	-5.168E-02	4.395E-02
US04	.599	6.936E-02	.116	.382	.309	.368
US05	.536	.571	-.211	.102	.792	.140
US06	.530	.557	-.337	.136	.828	2.374E-02
US07	.495	.155	.514	.158	.166	.693
US08	.497	-6.691E-02	-.127	.445	.249	446E-02
US09	.362	.105	.732	3.816E-02	-2.533E-02	.822

- **Extraction Method:** Principal Component Analysis. 3 components extracted Rotated Component Matrix.
- **Rotation Method:** Varimax with Kaiser Normalization. Rotation converged in 4 iterations.

Figure 20. Scree plot for user satisfaction (US)

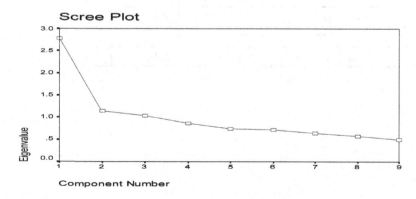

Table 61. Correlations for successful IS-IT alignment (AL)

QUESTION		AL01	AL02	AL03	AL04	AL05	AL06	AL07
AL01	Pearson Correlation	1	.366**	.429**	.392**	.388**	.383**	.367**
	Sig. (2-tailed)	.	.000	.000	.000	.000	.000	.000
AL02	Pearson Correlation	.366**	1	.303**	.477**	.446**	.368**	.470**
	Sig. (2-tailed)	.000	.	.000	.000	.000	.000	.000
AL03	Pearson Correlation	.429**	.303**	1	.311**	.399**	.369**	.381**
	Sig. (2-tailed)	.000	.000	.	.000	.000	.000	.000
AL04	Pearson Correlation	.392**	.477**	.311**	1	.353*	.397**	.441**
	Sig. (2-tailed)	.000	.000	.000	.	.000	.000	.000
AL05	Pearson Correlation	.386**	.446**	.399**	.353*	1	.346**	.463**
	Sig. (2-tailed)	.000	.000	.000	.000	.	.000	.000
AL06	Pearson Correlation	.383**	.368**	.369**	.397**	.346**	1	.352**
	Sig. (2-tailed)	.000	.000	.000	.000	.000	.	.000
AL07	Pearson Correlation	.367**	.470**	.381**	.441**	.463**	.352**	1
	Sig. (2-tailed)	.000	.000	.000	.000	.000	.000	.

** Correlation is significant at the 0.01 level (2-tailed).
N=604

Table 62. Reliability of questions (predictors) for successful IS-IT alignment (AL)

Question	Communality (Extraction)	Eigenvalue % Variance	Corrected Question-Total Correlation	Alpha if Question Deleted	Alpha	Sampling Adequacy (KMO and Bartlett's Test)	
AL01	468	47.80	.550	.794	0.818	Kaiser-Meyer-Olkin Measure of Sampling Adequacy =0.873	
AL02	.512	11.37	.582	.789		Bartlett's Test of Sphericity	Chi-Square = 1118
AL03	.424	10.10	.514	.800			Df=21
AL04	.489	65	.565	.792			Sig=0.000
AL05	.496	00	.571	.791			
AL06	.432	7.17	.522	.799			
AL07	.526	6.89	.594	.787			

N=604

Table 63. Component matrix ᵃ for AL

QUESTION	Component	
	1	**2**
AL01	.684	-
AL02	.715	-
AL03	.651	-
AL04	.699	-
AL05	.704	-
AL06	.657	-
AL07	.725	

- **Extraction Method:** Principal Component Analysis. 1 component extracted.
- **Rotation Method:** Varimax with Kaiser Normalization. Could not be rotated.

In the case of AL variable, the questions displayed one factor with reliability is of 0.818 which is acceptable. These questions remain same for all the three layers of subjects (AL-strategic, AL-tactical, and AL-operational) and therefore, responses are analysed with a single variable. Though question AL02 displayed the least communality (Table 62), communality of questions is mostly in proximity. Varimax method of rotation showed one components (Table 63) and the eigenvalues (47.80% and > 1) along with scree plot (Figure 21) supported this finding. Corrected-Question-Total correlation values indicated AL03 to be least, alpha-if-question-deleted not having shown a comparable increase in reliability, there being no multi-dimensionality and there being one component all variables were retained for the purpose.

As regards sampling plan, Kaiser-Meyer-Olkin (KMO) and Bartlett's test measures are examined for AL and found to be in conformity with requirements; KMO being 0.873 (expected value to be > 0.5) and Bartlett's test of specificity being significant (i.e. associated probability should be <0.05).

SUMMARY

This chapter is devoted for validation of tier-I variables. Methods used for understanding questions, variables and especially reliability of questions are discussed. Reliability of questions, multidimensionality of questions are tested for validation of tier-I variables for further use. Table 64 explains the variables and the questions retained for each question for further analyses.

Figure 21. Scree plot for successful IS-IT alignment (AL)

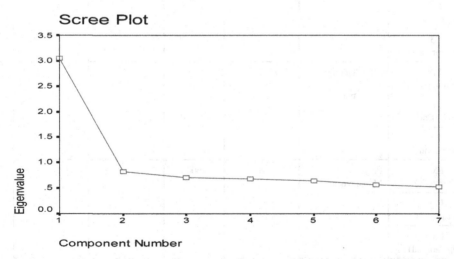

Table 64. Reliability of questions used for the model

Sl. No.	Variable Identification	Variable Description	Number of Questions	Sample Size	Cronbach Alpha	Questions Extracted	Revised Cronbach Alpha
1	U1	Strategic User Preparedness	6	74	0.87	-	0.87
2	U2	Tactical User Preparedness	6	210	0.83	-	0.83
3	U3	Operational User Preparedness	5	320	0.72	-	0.72
4	I1	IS Strategy	6	74	0.88	-	0.88
5	I2	Interface Strategy	4	210	0.79	-	0.79
6	I3	Transaction Strategy	4	320	0.76	-	0.76
7	T1	IT Strategy	7	74	0.89	-	0.89
8	T2	Component Strategy	8	210	0.86	-	0.86
9	T3	Interface Strategy	6	320	0.86	-	0.86
10	C1 (Strategic) C1 (Tactical) C1 (Operational)	User perception on Organisation	7	604	0.71	-	0.71
11	C2 (Strategic) C2 (Tactical) C2 (Operational)	User Perception on IT	8	604	0.69	-	0.69
12	C3 (Strategic) C3 (Tactical) C3 (Operational)	Decision Making Style	7	604	0.77	-	0.77
13	PP (Strategic) PP (Tactical) PP (Operational)	Planning and Policy	5	604	0.65	-	0.65
14	PM (Strategic) PM (Tactical) PM (Operational)	Project Management	6	604	0.82	-	0.82

continued on following page

Table 64. Continued

Sl. No.	Variable Identification	Variable Description	Number of Questions	Sample Size	Cronbach Alpha	Questions Extracted	Revised Cronbach Alpha
15	UM (Strategic)	User Motivation	5	604	0.75	-	0.75
	UM (Tactical)						
	UM (Operational)						
16	VC (Strategic)	Vendor Management	6	604	0.75	-	0.75
	VC (Tactical)						
	VC (Operational)						
17	AT (Strategic)	IT Acquisition	6	604	0.71	-	0.71
	AT (Tactical)						
	AT (Operational)						
18	LL (Strategic)	Life Cycle	7	604	0.81	-	0.81
	LL (Tactical)						
	LL (Operational)						
19	SA (Strategic)	Acquisition Success	6	604	0.82	-	0.82
	SA (Tactical)						
	SA (Operational)						
20	US (Strategic)	User Satisfaction	9	604	0.71	-	0.71
	US (Tactical)						
	US (Operational)						
21	AL (Strategic)	Alignment	7	604	0.82	-	0.82
	AL (Tactical)						
	AL (Operational)						

REFERENCES

Basili, V. R., Caldiera, G., & Rombach, H. D. (1994). Goal question metrics paradigm. In *Encyclopedia of Software Engineering* (*Vol. 1*, pp. 528–532). New York: Wiley.

Carmines, E. G., & Zeller, R. A. (1994). Reliability and validity assessment. In *International Handbook of Quantitative Applications in the Social Sciences* (*Vol. 4*, pp. 154–160). London: Sage Publications.

Fabrigar, L. R., Wegener, D. T., MacCallum, R. C., & Strahan, E. J. (1999). Evaluating the use of exploratory factor analysis in psychological research. *Psychological Methods*, *3*, 272–299. doi:10.1037/1082-989X.4.3.272.

Field, A. (2000). *Discovering statistics using SPSS for windows*. London: Sage Publications.

Kanter, J. (2000). *Managing with information* (4th ed.). New Delhi: Prentice Hall.

Mcliver, J. P., & Carmines, E. G. (1994). Unidimensional scaling. In *International Handbook of Quantitative Applications in the Social Sciences* (*Vol. 4*, pp. 154–160). London: Sage Publications.

Minieak, E., & Kurzeja, Z. D. (2001). *Statistics for business with computer applications*. Cincinnati, OH: Thomson Learning.

Mintzberg, H., Ahlstrand, B., & Lampel, J. (1988). *Startegy safri*. New York: The Free Press.

Nonaka, I. (1988). Toward middle-up-down management: Accelerating information creation. *Sloan Management Review*, *29*(3), 9–10.

Nunnally, J. C. (1978). *Psychometric theory*. New York: McGraw-Hill.

Pearce, J. A., & Robinson, R. B. (1996). *Strategic management: Formulation, implementation and control*. Burr Ridge, IL: Irwin.

Pedhazur, E. J. (1997). *Multiple regression in behavioral research* (3rd ed.). New York: Harcourt Brace College Publishers.

Rietveld, T., & Van Hout, R. (1993). *Statistical techniques for the study of language and language behaviour*. Berlin: Mouton de Gruyter. doi:10.1515/9783110871609.

Spector, P. E. (1988). Development of the work locus of control scale. *Journal of Operational Psychology*, *61*, 335–340.

Chapter 9
Validation of Model:
The Process for Tier–II Variables

ABSTRACT

The proposed IT acquisition model builds on the predictive behavior of Tier-I influencers and suggests that Tier-II influencers need to collectively contribute to attain organizational synergy. The most critical aspect of collectiveness is heterogeneous organizational behavior across the hierarchy in the organization. It is believed that strategic, tactical, and operational layers in the organization have different tasks, motivations, roles, and responsibilities. However, collective orientation of this heterogeneity needs to be achieved for this model for IT acquisition for its holistic success. Therefore, the model considers it important to identify the controlling agency in the hierarchy so that controlled elements contribute effectively in the IT acquisition process. Identification of "controlling" and "controlled" elements for assessment of collective contributions of users, information systems, and information technologies in the IT acquisition process needs in-depth studies through an appropriate stratified and unequal sampling plan for the proposed model. This chapter discusses validation of Tier-II influencers with quantitative methods.

VALIDATION OF PRE-ACQUISITION STAGE VARIABLES

It has been discussed earlier that stratified sampling processes provide enormous challenge to validate overall preparedness of the organization through sampling techniques and quantitative methods. In earlier chapters it was discussed and verified that methods adopted for the model validation are reliable since the data collected through the sampling process for Tier-I predictors have shown accepted

DOI: 10.4018/978-1-4666-4201-0.ch009

Cronbach alpha coefficient (α). The next challenge is to validate the higher layer of predictors assigned to the model. These are Tier-II predictors. These predictors use the reliable and validated data filtered from the Tier-I data sets. However, these data sets are governed by the variables that the model uses are "User Preparedness (U)", "IS preparedness (I)", "Technology Preparedness (T)", Climate Preparedness (C)". These variables display locus of control in the hierarchy explained earlier (Nonaka,1988). Such a situation recommends dummy coding methods in which locus of control is identified and then other controlled data are used for overall fitness of the variables so that further analyses can be carried for the model (Spector, 1988; Carmines & Zeller, 1994; Mcliver & Edward 1994;). For example, in Table 1, user preparedness (U) represents the overall group behavior constituted by U1, U2, U3 representing strategic, tactical and operational subject groups respectively. In this case U3 is considered as the control group to hypothesize that operational group is likely to influence the IT acquisition process the most in the organization (Pearce & Robinson, 1996; Pedhazur, 1997). It is thus imperative for U12 and U2 subjects respect the preparedness of U3 for successful IT acquisition.

VALIDATION OF USER PREPAREDNESS (U)

U as explained in Table 1 above is the mean of the responses obtained from the subjects through Likert scale. This summative nature of Likert scale is used since all the independent items are proved to be reliable and are not mostly non-dimensional (Nunnally, 1978; Pedhazur, 1997). The purpose of dummy coding is to understand whether collectively respondents across the three layers (strategic, tactical and operational) do collectively display their holistic understanding in projecting preparedness as hypothesised as "$H1_{U0}$". D1 and D2 are two dummy coded vectors associated with each group. In this case there are three independent groups such as $U_{strategic}$ (U1), $U_{tactical}$ (U2) and $U_{operational}$ (U3). Number of dummy vectors (N_D) were the same as the number of groups (N_G -1). A vector in a group is assigned "1" whereas other vectors are assigned "0". All the vectors in one group are assigned with "0" which is termed as control group. In this case choosing operational user group as the control group is arbitrary as explained above and in chapter 7. In order to test the null hypothesis formulated multiple regression analysis (MR) in conjunction with analysis of variance "ANOVA" was formulated. Whereas dummy coding prefers MR to ANOVA (Pedhazur, 1997) both are used here to provide a better analysis.

The regression equation for the analysis is:

$$U = a_0 + b_1 D1 + b_2 D2 \text{ (D1 and D2 assume the values 0,1)}$$

a_0 -> Mean of Control Group (U3)

b_1 -> Mean of Group U1

b_2 -> Mean of Group U2

Data analysed through SPSS-10.1 provides following results:

The regression equation for dependent variable:

$$U = 4.077 + 0.193*D1 - 0.043*D2 \text{ (Table 6.3)}$$

Table 1. Dummy coding for predicting user preparedness (U)

GROUP	Sample Size	No. of Items	User Preparedness (U)	Dummy Code (D1)	Dummy Code (D2)	Remarks
U1	74	6	U	1	0	U = ∑Uij /6; i=1, j=1-6 (Subject wise item- response mean)
U2	210	7	U	0	1	U = ∑Uij /7; i=2, j=1-7 (Subject wise item- response mean)
U3 (Control)	320	7	U	0	0	U = ∑Uij /7; i=3, j=1-7 (Subject wise item- response mean)

Table 2. ANOVA[b] user preparedness (U)

	Sum of Squares	df	Mean Square	F-Statistics	Sig.[a]
Regression	3.084	2	1.542	2.405	.091
Residual	385.241	601	.641		
Total	388.325	603			

- **Variables:** (Constant), D2, D1
- **Dependent Variable:** User Preparedness (U)

Table 3. Regression coefficients user preparedness (U)

	Unstandardized Coefficients		Standardized Coefficients	t-Statistics	Sig.
	B	Std. Error	Beta		
(Constant)	4.077	.045		91.105	.000
D1	.193	.103	.079	1.867	.062
D2	-043	.071	-.025	-.599	.549

- **Dependent Variable:** U

U_{D1}= 4.077+0.193-0 (putting values of D1 =1 and D2=0 for first group)

= 5.270 = Mean($U_{strategic}$)

U_{D2}= 4.077+0-0.043 (putting values of D1 =0 and D2=1 for second group)

= 4.034 = Mean($U_{tactical}$)

U_{D3}= 4.077+0-0 (putting values of D1 =0 and D2=0 for control group)

= 4.077 = Mean($U_{operational}$)

Analysing with the help of "Dunnet Table" which is a special table used for dummy variables for 2 treatments and 1 control group and degrees of freedom (df) as 603 but with upper 10 percent points;

F-value $_{(Expected)}$ = 2.3

F-value$_{(observed)}$ = 2.405 (Table 6.2)

F-value $_{(observed)}$ is more than the expected, it does not support the null hypothesis and $H1_{U0}$ is rejected in favour of $H1_{UA}$. This implies that $U_{strategic}$ (U1), $U_{tactical}$ (U2) and $U_{operational}$ (U3) collectively do predict "User preparedness (U)".

VALIDATION OF INFORMATION SYSTEM PREPAREDNESS (I)

"I" as explained in Table 4 above is the mean of the responses obtained from the subjects through Likert scale. As has been discussed for analysing "U" ; dummy coding is used here for the purpose. The purpose of dummy coding is to understand whether collectively respondents across the three layers (strategic, tactical and operational) do collectively display their holistic understanding in projecting IS preparedness as hypothesised as "$H1_{I0}$". D1 and D2 are two dummy coded vectors associated with each group. In this case there are three independent groups such as IS-strategy (I1), Interface-strategy (I2) and Transaction-strategy

Table 4. Dummy coding for predicting information system preparedness (I)

GROUP	Sample Size	No. of Items	IS Preparedness (I)	Dummy Code (D1)	Dummy Code (D2)	Remarks
I1	74	5	I	1	0	$I = \sum Iij /6$; i=1, j=1-5 (Subject wise item-response mean)
I2	210	4	I	0	1	$I = \sum Iij /4$; i=2, j=1-4 (Subject wise item-response mean)
I3 (Control)	320	3	I	0	0	$I = \sum Iij /3$; i=3, j=1-3 (Subject wise item-response mean)

(I3). Strategic, tactical and operational users responded to project I1, I2 and I3 respectively.

The regression equation for the analysis is:

$I = a_0 + b_1 D1 + b_2 D2$ (D1 and D2 assume the values 0,1) (Table 6)

a_0 -> Mean of Control Group (I3)

b_1 -> Mean of Group I1

b_2 -> Mean of Group I2

Data analysed through SPSS-10.1 provides following results:

The regression equation for dependent variable:

$I = 3.576 + 0.341*D1 - 0.029*D2$ (Table 6)

$I_{D1} = 3.576+0.341-0$ (putting values of D1 =1 and D2=0 for first group)

= 3.917 = Mean (I- IS Strategy)

$I_{D2} = 3.576+0-0.029$ (putting values of D1 =0 and D2=1 for second group)

= 3.547 = Mean (I- Interface Strategy)

$I_{D3} = 3.576+0-0$ (putting values of D1 =0 and D2=0 for control group)

= 3.576 = Mean (I-Transaction Strategy)

Analysing with the help of "Dunnet Table" which is a special table used for dummy variables for 2 treatments and 1 control group and degrees of freedom (df) as 603;

F-value $_{(Expected)}$ = 2.3

F-value $_{(observed)}$ = 4.912 (Table 5)

Table 5. ANOVA information system preparedness (I)

Model		Sum of Squares	df	Mean Square	F	Sig.
1	Regression	8.178	2	4.089	4.912	.008
	Residual	500.362	601	.833		
	Total	508.541	603			

- **Variables:** (Constant), DUMMY2, DUMMY1
- **Dependent Variable:** IS Preparedness (I)

Table 6. Regression coefficients information system preparedness (I)

Model		Unstandardized Coefficients			Standardized Coefficients	t	Sig.
		B	Std. Error		Beta		
1	(Constant)	3.576	.051			70.104	.000
	DUMMY1	.341	.118		.122	2.896	.004
	DUMMY2	-.029	.081		-.015	-.362	.717

- **Dependent Variable:** IS Preparedness (I)

F-value $_{(observed)}$ is greater than the expected, it does not support the null hypothesis and $H1_{I0}$ is rejected in favour of $H1_{IA}$. This implies that IS Strategy by strategic planners (I1), Interface Strategy by functional users(I2) and Transaction Strategy by operational users (I3) collectively do predict "IS preparedness (I)".

VALIDATION OF INFORMATION TECHNOLOGY PREPAREDNESS (T)

"T" as explained in Table 7 above is the mean of the responses obtained from the subjects through Likert scale. As has been for analysing "T" dummy coding is used for the purpose. The purpose of dummy coding is to understand whether collectively respondents across the three layers (strategic, tactical and operational) do collectively display their holistic understanding in projecting IT preparedness as hypothesised as "$H1_{T0}$". D1 and D2 are two dummy coded vectors associated with each group. In this case there are three independent groups such as IT-strategy (T1), Component-strategy (T2) and Interface-strategy (T3). Strategic, tactical and operational users responded to project T1,T2 and T3 respectively.

The regression equation for the analysis is:

$T = a_0 + b_1 D1 + b_2 D2$ (D1 and D2 assume the values 0,1)

a_0 -> Mean of Control Group (T3)

b_1 -> Mean of Group T1

b_2 -> Mean of Group T2

Data analysed through SPSS-10.1 provides following results:

Table 7. Dummy coding for predicting information technology preparedness (T)

GROUP	Sample Size	No. of Items	Technology Preparedness (T)	Dummy Code (D1)	Dummy Code (D2)	Remarks
T1	74	7	T	1	0	$T = \sum Tij /7$; i=1, j=1-7 (Subject wise item-response mean)
T2	210	8	T	0	1	$T = \sum Tij /8$; i=2, j=1-8 (Subject wise item-response mean)
T3 (Control)	320	6	T	0	0	$T = \sum Tij /6$; i=3, j=1-6 (Subject wise item-response mean)

Table 8. ANOVA information technology preparedness (T)

Model		Sum of Squares	df	Mean Square	F	Sig.
1	Regression	1.993	2	.997	1.119	.327
	Residual	535.160	601	.890		
	Total	537.153	603			

● **Variables:** (Constant), DUMMY2, DUMMY1
● **Dependent Variable:** Information Technology Preparedness (T)

Table 9. Regression coefficients information technology preparedness (T)

Model		Unstandardized Coefficients		Standardized Coefficients	t	Sig.
		B	Std. Error	Beta		
1	(Constant)	3.573	.053		67.732	.000
	DUMMY1	.132	.122	.046	1.082	.280
	DUMMY2	.108	.084	.055	1.289	.198

● **Dependent Variable:** T

The regression equation for dependent variable:

T= 3.573 + 0.132*D1 + 0.108*D2 (Table 6.9)

T_{D1}= 3.573+0.132+0 (putting values of D1 =1 and D2=0 for first group)

= 3.705 = Mean (T- IT Strategy)

T_{D2}= 3.573+0+0.108 (putting values of D1 =0 and D2=1 for second group)

= 3.681 = Mean (T- Component Strategy)

T_{D3}= 3.573+0+0 (putting values of D1 =0 and D2=0 for control group)

= 3.573 = Mean (T- Interface Strategy)

Analysing with the help of "Dunnet Table" which is a special table used for dummy variables for 2 treatments and 1 control group and degrees of freedom (df) as 603;

F-value $_{(Expected)}$ = 3.0

F-value$_{(observed)}$ = 1.119 (Table 8)

F-value $_{(observed)}$ is less than the expected, it does not support the null hypothesis and $H1_{T0}$ fails to reject. This implies that IT Strategy by strategic planners (T1), Component Strategy by functional users (I2) and Interface Strategy by operational users (I3) collectively may not predict "IT preparedness (T)".

VALIDATION OF USER PERCEPTION ON ORGANISATION (C1)

"C1" as explained in Table 10 above is the mean of the responses obtained from the subjects through Likert scale. The purpose of dummy coding is to understand whether collectively respondents across the three layers (strategic, tactical and operational) do collectively display their holistic understanding in projecting climate (User Per-

Table 10. Dummy coding for predicting user perception on organisation (C1)

GROUP	Sample Size	No. of Items	Cliamte Preparedness (I)	Dummy Code (D1)	Dummy Code (D2)	Remarks
C1-S	74	7	C1	1	0	$C1 = \sum C1ij /7$; i=1, j=1-7 (Subject wise item- response mean)
C1-T	210	7	C1	0	1	$C1 = \sum C1ij /7$; i=2, j=1-7 (Subject wise item- response mean)
C1-O (Control)	320	7	C1	0	0	$C1 = \sum C1ij /7$; i=3, j=1-7 (Subject wise item- response mean)

ception) as hypothesised as "$H1_{C10}$". D1 and D2 are two dummy coded vectors associated with each group.

The regression equation for the analysis is:

$C1 = a_0 + b_1 D1 + b_2 D2$ (D1 and D2 assume the values 0,1)

a_0 -> Mean of Control Group (C1-Operational)

b_1 -> Mean of Group C1-Strategic

b_2 -> Mean of Group C1-Tactical

Data analysed through SPSS-10.1 provides following results:

The regression equation for dependent variable:

$C1 = 4.557 + 0.016*D1 - 0.133*D2$ (Table 6.12)

$C1_{D1} = 4.557 + 0.016 + 0$ (putting values of D1 =1 and D2=0 for first group)

= 4.573 = Mean (C1- Strategic)

$C1_{D2} = 4.557 + 0 - 0.133$ (putting values of D1 =0 and D2=1 for second group)

= 4.424 = Mean (C1- Tactical)

$C1_{D3} = 4.557 + 0 - 0$ (putting values of D1 =0 and D2=0 for control group)

= 4.557 = Mean (C1-Operational)

Analysing with the help of "Dunnet Table" which is a special table used for dummy variables for 2 treatments and 1 control group and degrees of freedom (df) as 603;

F-value $_{(Expected)}$ = 2.3

F-value $_{(observed)}$ = 3.718 (Table 11)

Table 11. ANOVA user perception on organisation (C1)

Model		Sum of Squares	df	Mean Square	F	Sig.
1	Regression	2.564	2	1.282	3.718	.025
	Residual	207.195	601	.345		
	Total	20759	603			

- **Variables:** (Constant), DUMMY2, DUMMY1
- **Dependent Variable:** User Perception (C1)

Table 12. Regression coefficients user perception on organisation (C1)

Model		Unstandardized Coefficients		Standardized Coefficients	t	Sig.
		B	Std. Error	Beta		
1	(Constant)	4.557	.033		138.840	.000
	DUMMY1	.016	.076	.009	214	.831
	DUMMY2	-.133	.052	-.108	-2.557	.011

• **Dependent Variable:** User Perception (C1)

F-value $_{(observed)}$ is greater than the expected, it does not support the null hypothesis and $H1_{C10}$ is rejected in favour of $H1_{C1A}$. This implies that User Perception (C1) will be well reflected through strategic planners (C1-S), functional users (C1-Tactical) and operational users (C1-Operational).

VALIDATION OF USER PERCEPTION ON IT (C2)

"C2" as explained in Table 13 above is the mean of the responses obtained from the subjects through Likert scale. The purpose of dummy coding is to understand whether respondents across the three layers (strategic, tactical and operational) do collectively display their holistic understanding in projecting climate (User Perception on IT) as hypothesised as "$H1_{C20}$". D1 and D2 are two dummy coded vectors associated with each group.

The regression equation for the analysis is:

$C2 = a_0 + b_1 D1 + b_2 D2$ (D1 and D2 assume the values 0,1)

a_0 -> Mean of Control Group (C2-Operational)

b_1-> Mean of Group C2-Strategic

b_2-> Mean of Group C2-Tactical

Data analysed through SPSS-10.1 provides following results:

The regression equation for dependent variable:

$C2 = 4.163 - 0.178*D1 - 0.063*D2$ (Table 6.15)

$C2_{D1} = 4.163 - 0.178 + 0$ (putting values of D1 =1 and D2=0 for first group)

= 3.985 = Mean (C2- Strategic)

Table 13. Dummy coding for predicting user perception on IT (C2)

GROUP	Sample Size	No. of Items	Climate Preparedness (C2)	Dummy Code (D1)	Dummy Code (D2)	Remarks
C2-S	74	8	C2	1	0	C2 = $\sum$C2ij /8; i=2, j=1-8 (Subject wise item- response mean)
C2-T	210	8	C2	0	1	C2 = $\sum$C2ij /8; i=2, j=1-8 (Subject wise item- response mean)
C2-O (Control)	320	8	C2	0	0	C2= $\sum$C2ij /8; i=2, j=1-8 (Subject wise item- response mean)

Table 14. ANOVA of user perception on IT (C2)

Model		Sum of Squares	df	Mean Square	F	Sig.
1	Regression	2.030	2	1.015	2.836	.059
	Residual	215.06	601	.358		
	Total	217.08	603			

● **Variables:** (Constant), D2, D1
● **Dependent Variable:** User Perception on IT (C2)

Table 15. Regression coefficients of user perception on IT (C2)

Model		Unstandardized Coefficients		Standardized Coefficients	t	Sig.
		B	Std. Error	Beta		
1	(Constant)	4.163	.033		124.50	.000
	D1	-.178	.077	-.097	-2.31	.021
	D2	-.063	.053	-.050	-1.19	.233

● **Dependent Variable:** User Perception on IT (C2)

$C2_{D2} = 4.163 - 0 - 0.063$ (putting values of D1 =0 and D2=1 for second group)

$= 4.100 =$ Mean (C2- Tactical)

$C2_{D3} = 4.163 - 0 - 0$ (putting values of D1 =0 and D2=0 for control group)

$= 4.163 =$ Mean (C2-Operational)

Analysing with the help of "Dunnet Table" which is a special table used for dummy variables for 2 treatments and 1 control group and degrees of freedom (df) as 603;

F-value $_{(Expected)} = 2.3$

F-value$_{(observed)} = 2.836$ (Table 14)

F-value $_{(observed)}$ is greater than the expected, it does not support the null hypothesis and $H1_{C20}$ is rejected in favour of $H1_{C2A}$. This implies that User Perception on IT (C2) may be well reflected through strategic planners (C2-Strategic), functional users (C2-Tactical) and operational users (C2-Operational).

VALIDATION OF USER PERCEPTION DECISION MAKING STYLE (C3)

"C3" as explained in Table 16 is the mean of the responses obtained from the subjects through Likert scale. The purpose of dummy coding is to understand whether collectively respondents across the three layers (strategic, tactical and operational) do collectively display their holistic understanding in projecting climate (User Perception on Decision Making Style) as hypothesised as "$H1_{C30}$". D1 and D2 are two dummy coded vectors associated with each group.

The regression equation for the analysis is:

$C3 = a_0 + b_1 D1 + b_2 D2$ (D1 and D2 assume the values 0,1)

Table 16. Dummy coding for predicting user perception decision making style (C3)

GROUP	Sample Size	No. of Items	Climate Preparedness (C3)	Dummy Code (D1)	Dummy Code (D2)	Remarks
C3-S	74	7	C3	1	0	$C3 = \sum C3ij \, /7;\ i=3,\ j=1-7$ (Subject wise item-response mean)
C3-T	210	7	C3	0	1	$C3 = \sum C3ij \, /7;\ i=3,\ j=1-7$ (Subject wise item-response mean)
C3-O (Control)	320	7	C3	0	0	$C3 = \sum C3ij \, /7;\ i=3,\ j=1-7$ (Subject wise item-response mean)

a_0 -> Mean of Control Group (C3-Operational)

b_1 -> Mean of Group C3-Strategic

b_2 -> Mean of Group C3-Tactical

Data analysed through SPSS-10.1 provides following results:

The regression equation for dependent variable:

$C3 = 4.736 + 0.055*D1 + 0.108*D2$ (Table 18)

$C3_{D1} = 4.736 + 0.055 + 0$ (putting values of D1 =1 and D2=0 for first group)

= 4.791 = Mean (C3- Strategic)

$C3_{D2} = 4.736 + 0 + 0.108$ (putting values of D1 =0 and D2=1 for second group)

= 4.844 = Mean (C3- Tactical)

$C3_{D3} = 4.736 + 0 + 0$ (putting values of D1 =0 and D2=0 for control group)

= 4.736 = Mean (C3-Operational)

Analysing with the help of "Dunnet Table" which is a special table used for dummy variables for 2 treatments and 1 control group and degrees of freedom (df) as 603;

F-value $_{(Expected)}$ = 2.3

F-value $_{(observed)}$ = 2.472 (Table 17)

F-value $_{(observed)}$ is greater than the expected, it does not support the null hypothesis and $H1_{C30}$ is rejected in favour of $H1_{C3A}$. This implies that User Perception on Decision Making Style (C3) will be well reflected through strategic planners (C3-S), functional users (C3-Tactical) and operational users (C3-Operational).

Table 17. ANOVA[b] user perception decision making style (C3)

Model		Sum of Squares	df	Mean Square	F	Sig.
1	Regression	1.485	2	.743	2.472	.085[a]
	Residual	180.516	601	.300		
	Total	182.001	603			

- **Variables:** (Constant), D2, D1
- **Dependent Variable:** User Perception on Decision Making Style (C3)

Table 18. Regression coefficients user perception decision making style (C3)

	Model	Unstandardized Coefficients		Standardized Coefficients	t	Sig.
		B	Std. Error	Beta		
1	(Constant)	4.736	.031		154.575	.000
	D1	.055	.071	.033	.789	.056
	D2	.108	.108	.094	2.215	.055

• **Dependent Variable:** User Perception on Decision Making Style (C3)

VALIDATION OF VARIABLES USED FOR ASSESSMENT OF ORGANISATION PREPAREDNESS (O)

In this section the variables used for assessing organisational preparedness are tested for their suitability. Though organisational preparedness is predicted by a set of variables i.e. "U", "I", "T", and "C" as discussed in chapter 5 through causal analyses, a set of variables as defined and discussed in chapter 6 are used to understand the status through respondents and these become manifest variables for utilisation in multivariate analyses later through structural equation modelling. These variables are "Planning and Policy (PP)", "Project Management (PM)" and User Motivation (UM)".

VALIDATION OF VARIABLES TO ASSESS AVAILABILITY OF PLANNING AND POLICY FOR IT (PP)

"PP" as explained in Table 19 is the mean of the responses obtained from the subjects through Likert scale. The purpose of dummy coding is to understand whether collectively respondents across the three layers (strategic, tactical and operational) do collectively display their holistic understanding Planning and Policy for IT Acquisition as hypothesised as "$H1_{PP0}$". D1 and D2 are two dummy coded vectors associated with each group.

The regression equation for the analysis is:

$$PP = a_0 + b_1 D1 + b_2 D2 \text{ (D1 and D2 assume the values 0,1)}$$

Table 19. Dummy coding for predicting planning and policy for IT (PP)

GROUP	Sample Size	No. of Items	Planning and Policy Preparedness (PP)	Dummy Code (D1)	Dummy Code (D2)	Remarks
PP-S	74	4	PP	1	0	PP = PPij /5; i=1, j=1-5 (Subject wise item-response mean)
PP-T	210	4	PP	0	1	PP = ∑PPij /5; i=2, j=1-5 (Subject wise item- response mean)
PP-O (Control)	320	4	PP	0	0	PP = ∑PPij /4; i=3, j=1-4 (Subject wise item- response mean)

a_0 -> Mean of Control Group (PP-Operational)

b_1-> Mean of Group PP-Strategic

b_2-> Mean of Group PP-Tactical

Data analysed through SPSS-10.1 provides following results:

The regression equation for dependent variable:

PP= 3.414+ 0.362*D1 - 0.279*D2 (Table 6.21)

PP_{D1}= 3.414+0.362-0 (putting values of D1 =1 and D2=0 for first group)

= 3.776 = Mean (PP- Strategic)

PP_{D2}= 3.414+0-0.279 (putting values of D1 =0 and D2=1 for second group)

= 3.135 = Mean (PP- Tactical)

PP_{D3}= 3.414+0-0 (putting values of D1 =0 and D2=0 for control group)

= 3.414 = Mean (PP-Operational)

Analysing with the help of "Dunnet Table" which is a special table used for dummy variables for 2 treatments and 1 control group and degrees of freedom (df) as 603;

F-value $_{(Expected)}$ = 2.3

F-value$_{(observed)}$ = 3.166 (Table 20)

F-value $_{(observed)}$ is greater than the expected, it does not support the null hypothesis and $H1_{PP0}$ is rejected in favour of $H1_{PPA}$. This implies that involvement of Users strategic, tactical and operational level collectively report availability of Planning and Policy for IT Acquisition (PP).

VALIDATION OF UNDERSTANDING PROJECT MANAGEMENT ISSUES FOR IT ACQUISITION (PM)

"PM" as explained in Table 22 is the mean of the responses obtained from the subjects through Likert scale. The purpose of dummy coding is to understand whether collectively respondents

Table 20. ANOVA[b] planning and policy for IT (PP)

Model		Sum of Squares	df	Mean Square	F	Sig.
1	Regression	24.409	2	12.205	30.166	.000[a]
	Residual	243.149	601	.405		
	Total	267.558	603			

• **Dependent Variable:** Policy and Planning for IT Acquisition (PP)

Table 21. Regression coefficients planning and policy for IT (PP)

		Unstandardized Coefficients		Standardized Coefficients	t	Sig.
Model		B	Std. Error	Beta		
1	(Constant)	3.414	.036		96.008	.000
	DUMMY1	.362	.082	.178	4.411	.00
	DUMMY2	-.279	.056	-.200	-4.947	.000

• **Variables:** (Constant), DUMMY2, DUMMY1
• **Dependent Variable:** Policy and Planning for IT Acquisition (PP)

222

Table 22. Dummy coding for predicting project management issues for IT acquisition (PM)

GROUP	Sample Size	No. of Items	Project Management Preparedness (PM)	Dummy Code (D1)	Dummy Code (D2)	Remarks
PM-S	74	6	PM	1	0	PM = $\sum$ PMij /6; i=1, j=1-6 (Subject wise item- response mean)
PM-T	210	6	PM	0	1	PM = $\sum$ PMij /6; i=2, j=1-6 (Subject wise item- response mean)
PM-O (Control)	320	6	PM	0	0	PM=$\sum$PMij/6; i=3, j=1-6 (Subject wise item- response mean)

across the three layers (strategic, tactical and operational) do collectively display their holistic understanding on project management issues for IT Acquisition as hypothesised as "$H1_{PM0}$". D1 and D2 are two dummy coded vectors associated with each group.

The regression equation for the analysis is:

$PM = a_0 + b_1 D1 + b_2 D2$ (D1 and D2 assume the values 0,1)

a_0 -> Mean of Control Group (PM-Operational)

b_1 -> Mean of Group PM-Strategic

b_2 -> Mean of Group PM-Tactical

Data analysed through SPSS-10.1 provides following results:

The regression equation for dependent variable:

$PM = 3.650 - 0.069*D1 - 0.064*D2$ (Table 6.24)

$PM_{D1} = 3.650-0.069-0$ (putting values of D1 =1 and D2=0 for first group)

= 3.581 = Mean (PM- Strategic)

$PM_{D2} = 3.650-0-0.064$ (putting values of D1 =0 and D2=1 for second group)

= 3.586 = Mean (PM- Tactical)

$PM_{D3} = 3.650-0-0$ (putting values of D1 =0 and D2=0 for control group)

= 3.650 = Mean (PM-Operational)

Analysing with the help of "Dunnet Table" which is a special table used for dummy variables for 2 treatments and 1 control group and degrees of freedom (df) as 603;

Table 23. ANOVA^b project management issues for IT acquisition (PM)

Model		Sum of Squares	df	Mean Square	F	Sig.
1	Regression	1.103	2	.551	.885	.413^a
	Residual	374.337	601	.623		
	Total	375.440	603			

- **Variables:** (Constant), D2, D1
- **Dependent Variable:** Project Management issues for IT Acquisition (PM)

Table 24. Regression coefficients project management issues for IT acquisition (PM)

Model		Unstandardized Coefficients		Standardized Coefficients	t	Sig.
		B	Std. Error	Beta		
1	(Constant)	3.650	.044		82.732	.000
	DUMMY1	-6.892E-02	.102	-.029	-.677	.499
	DUMMY2	-6.429E-02	.070	.039	.917	.917

• **Dependent Variable:** Project Management Issues for IT Acquisition (PM)

F-value $_{(Expected)}$ = 2.3

F-value $_{(observed)}$ = 0.88 (Table 23)

F-value $_{(observed)}$ is greater than the expected, it does not support the null hypothesis and $H1_{PM0}$ fails to reject in favour of $H1_{PMA}$. This implies that involvement of Users strategic, tactical and operational level may not collectively report availability of Project Management Capability (PM).

VALIDATION OF UNDERSTANDING USER MOTIVATION ISSUES FOR IT ACQUISITION (UM)

"UM" as explained in Table 25 is the mean of the responses obtained from the subjects through Likert scale. The purpose of dummy coding is to understand whether collectively respondents across the three layers (strategic, tactical and operational) do collectively display their holistic understanding on project management issues for IT Acquisition as hypothesised as "$H1_{UM0}$". D1 and D2 are two dummy coded vectors associated with each group.

The regression equation for the analysis is:

$UM = a_0 + b_1 D1 + b_2 D2$ (D1 and D2 assume the values 0,1)

a_0 -> Mean of Control Group (UM-Operational)

b_1 -> Mean of Group UM-Strategic

b_2 -> Mean of Group UM-Tactical

Data analysed through SPSS-10.1 provides following results:

Table 25. Dummy coding for predicting user motivation issues for IT acquisition (UM)

GROUP	Sample Size	No. of Items	User Motivation (UM)	Dummy Code (D1)	Dummy Code (D2)	Remarks
UM-S	74	5	UM	1	0	UM = $\sum UMij$ /5; i=1, j=1-5 (Subject wise item- response mean)
UM-T	210	5	UM	0	1	UM = $\sum UMij$ /5; i=2, j=1-5 (Subject wise item- response mean)
UM-O (Control)	320	5	UM	0	0	UM = $\sum UMij$ /5; i=3, j=1-5 (Subject wise item- response mean)

Table 26. ANOVA user motivation issues for IT acquisition (UM)

Model		Sum of Squares	df	Mean Square	F	Sig.
1	Regression	4.973	2	2.487	5.729	.003
	Residual	260.841	601	.434		
	Total	265.814	603			

- **Variables:** (Constant), D2, D1
- **Dependent Variable:** User Motivation issues for IT Acquisition (UM)

Table 27. Regression coefficients user motivation issues for IT acquisition (UM)

Model		Unstandardized Coefficients		Standardized Coefficients	t	Sig.
		B	Std. Error	Beta		
1	(Constant)	3.793	.037		102.979	.000
	DUMMY1	.205	.085	.101	2.410	.016
	DUMMY2	.172	.059	.124	2.944	.003

- **Dependent Variable:** User Motivation issues for IT Acquisition (UM)

The regression equation for dependent variable:

$UM = 3.793 + 0.205*D1 + 0.172*D2$ (Table 6.27)

$UM_{D1} = 3.793 + 0.205 + 0$ (putting values of D1 =1 and D2=0 for first group)

= 3.998 = Mean (UM- Strategic)

$UM_{D2} = 3.793 + 0 + 0.172$ (putting values of D1 =0 and D2=1 for second group)

= 3.965 = Mean (UM- Tactical)

$UM_{D3} = 3.793 + 0 + 0$ (putting values of D1 =0 and D2=0 for control group)

= 3.793 = Mean (UM-Operational)

Analysing with the help of "Dunnet Table" which is a special table used for dummy variables for 2 treatments and 1 control group and degrees of freedom (df) as 603;

F-value $_{(Expected)}$ = 2.3

F-value $_{(observed)}$ = 5.729 (Table 26)

F-value $_{(observed)}$ is greater than the expected, it does not support the *null hypothesis* and $H1_{UM0}$ is rejected in favour of $H1_{UMA}$. This implies that involvement of Users at strategic, tactical and operational level collectively display motivation for IT acquisition (UM).

VALIDATION OF VARIABLES USED FOR ASSESSMENT OF PREPAREDNESS OF ORGANISATION IN IT-ACQUISITION STAGE (AQ)

As discussed in chapters seven, IT acquisition stage is subsequent to the pre-acquisition stage and it preparedness is well reflected through existence of a better vendor control mechanism (VC) as well as a better equipped IT cell to manage the process (AT). In this section these variables are tested for their ability to predict the preparedness.

Table 28. Dummy coding for predicting vendor management issues for IT acquisition (VC)

GROUP	Sample Size	No. of Items	Vendor Management (VC)	Dummy Code (D1)	Dummy Code (D2)	Remarks
VC-S	74	4	VC	1	0	VC = $\sum$VCij /4; i=1, j=1-4 (Subject wise item- response mean)
VC-T	210	4	VC	0	1	VC = $\sum$VCij /4; i=2, j=1-4 (Subject wise item- response mean)
VC-O (Control)	320	4	VC	0	0	VC = $\sum$VCij /4; i=3, j=1-4 (Subject wise item- response mean)

UNDERSTANDING VENDOR MANAGEMENT ISSUES FOR IT ACQUISITION (VC)

"VC" as explained in Table 28 is the mean of the responses obtained from the subjects through Likert scale. The purpose of dummy coding is to understand whether collectively respondents across the three layers (strategic, tactical and operational) do collectively display their holistic understanding on project management issues for IT Acquisition as hypothesised as "$H1_{VC0}$". D1 and D2 are two dummy coded vectors associated with each group.

The regression equation for the analysis is:

VC = a_0+ b_1 D1 + b_2 D2 (D1 and D2 assume the values 0,1)

a_0 -> Mean of Control Group (VC-Operational)

b_1-> Mean of Group VC-Strategic

b_2-> Mean of Group VC-Tactical

Data analysed through SPSS-10.1 provides following results:

The regression equation for dependent variable:

VC= 3.568+ 0.015*D1 + 0.013*D2 (Table 30)

VC_{D1}= 3.568+0.015+0 (putting values of D1 =1 and D2=0 for first group)

= 3.583 = Mean (VC- Strategic)

VC_{D2}= 3.568+0+0.013 (putting values of D1 =0 and D2=1 for second group)

= 3.581 = Mean (VC- Tactical)

Table 29. ANOVA[b] vendor management issues for IT acquisition (VC)

Model		Sum of Squares	df	Mean Square	F	Sig.
1	Regression	.029	2	.015	.027	.973[a]
	Residual	325.132	601	.541		
	Total	325.161	603			

- **Variables:** (Constant), D2, D1
- **Dependent Variable:** Vendor Management issues for IT Acquisition (VC)

Table 30. Regression coefficients vendor management issues for IT acquisition (VC)

Model		Unstandardized Coefficients			Standardized Coefficients	t	Sig.
		B	Std. Error		Beta		
1	(Constant)	3.568	.041			86.783	.000
	DUMMY1	.015	.095		.007	.159	.0874
	DUMMY2	.013	.065		.009	.207	.836

● **Dependent Variable:** Vendor Management issues for IT Acquisition (VC)

$VC_{D3} = 3.568+0+0$ (putting values of D1 =0 and D2=0 for control group)

= 3.568 = Mean (VC-Operational)

Analysing with the help of "Dunnet Table" which is a special table used for dummy variables for 2 treatments and 1 control group and degrees of freedom (df) as 603;

F-value $_{(Expected)}$ = 2.3

F-value$_{(observed)}$ = .027(Table 29)

F-value $_{(observed)}$ is greater than the expected, it does not support the null hypothesis and $H1_{VC0}$ fails to reject in favour of $H1_{VCA}$. This implies that involvement of Users at strategic, tactical and operational level collectively may not display Vendor Management for IT acquisition (VC).

VALIDATION OF UNDERSTANDING IT ACQUISITION PROCESS ISSUES (AT)

"AT" as explained in Table 31 is the mean of the responses obtained from the subjects through Likert scale. The purpose of dummy coding is to understand whether collectively respondents across the three layers (strategic, tactical and operational) do collectively display their holistic understanding on project management issues for IT Acquisition as hypothesised as "$H1_{AT0}$". D1 and D2 are two dummy coded vectors associated with each group.

The regression equation for the analysis is:

$AT = a_0 + b_1 D1 + b_2 D2$ (D1 and D2 assume the values 0,1)

a_0 -> Mean of Control Group (AT-Operational)

Table 31. Dummy coding for predicting understanding IT acquisition process issues (AT)

GROUP	Sample Size	No. of Items	IT Acquisition Process (AT)	Dummy Code (D1)	Dummy Code (D2)	Remarks
AT-S	74	4	AT	1	0	AT = $\sum$ATij /4; i=1, j=1-4 (Subject wise item- response mean)
AT-T	210	4	AT	0	1	AT = $\sum$ATij /4; i=2, j=1-4 (Subject wise item- response mean)
AT-O (Control)	320	4	AT	0	0	ATI = $\sum$ATij /4; i=3, j=1-4 (Subject wise item- response mean)

b_1 -> Mean of Group AT-Strategic

b_2 -> Mean of Group AT-Tactical

Data analysed through SPSS-10.1 provides following results:

The regression equation for dependent variable:

AT= 3.597+ 0.167*D1 - 0.033*D2 (Table 33)

AT_{D1} = 3.597+0.167-0 (putting values of D1 =1 and D2=0 for first group)

= 3.764 = Mean (AT- Strategic)

AT_{D2} = 3.597+0-0.033 (putting values of D1 =0 and D2=1 for second group)

= 3.564 = Mean (AT- Tactical)

AT_{D3} = 3.597+0-0 (putting values of D1 =0 and D2=0 for control group)

= 3.597 = Mean (AT-Operational)

Analysing with the help of "Dunnet Table" which is a special table used for dummy variables for 2 treatments and 1 control group and degrees of freedom (df) as 603;

F-value $_{(Expected)}$ = 2.3

F-value$_{(observed)}$ = 2.495 (Table 32)

F-value $_{(observed)}$ is greater than the expected, it does not support the null hypothesis and H1$_{AT0}$ is rejected in favour of H1$_{ATA}$. This implies that involvement of Users at strategic, tactical and operational level do collectively display concern for IT acquisition issues (AT).

VALIDATION OF PREDICTOR ASSESSING POST-ACQUISITION STATUS IN THE ACQUIRING ORGANISATION (G)

Success of IT acquisition in an organisation is dependent on various factors as discussed in chapter seven. The proposed model attempts to

Table 32. ANOVA[b] understanding IT acquisition process issues (AT)

Model		Sum of Squares	df	Mean Square	F	Sig.
1	Regression	2.231	2	1.115	2.495	.083[a]
	Residual	268.688	601	.447		
	Total	270.918	603			

- **Variables:** (Constant), D2, D1
- **Dependent Variable:** IT Acquisition issues (AT)

Table 33. Regression coefficients[a] understanding IT acquisition process issues (AT)

Model		Unstandardized Coefficients		Standardized Coefficients	t	Sig.
		B	Std. Error	Beta		
1	(Constant)	3.597	.037		96.395	.000
	DUMMY1	.167	.087	.081	1.931	.054
	DUMMY2	-.033	.059	-.024	-.558	.577

- **Dependent Variable:** IT Acquisition issues (AT)

assess this success in post acquisition stage and relates to the status predicted by using structural equation modelling. Various variables used for the assessment are "Longer life cycle (LL)", "Software acquisition success (SA)", "User Satisfaction (US)" and "IS–IT Alignment (AL)".

VALIDATION OF LONGER LIFE CYCLE PREDICTOR (LL)

"LL" as explained in Table 34 is the mean of the responses obtained from the subjects through Likert scale. The purpose of dummy coding is to understand whether collectively respondents across the three layers (strategic, tactical and operational) do collectively display their holistic understanding on life cycle of IT acquired as hypothesised as "$H1_{LL0}$". D1 and D2 are two dummy coded vectors associated with each group.

The regression equation for the analysis is:

$LL = a_0 + b_1 D1 + b_2 D2$ (D1 and D2 assume the values 0,1)

a_0 -> Mean of Control Group (LL-Operational)

b_1 -> Mean of Group LL-Strategic

b_2 -> Mean of Group LL-Tactical

Data analysed through SPSS-10.1 provides following results:

The regression equation for dependent variable:

$LL = 3.660 - 0.220*D1 - 0.132*D2$ (Table 36)

$LL_{D1} = 3.660 - 0.220 - 0$ (putting values of D1 =1 and D2=0 for first group)

= 3.440 = Mean (LL- Strategic)

$LL_{D2} = 3.660 - 0 - 0.132$ (putting values of D1 =0 and D2=1 for second group)

Table 34. Dummy coding for predicting longer life cycle predictor (LL)

GROUP	Sample Size	No. of Items	IT Acquisition Life Cycle (LL)	Dummy Code (D1)	Dummy Code (D2)	Remarks
LL-S	74	7	LL	1	0	LL = ∑LLij /7; i=1, j=1-7 (Subject wise item- response mean)
LL-T	210	7	LL	0	1	LL = ∑LLij /7; i=2, j=1-7 (Subject wise item- response mean)
LL-O (Control)	320	7	LL	0	0	LL = ∑LLij /7; i=3, j=1-7 (Subject wise item- response mean)

Table 35. ANOVA[a] longer life cycle predictor (LL)

Model		Sum of Squares	df	Mean Square	F	Sig.
1	Regression	4.030	2	2.015	3.652	.027
	Residual	331.609	601	.552		
	Total	335.640	603			

- **Variables:** (Constant), D2, D1
- **Dependent Variable:** Life Cycle issues of IT Acquired (LL)

Table 36. Regression coefficients longer life cycle predictor (LL)

Model		Unstandardized Coefficients		Standardized Coefficients	t	Sig.
		B	Std. Error	Beta		
1	(Constant)	3.660	.042		88.148	.000
	DUMMY1	-.220	.096	-.097	-2.297	.022
	DUMMY2	-.132	.066	-.084	-1.996	.046

- **Dependent Variable:** Life Cycle issues of IT Acquired (LL)

= 3.528 = Mean (LL- Tactical)

LL_{D3}= 3.660-0-0 (putting values of D1 =0 and D2=0 for control group)

= 3.660 = Mean (LL-Operational)

Analysing with the help of "Dunnet Table" which is a special table used for dummy variables for 2 treatments and 1 control group and degrees of freedom (df) as 603;

F-value $_{(Expected)}$ = 2.3

F-value$_{(observed)}$ = 3.652 (Table 35)

F-value $_{(observed)}$ is greater than the expected, it does not support the *null hypothesis* and $H1_{LL0}$ is rejected in favour of $H1_{LLA}$. This implies that involvement of Users at strategic, tactical and operational level collectively describe life cycle of IT acquired (LL).

VALIDATION OF SOFTWARE ACQUISITION SUCCESS PREDICTOR (SA)

"SA" as explained in Table 37 is the mean of the responses obtained from the subjects through Likert scale. The purpose of dummy coding is to understand whether collectively respondents across the three layers (strategic, tactical and operational) do collectively display their holistic understanding on success of IT acquired as hypothesised as "$H1_{SA0}$". D1 and D2 are two dummy coded vectors associated with each group.

The regression equation for the analysis is:

$SA = a_0 + b_1 D1 + b_2 D2$ (D1 and D2 assume the values 0,1)

a_0 -> Mean of Control Group (SA-Operational)

b_1-> Mean of Group SA-Strategic

Table 37. Dummy coding for predicting software acquisition success predictor (SA)

GROUP	Sample Size	No. of Items	IT Acquisition Success (SA)	Dummy Code (D1)	Dummy Code (D2)	Remarks
SA-S	74	6	SA	1	0	SA = $\sum$SAij /6; i=1, j=1-6 (Subject wise item- response mean)
SA-T	210	6	SA	0	1	SA = $\sum$SAij /6; i=2, j=1-6 (Subject wise item- response mean)
SA-O (Control)	320	6	SA	0	0	SA = $\sum$SAij /6; i=3, j=1-6 (Subject wise item- response mean)

b_2-> Mean of Group SA-Tactical

Data analysed through SPSS-10.1 provides following results:

The regression equation for dependent variable:

SA= 3.581- 0.135*D1+ 0.099*D2 (Table 39)

SA_{D1}= 3.581-0.135+0 (putting values of D1 =1 and D2=0 for first group)

= 4.446= Mean (SA- Strategic)

SA_{D2}= 3.581-0+0.099 (putting values of D1 =0 and D2=1 for second group)

= 3.680 = Mean (SA- Tactical)

SA_{D3}= 3.581-0-0 (putting values of D1 =0 and D2=0 for control group)

= 3.581 = Mean (SA-Operational)

Analysing with the help of "Dunnet Table" which is a special table used for dummy variables for 2 treatments and 1 control group and degrees of freedom (df) as 603;

F-value $_{(Expected)}$ = 2.3

F-value$_{(observed)}$ = 2.575 (Table 38)

F-value $_{(observed)}$ is greater than the expected, it does not support the *null hypothesis* and $H1_{SA0}$ is rejected in favour of $H1_{SAA}$. This implies that involvement of Users at strategic, tactical and operational level collectively describe success of IT acquired (SA).

VALIDATION OF USER SATISFACTION PREDICTOR (US)

"US" as explained in Table 40 is the mean of the responses obtained from the subjects through Likert scale. The purpose of dummy coding is to understand whether collectively respondents across the three layers (strategic, tactical and operational) do collectively display their holistic understanding on user satisfaction as hypothesised as "$H1_{US0}$". D1 and D2 are two dummy coded vectors associated with each group.

The regression equation for the analysis is:

Table 38. ANOVA^a software acquisition success predictor (SA)

Model		Sum of Squares	df	Mean Square	F	Sig.
1	Regression	3.224	2	1.612	2.575	.077
	Residual	376.160	601	.626		
	Total	37384	603			

• **Variables:** (Constant), D2, D1
• **Dependent Variable:** Success of IT Acquired (SA)

Table 39. Regression coefficients software acquisition success predictor (SA)

Model		Unstandardized Coefficients		Standardized Coefficients	t	Sig.
		B	Std. Error	Beta		
1	(Constant)	3.581	.044		80.965	.000
	DUMMY1	-.135	.102	-.056	-1.321	.187
	DUMMY2	.099	.070	.060	1.415	1.415

• **Dependent Variable:** Success of IT Acquired (SA)

Table 40. Dummy coding for predicting user satisfaction predictor (US)

GROUP	Sample Size	No. of Items	User Satisfaction (US)	Dummy Code (D1)	Dummy Code (D2)	Remarks
US-S	74	9	US	1	0	SAI = $\sum$SAij /9; i=1, j=1-9 (Subject wise item- response mean)
US-T	210	9	US	0	1	SA = $\sum$SAij /9; i=2, j=1-9 (Subject wise item- response mean)
US-O (Control)	320	9	US	0	0	SA = $\sum$SAij /9; i=3, j=1-9 (Subject wise item- response mean)

$US = a_0 + b_1 D1 + b_2 D2$ (D1 and D2 assume the values 0,1)

a_0 -> Mean of Control Group (US-Operational)

b_1 -> Mean of Group US-Strategic

b_2 -> Mean of Group US-Tactical

Data analysed through SPSS-10.1 provides following results:

The regression equation for dependent variable:

$US = 4.439 - 0.174*D1 + 0.065*D2$ (Table 42)

$US_{D1} = 4.439 - 0.174 + 0$ (putting values of D1 =1 and D2=0 for first group)

$= 4.265 =$ Mean (US- Strategic)

$US_{D2} = 4.439 - 0 + 0.065$ (putting values of D1 =0 and D2=1 for second group)

Table 41. ANOVA[a] user satisfaction predictor (US)

Model		Sum of Squares	df	Mean Square	F	Sig.
1	Regression	3.125	2	1.562	5.232	.006
	Residual	17463	601	.299		
	Total	182.588	603			

- **Variables:** (Constant), D2, D1
- **Dependent Variable:** User Satisfaction (US)

Table 42. Regression coefficients user satisfaction predictor (US)

Model		Unstandardized Coefficients		Standardized Coefficients	t	Sig.	95% Confidence Interval for B	
		B	Std. Error	Beta			Lower Bound	Upper Bound
1	(Constant)	4.439	.031		145.300	.000	4.379	4.499
	DUMMY1	-.174	.070	-.104	-2.469	.014	-.312	-.036
	DUMMY2	6.486E-02	.049	.056	1.337	.182	-.030	.160

- **Dependent Variable:** User Satisfaction (US)

= 4.504 = Mean (US- Tactical)

US_{D3}= 4.439-0+0 (putting values of D1 =0 and D2=0 for control group)

= 4.439 = Mean (US-Operational)

Analysing with the help of "Dunnet Table" which is a special table used for dummy variables for 2 treatments and 1 control group and degrees of freedom (df) as 603;

F-value $_{(Expected)}$ = 2.3

F-value$_{(observed)}$ = 5.232 (Table 41)

F-value $_{(observed)}$ is greater than the expected, it does not support the *null hypothesis* and $H1_{US0}$ is rejected in favour of $H1_{USA}$. This implies that involvement of Users at strategic, tactical and operational level collectively describe user satisfaction (US).

VALIDATION OF IS-IT ALIGNMENT PREDICTOR (AL)

"AL" as explained in Table 43 is the mean of the responses obtained from the subjects through Likert scale. The purpose of dummy coding is to understand whether collectively respondents across the three layers (strategic, tactical and operational) do collectively display their holistic understanding on IS-IT alignment issues as hypothesised as "$H1_{AL0}$". D1 and D2 are two dummy coded vectors associated with each group.

The regression equation for the analysis is:

$AL = a_0 + b_1 D1 + b_2 D2$ (D1 and D2 assume the values 0,1)

a_0 -> Mean of Control Group (AL-Operational)

b_1-> Mean of Group AL-Strategic

b_2-> Mean of Group AL-Tactical

Data analysed through SPSS-10.1 provides following results:

The regression equation for dependent variable:

AL= 3.607- 0.111*D1 - 0.157*D2 (Table 45)

AL_{D1}= 3.607-0.011-0 (putting values of D1 =1 and D2=0 for first group)

= 3.596= Mean (AL- Strategic)

AL_{D2}= 3.607-0-0.157 (putting values of D1 =0 and D2=1 for second group)

Table 43. Dummy coding for predicting IS-IT alignment predictor (AL)

GROUP	Sample Size	No. of Items	IS-IT Alignment (AL)	Dummy Code (D1)	Dummy Code (D2)	Remarks
AL-S	74	7	AL	1	0	I =∑ ALij /7; i=1, j=1-7(Subject wise item- response mean)
AL-T	210	7	AL	0	1	I = ∑ALij /7; i=2, j=1-7 (Subject wise item- response mean)
AL-O (Control)	320	9	AL	0	0	I = ∑ALij /7; i=3, j=1-7 (Subject wise item- response mean)

Table 44. ANOVA[b] IS-IT alignment predictor (AL)

Model		Sum of Squares	df	Mean Square	F	Sig.
1	Regression	5.077	2	2.538	5.113	.006[a]
	Residual	298.363	601	.495		
	Total	303.440	603			

- **Variables:** (Constant), D2, D1
- **Dependent Variable:** IS-IT alignment Issues (AL)

Table 45. Regression coefficients IS-IT alignment predictor (AL)

		Unstandardized Coefficients		Standardized Coefficients	t	Sig.
Model		B	Std. Error	Beta		
1	(Constant)	3.607	.039		91.584	.000
	DUMMY1	-.111	.091	-.051	-1.223	.222
	DUMMY2	-.157	.063	.105	2.509	.012

- **Dependent Variable:** IS-IT alignment Issues (AL)

= 4.450 = Mean (AL- Tactical)

AL_{D3}= 3.607-0-0 (putting values of D1 =0 and D2=0 for control group)

= 3.607 = Mean (AL-Operational)

Analysing with the help of "Dunnet Table" which is a special table used for dummy variables for 2 treatments and 1 control group and degrees of freedom (df) as 603;

F-value $_{(Expected))}$ = 2.3

F-value$_{(observed)}$ = 5.113 (Table 44)

F-value $_{(observed)}$ is less than the expected, it does support the null hypothesis and $H1_{US0}$ is rejected in favour of $H1_{USA}$. This implies that involvement of Users at strategic, tactical and operational level do collectively describe IS-IT alignment issues (AL).

SUMMARY

Table 46 describes the hypotheses tested for the purpose of understanding the predictable behaviour of the variables. In this chapter all the null hypotheses are tested with the help of dummy variables since unequal sample sizes are dealt with in addition to the fact that the sample respondents are in distinct groups with specific deliverables. Testing of the null hypotheses formulated provides information in support of the data validated for further analyses for the variables. Validation of the model through SEM is done in the subsequent chapter.

Rejection of null hypotheses in favour of respective alternate hypotheses leads to a conclusion that the means of respective predictor groups would be representative enough to predict the summative behaviour of the sample. As shown in table 48, except in the case of "Technology pre-

Table 46. Hypotheses for tier-II variables

F_c (Critical) = 2.3 (Dunnet Table)					
Df=603	α=0.05	2 treatments			
Sl. No.	Variable Identification	Variable Description	Variable	F_c - Statistics	Null Hypothesis (H_0)
1	U1	Strategic User Preparedness	U	2.405	$H1_{U0}$: Rejected in favour of $H1_{UA}$
	U2	Tactical User Preparedness			
	U3	Operational User Preparedness			
2	I1	IS Strategy	I	4.912	$H1_{I0}$: Rejected in favour of $H1_{IA}$
	I2	Interface Strategy			
	I3	Transaction Strategy			
3	T1	IT Strategy	T	1.119	$H1_{T0}$: Fails to reject
	T2	Component Strategy			
	T3	Interface Strategy			
4	C1 (Strategic)	User perception on Organisation	C1	3.718	$H1_{C10}$: Rejected in favour of $H1_{C1A}$
	C1 (Tactical)				
	C1 (Operational)				
5	C2 (Strategic)	User Perception on IT	C2	2.836	$H1_{C20}$: Rejected in favour of $H1_{C2A}$
	C2 (Tactical)				
	C2 (Operational)				
6	C3 (Strategic)	Decision Making Style	C3	2.472	$H1_{C30}$: Rejected in favour of $H1_{C3A}$
	C3 (Tactical)				
	C3 (Operational)				
7	PP (Strategic)	Planning and Policy	PP	0.027	$H1_{PP0}$: Fails to reject
	PP (Tactical)				
	PP (Operational)				
8	PM (Strategic)	Project Management	PM	0.885	$H1_{PM0}$: Fails to reject
	PM (Tactical)				
	PM (Operational)				

continued on following page

Table 46. Continued

F_c (Critical) = 2.3 (Dunnet Table)					
9	UM (Strategic)	User Motivation	UM	5.729	$H1_{UM0}$: Rejected in favour of $H1_{CMA}$
	UM (Tactical)				
	UM (Operational)				
10	VC (Strategic)	Vendor Management	VC	0.027	$H1_{VC0}$: Fails to reject
	VC (Tactical)				
	VC (Operational)				
11	AT (Strategic)	IT Acquisition	AT	2.495	$H1_{AT0}$: Rejected in favour of $H1_{ATA}$
	AT (Tactical)				
	AT (Operational)				
12	LL (Strategic)	Life Cycle	LL	3.562	$H1_{AL0}$: Rejected in favour of $H1_{ALA}$
	LL (Tactical)				
	LL (Operational)				
13	SA (Strategic)	Acquisition Success	SA	2.575	$H1_{SA0}$: Rejected in favour of $H1_{SAA}$
	SA (Tactical)				
	SA (Operational)				
14	US (Strategic)	User Satisfaction	US	5.232	$H1_{US0}$: Rejected in favour of $H1_{USA}$
	US (Tactical)				
	US (Operational)				
15	AL (Strategic)	Alignment	AL	5.113	$H1_{AL0}$: Rejected in favour of $H1_{ALA}$
	AL (Tactical)				
	AL (Operational)				

paredness (T)", "Planning and Policy (PP)", "Vendor Control and Management (VC)" and "Project Management Capability (PM)" other variables do collectively predict the summative representation of their respective variables.

REFERENCES

Carmines, E. G., & Zeller, R. A. (1994). Reliability and validity assessment. In *International Handbook of Quantitative Applications in the Social Sciences* (*Vol. 4*, pp. 154–160). London: Sage Publications.

Mcliver, J. P., & Carmines, E. G. (1994). Unidimensional scaling. In *International Handbook of Quantitative Applications in the Social Sciences* (*Vol. 4*, pp. 154–160). London: Sage Publications.

Nonaka, I. (1988). Toward middle-up-down management: Accelerating information creation. *Sloan Management Review*, *29*(3), 9–18.

Nunnally, J. C. (1978). *Psychometric theory*. New York: McGraw-Hill.

Pearce, J. A., & Robinson, R. B. (1996). *Strategic management: Formulation, implementation and control*. Burr Ridge, IL: Irwin.

Pedhazur, E. J. (1997). *Multiple regression in behavioral research* (3rd ed.). New York: Harcourt Brace College Publishers.

Spector, P. E. (1988). Development of the work locus of control scale. *Journal of Operational Psychology*, *61*, 335–340.

Chapter 10
The Validation Process for Tier–III Variables and Fitness of the Model

ABSTRACT

The validation of the model is dependent on the strength of the relationships established through variables, and Tier-III influencers are designed to ensure the validation process at a macro level. Tier-III influencers of the model help us understand the relations between variables matching (fitting) the data (Tier-I and II) and the way they influence the appropriateness of the model. Tier-III influencers characterize theoretical testing of the model and are mostly based on theory-driven search for the important antecedents of one or more focal variables. Tier-III influencers help us understand the relationship among the variables governing the outcome of the proposed model. It is agreed that the process of testing or validating theoretical models with survey data is addressed by first determining the adequacy of the measures of the unobserved variables in the model and then determining the reasonableness or adequacy of the hypothesized model. Measurements of Tier-III use conceptual definitions of the unobserved or latent variables, along with observed variables or items that measure these unobserved or latent variables. This chapter discusses model-to-data fit and parameter estimates by utilizing structural equation analysis. Model adequacy is determined by using hypotheses and model-to-data fit and parameter estimates from structural models.

VALIDATIONS OF TIER-III VARIABLES

For theoretical model testing researchers tend to agree that specifying and testing models using unobserved variables with multiple item measures of these unobserved variables and survey data involve: *1)* defining model Variable, *2)* stating

relationships among these variables, *3)* developing appropriate measures of these variables, *4)* gathering data using these measures, *5)* validating these measures, and *6)* validating the model (i.e., testing the stated relationships among the variables) (Bollen, 1991).

As shown in Figure 1 (reproduced from chapter six), Tier-I variables are examined for their applicability to predict the respective independent variables through summative nature of these items

DOI: 10.4018/978-1-4666-4201-0.ch010

(Nunnally, 1978) as explained in detail in Chapter 8. Tier-II variables representing independent variables are tested through hypotheses formulated for its predictability as discussed in Chapter 9. It is seen that these independent variables, otherwise termed as observed variables measured through the items of the questionnaire have collectively predicted its summated Tier-II variables. Tier-III variables are the unobserved variables ("latent variables") of the model. These Tier-III variables are tested and validated for their relationships in order to measure the overall fitness of the model. Besides discussing the application of Structural Equation Modelling (SEM) principles for the proposed model, its overall fitness is also tested in this chapter.

The relationship is generated through structural equation modelling. Application of structural equation modelling provides the relationship through two types of equations i.e. measurement equations and structural equations (Pedhazure, 1997). It brings the advantages over multiple regressions because of its flexibility to predict the validity of model in the face of multi-colinearity; and use of Confirmatory Factor Analysis (CFA)

to reduce measurement error. SEM techniques incorporate and integrate path analysis and factor analysis. Besides, as SEM supports "causal thinking", it prepares correlation matrix and covariance matrix for analyses as desired for understanding the "goodness-of-fit" of the model. SEM tries to address some limitations/ shortcomings experienced in multiple regressions. First, multiple regression assumes "one dependent variable" though there could be a number of "predictors". Second, multiple regressions do not use a dependent variable as a predictor for the next stage which is rather a reality in most of the problem statements. Third, measurement of error for dependent variables in regression analysis is mostly ignored. Latent variables are difficult to measure or predict and therefore, would normally lead to having error in measuring these.

"Pre-acquisition process preparedness (P)", "Climate preparedness (C)", "Organisation preparedness (O)", "Acquisition Process (AQ)" and "IT Acquisition Success (G)" are difficult to measure and therefore, are considered as latent variables which are prone to have measurement errors.

Figure 1. Variables used for the model

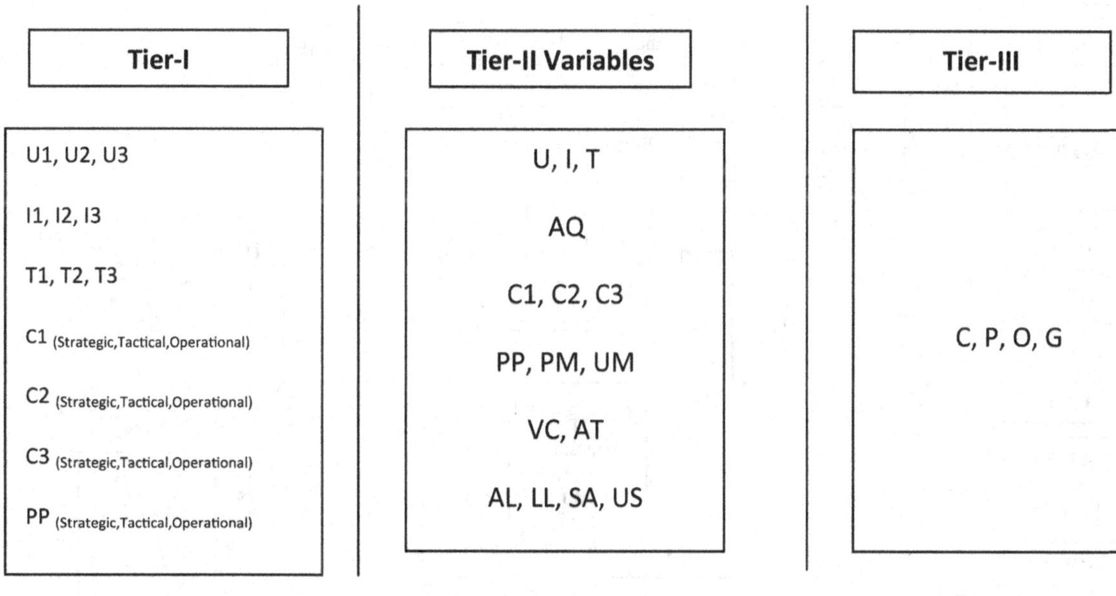

Tier-I	Tier-II Variables	Tier-III
U1, U2, U3 I1, I2, I3 T1, T2, T3 C1 (Strategic,Tactical,Operational) C2 (Strategic,Tactical,Operational) C3 (Strategic,Tactical,Operational) PP (Strategic,Tactical,Operational)	U, I, T AQ C1, C2, C3 PP, PM, UM VC, AT AL, LL, SA, US	C, P, O, G

Table 1. Variables for tier-III

Tier – II Variables *	Variable Notation	Tier-III**
User Preparedness	U	Pre-Acquisition Preparedness (P)
IS Preparedness	I	
Technology Preparedness	T	
User Perception on Organisation	C1	Climate Preparedness (C)
User Perception on IT	C2	
User Perception on Architecture	C3	
Planning and Policy	PP	Organisation Preparedness (O)
Project Management	PM	
User Motivation	UM	
Vendor Management	VC	IT Acquisition Preparedness (AQ)
Acquisition Process	AT	
Successful Acquisition	SA	Post Acquisition Status (G)
Life Cycle	LL	
User Satisfaction	US	
Alignment	AL	

* Independent Variables; ** Latent Variables

MODEL IDENTIFICATION

Path Analysis (PA) and SEM are used for identification and testing of models. PA and SEM are extensions to multiple regression and factor analysis. "Path diagrams" are used primarily to understand the SEM technique which visualise the relationships among the variables. In PA and SEM "independent" and "predictor" variables are termed as "exogenous" and "endogenous" respectively. Figure 2 later in this section describes the model and the relationships among these variables. Besides, it explains the path the variables traverse to explain the relationship. Hypotheses framed are already discussed in Chapter 3. These are represented in Figure 2 for better clarity. As described in Figure 1, Tier-II variables constitute "exogenous variables" and Tier-III variables constitute "endogenous variables". Table 2 represents these variables in detail. The basic framework of the model consists of endogenous variables which are not directly measurable and are based on unobservable theo-

Figure 2. The proposed model

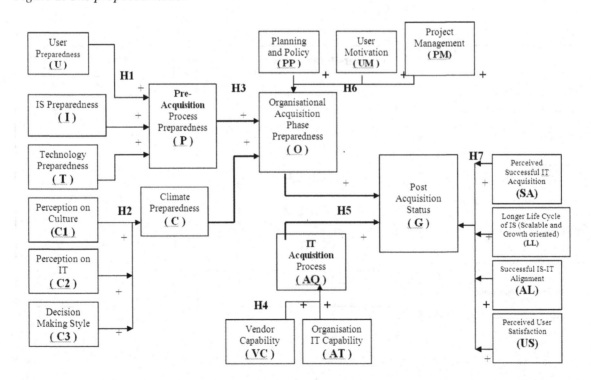

Table 2. Notations used for LISREL SEM

Symbol Used	Description	Notation
$- \cdot \blacktriangleright$	Error Measurement	δ
▭	Independent (Observed) Variable	U,I,T,C1,C2,C3,VC,AT,PP,PM,UM,AL,LLUS,SA
◯	Latent Dependent Ex-ogenous Variables	ξ (Unobserved) represented by P, C, AQ
◯	Latent Dependent En-dogenous Variables	η (Unobserved) represented by O,G
•••••••••▶	Path Coefficient	λ, denotes loading of indicator on Dependent Variable
——————▶	Path Coefficient	γ, denotes dependency between Dependent Variables

retical variables. These however, are measured through validation of hypothesised structural model using statistical techniques.

PATH ANALYSIS

Usually two strategies are used to tackle the problem of measuring latent variables. The first is selection of a single variable for each theoretical variable which is very rare in real life situation. The second approach is to have a group of indicators and assigning pre-determined weights to these indicators to predict the variable. Both these approaches are prone to errors and biases; and therefore, we have adopted Linear Structural Relationship (LISREL), an algorithm under SEM that adopts the process of latent structure analysis (Dillon and Goldstein, 1984). This adopts a structural framework with better results through confirmatory path analysis. In SEM technique PA is very important factor like factor analysis and multiple regressions. There is a limit to having a number of paths in SEM diagram in which number of parameters needs to be less than or equal to the number of observations.

Measurement Equations and Modelling in SEM

Structural equations express the relations among exogenous and endogenous variables. More often these variables are unobserved and therefore, called as latent or endogenous (true) variable. In LISREL, latent dependent (endogenous) variables are designated as "η", whereas latent independent (exogenous) variables are designated as "ξ". The model through LISREL is shown in Figure 3.

Table 2 and Figure 3 describe the generic representation of the modal through LISREL (Pedhazur, 1997).

ESTIMATION

Processing the data captured through survey is done through LISREL 8.7. Path diagram and path analysis are major deliverables of this software which translates the relationship among variables through path coefficients. It is a technique that explores simultaneous causal relationships among multiple variables. These variables are explained in Table 2. Reliability of these exogenous variables

Figure 3. LISREL path diagram for the proposed model

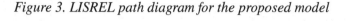

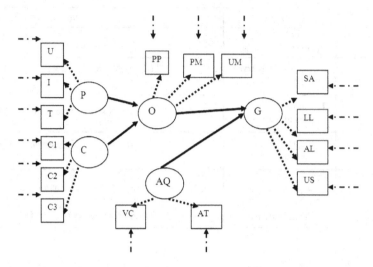

has been tested in chapters 8 and Figure 4 displays the model delivered by the LISREL software based on the model described in Figure 2. The exogenous and endogenous variables defined in Table 2 have described the path coefficients available with each arrow that relates these two variables. Exogenous variables have displayed their "disturbances" against each and these are "measurement errors" constrained. Using confirmatory analysis (CFA), the model is tested through

Figure 4. LISREL path diagram for the model

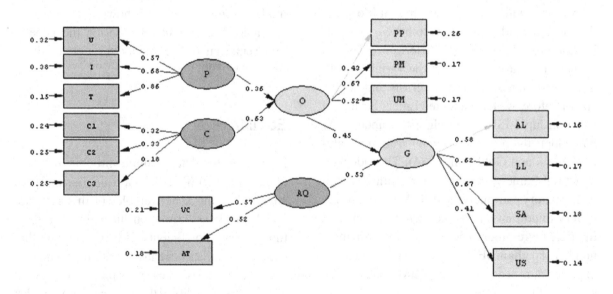

Chi-Square=202.83, df=83, P-value=0.00000, RMSEA=0.049

1. Hypothesising the relationships between variables.
2. Testing the relationships between theoretical variables and observations/measures used to define these.

Number of observations however, is not based on sample size, but number of variables in the model. The equation below shows the relationship for observations and number of variables.

Number of observations

$$N_o = \frac{[k(k+1)]}{2}$$

where k is number of variables.

In the proposed model, $N_o = 20$ and therefore, number of observations needs to be less than or equal to 2. Besides, a model needs to have less number of parameters than number of observations. In a model number of parameters is difficult to assess. Parameters aim to determine what affects endogenous variables through

1. Which paths are important.
2. What the variances of the exogenous variables are.
3. How the exogenous variables relate to each other (co-variances).
4. What the error terms (disturbances) of the endogenous variables are. (variances of endogenous variables are not important).

Number of parameters is determined as summation of *"number of paths (19)"* + *"number of variance of exogenous variables (15)"* + *"number of covariance (10)"* + *"number of disturbance terms (16)"*. In the proposed model number of paths is 19 which describes the relationship among the variables defined in Table 2. The number of variances of exogenous variables is 15 in this model and error terms (disturbances related to the endogenous variables are 5 (equal to the number of endogenous variables the model has). Total number of parameters therefore, is 60 and is well less than the number of observations (210) and thus we can go ahead for analysis of the model (Norman et al., 2003)

Table 3. Covariance matrix of exogenous variables

Variables	AL	LL	SA	US	PP	PM	UM	U	I	T	C1	C2	C3	VC	AT
AL	0.50														
LL	0.36	0.56													
SA	0.39	0.43	0.63												
US	0.24	0.25	0.27	0.30											
PP	0.24	0.28	0.29	0.15	0.44										
PM	0.39	0.41	0.44	0.28	0.27	0.62									
UM	0.31	0.31	0.34	0.23	0.21	0.36	0.44								
U	0.31	0.33	0.34	0.23	0.23	0.36	0.28	0.64							
I	0.37	0.41	0.43	0.28	0.33	0.45	0.35	0.42	0.84						
T	0.48	0.51	0.56	0.34	0.37	0.56	0.43	0.50	0.57	0.89					
C1	0.19	0.21	0.21	0.12	0.14	0.23	0.13	0.16	0.19	0.28	0.35				
C2	0.20	0.21	0.21	0.13	0.14	0.23	0.17	0.19	0.22	0.27	0.10	0.36			
C3	0.12	0.11	0.13	0.08	0.08	0.13	0.12	0.13	0.16	0.16	0.05	0.03	0.29		
VC	0.33	0.34	0.37	0.23	0.24	0.40	0.29	0.28	0.37	0.47	0.21	0.23	0.08	0.54	
AT	0.30	0.33	0.35	0.20	0.23	0.35	0.27	0.27	0.33	0.45	0.18	0.17	0.09	0.30	0.45

As regards covariance of the exogenous variables that the model produces, Table 3 provides the details. This covariance describes details regarding relationship that exogenous variables display with each other in the model.

Sample Size (N) = 604

Sample size of 604 respondents as described in chapters 5 and 6 has been considered for testing the model. Though covariance of endogenous variables is not important for analysis, these are shown in Table 4.

LISREL ESTIMATES (MAXIMUM LIKELIHOOD

Measurement Equations generated by the software LISREL are described in the Table 6.

Table 7 describes the possible effect on the Chi-Square value through modification of the path diagram.

Table 4. Covariance matrix of latent (endogenous variables)

Variables	O	G	P	C	AQ
O	1.00				
G	0.99	1.00			
P	0.97	0.95	1.00		
C	0.98	1.01	0.98	1.00	
AQ	1.02	0.99	0.97	1.07	1.00

Table 5. Correlation matrix of independent variables

Variables	P	C	AQ
P	1.00		
C	0.98 (0.02) 41.37	1.00	
AQ	0.97 (0.01) 68.84	1.07 (0.03) 41.79	1.00

FITNESS OF MODEL

Structural equation modeling is very general but very powerful multivariate analysis. These include "causal modeling through path analysis" with "Confirmatory Factor Analyses (CFA)" and "examining Goodness of Fit (*GoF*)". These are tested in order to understand the relationship through structural equation generated. While it is unreasonable to expect a structural model to fit properly because structural model with linear equation is a mere approximation, "fitness" of the model attempts to approximate this relationship.

CAUSAL MODELING THROUGH PATH ANALYSIS WITH CFA

Running the model through LISREL, generating path coefficients along with associated data, testing of hypotheses are the major deliveries of the model specified. Proposed hypotheses are already discussed in chapter 3 and are reproduced here along values obtained from LISREL modeling. Table 8 describes these in detail.

Table 8 above captures the hypotheses proposed, path coefficients each path displays to establish the relationship between latent endogenous variables and latent exogenous variables; loadings that each latent exogenous variable provides on each observed exogenous variable related to it (Pedhazur, 1997). Path analysis looks for a relationship through the "sign" attached to the coefficients. These path coefficients (standardized) are called "parameters" and are β's in a regression equation. Since hypotheses proposed expected a "positive" relationship among the variables with a direction attached to each and coefficients displayed the positive relationship, the result is in conformity with the hypotheses postulated. Besides, statistical tests can be applied to the paths mentioned in the model. In this process "theory of trimming" can be applied as is done in any "significance testing" for the hypotheses through regression analysis using F-test or

Table 6. Measurement equations and structural equations

Path Traced	Relationship	Error Variance	T-Statistics*	Standard Error	R²
U-P	U=0.57*P	0.32	19.52	0.029	0.50
I-P	I=0.68*P	0.38	20.85	0.033	0.55
T-P	T=0.86*P	0.15	28.54	0.030	0.84
C1-C	C1=0.32*C	0.24	14.26	0.023	0.30
C2-C	C2=0.33*C	0.25	14.39	0.023	0.30
C3-C	C3=0.18*C	0.25	8.49	0.021	0.11
VC-AQ	VC=0.57*AQ	0.21	22.15	0.026	0.60
AT-AQ	AT=0.52*AQ	0.18	21.96	0.024	0.59
PP-O	PP=0.43*O	0.26	16.74	0.015	0.42
PM-O	PM=0.67*O	0.17	17.98	0.037	0.72
UM-O	UM=0.52*O	0.17	16.81	0.031	0.61
AL-G	AL=0.58*G	0.16	15.14	0.011	0.68
LL-G	LL=0.62*G	0.17	24.83	0.025	0.69
SA-G	SA=0.67*G	0.18	25.43	0.026	0.72
US-G	US=0.41*G	0.14	20.81	0.020	0.54
O-P-C	O=0.36*P+0.63*C	0.035	1.98(P) 3.55 (C)	0.12 (P) 0.14 (C)	0.97
G-P-C-AQ	G = 0.16*P + 0.28*C + 0.53*AQ	0.031	1.35(P) 2.06 (C) 2.60 (AQ)	0.12 (P) 0.14 (C) 0.21 (AQ)	0.97

*Note: $p < 0.05$

Table 7. Modifications in path coefficients suggested by LISREL

Introduction of Path in Path Diagram		Possible Decrease in Chi-Square	Path Coefficient
From	To		
C	U	11.0	-0.45
C	T	14.2	0.66
P	C3	13.2	0.41

t-test. It is accepted that t-statistics values lower than tabled values are termed as unacceptable and need to be dropped from model. Though tests of the significance of path coefficients do not constitute a test of the model as a whole, it can be tested for individual equations generated by the model and suitably delete the equation or relationship from the model. This would specify that though over all model tests to be significant individual path does not. Researchers tend to chose an arbitrary criterion of meaningfulness for deletion of path coefficients having t-values smaller than 0.05. Though theory of trimming has serious limitations of being applied *post-hoc* for hypothesis testing, it provides rather an indication to understand the status of the path coefficients (Pedhazur, 1997). Further testing a parameter for its significance is as important to support a hypothesis as the applicability of theory of trimming. It is noted that "t-values" for parameter estimates larger than 2 (two) are normally judged to be different form zero and therefore, can be said to be significant (Joreskog & Sorbom, 1989). In some methods z-test are derived through the equation ($Z-Test = \frac{PathCeofficient}{SandardError}$) and is examined. Z-

Table 8. Testing of hypotheses proposed through the model

Hypothesis: Proposition	Path Coefficient	T-Statistics*	Z-Test	R^2	Remarks
$H1_0$: *Pre-acquisition preparedness is not positively associated with users' preparedness, IS preparedness and Technology preparedness in the organisation.*	0.57	19.52	19.65	0.50	Path coefficient is positive and t-statistics is significant, *Hypothesis $H1_0$ is rejected in favour of $H1_A$*
	0.68	20.85	20.60	0.55	
	0.86	28.54	28.60	0.84	
$H2_0$: *Organisation culture, Attitude of users towards IT and Decision making Style and Architecture do not collectively affect positively the IT acquisition process preparedness in the pre-acquisition phase.*	0.32	14.26	13.91	0.30	Path coefficient is positive and t-statistics is significant, *Hypothesis $H2_0$ is rejected in favour of $H2_A$*
	0.33	14.39	14.34	0.11	
	0.18	8.49	8.57	0.18	
$H3_0$**: *Organisational preparedness in the pre-acquisition phase do not positively depend on the climate preparedness and pre-acquisition preparedness of the organisation on users, IS and IT.*	0.36 (P) 0.63 (C)	1.98(P) 3.55(C)	2.0 (P) 3.5 (C)	0.97	Path coefficient is positive and t-statistics is significant, *Hypothesis $H3_0$ is rejected in favour of $H3_A$*
$H4_0$: *Capability of vendors and capability of IT acquisition organisation do not have positive effect IT acquisition process*	0.57	22.15	21.92	0.60	Path coefficient is positive and t-statistics is significant, *Hypothesis $H4_0$ is rejected in favour of $H4_A$*
	0.52	21.96	21.60	0.59	
$H5_0$**:*Delivery of IT in post-acquisition phase does not get influenced positively with preparedness of the organisation and proper IT acquisition process*	0.45 (O) 0.53 (AQ)	2.19(O) 2.60(AQ)	2.14 (O) 2.52 (AQ)	0.98	Path coefficient is positive and t-statistics is significant, *Hypothesis $H5_0$ is rejected in favour of $H5_A$*
$H6_0$: *Policy of the organisation on users, Planning and Policy on technology, User Motivation and Project Management Capability do not positively relate to organisational preparedness in the pre-acquisition phase.*	0.43	16.74	28.66	0.42	Path coefficient is positive and t-statistics is significant, *Hypothesis $H6_0$ is rejected in favour of $H6_A$*
	0.67	17.98	18.10	0.72	
	0.52	16.81	16.77	0.61	
$H7_0$: *Success of IT acquired in post-acquisition phase does not depend positively on technology acquisition, user satisfaction, longer life cycle, IS-IT alignment.*	0.58 (AL)	15.14(AL)	52.77	0.68	Path coefficient is positive and t-statistics is significant, *Hypothesis $H7_0$ is rejected in favour of $H7_A$*
	0.62(LL)	24.83(LL)	24.80	0.69	
	0.67(SA)	25.43(SA)	25.76	0.72	
	0.41(US)	20.81(US)	20.50	0.54	

Note: $p < 0.05$

value exceeding critical value of 1.96 is termed to be significant (Norman & Streiner, 2003).

As Table 8 describes all path coefficients are above 0.05 indicating usefulness of the relationships that each path portrays. Therefore, all the paths are to be retained in the model. Besides, all t-statistics are well above the threshold value of 2 except for the path coefficients of "latent exogenous variables P; value being 1.98". However, the z-tests reveal all values to be above 1.96 and therefore, parameters are significant. Though in the case of "P" value of t-statistics is below the critical values, this is retained since this parameter has a significant role and theory of trimming recommends for retaining these parameters.

ANALYSES ON HYPOTHESIS

Since values used for tests of significance are quite reasonably well satisfying, hypotheses are tested to be acceptable. Now the results need to be evaluated for each hypothesis proposed.

From Figure 5, it is quite evident that loading of pre-acquisition preparedness has been strongest through "technology preparedness" with a parameter estimate of 0.86 followed by "IS preparedness" having a value of 0.68 and the least is "user preparedness" having a value of 0.57. However, it implies that there is a "positive effect" on pre-acquisition preparedness through User preparedness (Rai et al., 2002), and IS preparedness (Segars & Grover, 1998) and technology preparedness (Venkatesh et al., 2003) and are established through the hypothesis that these need to be examined during the pre-acquisition phase for IT in an organization and cannot be overlooked. Hypothesis H1, is therefore established confirming the dependency proposed as $P = d*(U,I,T)$.

HYPOTHESIS H2

Figure 6 provides an indication for the relationship through loading of "climate preparedness" on "organization", "organization perception on technology" and "decision-making process in the organization". Estimated parameters are noted to be 0.32, 0.33 and 0.18 respectively. It establishes a positive relationship and confirms the dependency postulated as $C = d*(C1,C2,C3)$. It is further noted that organisation culture and organisation perception on technology provide an equally important effect in the process since organisation culture can inhibit or accelerate the process of adoption and acceptance of technology (Olson, 1982). User perception on technology also seems to be playing an equally important role in the assessing the climate (Evans, 2004). Decision making process in the organisation also finds a place in affecting the acquisition process and strategic managers do have an important role in the process (Jamsen et al., 1999).

Figure 7 displays a relationship between exogenous and endogenous variables required to understand the effect through parameters generated by the model. It is evident that parameter estimated for establishing the relationship between pre-acquisition preparedness thus arrived at pre-

Figure 5. Explanation of pre-acquisition preparedness

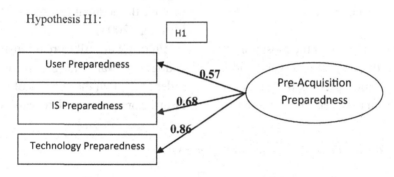

Figure 6. Explanation of climate preparedness

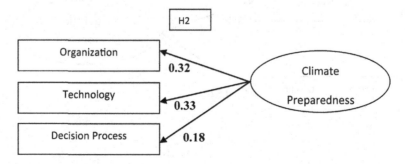

Figure 7. Explanation of organization preparedness

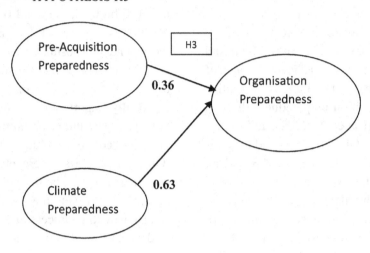

viously is quite significant (0.36) whereas user perception and culture in the organization play a dominant role in influencing the acquisition process compared to that of climate preparedness (0.18). Thus hypothesis H3 is established. Besides, both the variables display a positive relationship as hypothesized and dependency (Luftman, 2003; Rai et al., 2002) is proved to be true O= $d*$ (P,C). It is further noted that climate preparedness does not play a vital role in the pre-acquisition phase, but could influence.

Acquisition process is one of the most important processes for the acquiring organization. Loading of IT acquisition process preparedness is noted to be uniform between "Vendor control

and assessment" and "internal IT capability" having values 0.57 and 0.52 respectively as shown in Figure 8. This ensures a positive relationship and therefore, establishes the hypothesis H5 and dependency postulated as AQ= $d*$ (AT,VC). It confirms that these two factors are quite important to be assessed and this would establish organisation's internal capability to manage vendors and organise its own IT capabilities to define and manage the acquisition process (Pressman, 1997; Luftman, 2003).

Figure 9 describes relationship among latent endogenous variables generated by the model in order to explain the success of the acquisition of IT in the organization. It reveals that "organization

Figure 8. Explanation for measuring acquisition process

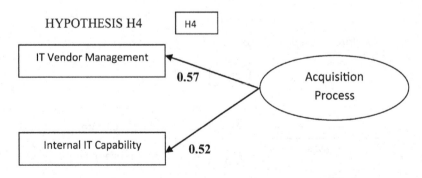

Figure 9. Explanation for measuring acquisition success

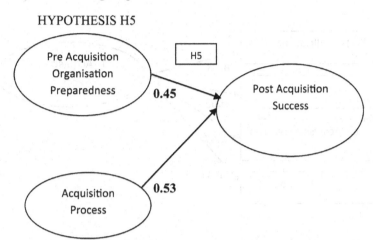

preparedness" and "acquiring process" affect positively the success of the IT acquired with parameters as 0.45 and 0.53 respectively. This establishes the hypothesis H6 and dependency postulated as G = d* (O,AQ). It is noted that IT acquisition process affects less the success in comparison to the organisation preparedness which establishes the reason behind postulation of this model and research. Therefore, acquiring organisation needs to make sincere effort to organise this preparedness prior to embarking on the acquisition process (Luftman et al., 2002).

Figure 10 provides a methodology to understand the existence of organization preparedness. Three exogenous variables "planning and policy", "project management" and "user motivation" are found to be loaded positively to understand orga-

nization preparedness with parameters as 0.43, 0.67 and 0.52 respectively. It is noted that planning and policy is having the least loading whereas other to variables are loaded uniformly. However, all the variables are "positively" loaded thus establishing the hypothesis H4. Planning and policy, project management and user motivation therefore, have definite effects on the organization preparedness (Luftman, 2003). This establishes the dependency postulated as O = d*(PP,PM,UM).

HYPOTHESIS H7

Figure 11 displays loading of exogenous variables "IS-IT alignment", "Life Cycle", System Acquisition success" and "User Satisfaction" by

Figure 10. Explanation for measuring organization preparedness

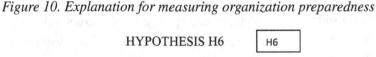

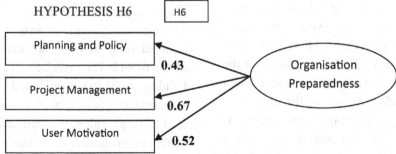

Figure 11. Explanation for understanding acquisition success

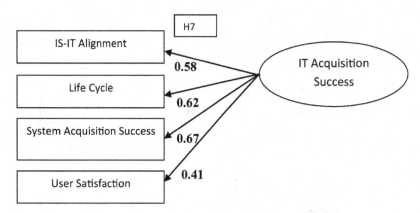

endogenous variable "Organization's IT Acquisition Success". It is important that IT acquired should have a better alignment between business and technology (Luftman, 2003). It should also ensure a better life cycle of the technology acquired and provide system usability besides giving user satisfaction (Jokela, 2001). The model derives positive relationship through parameters as 0.58, 0.62, 0.67 and 0.41 respectively. It therefore, establishes the hypothesis H7 and proved dependency $G = d*$ (SA, LL, AL, US).

It further establishes that these exogenous variables are loaded uniformly thereby forcing the IT acquiring organization to work effectively towards achieving these goals (Ward & Peppard, 2002).

GOODNESS OF FIT ASSESSMENT

Looking at the path coefficients in the path diagram provides an indication for individual relationship among variables thereby testing hypotheses postulated for each relationship. Significance level of each relationship is measured through t-statistics of the relationship. However, looking at the model proposed as a whole and testing it is another task that needs to be accomplished and this is done through "goodness-of-fit chi-square (χ^2_{GoF})". In normal regression analysis χ^2 is tested

to reject a null hypothesis so as to claim support for its alternative and the higher the value the better would be the difference between observed data and expected findings. (expected values are seen through null hypothesis having no relationship with variables). Because one usually aims to demonstrate that there is an association, observed values should differ from expected ones and more the difference, the better and larger would be the value of χ^2. However, in this fitness test for χ^2_{GoF}, it is assumed that the researcher does not wish to reject the model, but tries to test the model for its fitness with conceptual framework arrived at. It is because it is expected that difference between the observed data and hypothesised model needs to be small. Therefore, the smaller value of χ^2 is better (Joreskog and Sorbom, 1993). It is therefore, sometimes called as "badness-of-fit". In true sense χ^2 equal to 0 and p-value equal to 1 represents a perfect fit. This means that a non-significant χ^2 would lead to a better model.

Validity of a χ^2 test for the structural model has bagged a mixed response. Many dispute the findings while there are many test metrics and parameters found by researchers to test the fitness of the model. The premise of the dispute is that validity of χ^2 test is predicted based on sample size apart from other issues. A larger sample would lead to larger value. A small sample size would lead to an insignificant χ^2 (accepting the model to be fit) whereas a larger sample would lead to higher value of χ^2 (rejecting a null hypothesis). Therefore, χ^2_{GoF} test is sensitive to normality of data and to the sample size as wee; too many subjects will make it significant and too few subject would render it insignificant (Norman & Streiner, 2003). Since this is the only index that is attached with the test of significance, it is a serious concern and it is mostly observed that χ^2 is not valid in most empirical applications (Joreskog and Sorbom, 1993; Pedhazur, 1997).

It is observed by researchers that χ^2 is a measure of "fit" than a test-statistic. In other words, it tests the difference, discrepancy, and deviation between sample covariance matrix and correlation matrix (R^2). In many cases therefore, degrees of freedom (*df*) serves as a standard index by which χ^2 is judged, if small. In other words χ^2/df ratio determines the validity of the fitness of the model, lower is better and "three" is the threshold for its evaluation (Spector, 1988). It is argued that a value 2 or 3 for χ^2/df ration finds a good result for the model (Norman & Streiner, 2003). There is however, no agreement for the smallness of this ratio.

There are other indices to understand the fitness of the model, but mostly grouped in two categories: "comparative fit" and "variance explained". Among the comparative fit indices the most prominent are "Normed Fit Index (NFI)", "Non-Normed Fit Index (NNFI)". These tests are organized to understand if the model differs from the null hypothesis that none of the variables are related to each other. But the problem is that alike in R^2; better outcome is there with the increase in number of parameters for the model. Though there are many comparative fit indices, these are based on the ideas of 1) how much the model deviates from the null hypothesis of no relationships and 2) reduction in the index with increase in number of variables (Norman & Streiner, 2003). It is assumed that a value near to 1 (range is 0 through 1) for the model finds its fitness to be of acceptable limit (Kline, 1998; Mcliver and Carmines, 1994).

As regards variance explained, the measures are Goodness-of-fit Index (GoF), Adjusted Goodness-of-fit (AGFI). These depend on the number of parameters (the fewer the better) and sample size (the more is better). It should take the values between 0 (displaying total lack of fit) and 1 (displaying perfect fit). This has also an analogy between R^2 measured and GFI/AGFI (Tanaka, 1993).

Apart from the above indices, Root mean square residual (RMR) and standardized root mean square residual (SRMR) are two indices used for evaluation. These depend on the variance matrix and correlation matrix and its values range between 0 (specifying perfect fit) and 1 (meaning no model at all) where all the correlations are zero. It is also argued that RMR is an inferior index compared to GFI/AGFI (Joreskog, and Sorbom, 1989). It is also argued that there is no straight forward assessment of fit for the model and it is argued that there should be much faith in any fit-index in isolation (Selvin, 1991).

RESULTS AND ANALYSIS

Table 9 shows the "goodness-of-fit" statistics for the model generated through LISREL/PRELIS.

Analyzing the fitness of model of this kind is always contested by various researchers. A plethora of indices are in circulation for understanding and evaluating the fitness of the model. It is quite evident from various researches that an index strongly argued in favor is at times refuted by another researcher. Therefore, while there is no assured index to base the findings and prove in favor, it is essential to understand the underlying principle of its applicability and make the finding contextual.

The Comparative Fit Index (CFI) falls under the category of non-centrality indices and the critical value is $>= 0.90$ (Bollen & lennox, 1991). This value provides a non-centrality to argue in favour of accepting χ^2 for the null hypothesis

Table 9. Goodness of fit statistics

Sl. No.	Indicator	Observed Value	Critical Value
1	CFI	0.99	>= 0.90 (value near to 1) (Bollen & lennox, 1991)
2	Relative Chi- Square (χ^2:*df*)	(202.83:83) 2.5: 1	3:1 (Kline, 1998; Spector, 1988)
3	Goodness of Fit Index (GFI)	0.96	>= 0.90 (value near to 1) (Bentler,1992)
	Adjusted Goodness of Fit Index (AGFI)	0.94	
	Root Mean Square Error of Approximation (RMSEA)	0.049	<= 0.08: Acceptable Fit <= 0.06: Good Fit (Bentler,1992; Browne, Cudek,1993)
4	Normed Fit Index (NFI)	0.99	>= 0.90 (value near to 1) (Bentler,1992)
5	Non-Normed Fit Index (NNFI)	0.99	
4	Root Mean Square Residual (RMR)	0.013	Value between 0 & 1 (Near to 0) (Joreskog and Sorbom, 1989)
	Standardized RMR (SRMR)	0.027	

(the proposition is to understand the relationship among variables is true) as discussed above. In this case the value is 0.99 and therefore, is acceptable in testing the model. As discussed above, χ^2/*df* ratio determines a better index for assessing the fitness of the model (though it is argued at times against). In this case against a critical value of 3:1, the result is found to be 2.5:1. This goes in favour of the fitness of the model. Table 7 however, suggests reduction in χ^2 by introducing parameters and paths in the model. It may be seen that introducing path between "U" and "C" reduces the χ^2 by 11 and other prominent paths that cause such reductions are "T" and "C" (by 14.2) followed by "C3" and "P" (by 13.2). Such additions are examined to be infeasible because the model does not provide any meaning to the objective of finding a relationship. Since there is an acceptable ratio of 2.5:1, these modifications are not considered.

Goodness-of-Fit Index (GFI) and Adjusted Goodness-of-Fit Index (AGFI) are at times called as absolute fit indices and are not used for comparison purpose, but for evaluation. Results as obtained and described in Table 7.9 are quite

above the critical values and therefore, explains the fitness of the model (Bentler, 1992). Root Mean Square Error of Approximation (RMSEA) is again a non-centrality based index and result (0.049) indicates to be within the critical values suggested to be acceptable-fit if <0.08 (Bentler,1992) and good fit if <0.06 (Browne,1993). Normed Fit Index (NFI) and Non-Normed-Fit Index (NNFI) are relative fit indices used for assessment of fit of the model. The values generated by the test (0.99 each) are well above the critical values (0.90) and therefore, support the fitness of the model proposed (Bentler,1992). Root Mean Square Residual (RMR) and Standardised Root Mean Square Residual (SRMR) are relative fit indices used for testing the model and values near to zero (0.013 and 0.027 respectively) indicates a better fit (Joreskog and Sorbom, 1989).

SUMMARY

It is observed that most of the indices generated for the model are acceptable based on having an acceptable χ^2/*df*. Path coefficients as discussed above also supported the fitness of the model. It is to be noted that path coefficients measured the model and other indices provided the support for the model as a whole. PA and SEM are quite powerful techniques. Though these are named as causal modelling, these do not prove causation (Norman & Streiner, 2003). The maximum likelihood test for the model done through the software is sensitive to deviations from the normal values suggested by research. Therefore, PA and SEM are model testing procedures and not model-building ones. This is in tune with the objective of the research done for the model and it is construed that there is not only an overall fit for the model, but it clarifies the hypothesised relationship among the variables in the model proposed.

REFERENCES

Bentler, P. M. (1992). On the fit of models to covariances and methodlogy to the bulletin. *Psychological Bulletin*, (112): 400–404. doi:10.1037/0033-2909.112.3.400 PMID:1438635.

Bollen, K. A., & Lennox, R. (1991). Conventional wisdom on measurement: A structural equation perspective. *Psychological Bulletin*, *110*(2). doi:10.1037/0033-2909.110.2.305.

Browne, M. W., & Cudek, R. (1993). Alternative ways of assessing model fit. In Bollen, K. A., & Log, J. S. (Eds.), *Testing Structural Equation Models* (pp. 136–162). Newbury Park, CA: Sage Publications.

Dillon, W. R., & Goldstein, M. (1984). *Multivariate analysis: Methods and applications*. New York: John Weily & Sons.

Evans, N. (2004). *Promoting fusion in the business-IT relationship. Paper presented in Issues in Informing Science and Information Technology Education Joint Conference*. Australia: Rock Hampton.

Jamsen, P., Ikaheimo, S., & Malinen, P. (1999). Capital formation in Kenyan farmer-owned co-operatives: A case study. Turku, Finland. ISBN 92-5-104330-2

Jokela, T. (2001). *Review of usability capability assessment approaches*. Paper presented at the 24th Information Systems Research Seminar. Scandinavia, Norway.

Joreskog, K. G., & Sorbom, D. (1989). *LISREL 8: Structural equation modelling with SIMPLIS command language*. Hillsdale, NJ: Lawrence Erlbaum.

Kline, R. B. (1998). *Principles and practice of structural equation modeling*. New York: The Guilford Press.

Luftman, J. (2003). Assessing IT/business alignment. *Information Systems Management*, *20*(4), 9–21. doi:10.1201/1078/43647.20.4.20030901/77287.2.

Luftman, J. N., Papp, R., & Brier, T. (2002, September). Enablers and inhibitors of business-IT alignment. *AB Insight*.

Mcliver, J. P., & Carmines, E. G. (1994). Unidimensional scaling. In *International Handbook of Quantitative Applications in the Social Sciences* (Vol. 4, pp. 154–160). London: Sage Publications.

Norman, R. G., & Streiner, L. D. (2003). *PDQ statistics* (3rd ed.).

Nunnally, J. C. (1978). *Psychometric theory*. New York: McGraw-Hill.

Olson, M. H. (1982). New information technology and organsiational culture. *Management Information Systems Quarterly*, 71–92. doi:10.2307/248992.

Pedhazur, E. J. (1997). *Multiple regression in behavioral research* (3rd ed.). New York: Harcourt Brace College Publishers.

Pressman, R. S. (1997). *Software engineering: A practitioner's approach* (4th ed.). Singapore: McGraw-Hill.

Rai, A., Lang, S. S., & Welker, R. B. (2002). Assessing the validity of IS success models: An empirical test and theoretical analysis. *Information Systems Research*, *13*(1), 50–69. doi:10.1287/isre.13.1.50.96.

Segars, A. H., & Grover, V. (1998, June). Strategic information systems planning: An investigation of the construct and its measurement. *Management Information Systems Quarterly*, 139–163. doi:10.2307/249393.

Selvin, S. (1991). *Statistical analysis of epidemiologic data*. New York: Oxford University Press.

Spector, P. E. (1988). Development of the work locus of control scale. *Journal of Operational Psychology*, *61*, 335–340.

Tanaka, J. S. (1993). Multifaceted conceptions of fit in structural equation models. In Bollen, K. A., & Long, J. S. (Eds.), *Testing Structural Equation Models* (pp. 19–20). Thousand Oaks, CA: Sage.

Venkatesh, V., Morris, M. G., Davis, G. B., & Davis, F. D. (2003). User acceptance of information technology: Toward a unified view. *Management Information Systems Quarterly*, *27*(3), 425–478.

Ward, J., & Peppard, J. (2002). *Strategic planning for information systems*. London: John Wiley and Sons.

Section 4
Application of Model

Chapter 11
Application of the Model:
Case–Based Studies

ABSTRACT

It is argued that models are conceptualized, designed, developed, and validated to understand complex behaviour of larger entities. Models provide indicative measurements, and their validations in real life situation need careful considerations of relevant ambient conditions. Models also provide suggestive and causal relationships among their qualitative and quantitative influencers for better predictability. Generally, predictive models provide structural equations, measurement equations with associated random errors. These errors do play vital roles in relating abstracted behavior of the model outputs with the real life situations. In order to reduce these errors to an agreed level, case-based validations of models are quite important. This chapter discusses derived measurement and structural equations that the model has produced and presents some cases to examine the appropriateness of the application of the model developed.

DERIVED MEASUREMENT EQUATIONS OF THE MODEL

Measurement equations show the relationships among latent and exogenous variables. "Classical test theory" is the basis for establishing this relationship (Cronbach et al., 1972; Linn and Werts, 1979; Susan et al., 2008; España et al., 2010). The general form of the measurement equation is shown in Figure 1.

The measurement equation here is $X = \xi + \delta$ where X is the exogenous variables which is the mean of the items summated through dummy

coding as explained in chapters eight and nine. ξ represents the endogenous variable in the equation. Each variable X thus represents a set of independent indicators (questions) administered to the respondents and ordinal data are acquired. Classical test theory considers measurement errors (δ) and provides a predictive ability to the relationship between exogenous variable and predictors. Table 1 describes the relationships and displays the foundation for such predictions.

This table provides set of questions for each of the variables. Its values are obtained from the survey instruments administered among the respondents. Using these data the values of the predicted latent exogenous variables were com-

DOI: 10.4018/978-1-4666-4201-0.ch011

Figure 1. Measurement equation (SEM) (España et al., 2010)

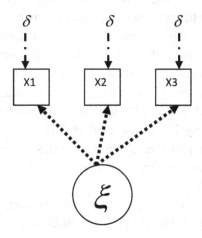

puted through measurement equations shown in the Table 1. The variable "X" with its measurement errors is obtained for each respondent for each variable and its mean across the variables in each category is computed for analysis. Table 1 indicates that latent exogenous variables U, I, T compute latent endogenous variables (ξ) P. Similarly, C1, C2, C3 variables compute C and VC, AT variables compute AQ. These variables are computed based on the summative nature of the structural equation model (Pedhazur, 1997). For example, in order to compute pre-acquisition preparedness (P), P_U, P_I, P_T are computed for the

Table 1. Measurement equation

Stratified Independent Indicators *Questions*	Dummy Codes Used *Item*	Summated Independent Indicator *Variable* x	Description of Exogenous Variable X	Latent Endogenous Variables ξ	Measurement Equation (Classical Test Theory) $(X = \xi + \delta)$
U101-U106	U1	U	User Preparedness	P Pre-Acquisition Preparedness	$U = P_U + \delta$ $I = P_I + \delta$ $T = P_T + \delta$ $(P_{mean}) = \frac{Pu+Pi+Pt}{3}$
U201-U207	U2				
U301-U307	U3				
I101-I106	I1	I	IS Preparedness		
I201-I204	I2				
I301-I306	I3				
T101-T107	T1	T	Technology Preparedness		
T201-T209	T2				
T301-T307	T3				
C101-C108	C1	C1	User Perception on Organization	C Climate Preparedness	$C1 = Cc_1 + \delta$ $C2 = Cc_2 + \delta$ $C3 = Cc_3 + \delta$ $(C_{mean}) = \frac{Cc1+Cc2+Cc3}{3}$
C201-C207	C2	C2	User Perception on IT		
C301-C307	C3	C3	User Perception on Decision Making Process		
VC01-VC06	VC	VC	Vendor Management	AQ Acquisition Process	$VC = AQ + \delta$ $AT = AQ + \delta$ $(AQ_{mean}) = \frac{AQvc+AQat}{2}$
AT01-A06	AT	AT	Acquisition Process		

users with due consideration of measurement error for each (the equation for $P_U = U - \delta$). The mean of P_U, P_I, and P_T provides the value for P as shown in Table 1. Similarly, all other variables are computed through the measurement equation.

DERIVED STRUCTURAL EQUATIONS OF THE MODEL

Apart from measurement equations, structural equations provide the predictive ability among latent exogenous variables and latent endogenous variables in the proposed model. Structural equations are represented in terms of relationships as shown in Figure 2. In the structural equations, η is denoted as latent endogenous variables predicted by associated exogenous variables ξ. The structural equations also do have errors denoted as ε.

Table 2 explains various structural equations produced through LISREL software version 8.7. These two equations are related to understand the relations for "organization's pre-acquisition preparedness" (O) in the pre-acquisition scenario and "organization's IT acquisition scenario" (G) assessed during post acquisition stage. "G" therefore, takes care of the IT acquisition process "AQ" adopted by the acquiring organization.

The first equation represented as O = 0.36*P+0.63*C+0.035 (vide Table 2) provides the tool to assess pre-acquisition preparedness in the acquiring organization. From the Table 2 in association with Figure 2, it is noted that path coefficients (γ) for the latent endogenous variable "O" are due to latent exogenous variables "P", "C" and these coefficients are 0.36 and 0.63 respectively. These are considered as factor loadings for each path the equation generates through the SEM method. Error variance (ε) for this equation is 0.035.

The second equation is the structural equation for evaluating IT acquisition status in post acquisition stage in the organization (G) and has relationship with organization's pre-acquisition stage preparedness (O) and the acquisition stage (AQ). This equation is noted to be

G=0.45*O+0.53*AQ+0.024.

The alternate equation is not considered in this discussion since it provides detailed relationship. Table 3 provides these indicators for all the sample organizations. This equation also provides the path coefficients (γ) attached to each relationship that latent exogenous variables have with latent endogenous variables used in this predictive equation (Pedhazur, 1997). These are 0.45, 0.53 in this equation. Structural equation with indirect

Figure 2. Structural equation modelling (Pedhazur, 1997)

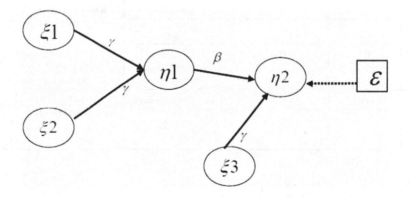

Table 2. Structural equation for predicting latent endogenous variable

Latent Exogenous Variables ξ	Description	Latent Endogenous Variables η	Description	Structural Equation $(\eta = \xi + \varepsilon)$
P ($\xi 1$)	Pre-Acquisition Preparedness	O ($\eta 1$)	Organization's IT Pre-Acquisition Preparedness	O = 0.36*P+0.63*C+0.035
C ($\xi 2$)	Climate Preparedness			
AQ ($\xi 3$)	Acquisition Process	G ($\eta 2$)	Organization's Acquisition Scenario (Post Acquisition Stage)	G = 0.45*O + 0.53 *AQ + 0.024. Alternately G = 0.16*P + 0.28*C + 0.53*AQ + 0.031

effect of the latent exogenous variables on G is considered since it provides the relationship with unobservable latent, but independent variables. (O) $\eta 1$ and (G) $\eta 2$ have three and four manifest variables respectively which are taken into consideration by the structural equations formulated through LISREL software and hence are not discussed here since the objective is to understand the relationship among three stages of the acquisition process.

Table 3. Prediction of organization's IT acquisition success (G)

Organization Number	User Preparedness (U)	IS Preparedness (I)	Technology Preparedness (T)	Pre-Acquisition User Preparedness (P)	Organization's Culture (C1)	Organization's Perception on IT (C2)	Organization's Decision Style (C3)	Organization's Climate Preparedness (C)	Pre-Acquisition Preparedness of the Organization (O)	Acquisition Process: Vendor Management (VC)	Acquisition Process: Technology Project Management (AT)	Organization's Acquisition Process Preparedness (AQ)	Organization's Acquisition Success (G)
Org.1	3.20	3.18	2.77	3.05	3.61	3.35	4.01	3.66	3.37	2.53	3.24	3.06	3.10
Org.2	3.63	3.32	3.05	3.33	3.86	3.58	4.36	3.93	3.64	2.76	3.27	4.10	3.24
Org.3	3.40	2.92	2.88	3.07	4.11	3.62	4.63	4.12	3.66	3.10	3.36	4.10	3.30
Org.4	3.48	2.56	3.08	3.04	3.99	3.61	4.17	3.92	3.53	2.78	3.36	3.86	3.24
Org.5	3.41	2.72	3.49	3.21	4.47	3.98	4.15	4.20	3.77	3.78	4.05	4.23	3.71
Org.6	3.91	3.36	3.44	3.57	4.26	3.62	4.47	4.12	3.84	3.53	3.75	4.19	3.59
Org.7	3.43	2.60	2.67	2.90	3.98	3.32	4.30	3.87	3.45	3.04	2.97	3.71	2.99
Org.8	4.04	3.16	3.59	3.60	4.31	3.57	4.71	4.20	3.90	3.41	3.98	4.31	3.73
Org.9	5.12	4.51	4.93	4.85	4.68	4.78	4.87	4.77	4.72	4.41	4.43	4.67	4.33
Org.10	3.44	3.42	2.70	3.19	3.82	3.96	4.50	4.09	3.69	3.03	3.06	3.70	3.15
Org.11	2.92	2.10	2.66	2.56	4.24	3.42	4.43	4.03	3.42	2.70	2.94	3.48	2.97
Org.12	4.37	4.30	4.84	4.50	4.98	4.32	4.99	4.76	4.59	4.16	4.35	4.49	4.23
Org.13	5.00	4.80	5.13	4.98	4.89	4.32	4.98	4.73	4.74	4.44	4.36	4.52	4.31

Table 3 provides the values obtained for each variable through measurement equation as well as structural equation. These values are analyzed hereafter.

CAUSAL ANALYSIS OF THE MODEL

Strategic alignment of business IS and IT is a major concern (Luftman, 2003) and has remained a perennial business priority. Success of IT acquisition largely depends on a successful alignment of IT with the business process. Though capability maturity model (CMM) provides a basis to assess the organization for alignment (Pressman, 2000), Luftman's strategic alignment studies advocate that IT alignment strategies are still devoid of focusing on business strategies and IT practices. Luftman's assessment model applied to 60 global 2000 companies is an attempt to assess the business strategies and IT practices. Luftman's model measures how well the IT service providers and business process owners work together or even create effective link between IT department and other department in the organization. Luftman's assessment model effectively uses Likert scaling. It suggests that assessment value as noted below in Table 4 should be used for studying the scenario.

The scale used for the proposed model is 7-point scale in Likert scaling which is in consonance with the scaling used for assessing independent variables. As shown in Table 4, score in the range $> 4.2 \leq 5.6$ in 7-point scale is appreciated in an organization to term the acquisition as success. Table 3 if read in conjunction with Table 4, provides an impression on the IT acquisition stages for the thirteen sample organizations.

INTER-SAMPLE ORGANIZATIONAL ANALYSIS

This section is devoted to assessing preparedness of the sample organizations based on the proposed framework and model. This assessment spans across all the three stages of the acquisition process i.e. Pre-Acquisition, Acquisition and Post Acquisition stages.

Assessment of Preparedness in Pre-Acquisition Stage

In this stage users, information systems, information technology and climate are assessed in the organization for fit at each level and in the process the resultant assessment of the variable is captured.

Table 4. Scaling attributes in Luftman's strategic IS-IT alignment model

Scale in Percent*	Organizational Assessment Description	Scale for Assessment in Proposed Model**
$> 1 \leq 20$ Percent	Fit does not exist, organization is ineffective	≤ 1.4
$>20 \leq 40$ Percent	Low level of Fit	$> 1.4 \leq 2.8$
$>40 \leq 60$ Percent	Moderate Fit, moderately effective	$> 2.8 \leq 4.2$
$> 60 \leq 80$ Percent	Mostly Fit	$> 4.2 \leq 5.6$
≥ 80 Percent	Strong level of Fit	≥ 5.6

(* Note: Percent of the highest value in the scale; ** The values are computed on 7-point Likert scale used in the study)

Table 5 and Figure 3 explain the user level assessment for understanding their involvement in the IT acquisition process. It is noted that strategic level involvement is moderately fit in eight and mostly fit in five organizations. It is essential that of strategic users need to involve themselves in this alignment exercise (Ward & Peppard, 2002). Interestingly, in four organizations the involvement of tactical managers is mostly fit whereas in eight organizations it is moderate. Only one organization showed strong fit in the tactical level. As regards operational users, three organizations have shown a good fit and remaining ten organizations have displayed "moderate fit". As an overall assessment, eight organizations appear to have a "moderate fit" across all the three layers of the decision making process whereas five have shown a good fit. In an IT pre-acquisition process, a moderate

Table 5. User level assessment

Org.No.	Us	Assessment	Ut	Assessment	Uo	Assessment	U	Assessment
1	3.88	Moderate Fit	3.28	Moderate Fit	3.39	Moderate Fit	3.52	Moderate Fit
2	3.55	Moderate Fit	4.24	Mostly Fit	4.06	Moderate Fit	3.95	Moderate Fit
3	3.50	Moderate Fit	3.60	Moderate Fit	4.06	Moderate Fit	3.72	Moderate Fit
4	4.08	Moderate Fit	3.50	Moderate Fit	3.83	Moderate Fit	3.80	Moderate Fit
5	4.14	Moderate Fit	3.36	Moderate Fit	3.69	Moderate Fit	3.73	Moderate Fit
6	5.00	Mostly Fit	3.92	Moderate Fit	3.77	Moderate Fit	4.23	Mostly Fit
7	3.47	Moderate Fit	4.23	Mostly Fit	3.54	Moderate Fit	3.75	Moderate Fit
8	4.31	Mostly Fit	4.67	Mostly Fit	4.11	Moderate Fit	4.36	Mostly Fit
9	5.57	Mostly Fit	5.70	Strong level of Fit	5.04	Mostly Fit	5.44	Mostly Fit
10	3.83	Moderate Fit	3.71	Moderate Fit	3.75	Moderate Fit	3.76	Moderate Fit
11	2.90	Moderate Fit	3.17	Moderate Fit	3.64	Moderate Fit	3.24	Moderate Fit
12	4.64	Mostly Fit	4.19	Moderate Fit	5.25	Mostly Fit	4.69	Mostly Fit
13	5.56	Mostly Fit	5.26	Mostly Fit	5.15	Mostly Fit	5.32	Mostly Fit

Us: Strategic User; Ut: Tactical User; Uo: Operational User; U: Overall User Assessment

Figure 3. User level assessment in sample organizations

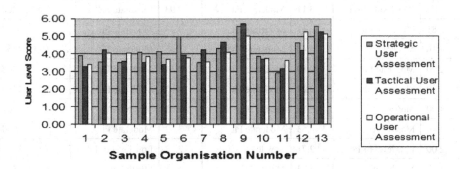

Figure 4. IS assessment in sample organizations

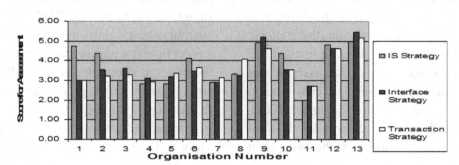

involvement is not adequate and it means that all the organizations seem to be lacking in motivating the users at all levels and strategic decision makers seem to be lacking in drive to deploy IT in the organization.

Organizing information systems, understanding interfaces among information systems and exploring formalizations of transactions are necessary pre-requisites for an organization to prioritize technology interventions (Ward & Peppard, 2002; Luftman et al., 2002; Monarch et al., 2004). It is observed from Table 6 and Figure 4 that information system fit is moderate in nine sample organizations whereas two have shown a good fit and one has shown a low fit. IS strategy in particular, has shown a low-fit in two sample organizations, moderate in five and most fit in six sample organizations. Interface strategy is moderately fit in nine sample organizations, most fit in three organizations and low fit in one organiza-

Table 6. Information systems assessment

Org.No	I1	Assessment	I2	Assessment	I3	Assessment	I	Assessment
1	4.71	Mostly Fit	2.99	Moderate Fit	2.97	Moderate Fit	3.56	Moderate Fit
2	4.38	Mostly Fit	3.51	Moderate Fit	3.21	Moderate Fit	3.70	Moderate Fit
3	3.00	Moderate Fit	3.61	Moderate Fit	3.28	Moderate Fit	3.30	Moderate Fit
4	2.79	Low level of Fit	3.11	Moderate Fit	2.93	Moderate Fit	2.94	Moderate Fit
5	2.81	Moderate Fit	3.17	Moderate Fit	3.33	Moderate Fit	3.10	Moderate Fit
6	4.10	Moderate Fit	3.46	Moderate Fit	3.65	Moderate Fit	3.74	Moderate Fit
7	2.90	Moderate Fit	2.89	Moderate Fit	3.14	Moderate Fit	2.98	Moderate Fit
8	3.30	Moderate Fit	3.27	Moderate Fit	4.05	Moderate Fit	3.54	Moderate Fit
9	4.90	Mostly Fit	5.16	Mostly Fit	4.62	Mostly Fit	4.89	Mostly Fit
10	4.36	Mostly Fit	3.53	Moderate Fit	3.52	Moderate Fit	3.80	Moderate Fit
11	2.00	Low level of Fit	2.71	Low level of Fit	2.72	Low level of Fit	2.48	Low level of Fit
12	4.81	Mostly Fit	4.63	Mostly Fit	4.61	Mostly Fit	4.68	Mostly Fit
13	4.96	Mostly Fit	5.44	Mostly Fit	5.15	Mostly Fit	5.18	Mostly Fit

I1: IS Strategy; I2: Interface Strategy; I3: Transaction Strategy

tion. Transaction strategy shows a similar assessment and this is not a good trend either. It reveals that most sample organizations have inducted technology without much preparation in pre-acquisition stage.

Acceptance of technology in any form is quite important for an organization. In order to deploy and absorb the technology planned, strategy should be in place even before the acquisition plan is initiated. This provides an avenue for bridging the gap between delivery of technology to meet the business requirements (Broadbent and Weill, 1996). In the proposed model the components outlined to understand the strategy. Table 7 and Figure 5 explain status of IT in sample organizations. It is noted that two sample organizations display lack of any IT strategy whereas in three organizations there is a strong evidence of IT strategy. Remaining eight organizations do have a moderate existence of the strategy. It tends to project that IT acquisitions are taking place without any strategic planning for the technology. Component strategy is an important deliverable of IT strategy and it displays process of acquisition of IT components besides providing

a detail account of the use of each component. It is seen that three organizations have a purposeful component acquisition whereas nine of the organizations have a moderate planning. One of these sample organizations displayed a very poor strategy for components. Similarly interface among components acquired needs a clear strategy since it might affect integration of the applications developed for the organization. It is noted that one organization has shown a poor strategy to interface the components, whereas four organizations have shown a well planned existence of the interface and rest nine organizations have a moderate plan. However, overall IT strategy is moderate in ten out of thirteen organizations and these organizations need special attention since moderate planning process might lead to a bad acquisition of technology.

Acceptance and use of information technology in organization as an infrastructure largely depend on user's attitude towards technology, strategic decision makers' patronage to use the technology and their way of deciding the very introduction of technology (Olson, 1982; Grover et al., 1998; Yaverbaum, 1988; Karahanna et al.,

Table 7. Information technology assessment

Org.No	T1	Assessment	T2	Assessment	T3	Assessment	T	Assessment
1	2.89	Moderate Fit	3.22	Moderate Fit	2.65	Low level of Fit	2.92	Moderate Fit
2	2.92	Moderate Fit	3.36	Moderate Fit	3.33	Moderate Fit	3.20	Moderate Fit
3	2.86	Moderate Fit	3.25	Moderate Fit	2.99	Moderate Fit	3.03	Moderate Fit
4	3.21	Moderate Fit	3.30	Moderate Fit	3.19	Moderate Fit	3.23	Moderate Fit
5	3.90	Moderate Fit	2.80	Moderate Fit	4.21	Mostly Fit	3.64	Moderate Fit
6	3.89	Moderate Fit	3.90	Moderate Fit	2.99	Moderate Fit	3.59	Moderate Fit
7	2.77	Low level of Fit	2.82	Moderate Fit	2.88	Moderate Fit	2.82	Moderate Fit
8	3.69	Moderate Fit	3.86	Moderate Fit	3.67	Moderate Fit	3.74	Moderate Fit
9	4.92	Mostly Fit	5.10	Mostly Fit	5.22	Mostly Fit	5.08	Mostly Fit
10	2.83	Moderate Fit	2.84	Moderate Fit	2.89	Moderate Fit	2.85	Moderate Fit
11	2.77	Low level of Fit	2.78	Low level of Fit	2.88	Moderate Fit	2.81	Moderate Fit
12	4.98	Mostly Fit	5.15	Mostly Fit	4.83	Mostly Fit	4.99	Mostly Fit
13	5.13	Mostly Fit	5.42	Mostly Fit	5.30	Mostly Fit	5.28	Mostly Fit

Figure 5. IT assessment in sample organizations

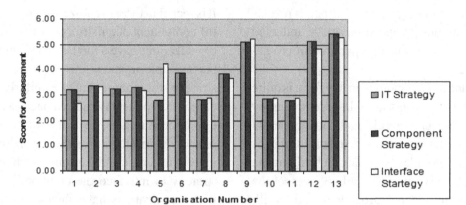

1999). Figure 6 and Table 8 discuss the situation in thirteen sample organizations. It is noted that employee's perception on the organization so far as the purpose for which the organization exists seems to be clear in seven organizations whereas in the remaining organizations it is not quite clear. This has an effect on clarity in the role that an employee plays for the organization and this, in turn, affects the use of technology. Interestingly however, perception on usefulness of IT is quite moderate in ten organizations and high in only three organizations. Barring three organizations where decision making style is moderately transparent, all the sample organizations displayed a better ambience in displaying predicted decision making behaviour. Overall assessment of climate

Figure 6. Climate assessment in sample organizations

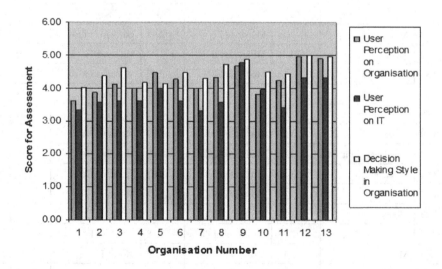

Table 8. Climate assessment

Org.No.	Cc1	Assessment	Cc2	Assessment	Cc3	Assessment	C	Assessment
1	3.61	Moderate Fit	3.35	Moderate Fit	4.01	Moderate Fit	3.66	Moderate Fit
2	3.86	Moderate Fit	3.58	Moderate Fit	4.36	Mostly Fit	3.93	Moderate Fit
3	4.11	Moderate Fit	3.62	Moderate Fit	4.63	Mostly Fit	4.12	Moderate Fit
4	3.99	Moderate Fit	3.61	Moderate Fit	4.17	Moderate Fit	3.92	Moderate Fit
5	4.47	Mostly Fit	3.98	Moderate Fit	4.15	Moderate Fit	4.20	Mostly Fit
6	4.26	Mostly Fit	3.62	Moderate Fit	4.47	Mostly Fit	4.12	Moderate Fit
7	3.98	Moderate Fit	3.32	Moderate Fit	4.30	Mostly Fit	3.87	Moderate Fit
8	4.31	Mostly Fit	3.57	Moderate Fit	4.71	Mostly Fit	4.20	Moderate Fit
9	4.68	Mostly Fit	4.78	Mostly Fit	4.87	Mostly Fit	4.77	Mostly Fit
10	3.82	Moderate Fit	3.96	Moderate Fit	4.50	Mostly Fit	4.09	Moderate Fit
11	4.24	Mostly Fit	3.42	Moderate Fit	4.43	Mostly Fit	4.03	Moderate Fit
12	4.98	Mostly Fit	4.32	Mostly Fit	4.99	Mostly Fit	4.76	Mostly Fit
13	4.89	Mostly Fit	4.32	Mostly Fit	4.98	Mostly Fit	4.73	Mostly Fit

however, is not good since almost nine sample organizations showed a moderate preparedness and only four of these organizations showed a better preparedness. This provides an impression that there is a kind of overall chaos in accepting information technology. Besides, poor inclination among strategic users to direct and support such acquisition and frequent change in decision making process affecting formalization process are also not uncommon.

Assessment of the preparedness of the acquiring organization in the pre-acquisition stage is considered important since it might increase success of the outcome of the acquisition process. This assessment therefore takes into consideration of the variables that the model uses to capture the level of preparedness at these levels.

Figure 7 and Table 9 explain the preparedness of the sample organizations in their respective pre-acquisition stages. While IT acquisition is a

Figure 7. Assessment of pre-acquisition preparedness in sample organizations

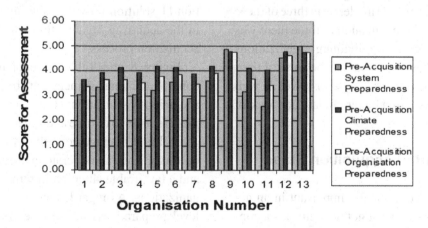

Table 9. Assessment of pre-acquisition preparedness of sample organization

Org.No.	P*	Assessment	C*	Assessment	O*	Assessment	Remarks
1	3.05	Moderate Fit	3.66	Moderate Fit	3.37	Moderate Fit	
2	3.33	Moderate Fit	3.93	Moderate Fit	3.64	Moderate Fit	
3	3.07	Moderate Fit	4.12	Moderate Fit	3.66	Moderate Fit	
4	3.04	Moderate Fit	3.92	Moderate Fit	3.53	Moderate Fit	
5	3.21	Moderate Fit	4.20	Mostly Fit	3.77	Moderate Fit	ERP implemented
6	3.57	Moderate Fit	4.12	Moderate Fit	3.84	Moderate Fit	
7	2.90	Moderate Fit	3.87	Moderate Fit	3.45	Moderate Fit	
8	3.60	Moderate Fit	4.20	Moderate Fit	3.90	Moderate Fit	ERP being implemented
9	4.85	Mostly Fit	4.77	Mostly Fit	4.72	Mostly Fit	ERP implemented
10	3.19	Moderate Fit	4.09	Moderate Fit	3.69	Moderate Fit	ERP implemented
11	2.56	Low level of Fit	4.03	Moderate Fit	3.42	Moderate Fit	
12	4.50	Mostly Fit	4.76	Mostly Fit	4.59	Mostly Fit	ERP implemented
13	4.98	Mostly Fit	4.73	Mostly Fit	4.74	Mostly Fit	ERP implemented

* Note: "P": Pre-acquisition System Preparedness, "C": Climate Preparedness, "O": Organization Preparedness in Pre-acquisition stage.

continuous process, it normally traverses through these stages and therefore, it was considered useful to assess preparedness through the discussed variables of the model. Most of these sample organizations taken up for study found to have acquired and used IT in some form. Out of thirteen organizations, five have acquired and implemented ERP modules and in one of the remaining organizations it is in the process of acquiring ERP. It may be noted here that despite attempting to acquire ERP organization's pre-acquisition preparedness has remained moderate in three of these organizations whereas in another three there was better preparedness. In remaining organizations preparedness has been moderate because of their moderate preparedness in systems level as well as due to absence of a better climate and lack of strategic support.

Assessment of Acquisition Stage

Acquisition stage is equally important in an acquisition process since it not only ensures a controlled acquisition process, but attempts to deploy

resources with a scope to meet the required results. This stage therefore, demands a close coordination among various stakeholders, such as, business process owners, IT practitioners, IT vendors, etc. Preparedness of these stakeholders is therefore, captured through this model to understand the acquisition process and its likely contribution to successful acquisition. Through this model two variables are measured i.e. "Vendor capability" and "IT-Solution provider capability." While vendor is expected to be engaged for IT acquisition IT solution provider is an internal resource in the acquiring organization who manages this acquisition process.

Figure 8 and Table 10 explain the vendor control and management capability of sample acquiring organizations. It is noted that strategic preparedness to outline and spearhead the vendor control and management shows a low level fit one organization, moderate in nine organizations and a favourable situation in remaining three organizations. As regards tactical and operational level preparedness to exercise control over the IT vendors, the situation is quite discouraging

Figure 8. Assessment of vendor management and control in sample organizations

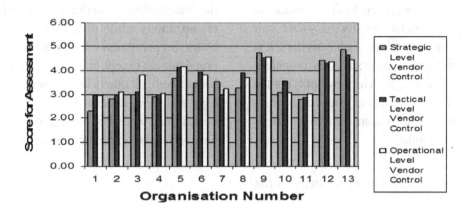

Table 10. Vendor management and control preparedness (VC)

Org. No.	VCs*	Assessment	VC$_t$*	Assessment	VCo*	Assessment	VC*	Assessment
1	2.29	Low level of Fit	2.96	Moderate Fit	2.98	Moderate Fit	2.53	Low level of Fit
2	2.83	Moderate Fit	2.97	Moderate Fit	3.11	Moderate Fit	2.76	Low level of Fit
3	3.00	Moderate Fit	3.11	Moderate Fit	3.81	Moderate Fit	3.10	Moderate Fit
4	2.92	Moderate Fit	2.99	Moderate Fit	3.07	Moderate Fit	2.78	Low level of Fit
5	3.67	Moderate Fit	4.15	Moderate Fit	4.16	Moderate Fit	3.78	Moderate Fit
6	3.47	Moderate Fit	3.93	Moderate Fit	3.83	Moderate Fit	3.53	Moderate Fit
7	3.53	Moderate Fit	2.98	Moderate Fit	3.23	Moderate Fit	3.04	Moderate Fit
8	3.25	Moderate Fit	3.9	Moderate Fit	3.70	Moderate Fit	3.41	Moderate Fit
9	4.74	Mostly Fit	4.55	Mostly Fit	4.58	Mostly Fit	4.41	Mostly Fit
10	3.08	Moderate Fit	3.54	Moderate Fit	3.10	Moderate Fit	3.03	Moderate Fit
11	2.80	Moderate Fit	2.88	Moderate Fit	3.04	Moderate Fit	2.70	Low level of Fit
12	4.42	Mostly Fit	4.31	Mostly Fit	4.38	Mostly Fit	4.16	Moderate Fit
13	4.85	Mostly Fit	4.65	Mostly Fit	4.45	Mostly Fit	4.44	Mostly Fit

*Note: VCs: Vendor Control at strategic level, VCt: Vendor Control at Tactical level, VCo: Vendor Control at Operational Level.

in ten organizations and good in the remaining three organizations. Interestingly ERP has been implemented in these three organizations.

While assessing overall IT acquisition process preparedness to execute IT projects, it is noted that four organizations have demonstrated low preparedness whereas two have displayed a good fit. Remaining seven have shown moderate preparedness in vendor management issues during IT acquisition.

It is quite important that IT solution providers in an organization develop expertise and knowledge of the business processes and also in relevant technology deployed for the purpose. Today most of the organizations have their IT cells to oversee various activities related to IT acquisitions. Sample organizations taken up for study have their own IT cells for undertaking such activities. It is therefore, pertinent to understand its preparedness to undertake such activities by applying the model and testing the results captured through its variables. Table 11 and Figure 9 discuss various variables of the model.

It is noted that preparedness of the IT cell at the strategic level is moderate in ten out of thirteen organizations while only three of them have a better preparedness. As regards tactical level preparedness except one organization that have a better result, all others have a moderate preparedness and this situation is not encouraging. At operational level however, three organizations have shown better preparedness whereas remain-

Table 11. IT-solution provider preparedness (AQ)

Org. No.	ATs*	Assessment	ATt*	Assessment	ATo*	Assessment	AQ*	Assessment
1	3.17	Moderate Fit	3.24	Moderate Fit	3.32	Moderate Fit	3.06	Moderate Fit
2	3.48	Moderate Fit	3.26	Moderate Fit	3.08	Moderate Fit	3.09	Moderate Fit
3	3.43	Moderate Fit	3.22	Moderate Fit	3.43	Moderate Fit	3.18	Moderate Fit
4	3.33	Moderate Fit	3.47	Moderate Fit	3.27	Moderate Fit	3.18	Moderate Fit
5	3.89	Moderate Fit	4.12	Moderate Fit	4.14	Moderate Fit	3.87	Moderate Fit
6	3.83	Moderate Fit	3.97	Moderate Fit	3.45	Moderate Fit	3.57	Moderate Fit
7	2.90	Moderate Fit	2.94	Moderate Fit	3.07	Moderate Fit	2.79	Low level of Fit
8	4.06	Moderate Fit	3.91	Moderate Fit	3.97	Moderate Fit	3.80	Moderate Fit
9	4.57	Mostly Fit	4.14	Moderate Fit	4.58	Mostly Fit	4.25	Mostly Fit
10	3.33	Moderate Fit	2.88	Moderate Fit	2.97	Moderate Fit	2.88	Moderate Fit
11	2.97	Moderate Fit	2.92	Moderate Fit	2.93	Moderate Fit	2.76	Low level of Fit
12	4.56	Mostly Fit	4.09	Moderate Fit	4.39	Mostly Fit	4.17	Moderate Fit
13	4.54	Mostly Fit	4.24	Mostly Fit	4.30	Mostly Fit	4.18	Moderate Fit

*Note: ATs: Strategic IT Solution Provider; ATt: Tactical IT Solution Provider; ATo: Operational IT Solution Provider

Figure 9. Assessment of preparedness of IT solution providers in sample organizations

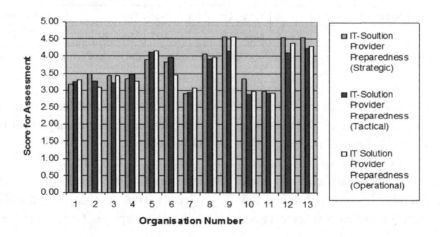

ing ten organizations have moderate preparedness in the IT acquisition process. In the overall IT acquisition scenario, the impression is also not encouraging since two of thirteen organizations have low preparedness, ten of these have moderate and only one has better preparedness.

IT ACQUISITION ASSESSMENT IN SAMPLE ORGANIZATION

Preparedness in each stage of the acquisition process is analyzed for the 13 sample organizations considered for the study. In this developed model success of the IT acquisition process is mostly assessed through the success of the pre-acquisition preparedness and a better management in IT acquisition stage.

Figure 10 and Table 12 explain overall IT acquisition scenario in the sample organizations. It has been noted that overall IT acquisition success has been moderate in ten out of thirteen organizations whereas only in three organizations (organization number 9, 12, and 13) the situation is somewhat better. In these three organizations ERP has been deployed for some business processes. These three organizations

are in manufacturing sector with highly formalized processes. Despite a moderate success in IT acquisition process, a highly dedicated strategic management has made the process automation successful. For the organization number 8, though it is in a manufacturing sector and having formalized processes, its acquisition of ERP has not been so far successful because of indifferent attitude of strategic management and inadequate exposure of IT-service providers. It heavily depends upon IT vendor in general and ERP vendor in particular. Organization number 5 which is also in manufacturing sector and has very highly formalized processes, a dedicated workforce, and an IT cell to look after the services of ERP enabled processes, its IT acquisition success seems to be moderate. This is because of poor acceptance of technology at the operational level and poor specifications of the ERP acquired. An effort has been made in this organization to replace existing ERP. In the remaining sample organizations the situation is not encouraging since the process automation is mostly disjoint and due to lack of adequate support from the management, there is no IT-service providing cell, thus leading to poor IT acquisition process. This aspect is evident from the table.

Figure 10. Assessment of IT acquisition success in sample organizations

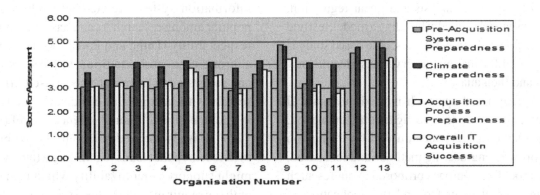

Table 12. IT acquisition success assessment in acquiring organizations (G)

Org. No.	P*	Assessment	C*	Assessment	AQ*	Assessment	G*	Assessment
1	3.05	Moderate Fit	3.66	Moderate Fit	3.06	Moderate Fit	3.10	Moderate Fit
2	3.33	Moderate Fit	3.93	Moderate Fit	3.09	Moderate Fit	3.24	Moderate Fit
3	3.07	Moderate Fit	4.12	Moderate Fit	3.18	Moderate Fit	3.30	Moderate Fit
4	3.04	Moderate Fit	3.92	Moderate Fit	3.18	Moderate Fit	3.24	Moderate Fit
5	3.21	Moderate Fit	4.20	Mostly Fit	3.87	Moderate Fit	3.71	Moderate Fit
6	3.57	Moderate Fit	4.12	Moderate Fit	3.57	Moderate Fit	3.59	Moderate Fit
7	2.90	Moderate Fit	3.87	Moderate Fit	2.79	Low level of Fit	2.99	Moderate Fit
8	3.60	Moderate Fit	4.20	Moderate Fit	3.80	Moderate Fit	3.73	Moderate Fit
9	4.85	Mostly Fit	4.77	Mostly Fit	4.25	Mostly Fit	4.33	Mostly Fit
10	3.19	Moderate Fit	4.09	Moderate Fit	2.88	Moderate Fit	3.15	Moderate Fit
11	2.56	Low level of Fit	4.03	Moderate Fit	2.76	Low level of Fit	2.97	Moderate Fit
12	4.50	Mostly Fit	4.76	Mostly Fit	4.17	Moderate Fit	4.23	Mostly Fit
13	4.98	Mostly Fit	4.73	Mostly Fit	4.18	Moderate Fit	4.31	Mostly Fit

*Note: P: Pre-Acquisition System Preparedness, C: Climate Preparedness, AQ: Acquisition Process Preparedness, G: Overall IT Acquisition Success

CASE-BASED STUDIES

Case based research is quite often used for quantitative as well qualitative empirical research (Wohlin, et al., 2000). While a case based study is normally organized to track a specific task at hand, it is difficult to display generalization. However, it provides a base for building a model to predict a specific outcome. Case based research can use multivariate data analyses methods such as principal component analysis and linear regression. This research is aimed at building a model, test and uses it for prediction. Besides, case based study is beneficial for making observations, documentation and then analyses.

A case based approach is used in empirical research in order to investigate a phenomenon. This method is very much useful for evaluation of software engineering methods and tools used. The modeling approach proposed in our research is an attempt to understand the application of software engineering principles to examine outcome. Though it provides an advantage to easily plan the study and can be carried out in an ongoing activity, it has a disadvantage in arriving at generalizations as discussed above and one does not have control over the effects as is normally available in experiments. It is however, strongly recommended by researchers to undertake case based studies in software engineering. In our case, since controlled studies are not expected and this study would be used to understand characteristics of problems, a case study based research is suitable.

Case-based studies for causal analysis in an information systems related research is quite popular among researchers and has commanded respectability (Dube and Pare, 2003). There is a strong case-study tradition in MIS research and suggested in favour of "case-based MIS research" while recognizing criticism leveled from the perspective of natural science model (Lee, 1989). It is also argued in favour of case-based MIS research that leads to building a theory that might support generalizability which is in tune with the requirement of natural science model as well as meeting requirements of scientific methodology. It is argued that MIS case study based research is capable of achieving the scientific objectives without any dilution as it is able to provide natural controls, meet the objective of controlled or logical deduction that might have been derived by mathematical/statistical proposition. It also supports replicable observations that might lead to confirmatory conclusions or otherwise (Benbasat et al., 1987). It provides a scope to identify the causal chain that led to the success or failure of the information system. It is also argued that undertaking multiple case studies to ascertain relationship between the IT and the organization is possible and case based research provides an ambience to investigate a contemporary phenomenon (Yin, 1994). Since there is a danger in depending solely on case based research that has some limitation in generalization, case based study is used because of its strong usability in IS research as discussed above supported by quantitative analysis with large sample size spanning across organizations. In this chapter we discuss two case studies related to IT acquisition through application of the model developed and validated. Discussions of these two cases demonstrate the inadequacy in the IT acquisition process that created undesirable situations.

TWO CASE STUDIES

Case 1: Cement Manufacturing Company

The cement company, a state public sector undertaking[1], was set up with an installed licensed capacity 0.4 Million Metric Tonnes of Portland cement per annum in the year 1962 and went into production in 1968. Organization structure of the company is shown in Figure 11.

In 1985 it expanded it production capacity to 0.56 million MT per annum. The technology chosen for this plant initially was of wet-process technology and was therefore, not energy efficient. In order to survive stiff competition from private sectors who rather expanded their base in the state, the management was forced to consider complete change in the production system to dry-process and this change was effective in 1995 with an increased production capacity of 0.96 million MT of Portland slag cement. This plant during modernization introduced latest technology with centralized process control system based on Supervisory Control and Data Acquisition (SCADA) with programmable Logic Controls (PLC) with a project cost of 1860 million rupees. The Plant

Figure 11. Organization structure of the company

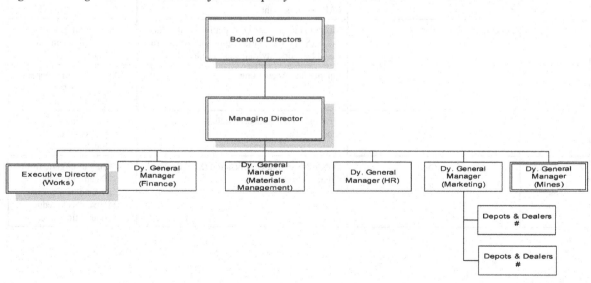

271

had been certified with quality standard confirming to ISO-9001:2000 and ISO-14001. The market network depended on dealer network who were managed though branch offices manned by marketing managers of the company. As regards human resource, it had strength of 816 directly employed and around 2000 indirectly employed persons. Training was a part of the HR policy in the company. The company showed decline in net profit despite capacity utilization mainly due to high cost of capital acquisition during modernization and sluggish market conditions. In order to improve performance, the company took some strategic steps in marketing area by re-organizing its network into 6 zones headed by a zonal manager apart from existing 12 branch managers. Steps were taken to reduce transaction cost and the variable cost of sales. Emphasis was given on realizing debtors who had not even paid during the last three years.

IT Acquisition Process

In the year 1989-90 the company started its computerized activities and details of IT acquisition scenario is shown Table 13.

Following induction of a programmer to the company, DOS based system was tried for "pay-roll" processing for its employees. It was without any planning, but the programmer was allowed to undertake the job on his own. Since the programmer was exposed to DOS based Fox-Base database, he undertook the job and implemented a batch application program. This trend continued and "Inventory Management" was introduced completely in-house on the same platform during the period from 1993 to 1997 as described in

Table 13. History of IT acquisition in the company (case 1)

Year	Description of IT Activity	Component	Remarks
1989-90	Pay-Roll System	DOS / Fox-Base	In-House activity and batch processing
1991-93	Inventory Management and Finance-Accounting Systems	DOS/ Fox Base.	-do-
1993-97	Sales and Marketing Management. Modules replicated at the mines as well as zonal offices.	OS upgraded to SCO-Unix	-do-
1998	MIS Plan	CMC as consultant	User Involvement low
1999	Execution of MIS Plan	Migration to Oracle+D2K platform with Unix as OS (Sales and Marketing modules); Ethernet based Network environment introduced	Vendor developed applications on-site. Batch Processing
2000	-do-	Finance and Accounting	Application developed on-site. Batch Processing
2001	-do-	Inventory Management, Purchase, Stores accounting	Application developed on-site. Batch Processing
2002-03	-do-	Query Processing Optimisation (Modules) and Attempt for Integration	Attempt to migrate from Batch-processing (Off-Line) to On-Line. Motive was to reduce transaction time.

Table 13. Later OS platform was migrated from DOS to SCO-Unix retaining the database. In the year 1997, management information systems (MIS Plan) proposal was put up before the managing director and a consulting agency's offer was approved through a tendering process. Later the plan submitted by the agency was also approved for implementation. However, acquisition strategy was deviated from the recommended strategy during execution. Acquisition strategy was aimed at automation of material management function, which formed around 55% of its cost of production, sales and marketing function to reduce transaction and coordination costs. "Sales and Marketing System" was developed under supervision of the in-house IT professionals but through a hired software vendor/developer on-site under SCO-UNIX; ORACLE and D2K platform. Whole plant was networked with Ethernet backbone. While choice of this platform was in line with the MIS plan recommendations, plan to expose in-house IT team to the tools and database was not available and source coding rested with the vendor working on-site. System Development Life Cycle (SDLC) approach was adopted to complete the project. Post installation maintenance and product tuning were also the responsibility of the software consultant. Following this, "Inventory" and "finance accounting" functions were IT enabled by the company but through another vendor keeping the project execution methodology same. Because of the investment on IT infrastructure, management tried to leverage and pressed for MIS reports from these systems. IT cell now headed by Dy. Manager, (the programmer had got the promotion) and two other programmers tried to generate the MIS reports which rather became very urgent and immediate in nature. Need for integrating all the IT enabled functions in order to have on-line invoicing; order tracking and dispatching of product to customers was felt. However, this was a daunting task for the IT cell, because of these disjoint systems, lack of training of IT manpower, the attempt did not provide the management the desired result and process la-

tency could not be addressed. Gradually user department which depended heavily on IT cell demanded service as well operational support. Users were also not trained to accommodate the technological impact. For example "Sales software" could not accommodate the requirement raised by user department for inclusion of dealer and depot management spread across the state. Sales figures could not be transacted on-line with finance accounting module and dispatching of product had problems with on-line invoicing module. Integration of these modules became absolutely essential and therefore the blame was on the consultant for its disjointed nature of work. Sources revealed that cost of implementation of the material management system, finance accounting system and sales accounting system was around 2 million, 1.5 million, and 1.8 million rupees respectively. Enough money had been spent along with many months of engagement in putting infrastructure in place and management is not satisfied on the outcome of all the efforts made so far.

Analysis of the Case 1 Based on the Model

Analysis of the described case followed the model developed. In the case of this cement company, a monolithic approach was taken for each of the systems keeping user's priorities in view. Immediate adoption of software process (Pressman, 1997) methodology resulted into disparate systems. These were well executed individually, but in phases. One critical but major issue which remained un-addressed was the integration plan for all the systems. When considered for integration, these systems could not bear the consequences that are incidental to the interfacing. MIS plan prepared had been ignored and this had created a gap in executing the recommendations. Since the organization dealt with standardized processes and did not envisage much change in the business rules, integration could have been well conceived while initiating

273

such approach. Table 14 explains the variables quantified through application of the model.

Table 14 reflects on the strength of the organization described in the form of strategic users' preparedness with a score of 3.88, presence of IS strategy with a score of 4.71, decision style of the organization with a score of 4.01. Though scores are moderately placed in the scorecard, these have played a supportive role in bringing the technologies in to its present form. User perception on IT (score of 3.35), user perception on organization (score of 3.61) also display a supportive role in accepting the technology. However, the

disturbing factors in the organization are poor vendor control and management capability (score of 2.53), strategy for interface and integration among information systems (score of 2.99) and technology (score of 2.65). Deficiency in executing the plan formulated led to a disjoint mode of implementation of technology.

The application of model indicated that there was support from the strategic decision makers to the IT projects. However, functional managers and operational cadre employees were not geared to use the services. In addition to this the competence of IT cell including the IT manager

Table 14. Application of model for assessment of IT acquisition (case 1)

IT-Acquisition Scenario in the Organization	Preparedness of Organization	Attributes of Organization	Components of Organization Preparedness	Constructs
Effectiveness of the IT-Acquisition (3.10)	Organizational Preparedness in Pre-IT Acquisition process (3.37)	Pre-Acquisition Process (3.05)	User Preparedness (3.20)	Strategic User (3.88)
				Functional User (3.28)
				Operational User (3.39)
			IS Preparedness (3.18)	IS Strategy (4.71)
				Interface Strategy (2.99)
				Transaction Strategy (2.97)
			Technology Preparedness (2.77)	IT Strategy (2.89)
				Component Strategy (3.22)
				Interface Strategy (2.65)
		Climate Preparedness (3.66)		User Perception on Organization (3.61)
				User Perception on IT (3.35)
				Decision Style of organization (4.01)
	IT-Acquisition Process (3.06)			Vendor Control and Management (2.53)
				IT-Service Providers Capability (3.24)

were not adequately exposed to the tools deployed during the acquisition process. Though there was a MIS plan, execution of interface planning for various modules was poorly managed. There were multiple vendors executing the projects and they are disjoint to each other. The entire IT acquisition therefore, was not remunerative because of poor capability of IT cell, IT vendors, and poor interface strategy. Besides, functional and operational employees did not show any eagerness to use the IT enabled systems. Therefore, the model, when applied appropriately diagnosed the preparedness issues and indicated the issues that should be taken up for the next IT projects being planned. It supported the finding of the model that it was not the technology, but the management style which led to such consequence. The model therefore, suggested that the organization should enhance the capability of IT cell, motivate the users to list their requirements and above all a vendor with adequate capability and have exposure to similar projects should be engaged.

Case 2: A Public Sector Business Organization

Another example of different nature was that of a giant public sector business organization. Though it was under the direct control of the government, it was primarily conducting commercial operations through manufacturing, marketing various products in geographically dispersed locations having centralized control at its corporate office. Major products of the company were steel, cement, iron ore mining, steel condenser tubes, power transmission equipments etc. The businesses were heterogeneous and disjoint in nature. The organization had an annual turnover of 4000 million rupees and there were around 8000 workforce. Incorporated in the year 1962 under companies act, the company was directly controlled by the government. Geographically dispersed business units having no relationship with each other made the organization complex. Organization structure of the company is shown in Figure 12.

Figure 12. Organization structure of the corporation

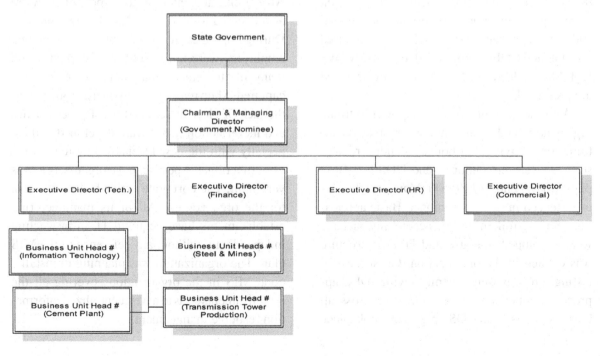

The decision making process though centralized at its corporate headquarters, each business unit took its routine decisions locally and therefore, demand on MIS was quite high at all levels. However, the organization in general and each business unit in particular did boast of standard procedures and process knowledge. Human resource was claimed to be highly professional and cooperative and there was neither any instance of strike nor lockout in the last decade.

IT Acquisition Process

The organization till 1988 did not have any intention to have computerization plan for itself. With the directive from the government and support from nodal agency appointed by the government to oversee IT infrastructure for the government agencies, the organization acquired computers with a view to bring in awareness among its employees. Employees were also given training in groups about the computers and its role in enabling business applications. Brief history of the IT acquisition in the organization is as described in Table 16. Following purchase of computers, the management decided to engage an application service provider to provide services on pay-roll and stores management system. This service based on DOS and COBOL continued for some period. In Table 15, details of IT infrastructure acquired are presented.

With the induction of IT manpower in to the organization and an intention to organize its automation activities in-house, Vendor related services were discontinued and DOS/Fox-Base platform was chosen by the IT-Manager who was experienced in this environment. Basic applications for pay-roll, inventory, accounting package were developed in-house and IT infrastructure was created in the organization. On successful testing (projects were organized with SDLC approach) applications were replicated across all business units. Later OS migration took place from DOS to UNIX for the applications. In order to benefit from the applications developed, it was planned to use the applications to track inventory-holding costs, streamline the flow of daily MIS reports on production, sales, work-in-process (WIP), cash and funds flow, etc., from those units to the head office. The head office also simultaneously planned for integrated software to provide an office automation system that would provide its operational and middle management a scope to gear its functions for a timely analyses of data captured and enable an atmosphere for better decision making. An MIS plan was prepared by engaging a consultant, which provided a scheme for short as well as long term acquisition plan for the organization. Since offices of all the strategic managers were in the head office and all the decisions were taken there, the management decided to automate the functions of head office in the first phase. Priority was set for having integrated office automation software that would address all the issues of Finance and Accounts, HR, Materials Management, Production and Operations. Data from business/ manufacturing units were planned to follow as per the agreed reporting structure. All official and internal correspondences were also decided to be on-line and through intranet. During implementation of the plan, it was felt that employees were not geared for the change and many of the transactions were not effectively captured. Main reason behind such a problem was the lack of clear understanding of process rules and its reflection in software developed and especially with the new IT enabled system. However, functional expertise in the organization was very high. The corporate office had a MIS plan for the organization. All of its manufacturing establishments have acquired IT infrastructure independently without any reference to the MIS plan. The organization was planning to install a good MIS in the organization covering all the establishments so as to have a centralized information resource management.

Table 15. History of IT acquisition in the organization (case 2)

Year	Description of IT Activity	Component	Remarks
1988	PCs are procured as per Govt. directive	DOS / Fox-Base	Awareness programme through a nodal agency
1989	Pay-Roll and Stores Accounting System introduced.	DOS and COBOL	Through a vendor across its business units but processed centrally.
1990	Two IT managers, Four Programmers inducted	-	Objective was to automate business applications in-house
1991-95	Pay-roll, Inventory, Finance and Accounting Systems developed; Replicated across all locations.	DOS / FOX-Base on which the IT manpower had earlier experience. Hardware and Networks were installed in each business unit along with headquarters.	Applications were independent, developed in-house.
1996	Migration of Applications	SCO-Unix and Fox-Base	-
1997	MIS Plan	-	-
1998	Application Integration	-	Did not take off
1999-2000	IT cell converted to a separate Business unit for IT infrastructure development	-	Focus shifted to IT business

Analysis of Case 2 Based on the Model

In the second case, the organization followed the right path of having a plan, organized interfaces and tried to implement systems in phased manner. However, people from multi-domain specialties were at a loss to take the instant burden of change while migrating from manual system to an IT enabled environment. Business rules could not be embedded into the software developed and failure occurred during integration. People were not taken into confidence and inadequate assessment of the capability of users was done. There was a lack of clear understanding of the processes, rules and logics by the operational and tactical groups (both the CIO and the Users) of the organization while aligning IT in to the processes. Table 16 indicates the scores of the variables obtained through application of the model.

Results from the model indicated that organization had a formalized organization structure with high degree of clarity, clear decision making process (score 4.36). People in this organization were not much averse to adopting IT since its employees were gradually being introduced to the technology since 1988 (score 3.58). There was a MIS plan and IS strategy was well defined in the organization (score 4.38) along with a moderate interface and integration strategy (score 3.51 and 3.21, respectively). Formalized processes had developed a good knowledgebase among functional and operational level employees who were able to list their requirements and priorities (score of 4.24 and 4.06 respectively). However, strategic level users were unable to leverage this strength due to their short stay in the position. Highly unstructured requirements had also made them vulnerable to list out requirements to capture these in a IS plan (score 3.55). The weakest part of the IT acquisition process was lack of an IT strategy in the organization (score 2.92) which had led to a moderate component planning and interfacing these during execution (score 3.36 and 3.33 respectively). A poorly formed IT-service provider (IT Cell) had been moderately able to select vendors and managing them (score 2.76)

Table 16. Application of model for assessment of IT acquisition in case 2

IT-Acquisition Scenario in the Organization	Preparedness of Organization	Attributes of Organization	Components of Organization Preparedness	Constructs
Effectiveness of the IT-Acquisition (3.24)	Organizational Preparedness in Pre-IT Acquisition process (3.64)	Pre-Acquisition Process (3.33)	User Preparedness (3.63)	Strategic User (3.55)
				Functional User (4.24)
				Operational User (4.06)
			IS Preparedness (3.32)	IS Strategy (4.38)
				Interface Strategy (3.51)
				Transaction Strategy (3.21)
			Technology Preparedness (3.05)	IT Strategy (2.92)
				Component Strategy (3.36)
				Interface Strategy (3.33)
		Climate Preparedness (3.93)		User Perception on Organization (3.86)
				User Perception on IT (3.58)
				Decision Style of organization (4.36)
	IT-Acquisition Process (3.09)			Vendor Control and Management (2.76)
				IT-Service Providers Capability (3.27)

and providing leadership for the project (score 3.27). This had resulted in having disjointed and poorly implemented information systems in the organization without any focus. Overall IT acquisition success was moderate having a score of 3.24.

The model was therefore, appropriate to be applied. It could be noted that information systems were disjoint and specific to the establishments. Poor technology planning and system development practices were reflected in the IT enabled systems. As a result of poor planning, transactions were not effectively managed and inter process

transactions were not effective at all. Though various packages were developed, its use had not been as expected due to less interest shown by the employees. This had been mainly due to inadequate patronage from the strategic management and their frequent change in management as well decision making style. Involvement of users in the systems development process since there was no coordination between the IT cell and the functional managers. Besides, the IT resource persons were not exposed to the IT components adequately before the IT projects started. This resulted in poor administration of the components deployed in the post acquisition stage. The model therefore, appropriately indicated that the organization did not have a proper involvement of the users across the layers identified by the model i.e. strategic, functional, and operational. The transactions and interfaces were also poorly managed indicating poor IS preparedness. The IT cell also was not properly equipped to handle the projects which led to disjoint IT infrastructure, poor handling of transactions and interfaces. User perception on organization's climate was low because of fast change in decision style, bad management of IT. Therefore, the organization would need to overcome these deficiencies before the integration plan was executed.

SUMMARY

In this chapter, the fitness and applicability of the structural model proposed are tested. It is seen that data captured through respondents have shown reliable analyses and also predictability of the attributes responsible for understanding the status of an IT acquisition process. It is also seen that the model is aplicable across a heterogeneous sample of organizations. In all the cases it could be inferred that good technology does not influence the success, but organization's ability to plan its IS and align these systems with the technology influences.

This chapter discussed two cases drawn from manufacturing sector which had all the functional exposures such as marketing, human resources, production, sales, finance and accounting. Both the organizations seemed to have a better exposure and expertise to its functional set up whereas IT acquisition processes were just treated very casually. User involvement was found to be very casual as well. This was a serious problem that both the organizations encountered in the post acquisition phases. Therefore, it was of much importance that an acquiring organization should take enough in-

terest in safeguarding the IT resources through a planned acquisition process and users at all levels must be prepared to actively participate in all the phases of IT acquisition.

The model applied to these two cases could effectively analyze the pre-acquisition preparedness and its possible effects on subsequent stages of the acquisition process. It also justified the relationships among various variables validated.

REFERENCES

Benbasat, I., Goldstein, D. K., & Mead, M. (1987, September). The case research strategy in studies of information systems. *Management Information Systems Quarterly*, 369–386. doi:10.2307/248684.

Broadbent, M., & Weill, P. (1996). *Management by maxim: Creating business driven information technology infrastructure*. Carlton, Australia: University of Melbourne.

Cronbach, L. J., Glester, G. C., Nanada, H., & Rajaratnam, N. (1972). *The dependability of behavioural measurements: Theory of generalizability for scores and profiles*. New York: Wiley.

Dube, L., & Pare, G. (2003). Rigor in information systems positivist case research: Current practices, trends, and recommendations. *Management Information Systems Quarterly*, 27(4), 597–635.

España, S., Condori-Fernandez, N., & González, A., & Pastor, O. (2010). An empirical comparative evaluation of requirements engineering methods. *Journal of the Brazilian Computer Society*, 16(1), 3–19. doi:10.1007/s13173-010-0003-5.

Grover, V., Teng, J., Segars, A., & Fiedler, K. (1998). The influence of information technology and business process changes in perceived producitivity: The IS executive's perspective. *Information & Management*, 34(3), 141. doi:10.1016/S0378-7206(98)00054-8.

Karahanna, E., Straub, D. W., & Chervany, N. L. (1999). Information technology adoption across time: A cross-sectional comparison of pre-adoption and post-adoption beliefs. *Management Information Systems Quarterly, 23*(2), 183–213. doi:10.2307/249751.

Land, S. K., Smith, D. B., & Walz, J. W. (2008). *Practical support for lean six sigma software process definition: Using IEEE software engineering standards*. New York: John Wiley & Sons, Inc. doi:10.1002/9780470289969.

Lee, A. S. (1989, March). A scientific methodology for MIS case studies. *Management Information Systems Quarterly*, 33–50. doi:10.2307/248698.

Leffingwell, D. (2007). *Scaling software agility: Best practices for large enterprises*. Boston: Addison-Wesley.

Linn, R. L., & Werts, C. E. (1979). Covariance structures and their analysis. In Traub, R. E. (Ed.), *New directions for testing and measurement: methodological developments* (Vol. 4, pp. 53–73). San Francisco, CA: Jossey-Bass.

Luftman, J. (2003). Assessing IT/business alignment. *Information Systems Management, 20*(4), 9–21. doi:10.1201/1078/43647.20.4.20 030901/77287.2.

Luftman, J. N., Papp, R., & Brier, T. (2002, September). Enablers and inhibitors of business-IT alignment. *ABInsight*.

Monarch, I., Sisti, F., Ambrose, K., & Blanchette, S. (2004). *Why not network centric acquisition?* Paper presented at the Conference on Acquisition of Software Centric Systems. Pittsburgh, PA.

Olson, M. H. (1982). New information technology and organsiational culture. *Management Information Systems Quarterly*, 71–92. doi:10.2307/248992.

Pedhazur, E. J. (1997). *Multiple regression in behavioral research* (3rd ed.). New York: Harcourt Brace College Publishers.

Pressman, R. S. (1997). *Software engineering: A practitioner's approach* (4th ed.). Singapore: McGraw-Hill.

Ward, J., & Peppard, J. (2002). *Strategic planning for information systems*. London: John Wiley and Sons.

Wohlin, C., Runeson, P., Host, M., Ohlsson, M. C., Regnell, B., & Wesslen, A. (2000). *Experimentation in software engineering: An introduction*. London: Kluwer Academic Publishers. doi:10.1007/978-1-4615-4625-2.

Yaverbaum, G. J. (1988, March). Critical factors in the user environment: An experimental study of users, organisation and tasks. *Management Information Systems Quarterly*, 75–88. doi:10.2307/248807.

Yin, R. K. (1994). *Case study research: Design and methods*. Thousand Oaks, CA: Sage.

ENDNOTES

[1] A public sector undertaking is a system of working in India which is formed by different acts of the union government in order to provide an ambience to execute projects and serve citizen with definite roles. These are indirectly controlled by the government system.

Chapter 12
Model Representation through UML and SPEM

ABSTRACT

Establishing strategic fit dynamically between information systems and information technologies for having a well managed IT acquisition life cycle in the organization is quite challenging. Despite advancements in software engineering process modeling techniques and the existence of maturity in handling multi-disciplinary challenges in designing appropriate information systems, there is growing popularity in developing model-driven methods. This chapter discusses application of a model-driven method that aims to use software engineering process modeling. It also aims to showcase the appropriateness of the application of the model in software engineering. The chapter discusses the role of SDLC-driven approaches for IT services acquisitions and relates to the UML and SEPM principles while discussing the deliverables of the model.

INTRODUCTION

The conceptualized, designed and developed model recognises the fact that each organization is unique and its requirements are dynamic. Thus generic IT infrastructure and services have to undergo process re-engineering adequately before deployment. Such a process needs internal capabilities to organize issues related to development and management of IS with an aim to capture dynamic needs in an organisation. The model also includes many factors such as understanding the

process itself, aligning technology to the process, IT usage, and usability contributes to the success of IT acquisition. These factors, even if addressed properly do not necessarily lead to successful IT acquisition. While discussing various stages of the acquisition process and understanding the roles of various stakeholders, the model recognized that organization and service providers work collectively and collaborate. In order to make this collaboration successful, there should be a level playing situation to derive synergic effects. It is, therefore, pertinent to understand the issues that might affect the success of IT acquisition in an organisation. Software engineering principles iden-

DOI: 10.4018/978-1-4666-4201-0.ch012

tify these issues to be analysis, design, construction, verification, and management of technical entities. However, understanding other soft issues like user's attitude and acceptability at each stage of acquisition are perhaps less addressed. Models available in the software engineering discipline can be chosen depending on their suitability and applicability to a project. But, at the organisation level, these processes could be many and atomic. This situation creates a complex buyer-supplier relationship where the IT cell in the organisation assumes the buyer's role and leads the entire process of acquisition.

Quality models though are available to understand the supplier behaviour as well as to keep control over the acquisition process, are again process specific. It is often argued that quality in the IT acquisition process might not lead to producing quality product. But adherence of quality in all stages of IT acquisition—definition, development, and maintenance—would provide some indications about the product being produced (Jiang et al. 2001). Mostly organisations become complex as they grow. This growth coupled with dynamic ambient conditions does impose limitations to the quality process attributes adopted for IT acquisition. On the other hand, suppliers who mostly are technology and service providers do not have prior exposure to the issues relevant to the organisation and might not be interested in doing so. The simple intention might be to execute and sign off for the next project. Capability of the service provider/supplier is of paramount importance that could have a direct bearing on the IT acquisition process. It is also apprehended that acquisition of a quality certified product and engaging a quality certified service provider could be costly.

A successful IT acquisition must deliver business value, whether it is on project mode or otherwise. This business value is possible even if IT acquisition is late, over budget, and delivers expected functionality only partly. A project delivered on time, on budget, but without any business value will be termed as ineffective and consequently a failure. Therefore, it is pertinent to understand that any IT acquisition is not simply a project, but a sizable organisational paradigm. It is invariably seen that failures in IT acquisition is not because of tools and/or technology termed as the hard issues, but soft issues like rightly choosing the technology and/or tools, organisational planning, and communication among the supplier and the acquirer. It is also argued that different technologies and/or tools chosen depending on the expertise of the acquirer/vendor who are actively involved in the process would not affect business value if adequate planning is done.

Despite the challenges and limitations in capturing user capabilities, software engineering principles are deployed constantly in organisations. The organisation goes through various Systems Development Life Cycle (SDLC) driven projects to acquire IT infrastructure. Though SDLC driven projects have their advantages for a project management and other various models do provide project management techniques, they are not free from limitations in capturing organisational business value at macro level (Jiang *et al.* 2001; Lamb and Kling 2003). These limitations include failure of user to educate the developer and vice versa. SDLC recognises the fact that ultimate success of any IT infrastructure acquired would depend on the way end-users use it. End-user competence and their attitude towards the IT usage have direct impact on its successful use. Thus there is a scope to understand user's involvement in the IT acquisition process. This is a complex phenomenon since users span across all layers in the organisation, they involve in technology driven processes and also liaise with technology providers.

SDLC APPROACH

During the early stage of IT acquisition, managing IT activities relating to operation, programming, and data collection were the major areas of concern. In later stages the focus was on establishing a unit to look after various types of applications over an extended lifecycle, despite change in technology. Simultaneously, emphasis to involve users developed not because of business priorities, but to enable easy use of applications computerized. However, a review of IS/IT has been occasional in organisations (Frank 1998). Two areas of concern, emerged in the early 1970s, "Data Processing (DP)" and "Management Information System (MIS)". In the early 1980s, a third area of concern evolved, i.e., strategy for leveraging lessons learned from DP and MIS (Flynn 1998). DP approach was focused to ensure automation through IS/IT of the processes to achieve required efficiency.

Most IT departments started involving users by specifying their roles. But MIS could not be integrated with DP. Frequently MIS applications got divorced from DP systems resulting in using different sources of data from different MIS applications. This led to providing a link between DP and MIS. Thus DP and MIS became a subset of the Strategic Information System (SIS). This talked about business process, business network redesign, and business scope redefinition, all using IS/IT. This also talked about Executive Information System (EIS), Electronic Data Interchange (EDI), and Business Process Reengineering (BPR). Figure 1 shows the relationship among DP, MIS and SIS. It also shows a strong relationship between business strategy and IS/IT. In this relationship it is recognised that user management, user operations in general, and executive management in particular are important contributors to an effective IS driven business strategy in the organisation.

Ideally systems design commences at the fag-end of the strategic planning process and should be on project mode after this point of time. But normally the project cycle starts immediately after some requirements are set for the organisation and the vendor embarks on executing the project. Researchers argue that IS need not be IT-centric, but efficient and/or effective operation of IS depends on the use of IT. Therefore, there should be a strong orientation of IS towards work system rather than becoming IT-centric. In this context the organisation and IT just coexist and need not be independent (Wang and Tai 2003). In order to make an application or IT acquisition successful, focusing on technology alone will not help, but there should be clear understanding on the distinction between "IS Strategy" and "IT

Figure 1. End users of IT and decision making process. Source: adapted from Davis and Olson (2000).

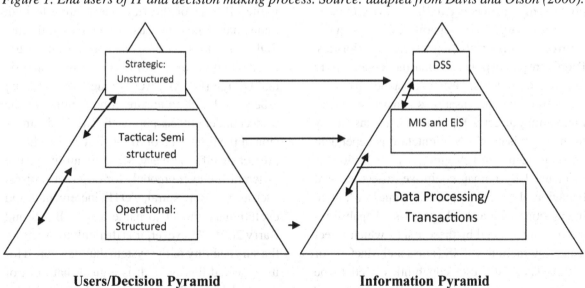

Users/Decision Pyramid   **Information Pyramid**

Strategy". However, in reality, organisations grow to be complex and this becomes more complex when users at all levels demand pervasive use of IT (Basili et al. 1994; Nuseibeh and Easterbrook 2000). This leads to a phenomenon called "IS demand" and "IT supply". An alignment between these two elements is vital for an organisation.

Modern Systems Analysis and Design (SA&D) and SDLC methods recognise user-interface designs (Lycett *et al.* 2003). However, these issues are addressed during the design stages of SDLC. In this stage the users interact with the project team. But it is essential that the requirement engineering stage is meticulously followed prior to embarking on SDLC. In this stage the acquiring organisation needs to strategize involvement of users to capture their requirements. The capabilities of users to collaborate in the process are important at this stage to bridge the gap among IT experts, process owners, and IT users in general. Involvement of users at this stage is expected to influence their usability behaviour to a great extent in the subsequent stages of SDLC.

In a SDLC-led IT acquisition scenario, user capabilities are usually perceived to be limited to eliciting user involvement in screen design, report format finalization, menu detailing, choice of fonts and colours, etc. But IS development process, though needing all these inputs, expects to address larger user capabilities issues in the form of overall organisational systemic priorities. People are part of organisational models and so are information systems. Any inconsistency in matching IS with the organisation's consistent mental models may affect SDLC deliveries. Consistency in the organisation's IS orientation is dependent on socio-technical behaviour. This behaviour is influenced by human cognitive, affective, and behavioural factors and the dynamics of human interactions with technologies. User capabilities are also influenced by these issues which affect users' interaction with IS (Ditsa and MacGregor 1995). Therefore, user capabilities need to be addressed as early as possible (Broadbent *et al*

1996; Herron 2002). Systems development life cycle (SDLC) process provides an opportunity to systems planners to install IS through user participation, capturing user requirements and incorporating them appropriately (Balint 1995). Modern SDLC models are based more on organisational needs than human needs. People play different roles in SDLC in which their roles carry immense value. These roles are primarily end-users, planners, and domain experts (IT and non-IT). However, usually it is experienced that either end-users contribute too little in the process or domain experts inadequately collaborate. Often it is also found that limited capabilities in the organisation lead to ineffective rollout of systems. This problem can be addressed by carefully integrating user capabilities into the SDLC process to achieve a truly user-centred IS development scenario. In order to ensure such scenario, the acquiring organisation needs to provide an enabling environment.

SDLC, though is organisation-centric with strong bias to information systems than information technology, it is not free from some serious limitations. One of them is the way the SDLC is organised for freezing the milestones and then referring back in case it is needed after execution of the stage. Another dimension of the criticism is the offshoot of the first one leading to high maintenance cost because of lack of time that SDLC provides for analysis and design. Structured analysis and Object Oriented Analysis and Design (OOAD) were thought of providing a better solution to ensure good conduct of the project under process approach. The third dimension of the limitation of SDLC is its suitability in project specific delivery. Most organisations use different life cycle models for different projects such as waterfall, spiral, COTS, incremental, and evolutionary model to name a few (Basili and Barry 2001). However, it is difficult to ascertain the survivability of the system thus developed for its expected life cycle. It is argued that most of the models popularly coming under SDLC have limitations in delivering good result in a complex scenario, but are successful in a tightly specified domain. All software models under SDLC can be characterized as a problem-solving loop, which may go through four distinct stages: status quo, problem definition, solution integration, post-acquisition assessment. Status quo represents current status, problem definition identifies the specific problem to be solved, and technical development solves the problem through application of some technology (Boehm and Hansen 2001).

Application of the Model for User Capabilities Mapping

IT acquisition in an organisation is termed successful if its people can leverage the presence of IT through effective use and can understand the way IT needs to be used. Definition of user is broadbased. Users assume the role of end-users, technology managers, and technology suppliers as well. In this section we look at users in an acquiring organisation. Users span across all levels in the organisation: "strategic", "tactical" and "operational levels"; IT managers, and developers representing the acquiring organisation. Figure 1 shows that users perform their roles differently at different levels and their requirement varies. This is also true when we discuss about IT requirements which need to be detailed for the organisation. One of the issues in the acquisition process is to involve users to understand the purpose of providing a systemic environment for their work. Operational users form the core group who perform iterative process oriented transactions. These transactions might grow in volume and frequency and the group needs to perform the task with ease provided there is structured-ness. "Structured-ness" calls for predicted behaviour of the transactions and provides a path for traceability in case there is a need to do so. Ownership of the users on the transactions provides an indication for the preparedness since it helps the IT service

provider to capture the transactions well with the help of these users. Maturity at this level provides the organisation a tool to organise data processing effectively. This in turn would help the next upper layer called "tactical users". These users are the functional users in the organisation who provide domain knowledge to the system of decision making process (Boehm and Hansen 2001).

Capability of these users leads to understanding the behaviour of information systems and the organisation of transactions and analysing the behaviour as well. This capability of tactical users provides a leadership to operational users and monitors the requirements of "strategic users". IT acquisition largely depends on the systemic approach provided by tactical users. Strategic users, often involved in the decision making process, tend to use the IT infrastructure sparingly, but depend heavily on tactical users to feed on (Corinne and Muthu 2008; Pervan 1998). This segment of users provides a dynamic ambient condition to information management and, therefore, must be well aware of exactly what IT being acquired is going to deliver. This dynamic ambient condition leads to "unstructured-ness" and ad hoc reporting environment in which there could be no standard pattern to follow.

This environment imposes restrictions on tactical users to meet the requirement at short notice. With the functional expertise they tend to focus on structured reports that get generated at the operational level, evaluate, and analyse as the situation demands. Tactical users, the interface layer between strategic and operational users, therefore, are the most critical mass in the decision-making process that provides analytical features to the data processed. There lies the importance of Management Information Systems (MIS) which is used by this layer of users through Executive Information Systems (EIS) and Decision Support System (DSS). A requirement analysis at this level will organise the direction for IT acquisition (Bowen *et al.* 2002).

Another set of users that should not be ignored is IT managers and related workforce. These users are not only the immediate beneficiary of IT but their role in the pre-acquisition process also is of paramount importance. Capacity building of these users would enhance the pre-acquisition IT planning process, manage IS-IT alignment process effectively at the strategic level and bridge the gap between IS and IT planned. Tactical level IT experts form the backbone of the IT architecture providing an interface between the tool specific users for developing the IT component based infrastructure. Exposure of these set of users to business processes would enhance the interaction and processes would be captured well. If managed properly during the pre-acquisition process, the organisation would draw "business maxim" as well as the "IT maxim" through these set of users in association with business domain functional users (Lee 2001; Luftman 2003).

In section one, we said that SDLC and user capabilities are important dimensions of the IT acquisition process in an organisation. SDLC-driven projects aim to conceptualize, design, develop, and deploy user-centered services which could survive a considerable life cycle so that desired services are garnered for meeting organisational objectives. SDLC activities provide a detailed and sequential approach to bringing together organisational priorities, user expectations, and system deliverables. These dimensions are presented in Table 1.

Table 1. Role of users in SDLC

SDLC Activities	Stage of SDLC	Critical Success Factors	User Roles (Capabilities)
Mission Definition	Pre-Acquisition Stage	Macro deliveries are captured	Able to formulate long term delivery plans
Concept of Operations		Formulation of standard operating procedure	Able to outline process capabilities
Project Planning		Processes are prioritized and sequenced	Able to engineer process deliveries and interface them
Requirement Definition		Process outputs and outcomes are organised	Able to fine tune process output, outcomes
Systems Specification		Development of road map for functional deliveries	Able to relate domain specific outputs to organisation's mandate
Systems Architecture	Acquisition Stage	"Fit" between organisation structure and systems structure	Able to relate overall systems deliveries to macro perspective of organisational deliveries
Systems Design		Proper development and verification of systems behaviour	Able to design systems behaviour
Systems Implementation		Efficient coding and operation of systems	Able to measure system deliveries
Systems Testing		Survive tests, quality parameters and standards	Able to test the systems as per organisational priorities
Systems Evolution		Proactive measures to specify improvement	Able to refine systems behaviour
Systems Usability	Post -Acquisition Stage	Systems are easy to use	Able to adapt to the environment
Systems Use		Physical behaviour of systems	Able to spread systems use
Systems Usefulness		Sustained use of systems	Able to provide inputs for systems improvement

Source: Adapted from Mead et al. (2000) and Piekarski and Plimmer (2007)

SDLC-driven projects have three distinct stages which could provide an insight to user capabilities as presented in Table 1. These stages are "pre-acquisition", "acquisition" and "post-acquisition". In Table 1, various dimensions are enumerated and placed in these three stages of SDLC. In the pre-acquisition stage SDLC envisages a well planned organisational approach to elicit systems requirements and long term delivery schedules. SDLC needs a careful articulation of system requirements through process mapping, establishing relationships among process as envisaged at the organisational architecture (Shaw and Garlan 1996), and binding all systemic parameters to these processes. In the post- acquisition stage, SDLC prepares the project planners and managers to test the planned deliveries and measure their successes through user-driven tests and feedback. This stage reflects an end-user motivation to use the IT enabled processes for a desired life cycle.

User Stratification under SDLC

It is evident from Table 1 that SDLC needs user support in all its three stages. As presented in Figure 2 there are three distinct levels of users in an organisation to carry out SDLC mandates.

Thus it is important to consider that IT infrastructure acquisition is a larger organisational issue and is viewed as an opportunity in which various stakeholders converge together to set up, own and maintain the acquired infrastructure. These stakeholders are primarily the users who assume the role of end-users, IT suppliers, IT managers, and functional planners. It is apparent from the last few decades of IS research that organisations face a plethora of user related challenges and user capability is one of them. In general, user capability is concerned with the way humans interact with information systems, the ways they prefer to use IT as a tool and accomplish tasks given to them. Therefore, user capability largely depends on maturity levels in the organi-

sation's processes, technology acquisition environment, and people.

UML-BASED MODELLING

As explained earlier in this chapter traditional SDLC is generally practised for systems development and acquisition in organisations. There are various SDLC models for the purpose of systems development. UML is often used for process modelling and is covered by ISO/IECS-19501 (Pervan 1998). UML provides modelling with platform independence. Since it is a process modelling tool and the framework is presented to understand and reflect the dependencies of various capability variables iteratively, UML is adopted to reflect them (Mellor and Marc 2002; Rumbaugh et al. 1999). Application of UML for reflecting capabilities in SDLC driven projects does have critical influence since user capabilities are agile and need to be captured iteratively.

UML-BASED SDLC USER CAPABILITY MODELLING

SDLC is a conceptual model having various methods for managing software engineering processes. It requires continuous requirement acquisition and user capabilities need to be assessed at these stages in an organisation. Business models often reflect various views of the processes and these views need to be well articulated in SDLC. Thus UML a modelling language, which can be used to specify, visualize, and construct these views of the business models can be used at any point of time of the SDLC process. This would be especially relevant in the initial stages of the IT acquisition cycle (Youssef et al. 2008).

UML has emerged as an industry standard which combines object orientation and component modelling. It provides a developer and the business modeller to collaborate and map organisational

Figure 2. Activity Diagram

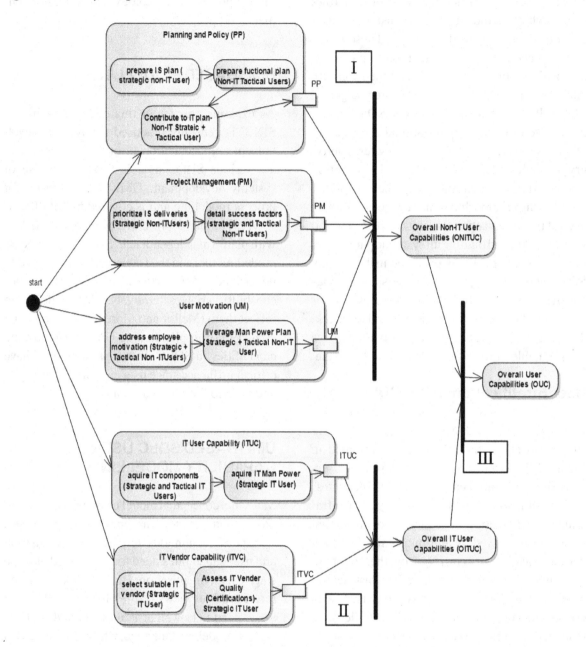

processes through various interactive components. It therefore provides a link for IT users and non-IT users to collaborate and bring in the right ambience to contribute to the larger complex process of mapping automation principles to existing and real organisational processes. Executable UML approach has now enabled the developer

to directly generate codes from abstracted UML driven models which can be modified at the micro level (Mellor and Marc 2002). This enables the non-IT user to collaborate and contribute to the abstracted models for organisational process and collaborate with IT users for effective development and deployment of applications. This also helps in incorporating changes arising from evolving end-user requirements. Therefore, there is a need for the acquiring organisation to support and motivate end users to collaborate and engage with IT-users continuously.

SDLC driven projects provide similar situations where all users collaborate in the project life cycle. In this table various activities of SDLC are described in which the defined users play their role specific to each activity. These activities are considered relevant in three stages of IT acquisition (pre-acquisition, acquisition, and post-acquisition). In these stages user responsibilities and unique and they need to deliver as per the demands of SDLC. Generally, organisations are agile and requirements change according to forces influencing internal processes and external interfaces (Larman 2004). Bringing all the agile issues into the ambit of application development projects is a complex phenomenon and UML supports this process through its various views and areas (Rumbaugh *et al.* 1999) as presented in Table 3. Various important views are "Static", "Use Case", Interaction", "Model Management", "State Machine", "Activity", "Implementation" and "Deployment". The areas are "Structural", "Dynamic", "Model Management" and "Extensibility". UML generates various diagrams which incorporates and represents user intentions and these are "Package", "Communication", "Uses Case", "Sequence", "Class", "Component", "Activity", State Machine" and "Deployment". Thus there is an opportunity created by UML process-driven projects to provide a model driven approach to users to effectively contribute to SDLC driven projects. This approach also provides an insight to user capability indicators in each stage of SDLC and the UML processes adopted for a project.

Discussions made above are presented for providing a panoramic view of the mapping process through deployment of SDLC-UML. Examples of various diagrams are presented for appreciation of the SDLC and UML driven processes. It is noted that various diagrams can be used in three distinct stages of SDLC driven projects.

- **Activity Diagrams:** UML uses activity diagrams to capture business process, activities in sequence, objects interfaced, and dependencies among activities (Rumbaugh et al. 1999). In this case this "activity diagram" is used for capturing the entire process of assessing organisational capabilities (OUC) which is assessed through the framework and explained in Figure 2.

In the presented activity diagram, three stages are involved to manage the SDLC in an organisation to capture capabilities. In stage I, non-IT user capabilities are captured and they can be assessed in each layer in the model. These capabilities are to be aggregated for further assessment. In stage II, IT capabilities are assessed through evaluation capabilities of the IT department, its acquisition capabilities including IT vendor identification and management. In stage III, aggregation of stages I and II are managed to understand the overall capabilities scenario in the organisation.

- **Capturing Business Structural Views (Sequence Diagrams):** This is an important exercise though UML modelling which captures capabilities requirements at various levels as described in Table 2. This is explained through a "sequence diagram" in Figure 3. In the diagram, prioritizations of activities are presented. Stage I is sequenced first since non-I users are expected to spearhead the IS planning process and prioritize the planning of IS deliveries. Stage II involves collaboration of all IT and non-IT users to manage the projects identified, requirements elicited, and reflection of organisational behaviour and processes in IT-enabled processes.

Figure 3. Sequence diagram

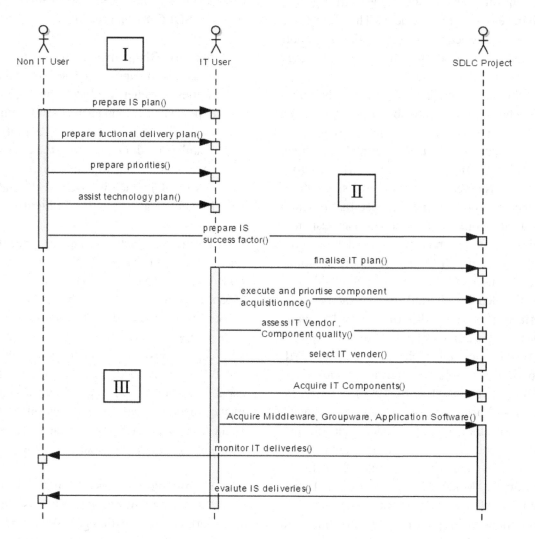

In stage III, monitoring and evaluation of IS and IT deliveries are in the agenda since investments already made in stages I and II are to be measured vis-à-vis expected success factors. Actors defined here are "IT users", "non-IT users", and "SDLC projects" and all participate in the SDLC process.

- **Capturing SDLC Behavioural Views:** In this view business process diagram is used with "class diagrams" in which user capabilities are aggregated through individual non-IT and IT capabilities. Any change in

the capability attributes would reflect in the overall capabilities in the organisation and demand a change management exercise for corrective measures.

In Figure 4 class diagram is explained. Stage I of the class diagram indicates non-IT user capabilities and these users form a class in the organisation. IT users form another class and they collaborate with non-IT users to implement IS designed services. IT vendors also collaborate as another class to support the SDLC process. In stage II these activities are captured for mapping delivery

Figure 4. Class diagram

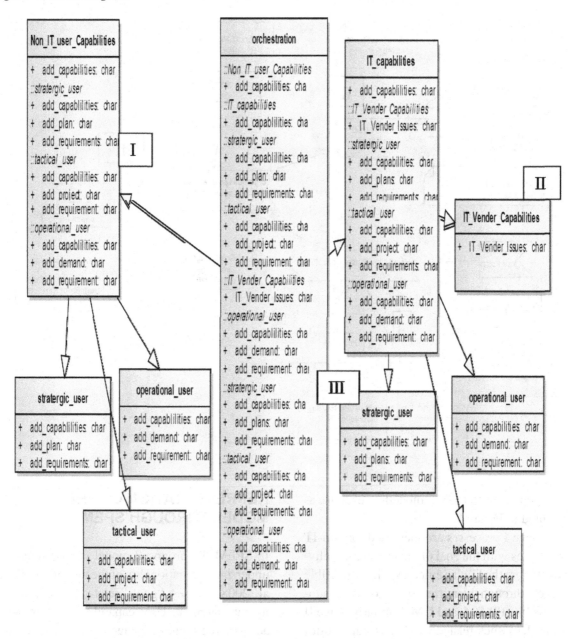

issues. In stage III, an orchestration is necessary at organisational level to meet the business goals and mapping the capabilities of stages I and II.

UML-BASED SDLC PROCESS MODELLING

SDLC projects are part of organisational processes since they are expected to align IS with IT services. Behaviour of SDLC driven process model

Figure 5. Process diagram

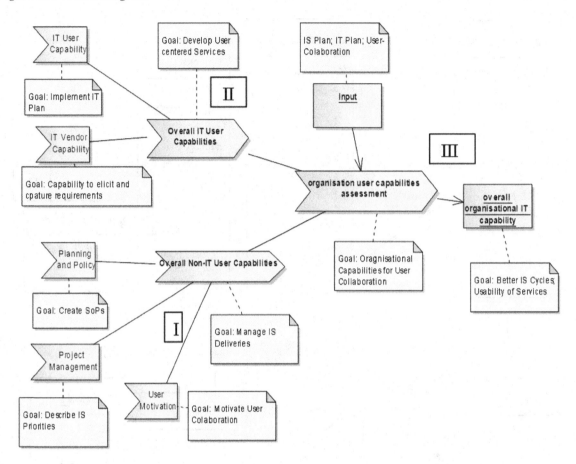

is developed through UML modelling exercise as presented in Figure 5.

In stage I processes are identified for non-IT capabilities with the goal of "managing IS deliveries" before the IT plan emerges. This is possible to track through identified goals of each sub-process like PP, PM, and UM. Similarly, stage II covers the issues related to IT user capabilities with the goal "develop user centered services" (ITUC and ITVC) so that in stage III, the overall process (OUC) is managed with the goal of "having organisational IT capabilities".

REPRESENTATION OF THE MODEL THROUGH SPEM

In SPEM the proposed model is represented to understand the rationality of the model (Seidita et al., 2008) to assess "goals" related to user capability management. User capabilities are assessed across three suggested stages for predictable success of EIS. SPEM supported conceptual model is explained in Figure 6 through a class diagram. This diagram uses the metrics discussed in Table 2.

As indicated in Table 2, stage-I of IT acquisition needs to capture non-IT user capabilities as a class. IT users form another class and they collaborate with non-IT users to implement EIS oriented services. IT venders also collaborate as a class to support the EIS. In stage-II these ac-

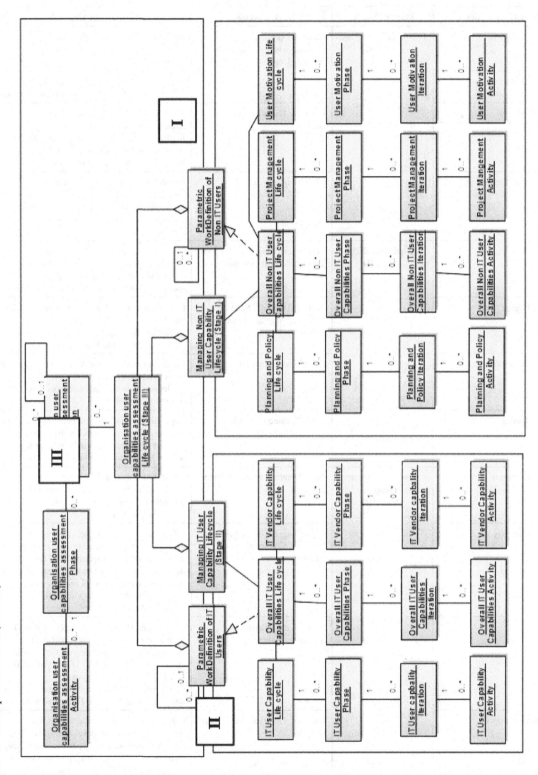

Figure 6. Conceptual model (SPEM)

Table 2. Mapping user capabilities in SDLC through UML

SDLC Activities	Stage of SDLC	UML Processes	Related User Capabilities
Mission Definition	Pre-Acquisition Stage (Stage I)	Package Diagram, Communication Diagram, Activity Diagram	Strategic Non-IT users' capability to contribute to static views for the system (Structural Areas)
Concept of Operations			Strategic users' capability to contribute to the meta model (Static View and Structural Areas)
Project Planning		Use Case Diagram, Sequence Diagram	Static views of strategic non-IT users and strategic IT-users for formalizing the meta model, relationships and generalization of deliveries at the enterprise level (Use Case View and Structural Areas)
Requirement Definition			
Systems Specification		Class Diagram	Capabilities of strategic IT-users and functional non-IT Users to contribute to enterprise systems design and deliverables for each system (Implementation View and Structural Areas)
Systems Architecture	Acquisition Stage (Stage II)	Component Diagram, Communication Diagram	Capabilities of strategic IT-users and functional non-IT users to contribute to establish relationships among systems specified (Static View and Structural Areas)
Systems Design		Activity Diagram, State Machine Diagram, Sequence Diagram	Capabilities of tactical IT –users and functional non-IT users to detail processes, process deliveries, and sequencing processes. (Dynamic Areas and Interaction view)
Systems Implementation		Deployment Diagram	Capabilities of strategic, tactical IT, and non-IT users to encourage common users for implementation of systems (Static views, Structural Areas)
Systems Testing		State Machine Diagram, Communication Diagram	Capabilities of tactical and operational non-IT users and IT users to validate the desired services of systems (Static Views, Deployment Views; Structural Areas and Dynamic Areas)
Systems Evolution	Post-Acquisition Stage (Stage III)	Class Diagram, State Machine Diagram	Capabilities of strategic IT and non-IT users to contribute to systems improvement and business process engineering (Model Management View)
Systems Usability		Class Diagram, Deployment Diagram, Communication Diagram	Capabilities of non-IT users (Strategic, Tactical and Operational) to contribute to make the systems usable; capabilities of IT users to ensure development of systems that are in conformity with non-IT users' expectations (Interaction View and Dynamic Area)
Systems Use		Deployment Diagram, Sequence Diagram	Capabilities of strategic and tactical non-IT users to ensure that systems developed are in use; operational users accept the systems automated. capabilities of IT users to motivate non-IT users to use the system. (Implementation View and Deployment View with Structural Area and Extensibility Area)
Systems Usefulness		Use Case Diagram, State Chart Diagram	Capabilities of non-IT Users to display the usefulness of systems developed and outline scope for improvement (State Machine View, Activity View, Interaction View with Dynamic Area; Model Management View)

Source: Rumbaugh et al. (1999) and Mellor and Marc (2002)

tivities are captured for mapping delivery issues through goals set. In stage-III, an orchestration is recommended to meet organizational business goals with effective metrics based mapping of the capabilities of stage-I and stage-II. Through SPEM, it is argued that each stage of the EIS acquisition process has a "*life cycle*" and has a metrics based "*WorkDefinition*". The *life cycle* determines the rationale behind including agile user centric services (Dean, 2007).

In Figure 6, each stage (I, II, III) is expected to have reasonably predicted life cycles in which agile relations among users are captured. Each stage is bound by relationships that converge in each step in the hierarchy to help traceability of the goal based metrics to fulfil organizational objectives. Through SPEM it is aimed to model the tasks that users can accomplish in Stage-I. This stage is quite important since the metrics used here would determine success of Stage-II and Stage-III. In Stage-II, these tasks are translated into IT enabled services by the IT service providers.. Success of Stage-III depends on how well collaborative efforts in TTF exercise have been carried out. Metrics used in this Stage-III are the outcomes of the strategic planning conducted in Stage-I and the way Stage-II is executed. Thus SPEM enabled model provides a holistic approach for determining organizational IT acquisition success.

SUMMARY

In this chapter two examples are show cased to use the model in software engineering processes. Its applicability is based on the SDLC approaches and thus there is scope to examine its applicability in other software process models. SDLC projects are managed with a mandate to align IS with IT components. This exercise needs active collaboration of users at all levels in the organisation. In this paper we state that identification of user capabilities is very important in the SDLC process and these are dynamic in nature. These capabili-

ties need to be continuously assessed through a mechanism and thresholds are to be monitored for corrective measures. UML itself has many limitations in managing user capabilities. However, this modelling tool provides the organisation an opportunity for motivating IT users and non-IT users to collaborate and contribute to agile application development and implementation processes. The UML driven model presented in this paper explains an approach to understand the capabilities of IT users and non-IT users to collaborate. Future work includes planning of capability thresholds, examining the capability parameters, and preparing a decision tree to track incapability, and address them at the organisational level.

REFERENCES

Balint, L. (1995). Computer-supported human-to-human interaction in information and decision systems: New perspectives of error-free interpersonal communication. In *Proceedings of the IEEE International Conference on Systems, Man and Cybernetics*, (pp. 1124-1129). Vancouver, Canada: IEEE.

Baslll, V. R., & Barry, B. (2001, May). COTS-based systems top 10 list. *Software Management*, 91-93.

Basili, V. R., Caldiera, G., & Rombach, H. D. (1994). Goal question metrics paradigm. In *Encyclopedia of Software Engineering* (pp. 528–532). Singapore: John Wiley.

Boehm, B., & Hansen, W. J. (2001, May). The spiral model as a tool for evolutionary acquisition. *Journal of Defense Software Engineering*, 4-11.

Bowen, P. L., Heales, J., & Vongphakdi, M. T. (2002). Reliability factors in business software: Volatility, requirements and end-users. *Information Systems Journal*, *12*(3), 185. doi:10.1046/j.1365-2575.2002.00128.x.

Broadbent, M., Weill, P., & O'Brien, T. (1996). Firm context and patterns of IT infrastructure capability. In *Proceedings of the 17th International Conference on Information Systems*, (pp. 174-194). Cleveland, OH: IEEE.

Corinne, M. K., & Muthu, K. (2008). Resilience of super users' mental models of enterprise-wide systems. *European Journal of Information Systems*, *17*, 29–46. doi:10.1057/palgrave.ejis.3000728.

Davis, B. G., & Olson, M. H. (2000). *Management information systems: Conceptual foundations, structure and development* (2nd ed.). Singapore: McGraw-Hill.

Ditsa, G., & MacGregor, G. E. (1995). Models of user perceptions, expectations and acceptance of information systems. In *Proceedings of the the Sixth International Conference of the Information Resource Management Association*, (pp. 221-229). Hershey, PA: IEEE.

Flynn, J. D. (1998). *Information systems requirements: Determination and analysis* (2nd ed.). Berkshire, UK: McGraw-Hill.

Frank, K. (1998). A contingency based approach to requirements elicitation and systems development. *Journal of Systems and Software*, *40*(1), 3–6. doi:10.1016/S0164-1212(97)00011-3.

Herron, D. (2002). *IT measurement: Practical advice from experts, international function point user group part-I*. Boston: Addison Wesley Professional.

Jiang, J. J., Klein, G., & Shepherd, M. (2001). The materiality of information system planning to project performance. *Journal of the Association for Information Systems*, *2*(5).

Lamb, R., & Kling, R. (2003). Re-conceptualising users as social actors in information systems research. *Management Information Systems Quarterly*, *27*(2), 197–235.

Larman, C. (2004). *Applying UML and patern*. Upper Saddle River, NJ: Prentice Hall.

Lee, C. S. (2001). Modelling the business value of information technology. *Information & Management*, *39*(3), 191–210. doi:10.1016/S0378-7206(01)00090-8.

Luftman, J. (2003). Assessing IT and business alignment. *Information Systems Management*, *20*(4), 9–21. doi:10.1201/1078/43647.20.4.20030901/77287.2.

Lycett, M., Macredie, R. D., Patel, C., & Paul, R. J. (2003). Migrating agile methods to standardised development practice. *Computer Magazine*, *36*(6), 79–85. doi:10.1109/MC.2003.1204379.

Mead, N. R., Ellison, R., Linger, R. C., Lipson, H. F., & McHugh, J. (2000). Life-cycle models for survivable systems. In *Proceedings of the Third Information Survivability, Workshop (ISW-2000)*. Boston, MA: ISW.

Mellor, S. J., & Balcer, M. J. (2002). *Executable UML: A foundation for model-driven architecture*. Boston: Addison Wesley.

Nuseibeh, B., & Easterbrook, S. (2000). Requirements engineering: A roadmap. In *Proceedings of the International Conference on Software Engineering (ICSE)*. Limerick, Ireland: ICSE.

Pervan, G. (1998). How the chief executive officers in large organisations view the management of their information systems. *Journal of Information Technology*, *13*, 95–109. doi:10.1080/026839698344882.

Piekarski, W., & Plimmer, B. (2007). A conceptual framework for explaining the value of end user maturity levels for IT management. In *Proceedings of the Eighth Australasian User Interface Conference (AUIC)*, (pp. 27-30). Ballarat, Australia: AUIC.

Rumbaugh, J., Jacobson, I., & Booch, G. (1999). *The unified modelling language reference manual*. Singapore: Addison Wesley Longman.

Seidita, V., Cossentino, M., & Gaglio, S. (2008). Using and extending the SPEM specifications to represent agent oriented methodologies. In *Proceedings of Agent-Oriented Software Engineering* (pp. 46–59). Estoril, Portugal: IEEE.

Shaw, M., & Garlan, D. (1996). *Software architecture: Perspectives on an emerging discipline.* Upper Saddle River, NJ: Prentice Hall.

Shehab, Sharp, Supramaniam, & Spedding. (2004). Enterprise resource planning: An integrative review. *Business Process Management Journal*, *10*(4), 359–386. doi:10.1108/14637150410548056.

Wang, E. T. G., & Tai, J. C. F. (2003). Factors affecting information systems planning effectiveness: Organizational contexts and planning systems dimensions. *Information & Management*, *40*(4), 287–303. doi:10.1016/S0378-7206(02)00011-3.

Youssef, W., Manuel, K., & Nicolas, N. (2008). *e-SPM: An online software project management game* (Working Paper, 08/02). Louvain School of Management.

Compilation of References

Abdul-Gader, A. H., & Kozar, K. A. (1995, December). The impact of computer alienation on information technology investment decisions: An exploratory cross-national analysis. *Management Information Systems Quarterly*, 535–559. doi:10.2307/249632.

Abrahamsson, P., & Jokela, T. (2001). *Implementing user-centred design in to a software development organsiation- a subcultural analysis*. Paper presented at the 24th Information Systems Research Seminar. Scandinavia, Norway.

Abramovsky, L., Kremp, E., Lopez, A., Schmidt, T., & Simpson, H. (2009). Understanding co-operative R&D activity: Evidence from four European countries. *Economics of Innovation and New Technology*, *18*(3), 243–265. doi:10.1080/10438590801940934.

AFEI. (2010). Industry perspective on the future of DoD IT acquisition (Industry Task Force Report). Arlington, VA: The Association of Enterprise Information (AFEI).

Agarwal, R., & Sambamurthy, V. (2002). Principles and models for organising the IT function. *MIS Quarterly Executive*, *1*(1), 1–16.

Ahen, D. M., Clouse, A., & Turner, R. (2001). *CMMI distilled: A practical introduction to integrated process improvement*. Boston: Addison-Wesley.

Ali, J., & Kumar, S. (2011). Information and communication technologies (ICTs) and farmers' decision-making across the agricultural supply chain. *International Journal of Information Management*, *31*, 149–159. doi:10.1016/j.ijinfomgt.2010.07.008.

Alter, S. (2003). 18 reasons why IT-related work systems should replace: The IT artifact as the core subject matter of the field. *Communications of the Association for Information Systems*, *12*, 365–394.

Anderson, S., & Felici, M. (2001). Requirements evolution: From process to product oriented management. In *Proceedings of the 3rd International Conference on Product Focused Software Profess Improvement* (LNCS), (vol. 2188, pp. 27-41). Kaiserslautern, Germany: Springer.

Anthony, R. N. (1965). *Planning and control: A framework for analysis*. Boston: Harvard University Press.

Anthony, R. N., & Govindarajan, V. (2004). *Management control systems*. New Delhi: Tata McGraw-Hill Publishing Company Limited.

Arvanitis, S., & Louikis, E. (2009). A comparative study of the effect of the ICT, organizational and human capital on labour productivity in Greece and Switzerland. *Information Economics and Policy*, *21*, 43–61. doi:10.1016/j.infoecopol.2008.09.002.

Awazu, Y., Baloh, P., Desouza, K. C., Wecht, C. H., Kim, J., & Jha, S. (2009). Information-communication technologies open up innovation. *Research Technology Management*, *52*(1), 51–58.

Bacon, C. J. (1992, September). The use of decision criteria in selecting information systems/ technology investments. *Management Information Systems Quarterly*, 335–353. doi:10.2307/249532.

Bakopoulos, Y. J. (1985). Toward a more precise concept of information technology. In *Proceedings of International Conference on Information Systems*, (pp. 17-24). IEEE.

Balint, L. (1995). Computer-supported human-to-human interaction in information and decision systems: New perspectives of error-free interpersonal communication. In *Proceedings of the IEEE International Conference on Systems, Man and Cybernetics*, (pp. 1124-1129). Vancouver, Canada: IEEE.

Barki, H., & Hartwick, J. (1989, March). Rethinking the concept of user involvement. *Management Information Systems Quarterly*, 53–63. doi:10.2307/248700.

Barnett, W. P., Mischke, G. A., & Ocasio, W. (2000). The evolution of collective strategies among organizations. *Organization Studies, 21*(2). doi:10.1177/0170840600212002.

Baroudi, J. J., Olson, M. H., & Ives, B. (1986). An empirical study of the impact of user involvement on system usage and information satisfaction. *Communications of the ACM, 29*(3), 232–238. doi:10.1145/5666.5669.

Barua, A., Konana, P., Whinston, A., & Yin, F. (2004). An empirical investigation of net-enabled business value. *Management Information Systems Quarterly, 28*(4), 585–620.

Basili, V. R, & Boehm, B. (2001, May). COTS-based systems top 10 list. *Software Management*, 91-93.

Basili, V. R., Caldiera, G., & Rombach, H. D. (1994). Goal question metrics paradigm. In *Encyclopaedia of Software Engineering* (*Vol. 1*, pp. 528–532). New York: Wiley.

Becerra-Fernandez, I., & Sabhewal, R. (2010). *Knowledge management: Systems and processes*. New Delhi: PHI Learning Pvt. Ltd..

Beer, S. (1974). *Decision and control: The meaning of operational research and management cybernetics*. London: John Wiley & Sons.

Benbasat, I., Goldstein, D. K., & Mead, M. (1987, September). The case research strategy in studies of information systems. *Management Information Systems Quarterly*, 369–386. doi:10.2307/248684.

Bentler, P. M. (1992). On the fit of models to covariances and methodlogy to the bulletin. *Psychological Bulletin*, (112): 400–404. doi:10.1037/0033-2909.112.3.400 PMID:1438635.

Bertalanffy, L. V. (2003). General systems theory. In Midgley, G. (Ed.), *General Systems* (*Vol. 1*). London: Sage Publications.

Bharadwaj, A. S. (2000). A resource based perspective on IT capability and firm performance: An empirical investigation. *Management Information Systems Quarterly, 24*(1), 169–196. doi:10.2307/3250983.

Bhattacherjee, A. (2001). Understanding information systems continuance: An expectation- confirmation model. *Management Information Systems Quarterly, 25*(3), 351–370. doi:10.2307/3250921.

Boehm, B., & Hansen, W. J. (2001, May). The spiral model as a tool for evolutionary acquisition. *Journal of Defense Software Engineering*, 4-11.

Boehm, B. W. (1981). *Software engineering economics*. Hoboken, NJ: Prentice Hall.

Bollen, K. A., & Lennox, R. (1991). Conventional wisdom on measurement: A structural equation perspective. *Psychological Bulletin, 110*(2). doi:10.1037/0033-2909.110.2.305.

Bowen, P. L., Heales, J., & Vongphakdi, M. T. (2002). Reliability factors in business software: Volatility, requirements and end-users. *Information Systems Journal, 12*(3), 18. doi:10.1046/j.1365-2575.2002.00128.x.

Broadbent, M., Weill, P., & O'Brien, T. (1996). Firm context and patterns of IT infrastructure capability. In *Proceedings of the 17th International Conference on Information Systems*, (pp. 174-194). Cleveland, OH: IEEE.

Broadbent, M., & Weill, P. (1993). Improving business and information strategy alignment: Learning from the banking industry. *IBM Systems Journal, 32*(1), 162–179. doi:10.1147/sj.321.0162.

Broadbent, M., & Weill, P. (1996). *Management by maxim: Creating business driven information technology infrastructure*. Carlton, Australia: University of Melbourne.

Broadbent, M., Weill, P., & St. Calir, D. (1999). The implications of information technology infrastructure for business process redesign. *Management Information Systems Quarterly, 23*(2), 159–182. doi:10.2307/249750.

Brown, I. (2010). *Strategic information systems planning: Comparing espoused beliefs with practice*. Paper presented at the 18th European Conference on Information Systems. Pretoria, South Africa.

Brown, D. R., & Harvey, D. (2006). *Experiential approach to organizational development*. Upper Saddle River, NJ: Prentice Hall.

Browne, M. W., & Cudek, R. (1993). Alternative ways of assessing model fit. In Bollen, K. A., & Log, J. S. (Eds.), *Testing Structural Equation Models* (pp. 136–162). Newbury Park, CA: Sage Publications.

Bruce, M. (1998). Understanding organizations: The dominance of systems theory. *International Journal of Organisational Behaviour, 1*(1), 1–12.

Brynjolfsson, E., & Hitt, M. (1998). Beyond the productivity paradox computers are the catalyst for bigger changes. *Communications of the ACM, 41*, 49. doi:10.1145/280324.280332.

Budhwar, P. S., Varma, A., Katou, A. A., & Narayan, D. (2009). The role of HR in cross-border mergers and acquisitions: The case of Indian pharmaceutical firms. *Multinational Business Review, 17*(2), 89–110. doi:10.1108/1525383X200900011.

Carlone, R.V., & Grosshans, W. (1992). Information technology: An audit guide for assessing acquisition risks. *GAO/IMTEC-8.1.6.*

Carmines, E. G., & Zeller, R. A. (1994). Reliability and validity assessment. In *International Handbook of Quantitative Applications in the Social Sciences* (Vol. 4, pp. 154–160). London: Sage Publications.

Casper, R., & Ghassan, A. (2000). *The orbital model: A methodology for development of interactive systems.* Melbourne, Australia: RMIT University. Retrieved from http://goanna.cs.rmit.edu.au/~ghasan/Orbital.doc

Cassidy, A. (2002). *A practical guide to planning for e-business success: How to e-enable your enterprise.* Boca Raton, FL: CRC Press.

Champian, D. J. (1975). *The sociology of organizations.* New York: McGraw-Hill Book Company.

Chandler, A. D. (1977). *The visible hand: The managerial revolutions in American business.* Cambridge, MA: Harvard Business.

Chandra, Y., & Coviello, N. (2010). Broadening the concept of international entrepreneurship: Consumers as international entrepreneurs. *Journal of World Business, 45*(3), 228–236. doi:10.1016/j.jwb.2009.09.006.

Chau, P. Y. C. (1994). Selection of packaged software in small business. *European Journal of Information Systems, 3*(4), 292–302. doi:10.1057/ejis.1994.34.

Chin, D. C.W. (1994, December). Organizational life cycle: A review and proposed directions for research. *Mid-Atlantic Journal of Business.*

Clark, C. E., Cavanaugh, N. C., Brown, C. V., & Sambamurthy, V. (1997, December). Building readiness capabilities in the organisation: Insights from the Bell Atlantic experience. *Management Information Systems Quarterly*, 425–454. doi:10.2307/249722.

Clegs, S. R. (1990). *Modern organizations.* New Delhi: Sage Publications.

Clemons, E. K., & Row, M. C. (1991). Sustaining IT advantage: The role of structural difference. *Management Information Systems Quarterly, 15*(3), 275–292. doi:10.2307/249639.

Coleman, P., & Papp, R. (2006). Strategic alignment: Analysis of perspectives. In *Proceedings of the 2006 Southern Association for Information Systems Conference,* (pp. 242 – 250). AISC.

Cooper, R. B., & Zmud, R. W. (1990). Information technology implementation research: A technology diffusion approach. *Management Science, 34*(2), 123–139. doi:10.1287/mnsc.36.2.123.

Corbett, A. C. (2005). Experiential learning within the process of opportunity identification and exploitation. *Entrepreneurship Theory & Practice, 29*, 473–491. doi:10.1111/j.1540-6520.2005.00094.x.

Corinne, M. K., & Muthu, K. (2008). Resilience of super users' mental models of enterprise-wide systems. *European Journal of Information Systems, 17*, 29–46. doi:10.1057/palgrave.ejis.3000728.

Cragg, P., Caldeira, M., & Ward, J. (2011). Organizational information systems competences in small and medium-sized enterprises. *Information & Management, 48*, 353–363. doi:10.1016/j.im.2011.08.003.

Cronbach, L. J., Glester, G. C., Nanada, H., & Rajaratnam, N. (1972). *The dependability of behavioural measurements: Theory of generalizability for scores and profiles.* New York: Wiley.

Cruz-Cunha, M. M. (2010). *Enterprise information systems for business integration in SMES, technological, organziational and social dimensions.* Hershey, PA: IGI Global Publications.

Cuena, J., & Molina, M. (2000). The role of knowledge modeling techniques in software development: A general approach based on a knowledge management tool. *International Journal of Human-Computer Studies, 52,* 385–421. doi:10.1006/ijhc.1999.0232.

Curtis, B., Hefley, W. E., & Miller, S. (1995). *People capability maturity model.* Pittsburgh, PA: Software Engineering Institute, Carnegie Melon University.

Curtis, B., Krasner, H., & Iscoe, N. (1988). A field study of the software design process for large systems. *Communications of the ACM, 31*(11), 1268–1287. doi:10.1145/50087.50089.

Daft, R. L. (2008). *Organization theory and design* (10th ed.). Cengage Learning.

Datnthanam, R., & Hartono, E. (2003). Issues in linking information technology capability to firm performance. *Management Information Systems Quarterly, 27*(1), 125–153.

Davis, B. G., & Olson, M. H. (2000). *Management information systems: Conceptual foundations, structure and development* (2nd ed.). Singapore: McGraw-Hill.

Davis, F. D. (1989, September). Perceived usefulness, perceived ease of use, and user acceptance of information technology. *Management Information Systems Quarterly,* 319–340. doi:10.2307/249008.

Davis, G. B., & Olson, M. H. (2000). *Management information systems.* New Delhi: Tata McGraw-Hill Publishing Company.

Defence Science Board. (2009). *Report of the task force on defense science board.* Washington, DC: Department of Defense Policies and Procedures for the Acquisition of Information Technology.

Deming, E. E. (2000). *Out of crisis.* Cambridge, MA: The MIT Press.

Dewire, T. D. (2003). From the editor. *Information Systems Management, 20*(4), 5–8. doi:10.1201/1078/43647.20.4.20030901/77286.1.

DHS. (2008). *Department of homeland security acquisition instruction/guidebook #102-01-001: Appendix B interim version 1.9 November 7 2008.* Washington, DC: DHS.

Díaz-Ley, M., García, F., & Piattini, M. (2010). MIS-PyME- Software measurement capability maturity model – Supporting the definition of software measurement programs and capability determination. *Advances in Engineering Software, 41,* 1223–1237. doi:10.1016/j.advengsoft.2010.06.007.

Dillon, W. R., & Goldstein, M. (1984). *Multivariate analysis: Methods and applications.* New York: John Weily & Sons.

Ditsa, G., & MacGregor, G. E. (1995). Models of user perceptions, expectations and acceptance of information systems. In *Proceedings of the Sixth International Conference of the Information Resource Management Association,* (pp. 221-229). IEEE.

Dodgson, M., Gann, D., & Salter, A. (2006). The role of technology in the shift towards open innovation: the case of Proctor & Gamble. *R & D Management, 36*(3), 334–346. doi:10.1111/j.1467-9310.2006.00429.x.

Dressler, S. (2004). *Strategy, organization and performance management: From basics to best practices.* Boca Raton, FL: Universal Publishers.

Drucker, P. (1969). *The age of discontinuity: Guidelines to our changing society.* London: Heinemann.

Drucker, P. F. (1990). *Managing the non-profit organizations practices and principles.* New Delhi: Macmillan India Limited.

Drucker, P. F. (1999). *Management challenges for the 21ˢᵗ century.* New York: Harper Business.

Dube, L., & Pare, G. (2003). Rigor in information systems positivist case research: Current practices, trends, and recommendations. *Management Information Systems Quarterly, 27*(4), 597–635.

Dunbar, R. J. M., & Starbuck, W. H. (2006). Learning to design organizations and learning from designing them. *Organization Science, 17*(2), 171–178. doi:10.1287/orsc.1060.0181.

Dvorak, R., Holen, E. E., Mark, D., & Meehan, W. F. (1997). Six principles of high-performance IT. *The McKinsey Quarterly, 3*, 164–177.

Earl, M. (1993, March). Experiences in strategic information systems planning. *Management Information Systems Quarterly.* doi:10.2307/249507.

Earl, M. J. (1987). Information systems strategy formulation. In Boland, R. J., & Hirschheim, R. A. (Eds.), *Critical Issues in Information Systems Research.* Chichester, UK: John Wiley & Sons.

Earl, M. J. (1992). Putting IT in its place: A polemic for the nineties. *Journal of Information Technology, 7*, 100–108. doi:10.1057/jit.1992.15.

Eckerson, W. W. (2006). *Performance dashboards: Measuring, monitoring and managing your business.* New York: John Wiley & Sons.

Eckes, G. (2001). *Making six-sigma last: Managing the balance between cultural and technical change.* New York: John Wiley & Sons.

Eilon, S. (1979). *Management control.* Oxford, UK: Pergamon Press.

Eskelin, A. (2001). *Technology acquisition: Buying the future of your business.* Reading, MA: Addison-Wesley.

España, S., Condori-Fernandez, N., & González, A., & Pastor, O. (2010). An empirical comparative evaluation of requirements engineering methods. *Journal of the Brazilian Computer Society, 16*(1), 3–19. doi:10.1007/s13173-010-0003-5.

Evans, N. (2004). *Promoting fusion in the business-IT relationship.* Paper presented at Issues in Informing Science and Information Technology Education Joint Conference. Rock Hampton, Australia.

Everdingen, Y., Hillergersberg, J., & Waarts, E. (2000). ERP adoption by European midsize companies. *Communications of the ACM, 43*(3), 27–31. doi:10.1145/332051.332064.

Fabrigar, L. R., Wegener, D. T., MacCallum, R. C., & Strahan, E. J. (1999). Evaluating the use of exploratory factor analysis in psychological research. *Psychological Methods, 3*, 272–299. doi:10.1037/1082-989X.4.3.272.

Fenton, N. E., & Pfleeger, S. L. (2002). *Software metrics: A rigorous & practical approach* (2nd ed.). Singapore: Thomson Asia Pte. Ltd..

Ferguson, J., Cooper, J., Falat, M., Fisher, M., Guido, A., & Marciniak, J. … Webster, R. (1997). Software acquisition process maturity questionnaire: The acquisition risk management initiative. Pittsburgh, PA: Software Engineering Institute, Carnegie Mellon University.

Fernandez, I. B., & Sabhrewal, R. (2010). *Knowledge management: Systems and processes.* New Delhi: PHI Learning Private Limited.

Fiedler, E. (1964). *A contingency model of leadership effectiveness.* Journal for Advances in Experimental Social Psychology.

Field, A. (2000). *Discovering statistics using SPSS for windows.* London: Sage Publications.

Fletcher, M., & Harris, S. (2012). Knowledge acquisition for the internationalization of the smaller firm: Content and sources. *International Business Review, 21*, 631–647. doi:10.1016/j.ibusrev.2011.07.008.

Flynn, J. D. (1998). *Information systems requirements: Determination and analysis* (2nd ed.). Berkshire, UK: McGraw-Hill.

Fowler, F., Rice, D., Foemmel, M., Hieatt, E., Mee, R., & Stafford, R. (2003). *Patterns of enterprise application architecture.* Boston: Addison-Wesley.

Frank, K. (1998). A contingency based approach to requirements elicitation and systems development. *Journal of Systems and Software, 40*(1), 3–6. doi:10.1016/S0164-1212(97)00011-3.

Franz, C. R., & Robey, D. (1986). Organizational context, user involvement and the usefulness of information systems. *Decision Sciences, 17*(4), 329–356. doi:10.1111/j.1540-5915.1986.tb00230.x.

Gable, G. (2010). Strategic information systems research: An archival analysis. *The Journal of Strategic Information Systems, 19*, 3–16. doi:10.1016/j.jsis.2010.02.003.

Galbraith, J. R. (1998). *Strategy implementation: The role of structure and process. St. Paul, MN.* MN: West.

Gallo, T. E. (1988). *Strategic information management and planning*. Englewood Cliffs, NJ: Prentice Hall.

Garlan, J., & Anthony, R. (2003). *Large-scale software architecture: A practical guide using UML*. New Delhi: Wiley Dreamtech India.

Gebauer, J. (1997). Modeling the IT-infrastructure of inter-organisational processes-automation vs. flexibility. In *Proceedings of Conference of International Society for Decision Support(IDSS)*. Lausanne, Switzerland: IDSS.

Geraldi, J. G., Kutsch, E., & Turner, N. (2011). Towards a conceptualisation of quality in information technology projects. *International Journal of Project Management*, *29*, 557–567. doi:10.1016/j.ijproman.2010.06.004.

Gibson, C. F., & Nolan, R. L. (1974, January/February). Managing the four stages of EDP growth. *Harvard Business Review*, 76–88.

Gollakota, K. (2008). ICT use by businesses in rural India: The case of EID Parry's Indiagriline. *International Journal of Information Management*, *28*, 336–341. doi:10.1016/j.ijinfomgt.2008.04.003.

Gómez, J., & Vargas, P. (2009). The effect of financial constraints, absorptive capacity and complementarities on the adoption of multiple process technologies. *Research Policy*, *38*(1), 106–119. doi:10.1016/j.respol.2008.10.013.

Gómez, J., & Vargas, P. (2012). Intangible resources and technology adoption in manufacturing firms. *Research Policy*, *41*, 1607–1619. doi:10.1016/j.respol.2012.04.016.

Grady, R. B. (1992). *Practical software metrics for project management and process improvement*. Upper Saddle River, NJ: Prentice Hall.

Grady, R. B., & Caswell, D. L. (1987). *Software metrics: Establishing company-wide programme*. Upper Saddle River, NJ: Prentice Hall.

Grehag, A. (2001). *Requirements management in a life cycle perspective- A position paper*. Paper presented at the 7th International Workshop on Requirement Engineering: Foundation for Software Quality (REFSQ:2001). Interlaken, Switzerland.

Greiner, L. E. (1997). Evolution and revolution as organizations grow: A company's past has clues for management that are critical to future success. *Family Business Review*, *10*(4). doi:10.1111/j.1741-6248.1997.00397.x.

Gross, P. H. B., & Ginzberg, M. J. (1984). Barriers to the adaptation of application software packages. *Systems, Objectives. Solutions*, *4*(4), 211–226.

Grover, V., Teng, J., Segars, A., & Fiedler, K. (1998). The influence of information technology and business process changes in perceived productivity: The IS executive's perspective. *Information & Management*, *34*(3), 141. doi:10.1016/S0378-7206(98)00054-8.

Gunasekaran, A. (Ed.). (2009). *Advances in enterprise information systems*. Hershey, PA: IGI Global.

Guttman, R., & Greenbaum, C. W. (1998). Facet theory: Its development and current status. *European Psychologist*, *3*(1), 13–36. doi:10.1027/1016-9040.3.1.13.

Haag, S., Baltzan, P., & Phillips, A. (2009). Business driven technology. New Delhi: Tata McGraw-Hill Education Private Limited. ISBN: 13: 978-0-07-067109-6

Halle, B. V. (2002). *Business rules applied: Building better systems using the business rules approach*. New York: John Wiley & Sons, Inc..

Handy, C. (1989). *The age of unreason*. London: Business Books.

Hansson, S. O. (2005). Decision theory – A brief introduction. Stockholm, Sweden: Royal Institute of Technology (KTH).

Hartwick, J., & Barki, H. (1999). Conflict management styles of users and analysts, and their impact on conflict resolution. In *Proceedings of 32nd Hawaii International Conference on Systems Sciences*. IEEE.

Hatry, H. P. (2006). *Performance measurement: Getting results*. Washington, DC: The Urban Institute Press.

Hearst, M. A. (2009). *Search user interfaces*. New York: Cambridge University Press. doi:10.1017/CBO9781139644082.

Henderson, J., & Venkatraman, N. (1990). *Strategic alignment: A model for organizational transformation via information technology* (Working Paper 3223-90). Cambridge, MA: Sloan School of Management, Massachusetts Institute of Technology.

Henderson, J. C., & Venkatraman, N. (1993). Strategic alignment: Leveraging information technology for transforming organisations. *IBM Systems Journal, 32*(1), 4–16. doi:10.1147/sj.382.0472.

Henderson, J., & Venkatraman, N. (1992). Strategic alignment: A model for organizational transformation through information technology. In Kochan, T., & Unseem, M. (Eds.), *Transforming Organisations*. New York: Oxford University Press.

Herron, D. (2002). *IT measurement: Practical advice from experts, international function point user group part-I*. Boston: Addison Wesley Professional.

Hicks, H. G., & Gullet, C. R. (1976). *Organizations: Theory and behavior*. Singapore: McGraw-Hill International Book Co..

Hoffer, J. A., George, J. F., & Valacich, J. S. (2001). *Modern systems analysis and design* (2nd ed.). Singapore: Addison Wesley Longman.

Holland, C. P., & Light, B. (1999, May/June). A critical success factors model for ERP implementation. *IEEE Software*, 30–36. doi:10.1109/52.765784.

Hong, K., & Kim, Y. (2002). The critical success factors for ERP implementation: An organizational fit perspective. *Information & Management, 40*(1), 25–40. doi:10.1016/S0378-7206(01)00134-3.

Hosier, W. A. (1961). Pitfalls and safeguards in real-time digital systems with emphasis on programming. *IRE Transactions on Engineering Management, 8*.

Hoving, R. (2003). Executive response: Project management process maturity as a secret weapon. *MIS Quarterly Executive, 2*(1), 29–30.

Huang, C., Derrick, C., & Hu, O. (2004). Integrating web services with competitive strategies: The balance scorecard approach. *Communications of AIS, 13*.

Huff, S. L., & Munro, M. C. (1985, December). Information technology assessment and adoption: A field study. *Management Information Systems Quarterly*, 327–340. doi:10.2307/249233.

Humphrey, W. S. (1989). *Managing the software process*. Englewood Cliffs, NJ: Addison Wesley.

Ibrahim, L. (2000). Using an integrated capability maturity model - The FAA experience. In *Proceedings of the Tenth Annual International Symposium of the International Council on Systems Engineering (INCOSE)*, (pp. 643-648). INCOSE.

IEEE. (1994). How ISO 9001 fits into the software's world. *IEEE S/W, 11*.

IFMA. (2011). A framework for facilities lifecycle cost management. *International Facility Management Association*. Retrieved November 25, 2011 from http://www.ifma.org/tools/research/Asset_Lifecyle_Model.pdf

IFPUG. (2002). *IT measurement: Practical advice from experts: International function point users group*. Boston: Addison-Wesley.

Iivari, J. (1992). The organisational fit of information systems. *Journal of Information Systems, 2*, 3–29. doi:10.1111/j.1365-2575.1992.tb00064.x.

International Function Point Users Group (IFPUG). (2002). *IT measurement: Practical advice from experts*. Reading, MA: Addison-Wesley.

Irani, Z. (2002). Information systems evaluation: Navigating through problem domain. *Information & Management, 40*(1), 11–24. doi:10.1016/S0378-7206(01)00128-8.

ISO. (1991). *International organisation for standardisation: ISO/IEC 9126*. Geneva: ISO.

Jackson, M. C. (2000). *Systems approach to management*. New York: Plenum Publishers.

Jalote, P. (2002). *CMM in practice: Process for executing software projects at infosys*. Delhi: Pearson Education.

Jamsen, P., Ikaheimo, S., & Malinen, P. (1999). Capital formation in Kenyan farmer-owned cooperatives: A case study. Turku, Finland. ISBN 92-5-104330-2

Jenkins, G. M. (1969). The systems approach. *Journal of Systems Engineering, 1*, 3–49.

Jeston, J., & Nelis, J. (2008). *Business process management*. New York: Elsevier.

Jiang, J. J., Klein, G., & Shepherd, M. (2001). The materiality of information system planning to project performance. *Journal of the Association for Information Systems, 2*(5).

Johnson, C. W. (2011). Identifying common problems in the acquisition and deployment of large-scale, safety–critical, software projects in the US and UK healthcare systems. *Safety Science, 49*, 735–745. doi:10.1016/j.ssci.2010.12.003.

Johnston, H. R., & Carrico, S. R. (1998, March). Developing capabilities to use information strategy. *Management Information Systems Quarterly*.

Jokela, T. (2001). *Review of usability capability assessment approaches*. Paper presented at the 24th Information Systems Research Seminar. Scandinavia, Norway.

Jokela, T., & Abrahamsson, P. (2000). Modelling usability capability-introducing the dimensions. In *Proceedings of PROFES 2000*. Oulu, Finland: PROFES.

Jones, G. R. (2004). *Organizational theory, design and change*. New Delhi: Pearson Education.

Joreskog, K. G., & Sorbom, D. (1989). *LISREL 8: Structural equation modelling with SIMPLIS command language*. Hillsdale, NJ: Lawrence Erlbaum.

Kalusopa, T. (2005). The challenges of utilizing information communication technologies (ICTs) for the small-scale farmers in Zambia. *Library Hi Tech, 23*, 414–424. doi:10.1108/07378830510621810.

Kanter, J. (2000). *Managing with information* (4th ed.). New Delhi: Prentice Hall.

Kanter, R. M. (1983). *The change masters*. London: University of Chicago Press.

Kaplan, R. S., & Norton, D. P. (1996). *Balanced scorecard: Translating strategy into action*. Boston: Harvard.

Kappel, T. A. (2001). Perspectives on roadmaps: How organizations talk about the future. *Journal of Product Innovation Management, 18*, 39–50. doi:10.1016/S0737-6782(00)00066-7.

Karahanna, E., Straub, D. W., & Chervany, N. L. (1999). Information technology adoption across time: A cross-sectional comparison of pre-adoption and post-adoption beliefs. *Management Information Systems Quarterly, 23*(2), 183–213. doi:10.2307/249751.

Kast, F. E., & Rosenzweig, J. E. (1972). *General systems theory: Applications for organization and management*.

Kettinger, W. V, & Grover, S. G., & Segars. (1994). Strategic information systems revisited: A study in sustainability and performance. *Management Information Systems Quarterly, 18*(1), 31–33. doi:10.2307/249609.

Kind, J. L., & Kraemer. (1984). Evolution and organisational information systems: An assessment of Nolan's stage model. *Communications of the ACM, 27*(5), 466–470. doi:10.1145/358189.358074.

King, W. R. (Ed.). (2009). *Planning for information systems*. New Delhi: PHI Learning Pvt. Ltd..

Klein, M., & Methile, L. B. (1992). *Expert systems: A decision support approach*. Cornwall, UK: Addison-Wesley Publishing Company.

Kline, R. B. (1998). *Principles and practice of structural equation modeling*. New York: The Guilford Press.

Koellinger, P. (2008). The relationship between technology, innovation, and firm performance – Empirical evidence form e-business in Europe. *Research Policy, 37*, 1317–1328. doi:10.1016/j.respol.2008.04.024.

Kohli, R., & Sherer, S. A. (2002). Measuring payoff information technology investments: Research issues and guidelines. *Communications of AIS, 9*.

Kohli, R., & Devaraj, S. (2004). Realising business value of information technology investments: An organisational process. *MIS Quarterly Executive, 3*(1), 53–68.

Kotler, P., & Keler, K. (2011). *Marketing management* (14th ed.). Hoboken, NJ: Prentice Hall.

Kown, T. H., & Zmud, R. W. (1987). Unifying the fragmented models of information systems implementation. In *Critical Issues in Information Systems Research*. New York, NY: John Wiley and Sons.

Kumar, K., & Hillegersberg, J. (2000). ERP experiences and evolution. *Communications of the ACM, 43*(3), 22–26. doi:10.1145/332051.332063.

Ladley, J. (2010). *Making enterprise information management (EIM) work for business: A guide to understanding information as an asset*. London: Elsevier.

Lamb, R., & Kling, R. (2003). Re-conceptualising users as social actors in information systems research. *Management Information Systems Quarterly, 27*(2), 197–235.

Land, S. K., Smith, D. B., & Walz, J. W. (2008). *Practical support for lean six sigma software process definition: Using IEEE software engineering standards*. New York: John Wiley & Sons, Inc. doi:10.1002/9780470289969.

Larman, C. (2004). *Applying UML and patern*. Upper Saddle River, NJ: Prentice Hall.

Lavole, D., & Culbert, S. A. (1978). Stages in organization and development. *Human Relations, 31*, 417–438. doi:10.1177/001872677803100503.

Lawler, E. E. III, & Worley, C. G. (2006). *Built to change*. San Francisco, CA: Jossey-Bass.

Lee, A. S. (1989, March). A scientific methodology for MIS case studies. *Management Information Systems Quarterly*, 33–50. doi:10.2307/248698.

Lee, C. S. (2001). Modeling the business value of information technology. *Information & Management, 39*(3), 191–210. doi:10.1016/S0378-7206(01)00090-8.

Lee, S., Kang, S., Park, Y., & Park, Y. (2007). Technology roadmapping for R&D planning: The case of the Korean parts and materials industry. *Technovation, 27*, 433–445. doi:10.1016/j.technovation.2007.02.011.

Lee, Y., Kozar, K. A., & Larsen, K. R. T. (2003). The technology acceptance model: Past, present and future. *Communications of AIS, 12*, 750–780.

Leffingwell, D. (2007). *Scaling software agility: Best practices for large enterprises*. Boston: Addison-Wesley.

Lester, D. L., Parnell, J. A., & Carraher, S. (2003). Organizational life cycle: A five-stage empirical scale. *The International Journal of Organizational Analysis, 11*(4). doi:10.1108/eb028979.

Levie, J., & Lichtenstein, B. B. (2008). *From stages of business growth to a dynamic states model of entrepreneurial growth and change (WP08-02)*. Glasgow, UK: Hunter Centre for Entrepreneurship, University of Strathclyde.

Lewis, J. I. (2007). Technology acquisition and innovation in the developing world: Wind turbine development in China and India. *Studies in Comparative International Development, 42*(3–4), 208–232. doi:10.1007/s12116-007-9012-6.

Lichtenthaler, U. (2007). Managing external technology commercialisation: A process perspective. *International Journal of Technology Marketing, 2*(3), 225–242. doi:10.1504/IJTMKT.2007.015202.

Lichtenthaler, U. (2010). Technology exploitation in the context of open innovation: Finding the right 'job' for your technology. *Technovation, 30*, 429–435. doi:10.1016/j.technovation.2010.04.001.

Lientz, B. P., & Chen, M. (1981). Assessing impact of new technology in information systems. *Long Range Planning, 14*(6), 44–50. doi:10.1016/0024-6301(81)90059-5.

Linn, R. L., & Werts, C. E. (1979). Covariance structures and their analysis. In Traub, R. E. (Ed.), *New directions for testing and measurement: methodological developments* (Vol. 4, pp. 53–73). San Francisco, CA: Jossey-Bass.

Linthicum, D. S. (2004). *Enterprise application integration*. New Delhi: Pearson Education Inc..

Li, Y., Liu, Y., & Liu, H. (2011). Co-opetition, distributor's entrepreneurial orientation and manufacturer's knowledge acquisition: Evidence from China. *Journal of Operations Management, 29*, 128–142. doi:10.1016/j.jom.2010.07.006.

Lokshin, B., Hagedoorn, J., & Letterie, W. (2011). The bumpy road of technology partnerships: Understanding causes and consequences of partnership mal-functioning. *Research Policy, 40*, 297–308. doi:10.1016/j.respol.2010.10.008.

Lorange, P., & Vanicl, R. F. (1977). *Strategic planning systems*. Englewood Cliffs, NJ: Prentice-Hall Inc..

Loudon, K. C., & Loudon, J. P. (2006). *Essentials of business information systems*. Upper Saddle River, NJ: Prentice Hall.

Loudon, K. C., Loudon, J. P., & Dass, R. (2010). *Management information systems*. New Delhi: Dorling Kindersley.

Lucas, H., & Baroudi, J. (1994, Spring). The role of information technology in organisation design. *Journal of Management Information Systems, 9.*

Luftman, J. (2000). Assessing business – IT alignment maturity. *Communications of the AIS, 4.*

Luftman, J. N., Papp, R., & Brier, T. (2002, September). Enablers and inhibitors of business-IT alignment. *AB Insight.*

Luftman, J. (2003). Assessing IT and business alignment. *Information Systems Management, 20*(4), 9–21. doi:10.1 201/1078/43647.20.4.20030901/77287.2.

Lycett, M., Macredie, R. D., Patel, C., & Paul, R. J. (2003). Migrating agile methods to standardised development practice. *Computer Magazine, 36*(6), 79–85. doi:10.1109/MC.2003.1204379.

Lynch, R. K. (1984). Implementing packaged application software: Hidden costs and new challenges. *Systems, Objectives. Solution, 4*(4), 227–234.

Lyytinen, K., & Robey, D. (1999). Learning failure in information systems development. *Information Systems Journal, 9*(2), 85. doi:10.1046/j.1365-2575.1999.00051.x.

Maciarielo, J. A., & Kirby, C. J. (2000). *Management control systems: Using adaptive systems to attain control.* New Delhi: Prentice-Hall of India Private Limited.

Madhok, A., & Keyhani, M. (2012). Acquisitions as entrepreneurship: Asymmetries, opportunities, and the internationalization of multinationals from emerging economies. *Global Strategy Journal, 2*(1), 26–40. doi:10.1002/gsj.1023.

Maier, M. W., & Rechtin, E. (2009). *The art of systems architecting.* Boca Raton, FL: CRC Press.

Mantel, M. M., & Teorey, T. J. (1989, September). Incorporating behavioural techniques into the systems development life cycle. *Management Information Systems Quarterly.*

Marble, R. P. (1992). A stage – theoretic approach to information systems planning in existing business entities of recently established market economies. In *Proceedings of the 10th International Conference of the System Dynamics Society 1992,* (pp. 405-414). Utrecht, Netherlands: IEEE.

Marino, J., & Rowley, M. (2010). Understanding SCA (service component architecture). Boston: Addison-Wesley. ISBN: 13: 978-0-321-51508

Markus, M. L., & Robey, D. (1988). Information technology and organisational change: causal structure in theory and research. *Management Science, 34*(5), 583–598. doi:10.1287/mnsc.34.5.583.

Marple, J., Clark, B., Jones, C., & Zubrow, D. (2001). *Measures in support of evolutionary acquisition.* Pittsburgh, PA: Software Engineering Institute, Carnegie Mellon University.

Martins, L., & Keillermanns, F. W. (2001). User acceptance of a web-based information system in a non-voluntary context. In *Proceedings of the 22nd International Conference on Information Systems (ICIS),* (pp. 607-612). New Orleans, LA: ICIS.

Masav, D. E. (1984). *Voluntary non-profit enterprise management.* New York: Plenum Press.

McFarlan, F. W., & McKenny, J. L. (1983). *Corporate information systems management: The issues facing senior executives.* Homewood, IL: Irwin.

Mcliver, J. P., & Carmines, E. G. (1994). Unidimensional scaling. In *International Handbook of Quantitative Applications in the Social Sciences* (Vol. 4, pp. 154–160). London: Sage Publications.

Mead, N. R., Ellison, R., Linger, R. C., Lipson, H. F., & McHugh, J. (2000). Life cycle models for survivable systems. In *Proceedings of Third Information Survivability Workshop, ISW-2000.* Boston: ISW.

Mellor, S. J., & Balcer, M. J. (2002). *Executable UML: A foundation for model-driven architecture.* Boston: Addison Wesley.

Melville, N., Kraemer, K., & Gurbaxani, V. (2004). Review: Information technology and organizational performance: An integrative model of IT business value. *Management Information Systems Quarterly, 28*(2), 283–322.

Merchant, K. A., & Van der Steede, W. A. (2007). *Management control systems – Performance, measurement, evaluation and incentives* (2nd ed.). Essex, UK: Prentice Hall.

Midgley, G. (2003). *Systems thinking: An introduction and overview*. London: Sage Publications.

Miller, D., & Toulouse, J. M. (1986). Chief executive personality and corporate strategy and structure in small, firms. *Management Science, 32*(11), 1389–1409. doi:10.1287/mnsc.32.11.1389.

Millett, B. (1998). Understanding organisations: The dominance of systems theory. *International Journal of Organisational Behaviour, 1*(1), 1–12.

Minieak, E., & Kurzeja, Z. D. (2001). *Statistics for business with computer applications*. Cincinnati, OH: Thomson Learning.

Mintzberg, H. (1979). *The structuring of organizations: A synthesis of the research*. Englewood Cliffs, NJ: Prentice Hall.

Mintzberg, H., Ahlstrand, B., & Lampel, J. (1988). *Startegy safri*. New York: The Free Press.

Mintzberg, H., Dury, R., & Andre, T. (1976). The structure of 'unstructured' decision processes. *Administrative Science Quarterly*, 21.

Misra, H., Satpathy, M., & Mohanty, B. (2003). A user centric IT-acquisition model. In *Proceedings of Sixth International Conference on Information Technology*, (pp. 439-445). IEEE.

Misra, H., Satpathy, M., & Mohanty, B. (2004). Organisation preparedness and information technology acquisition success: An assessment model. In *Proceedings of Tenth Americas Conference on Information Systems*, (pp. 3679-3692). New York: IEEE.

Misra, H. K. (2006). Role of human reource in information technology alignment in organizations: A metric based strategic assessment framework. *Journal of Information Technology Management, 17*(3).

Misra, H. K., Satpathy, M., & Mohanty, B. (2005). Assessment of IT acquisition process: A metrics based measurement approach. *Vilakshan: XIMB Journal of Management, 2*(2), 23–54.

Misra, H., Satpathy, M., & Mohanty, B. (2005). Stratified users and organisation preparedness for information technology acquisition: A causal model. *Vilakshan XIMB Journal of Management, 2*(1), 1–21.

Misra, H., Satpathy, M., & Mohanty, B. (2007). Measuring user's role to assess organisation preparedness in a systems acquisition life cycle: A cognitive framework. *International Journal of Information and Communication Technology, 1*(1), 50–61. doi:10.1504/IJICT.2007.013277.

Mithas, S., Ramasubbu, N., & Sambamurthy, V. (2011). How information management capability influences firm performance. *Management Information Systems Quarterly, 35*(1), 237–256.

Mockler, R. T. J. (1975). *The management control process*. New Delhi: Prentice-Hall Inc..

Monarch, I., Sisti, F., Ambrose, K., & Blanchette, S. (2004). *Why not network centric acquisition?* Paper presented at the Conference on Acquisition of Software Centric Systems. Pittsburgh, PA.

Morton, M., & Scott, S. (1991). *The corporation of the 1990s*. New York: Oxford University Press.

Mukherji, S. (2012). A framework for managing customer knowledge in retail industry. *IIMB Management Review, 24*, 95–103. doi:10.1016/j.iimb.2012.02.003.

National Research Council. (2007). *Improving disaster management: The role of IT in mitigation, preparedness, response, and recovery*. Washington, DC: National Academies Press.

Niu, J., & Atlee, J. M. (2003). Template semantics for model-based notations. *IEEE Transactions on Software Engineering, 29*(10).

Nolan, R. L. (1979). Managing the crises in data processing. *Harvard Business Review*.

Nonaka, I. (1988). Toward middle-up-down management: Accelerating information creation. *Sloan Management Review, 29*(3), 9–10.

Norman, R. G., & Streiner, L. D. (2003). *PDQ statistics* (3rd ed.).

Nunnally, J. C. (1978). *Psychometric theory*. New York: McGraw-Hill.

Nuseibeh, B., & Easterbrook, S. (2000). Requirements engineering: A roadmap. In *Proceedings of International Conference on Software Engineering (ICSE-2000)*. Limerick, Ireland: ICSE.

Olson, M. H. (1982). New information technology and organsiational culture. *Management Information Systems Quarterly*, 71–92. doi:10.2307/248992.

Orlikowski, W. J. (1992). The duality of technology: Rethinking the concept of technology in organizations. *Organization Science*, *3*(3). doi:10.1287/orsc.3.3.398.

Orlikowski, W. J., & Barley, S. R. (2001). Technology and institutions: What can research on information technology and research on organisations learn from each other? *Management Information Systems Quarterly*, *25*(2), 145–146. doi:10.2307/3250927.

Ould, M. A. (1995). *Business process: Modelling and analysis for re-engineering and improvement*. London: John Wiley and Sons.

Page, S. M. (1996). Organisational culture & information systems. In *Proceedings of the United Kingdom Academy for Information Systems, 1st Annual Conference*. AIS.

Palaniswamy, R. (2002). An innovation – diffusion view of implementation of enterprise resource planning (ERP) systems and development of a research model. *Information & Management*, *40*, 87–114. doi:10.1016/S0378-7206(01)00135-5.

Papp, R., & Luftman, J. (1995). Business and IT strategic alignment: New perspectives and assessments. In *Proceedings of the Association for Information Systems, Inaugural Americas Conference on Information Systems*. Pittsburgh, PA: AIS.

Papp, R., Luftman, J., & Brier, T. (1996). Business and IT in harmony: Enables and inhibitors to alignment. In *Proceedings of AMCIS*. Phoenix, AZ: AMCIS.

Parmenter, D. (2007). *Key performance indicators: Developing, implementing, and using wining KPIs*. New York: John Wiley & Sons.

Paulk, M. C. (1995). How ISO-9001 compares with the CMM. *IEEE Software*, *12*(1), 74–83. doi:10.1109/52.363163.

Paulk, M. C., Weber, C. V., & Curtis, B. (1994). *The capability maturity model for software: Guidelines for improving the software process*. Reading, MA: Addison-Wesley.

Pearce, J. A., & Robinson, R. B. (1996). *Strategic management: Formulation, implementation and control*. Burr Ridge, IL: Irwin.

Pedhazur, E. J. (1997). *Multiple regression in behavioral research* (3rd ed.). New York: Harcourt Brace College Publishers.

Peppard, J. (2001). Bridging the gap between the IS organisation and the rest of the business: Plotting a route. *Information Systems Journal*, *11*(3), 249. doi:10.1046/j.1365-2575.2001.00105.x.

Peppard, J., Lambart, R., & Edwards, C. (2000). Whose job is it anyway? Organisational competencies for value creation. *Information Systems Journal*, *10*(4), 291. doi:10.1046/j.1365-2575.2000.00089.x.

Pereira, J. V. (2009). The new supply chain's frontier: Information management. *International Journal of Information Management*, *29*, 372–379. doi:10.1016/j.ijinfomgt.2009.02.001.

Pervan, G. (1998). How the chief executive officers in large organisations view the management of their information systems. *Journal of Information Technology*, *13*, 95–109. doi:10.1080/026839698344882.

Peters, L. S. (1995). *The dimensions of strategic leadership in technical hybrid organizational relationships*. Advances in Global High-Technology Management.

Petligrew, A. M., Whittington, R., Melin, L., Sanchez-Runde, C., Ruigrok, W., & Numagami, T. (2003). *Innovative forms of organizing*. New Delhi: Sage Publications.

Pfeffer, J. (1997). *New directions for organizational theory: Problems and prospects*. New York: Oxford University Press.

Phelps, B. (2004). *Smart business metrics*. London: Pearson Education Limited.

Piekarski, W., & Plimmer, B. (2007). A conceptual framework for explaining the value of end user maturity levels for IT management. In *Proceedings of the Eighth Australasian User Interface Conference (AUIC)*, (pp. 27-30). Ballarat, Australia: AUIC.

Powell, T. C., & Dent-Micallef, A. (1997). Information technology as competitive advantage: The role of human, business and technology resources. *Strategic Management Journal, 18*(5), 375–405. doi:10.1002/(SICI)1097-0266(199705)18:5<375::AID-SMJ876>3.0.CO;2-7.

Pressman, R. S. (1997). *Software engineering: A practitioner's approach* (4th ed.). Singapore: McGraw-Hill.

Preston, K., & Karahanna, E. (2009). The antecedents of IS strategic alignment: A nomological network. *Information Systems Research, 20*(2), 159–179. doi:10.1287/isre.1070.0159.

Pucciarelli, J. C., & Waxman, J. (2008). *Financing options to improve IT acquisition and long-term management strategies* (White Paper). New York: IDC Corporate.

Quinn, J. B., & Baily, M. B. (1994). Information technology: Increasing productivity in services. *The Academy of Management Executive, 8*, 28.

Quinn, R. E., & Cameron, K. S. (1983). Organizational life cycles, and shifting criteria of effectiveness: Some preliminary evidence. *Management Science, 29*, 33–51. doi:10.1287/mnsc.29.1.33.

Radeke, F. (2011). Toward understanding enterprise architecture management's role in strategic change: Antecedents, processes, outcomes. In *Proceedings of Wirtschaftinformatik*. Wirtschaftinformatik.

Rai, A., Lang, S. S., & Welker, R. B. (2002). Assessing the validity of IS success models: An empirical test and theoretical analysis. *Information Systems Research, 13*(1), 50–69. doi:10.1287/isre.13.1.50.96.

Ramirez, R., Melville, N., & Lawler, E. (2010). Information technology infrastructure, organizational process redesign, and business value: An empirical analysis. *Decision Support Systems, 49*, 417–429. doi:10.1016/j.dss.2010.05.003.

Rampersad, G., Plewa, C., & Troshani, I. (2012). Investigating the use of information technology in managing innovation: A case study from a university technology transfer office. *Journal of Engineering and Technology Management, 29*, 3–21. doi:10.1016/j.jengtecman.2011.09.002.

Rangan, S., & Adner, R. (2001). *Profitable growth in internet-related business: Strategy tales and truths* (Working Paper, 2001/11/SM). Fontaineblueau, France: INSEAD.

Rao, R. R., Eisenberg, J., & Schmitt, T. (Eds.). (2007). *Improving disaster management: The role of IT in mitigation, preparedness, response, and recovery*. Washington, DC: National Academy of Sciences.

Rastogi, P. N. (1995). *Management of technology and innovation: Competing through technological excellence*. New Delhi: Sage Publications India.

Reuber, A. R., & Fischer, E. (2011). International entrepreneurship in Internet-enabled markets. *Journal of Business Venturing, 26*, 660–679. doi:10.1016/j.jbusvent.2011.05.002.

Review, M. I. E. A. (2011). *Maritime intelligence, surveillance, and reconnaissance enterprise acquisition (MIEA) review*. Washington, DC: Department of Defence.

Richardson, G. L., Jackson, B. M., & Dickson, G. W. (1990, December). A principles-based enterprise architecture: Lessons from texaco and star enterprise. *Management Information Systems Quarterly*, 380–403.

Riemenschneider, C. K., Harrison, D. A., & Mykytyn, P. P. Jr. (2003). Understanding it adoption decisions in small business: Integrating current theories. *Information & Management, 40*(4), 269–285. doi:10.1016/S0378-7206(02)00010-1.

Rietveld, T., & Van Hout, R. (1993). *Statistical techniques for the study of language and language behaviour*. Berlin: Mouton de Gruyter. doi:10.1515/9783110871609.

Robbins, S. P., & Judge, T. A. (2008). *Essentials of organizational behavior*. New Delhi: PHI Learning Private Limited.

Robillard, J., & Sambrook, R. (2008). USAF emergency and incident management systems: A systematic analysis of functional requirements. *EIM Requirements Study*, 1-13.

Rockart, J. (1988, Summer). The line takes leadership – IS management in a wired society. *Sloan Management Review*, 57–64.

Rogers, D. M. (1983). *Diffusion of innovations*. New York: The Free Press.

Ross, J. W., Beath, C. M., & Goodhue, D. (1996, Fall). Develop long-term competitiveness through IT assets. *Sloan Management Review*, 31–42.

Royce, W. W. (1970). Managing the development of large software systems. In *Proceedings of the 9th International Conference on Software Engineering*, (pp. 328-338). IEEE Computer Society.

Rumbaugh, J., Booch, G., & Jacobson, I. (2004). *The unified modeling language reference manual* (2nd ed.). Reading, MA: Addison-Wesley.

Rumbaugh, J., Jacobson, I., & Booch, G. (1999). *The unified modelling language reference manual*. Singapore: Addison Wesley Longman.

Sahgal, J. L. (1988). *Organization development*. Jaipur, India: Rupa Books International.

Scacchi, W. (2001). Process models in software engineering. In Marciniak, J. J. (Ed.), *Encyclopedia of Software Engineering* (2nd ed.). New York: John Wiley and Sons.

Scarbrough, H. (1996). Perspectives on innovation in organizations. *Organization Studies*, *17*(1), 107–129. doi:10.1177/017084069601700105.

Schimtt, J. W., & Kozar, K. A. (1978). Management's role in information system development failures: A case study. *Management Information Systems Quarterly*, 7–16. doi:10.2307/248937.

Seddon, P. B., Staples, S., Patnayakuni, R., & Bowtell, M. (1999). Dimensions of information systems success. *Communications of AIS Volume, 2*(20).

Seddon, P. B., Shanks, G., & Reynolds, P. (2011). How does enterprise architecture add value to organisations? *Communications of the Association for Information Systems*, 28.

Seeley, M. E., & Targett, D. (1997). A senior executive end-user framework. *Information Systems Journal*, *7*(4), 289. doi:10.1046/j.1365-2575.1997.00019.x.

Segars, A. H., & Grover, V. (1998, June). Strategic information systems planning: An investigation of the construct and its measurement. *Management Information Systems Quarterly*, 139–163. doi:10.2307/249393.

Seidita, V., Cossentino, M., & Gaglio, S. (2008). Using and extending the SPEM specifications to represent agent oriented methodologies. In *Proceedings of Agent-Oriented Software Engineering* (pp. 46–59). Estoril, Portugal: IEEE.

Selvin, S. (1991). *Statistical analysis of epidemiologic data*. New York: Oxford University Press.

Seth, N., Deshmukh, S., & Vrat, P. (2005). Service quality models: A review. *International Journal of Quality & Reliability Management*, *22*(9), 913–949. doi:10.1108/02656710510625211.

Shang, S., & Seddon. (2002). Assessing and managing benefits of enterprise systems: The business manager's perspective. *Information Systems Journal*, *12*(4), 271. doi:10.1046/j.1365-2575.2002.00132.x.

Sharma, S., & Rai, A. (2003). An assessment of the relationship between ISD leadership characteristics and IS innovation adoption in organizations. *Information & Management*, *40*(5), 391–401. doi:10.1016/S0378-7206(02)00049-6.

Shaw, M., & Garlan, D. (1996). *Software architecture: Perspectives on an emerging discipline*. New York: Prentice Hall.

Shayo, C., Olfman, L., & Teitrlroit, R. (1999). An exploratory study of the value of pre-training end-user participation. *Information Systems Journal*, *9*(1). doi:10.1046/j.1365-2575.1999.00049.x.

Sheard, S. A. (1996). The frameworks quagmire: A brief look. *Software Productivity Consortium*. Retrieved from http://www.software.org/quagmire/frampapr/FRAM-PAPR.HTML

Sheard, S. A. (1996). Twelve systems engineering roles. In *Proceedings of INCOSE*, (pp. 481-488). Minneapolis, MN: INCOSE.

Shehab, Sharp, Supramaniam, & Spedding. (2004). Enterprise resource planning: An integrative review. *Business Process Management Journal*, *10*(4), 359–386. doi:10.1108/14637150410548056.

Shimizu, K., & Hitt, M. A. (2004). Strategic flexibility: Organizational preparedness to reverse ineffective strategic decisions. *The Academy of Management Executive*, *18*(4), 44–59. doi:10.5465/AME.2004.15268683.

Shi, Y., Tian, Y., Kou, G., Peng, Y., & Li, J. (2011). *Optimization based data mining: Theory and applications.* New York: Springer. doi:10.1007/978-0-85729-504-0.

Simchi-Levi, D., Wu, D. S., & Shen, Z.-J. (Eds.). (2004). Handbook of quantitative supply chain analysis: Modeling in the e-business era. New York: Springer Science + Business Media Inc.

Simon, H. A. (1960). *The new science of management decision.* New York, NY: Harper and Row. doi:10.1037/13978-000.

Sinha, R. V., & Noble, S. H. (2008). The adoption of radical manufacturing technologies and firm survival. *Strategic Management Journal, 29*(9), 943–962. doi:10.1002/smj.687.

Smith, J. H., & Keil, M. (2003). The reluctance to report bad news on troubled software projects: A theoretical model. *Information Systems Journal, 13*(1), 69. doi:10.1046/j.1365-2575.2003.00139.x.

Smith, W. E. (2008). *The creative power: Transforming ourselves, our organizations, and our world.* London: Routledge. doi:10.4324/9780203888780.

Sohal, A. S., & Ng, L. (1998). The role and impact of information technology in Australian business. *Journal of Information Technology, 13*, 201–217. doi:10.1080/026839698344846.

Sommerville, I., & Sawyer, P. (1997). *Requirements engineering: A good practice guide.* New York: Wiley.

Spector, P. E. (1988). Development of the work locus of control scale. *Journal of Operational Psychology, 61*, 335–340.

Stamm, B. V. (2008). *Managing innovation, design and creativity.* Hoboken, NJ: John Wiley and Sons.

Standing, C., & Kiniti, S. (2011). How can organizations use wikis for innovation? *Technovation, 31*, 287–295. doi:10.1016/j.technovation.2011.02.005.

Staples, D. S., Wong, I., & Seddon, P. B. (2002). Having expectations of information systems benefits that match received benefits: Does it really matter? *Information & Management, 40*(2), 115–131. doi:10.1016/S0378-7206(01)00138-0.

Stoyanov, E. A., Wischy, M. A., & Roller, D. (2005). Cybernetics and general systems theory (GST) principles for autonomic computing design. In *Proceedings of the Second International Conference on Autonomic Computing (ICAC'05).* IEEE.

Strong, D. M., & Volkoff, O. (2004, June). A roadmap for enterprise system implementation. *IEEE Computer*, 22-29.

Strong, D., & Volkoff, O. (2010). Understanding organization-enterprise system fit: A path to theorizing the information technology artifact. *Management Information Systems Quarterly, 34*(4), 731–756.

Stucci, T. (2012). Emerging market firms: Acquisitions in advanced markets: Matching strategy with resource, institution and industry-based antecedents. *European Management Journal, 30*, 278–289. doi:10.1016/j.emj.2012.03.011.

Swan, J., Newell, S., & Robertson, M. (1999). The illusion of 'best practice' in information systems for operations management. *European Journal of Information Systems, 8*, 284–293. doi:10.1057/palgrave.ejis.3000336.

Swanson, E. B. (1988). *Information system implementation bridging the gap between design and utilization.* Homewood, IL: Irwin.

Szajna, B., & Scamell, R. W. (1993, December). The effects of information system user expectations on their performance and perceptions. *Management Information Systems Quarterly*, 493–516. doi:10.2307/249589.

Tait, P. (1988, March). The effect of user involvement on systems success: A contingency approach. *Management Information Systems Quarterly*, 91–108. doi:10.2307/248809.

Tanaka, J. S. (1993). Multifaceted conceptions of fit in structural equation models. In Bollen, K. A., & Long, J. S. (Eds.), *Testing Structural Equation Models* (pp. 19–20). Thousand Oaks, CA: Sage.

Team, C. P. (2002). *CMMI for systems engineering/ software engineering, version 1.1- Staged representation (CMU/SEI – 2002-TR-02, ADA339224).* Pittsburgh, PA: Software Engineering Institute, Carnegie Mellon University.

Thomsen, M. (2010). *Procurement competence in procurement and development of IT - the skills-emergence in the shadow of knowledge fragmentation.* (PhD Thesis). Halmstad University, Sweden.

Tor, G. M., Staples, D. S., & Mckeen, J. D. (2003). Emprically testing some main user-related factors for systems development quality. *American Society for Quality Journal, 10*(4), 39–54.

Torkzadeh, G., & Lee, J. (2003). Measures of perceived end-user computing skills. *Information & Management, 40*, 607–615. doi:10.1016/S0378-7206(02)00090-3.

Turban, E., Sharda, R., Aronson, J. E., & King, D. (2008). *Business intelligence: A managerial approach.* Upper Saddle River, NJ: Prentice Hall.

Umanath, N. S. (2003). The concept of contingency beyond 'it depends': Illustrations from IS research stream. *Information & Management, 40*(6), 551–562. doi:10.1016/S0378-7206(02)00080-0.

Venkatesh, V., Morris, M. G., Davis, G. B., & Davis, F. D. (2003). User acceptance of information technology: Toward a unified view. *Management Information Systems Quarterly, 27*(3), 425–478.

Venkatraman, N., Henderson, J. C., & Oldash, S. (1993). Continuous strategic alignment: Exploiting information technology capabilities for competitive success. *European Management Journal, 11*(2), 139 149. doi:10.1016/0263 2373(93)90037-I.

Volkoff, O. (1999). Using the structurational model of technology of analyse an ERP implementation. In *Proceedings of Academy of Management '99 Conference.* AM.

Wang, E. T. G., & Tai, J. C. F. (2003). Factors affecting information systems planning effectiveness: Organizational contexts and planning systems dimensions. *Information & Management, 40*(4), 287–303. doi:10.1016/S0378-7206(02)00011-3.

Ward, J. M. (2012). Information systems strategy: Quo vadis? *The Journal of Strategic Information Systems, 21*, 165–171. doi:10.1016/j.jsis.2012.05.002.

Ward, J., Griffiths, P., & Peppard, W. (1990). *Strategic planning for information systems.* Chichester, UK: John Wiely and Sons Ltd..

Ward, J., & Peppard, J. (2002). *Strategic planning for information systems.* London: John Wiley and Sons.

Watson, R. T., Pitt, L. F., & Kavan, B. C. (1998, March). Measuring information systems service quality: Lessons from two longitudinal case studies. *Management Information Systems Quarterly*, 61–79. doi:10.2307/249678.

Weber, C., & Layman, B. (2002). Measurement maturity and the CMM: How measurement practices evolve as processes mature. *Soft Qual Pract, 4*(3).

Weber, M. (1978). *Economy and society: An outline of interpretive sociology* (Roth, G., & Wiffich, C., Eds.). Berkeley, CA: University of California Press.

Weill, P., & Vitale, M. (2002). What IT infrastructure capabilities are needed to implement e-business models?. *MIS Quarterly Executive, 1*(1).

Weill, P., & Olson, M. H. (1989). An assessment of the contingency theory of management information systems. *Journal of Management Information Systems, 6*(1), 59–85.

Wiseman, C. (1985). *Strategy and computers.* Homewood, IL: Dow Jones-Irwin.

Wohlin, C., Runeson, P., Host, M., Ohlsson, M. C., Regnell, B., & Wesslen, A. (2000). *Experimentation in software engineering: An introduction.* London: Kluwer Academic Publishers. doi:10.1007/978-1-4615-4625-2.

Xu, K., Huang, K., & Gao, S. (2012). Technology sourcing, appropriability regimes, and new product development. *Journal of Engineering and Technology Management, 29*, 265–280. doi:10.1016/j.jengtecman.2012.03.003.

Yap, C. S., Soh, C. P. P., & Raman, K. S. (1992). Information systems success factors in small business. *Omega: International Journal of Information Management, 20*(5/6), 597–609. doi:10.1016/0305-0483(92)90005-R.

Yaverbaum, G. J. (1988, March). Critical factors in the user environment: An experimental study of users, organisation and tasks. *Management Information Systems Quarterly*, 75–88. doi:10.2307/248807.

Yeh, Q.-J., & Tsai, C.-L. (2001). Two conflict potentials during IS development. *Information & Management, 39*(2), 135–149. doi:10.1016/S0378-7206(01)00088-X.

Yetton, P., Martin, A., Sharma, R., & Johnston, K. (2000). A model of information systems development project performance. *Information Systems Journal, 10*(4), 263. doi:10.1046/j.1365-2575.2000.00088.x.

Yin, R. K. (1994). *Case study research: Design and methods*. Thousand Oaks, CA: Sage.

Youssef, W., Manuel, K., & Nicolas, N. (2008). *e-SPM: An online software project management game* (Working Paper, 08/02). Louvain School of Management.

Zeleny, M. (2005). *Human systems management: Integrating knowledge, management and systems*. Singapore: World Scientific Publishing. doi:10.1142/9789812703538.

Zey, M. (1992). *Decision making: Alternatives to rational choice models*. Thousand Oaks, CA: Sage Publications.

Zmud, R. W. (1982). Diffusion of modern software practices: Influence of centralization and formalisation. *Management Science, 28*(12), 1421–1431. doi:10.1287/mnsc.28.12.1421.

Zwikael, O., & Globerson, S. (2004). Evaluating the quality of project planning: A model and field results. *International Journal of Production Research, 42*(8), 1545–1556. doi:10.1080/00207540310001639955.

About the Authors

Harekrishna Misra is a professor in the IT & Information Systems Group at the Institute of Rural Management, Anand, India. He is an Electronics and Communication Engineer, has Post-Graduate Diploma in Business Management in Systems and Operations Management from XIM-Bhubaneswar, India, and has Masters Degree in Software Systems from BITS-Pilani, India. He also holds a Doctorate degree from Utkal University, Bhubaneswar, India, in the area of Information Systems Management. He has around 28 years of experience in industry and academia in the fields of IT infrastructure management, communication, and networks. His current research interests include software engineering (process modelling), e-governance, information systems management in development organisations, e-Business for rural enterprises, and ICT-enabled value chain in rural enterprises. His current interests include information systems modelling related to business and development processes with citizen participation. He is a life member of Institution of Engineers (India), member of IEEE, Association of Computing Machinery (ACM), and Association of Information Systems, USA. He is in the reviewers' panel of the *Computing Reviews*-ACM. He has widely published in national and internationally reputed and refereed journals. He has also participated in technical as well as programme committees and presented papers in national and international refereed academic conferences.

Hakikur Rahman (PhD) is the Principal of the Institute of Computer Management & Science (ICMS) and President of ICMS Foundation. He is currently an Adjunct Faculty member of Bangabandhu Sheikh Mujibur Rahman Agricultural University and the secretary of the South Asia Foundation Bangladesh Chapter. In December 1999, Dr. Rahman worked as the National Project Coordinator for the transformed entity of the Sustainable Development Networking Programme (SDNP) in Bangladesh. From January through December of 2007, he served Sustainable Development Networking Foundation (SDNF) as its Executive Director (CEO). On December 31, 2006, SDNP, a global initiative of UNDP, completed its activity in Bangladesh. Before joining SDNP, Rahman worked as the Director of the Computer Division at Bangladesh Open University. After graduating from the Bangladesh University of Engineering and Technology (1981), he completed his Master's of Engineering from the American University of Beirut (1986) and his PhD in Computer Engineering from the Ansted University, UK (2001).

Index

A

acquisition process (AQ) 153, 239
acquisition stage 49, 67, 74, 225, 229, 258, 266, 269, 279, 287
acquisition stage (AQ) 258
Activity Diagrams 288-289
Adjusted Goodness-of-fit (AGFI) 251
Application Specific Integrated Circuits (ASIC) 38

B

Business Intelligence (BI) 20, 27
Business Process Re-engineering (BPR) 20, 28
business-to-business (B2B) 101
business-to-customer (B2C) 101

C

Capability Maturity Model (CMM) 50, 260
Chief Executive Officer (CEO) 39
Chief Information Officer (CIO) 39
climate preparedness 106, 109, 132, 134-136, 138-139, 147, 150, 211, 239, 247-248, 266, 270
CMM- Integrated (CMM-I) 130
Commercial Off The Shelf (COTS) 49
Comparative Fit Index (CFI) 251
Computer Aided Design and Manufacturing (CAD&M) 3
Computer Aided Designs (CAD) 10
Computer Aided Manufacturing (CAM) 10
Computer Aided Software Engineering (CASE) 51
Computer Based Information Systems (CBIS) 44
Confirmatory Factor Analysis (CFA) 166, 239
Corrected-Question-Total 169, 173-174, 176, 179, 181-182, 184, 186-188, 190, 192, 200, 202, 207
Cronbach alpha coefficient 169, 211
cybernetic paradigm 18

D

dashboards 17, 29-32, 37
data processing (DP) 99, 283
decision making style 109, 135, 138-139, 147, 186, 191-192, 219-221, 264, 278
Decision Support Systems (DSS) 20, 80
degrees of freedom (df) 213-214, 216-217, 219-220, 222-223, 225, 227-228, 230-231, 233-234, 251
dummy coding 164-165, 211-224, 226-227, 229-233, 256
Dunnet Table 213-214, 216-217, 219-220, 222-223, 225, 227-228, 230-231, 233-234

E

Electronic Data Interchange (EDI) 100, 283
Emerging Market (EM) 17
Enterprise Application Integration (EAI) 128
Enterprise Resource Planning (ERP) 3, 10, 20, 70, 88, 120
entrepreneurial orientation (EO) 93
evaluation-choice 25
Evolutionary acquisition strategy 52
Executive Information System (EIS) 100, 283
Executive Support System (ESS) 130
External Service Providers (ESP) 69

F

Factor Analysis (FA) 164
Federal Aviation Administration (FAA) 130

G

gap analysis 63
General Accounting Office (GAO) 96
general systems theory (GST) 11, 15, 21, 34
Goal-Question-Metrics (GQM) 124, 144
Goodness-of-Fit Index (GFI) 252